The Hamlyn Guide to
the Seashore
and Shallow Seas
of Britain and Europ

A.C.Campbell D.Phil.

illustrated by
James Nicholls

HAMLYN
London · New York · Sydney · Toronto

Preface

This book is intended to provide the layman and the student with a simple means of identifying most of the common marine plants and animals in the field. The accurate determination of certain species often depends on the correct use of an identification key in a specialist's monograph. Unfortunately the use of such identification keys frequently presupposes some knowledge of the group of organisms in question and may not therefore be of great help to the beginner. As an alternative, this book provides illustrations and simple accounts of the form, habitats and distribution of a number of species to be found on the shores and in the shallow seas around Britain and Europe. It must be said, however, that a book of this size cannot always provide an exact identification, especially where some of the more obscure groups are concerned. For this reason the reader is directed to other sources at certain points in the text.

Many thousands of species have been recorded in the European seas and it would be impossible to include them all in this book. The thousand or so selected for inclusion have been chosen because they are relatively common, and because they can generally be identified without the aid of a microscope. In a number of cases the use of a hand lens is called for.

A. C. Campbell

Acknowledgements

The author and artist wish to acknowledge the great help given by so many friends and colleagues. Special thanks must be given to the following for criticism, advice and loan of material: Dr G. Boalch, Professor M. Godward, Dr J. Fraser, Dr A. G. Hildrew, Dr P. Holigan, Professor M. S. Laverack, Dr J. R. Lewis, The Manchester Museum, Professor N. B. Marshall, Dr T. Norton, Professor D. Nichols, Mr P. Oliver, Mr and Mrs T. Pain, Queen Mary College, The University of London, The Royal Scottish Museum, Dr P. S. Rainbow, Dr J. S. Ryland, Dr N. Tebble and Mr A. Wheeler.

The publishers would like to acknowledge the valuable assistance given by Dr G. W. Potts of the Marine Biological Association of the United Kingdom in the preparation of this book, and in the provision of reference material for a number of illustrations.

Line drawings by James Nicholls and Linda Rogers Associates

Published by
The Hamlyn Publishing Group Limited
London · New York · Sydney · Toronto
Astronaut House, Feltham, Middlesex, England

Copyright © The Hamlyn Publishing Group Limited 1976
ISBN 0 600 34396 0
ISBN 0 600 34019 8 (cased edition)

Text set in Univers by Keyspools Limited, Golborne, Lancashire
Printed in Italy by Officine Grafiche A. Mondadori, Verona

Contents

Introduction

For generations, people living by the shores of Europe have looked to the sea as a source of food and a means of trading, and consequently have become aware of the diversity of plants and animals existing there. For the biologist the seashore is an excellent training ground; for the layman it is a fascinating area for exploration. Although Aristotle was one of the first to describe marine organisms, our knowledge of them developed slowly. Today it is considerable, and almost entirely due to work undertaken in the last two hundred years. In 1758 the Swedish Botanist, Linnaeus, published *Systema Naturae* and established a method for classifying organisms which survives today. Later, in 1788, O. F. Müller described and illustrated marine animals from Scandinavia for the first time. A number of devoted and energetic naturalists emerged in the nineteenth century, and in almost every European maritime nation they collected, described and classified the easily obtainable plants and animals. In 1832 two Frenchmen, Audouin and Milne-Edwards, realized that animals and plants do not occur at random on the shore, and they produced the first scheme for zonation. Zonation was discussed further by Forbes in 1841. Later, in 1859, he published *The Natural History of the European Seas* which provided a general account of the marine biology of Europe. The Norwegian, M. Sars, continued the process of describing the Scandinavian fauna in 1845, when the first part of *Fauna Littoralis Norwegia* appeared.

Meanwhile in England Gosse was writing popular books about seashore life. These greatly influenced his Victorian readers, many of whom were sadly ignorant of conservation. As a result, many beaches were stripped of the rarer species by the ardent collectors he inspired. Four of his books, *A Naturalist's Rambles on the Devonshire Coast*, 1853; *The Aquarium*, 1854; *Tenby; A Seaside Holiday*, 1856; and *A Year at the Shore*, 1865 must be mentioned. In 1859 Darwin's *Origin of Species* was published. This had a profound effect on the future course of biological science. It may have led Dr Anton Dohrn among others to study the development and growth of animals. Dohrn required a marine laboratory where live animals could be kept for study and experiment. He ultimately succeeded in setting up such an establishment at Naples in 1874. Although a marine station had been established at Kristineberg in Sweden much earlier in 1830, the Naples laboratory was the first to be specifically designed for experimental purposes. The potential for such work in marine laboratories was quickly realized, and towards the end of the century similar institutions began to appear all over Europe.

The first in Britain was established at St Andrew's University in 1884, although Sir John Murray had already started work in his floating laboratory 'The Ark', which was moored at Granton. Also in 1884 the Marine Biological Association of the United Kingdom was formed to promote scientific research and to increase knowledge of fishes and fisheries. It opened its famous laboratory at Plymouth in 1888. Now over forty such laboratories are run by universities and governments in Europe. Most are engaged in academic or applied research and their influence on the development of marine science has been enormous. Consequently there exists today a wealth of literature in the form of books and scientific papers, some of which are referred to in the bibliography at the end of this book. Four must be mentioned here, however. *The Sea Shore* by Sir Maurice Yonge was first published in 1949. It gives an excellent account of intertidal life, whilst the companion volumes entitled *The Open Sea* (parts I and II) by Sir Alister Hardy tell of life in the seas and oceans. These appeared in 1956 and 1959. In 1964 J. R. Lewis produced an important work *The Ecology of Rocky Shores* which sets out in a modern, scientific fashion the principles of zonation, and which builds on earlier theories such as those established by T. A. and A. Stephenson in 1949. Experimental marine biology is still a comparatively young science, but rapidly developing techniques, together with man's increasing dependence on the resources of the sea, assure it an important future.

How to use this book

This book describes the more common plants and animals which may be found on the European shores and in the adjacent shallow seas. The use of a hand lens will be helpful in dealing with some of the smaller species, but in general the naked eye should suffice. Many marine plants and animals lack the common names of their terrestrial counterparts, thus the only one that can normally be used is the scientific name, but where a common name exists it has been included in the text and index. Scientific names are written in italics. Sometimes two scientists have independently given an organism different names. Normally one of these takes preference by common consent, but where an alternative name or synonym persists in use, it is given here. To help further, the author who first used the species name has his name written after it. If his species has subsequently been transferred to another genus the author's name is placed in brackets. In the case of many plants the name of the author who made the transfer is usually also given.

If you think you know the name of a plant or animal you have found, it can be checked in the index. If you wish to identify a specimen for the first time, use the outline key on pages 14–17 to establish where in the book the organism you have found is described, then turn to the page(s) mentioned and make your identification. Almost all the species described in the text are illustrated, and key anatomical features have been given in many cases to help distinguish between similar species; these features will not always be consistent from group to group, however. Line drawings are also used in the text in certain cases. Very often the geographical locality or the habitat, for instance *upper shore* or *in mud*, will assist in helping with the correct identification, so the text and the illustrations must be used together. It will be noted that the distribution of organisms in the sea with regard to depth is not given with equal precision in every case. This is because records themselves are variable. In some cases the exact depths at which organisms occur are known; in other cases only a general impression is available, for instance shallow water. Unfortunately, various authorities have different interpretations of the words *shallow* and *deep*. In this book *shallow* is broadly taken to mean down to 10m, while *deep* means below 10m, but still on the continental shelf and therefore not the deep sea.

In addition to the outline shape, many other factors are important when identifying specimens. The illustrations do not themselves indicate size, but a guide to the general proportions of the various species is given in the text. It must be remembered that juveniles are frequently smaller than the average size of adults, however, and occasionally abnormally large specimens may be found. Colours in marine organisms can be surprisingly variable, and although the artist has taken great trouble to produce life-like impressions of colour, a book of this size cannot include all the variations. Some invertebrates – notably the octopus and cuttlefish – as well as certain fishes, can change their colour rapidly at will. Other specimens alter their coloration when removed from the sea even after a short period of time. Where colour changes are likely to cause confusion reference to alternative characters will usually assist with identification. Growth form and behavioural characters such as locomotion patterns also help in some cases. It should be remembered that the appearance of many species around our coasts is related to the seasons. A number of plants are at their peak in Spring and Summer, and most animals have seasonal breeding cycles. These may involve migration in fishes. Remember also that many marine organisms are nocturnal, so the experienced marine naturalist should note that some organisms may only be found at night.

From time to time the text includes a reference to a work which will be of particular assistance for the group of organisms in question. A more detailed list of reference sources for all groups is given in the bibliography.

Finally, it should be noted that the male and female of some species have a different external appearance. Where a particular sex is illustrated, ♂ denotes male, and ♀ denotes female.

The European seas

This book covers an area which includes several widely differing marine regions. These range from the Atlantic Ocean bordering the Iberian Peninsula (this region is sometimes known as the Lusitanian region – Lusitania being an ancient name for Portugal), Ireland, Scotland and Norway, as well as the almost enclosed Mediterranean and Baltic Seas. Between these extremes of open ocean and enclosed sea lie the North Sea, the Irish Sea and the English Channel, all of which are influenced by ocean and by land. The size of the European continent means that the climatic conditions vary greatly over the whole area, so increasing the diversity of habitats.

The geography of Europe today is very different from what it was during the geological era known as the Tertiary period (15 to 70 million years ago). Then, a large sea known as the Tethys, which was considerably greater than the present-day Mediterranean, linked what are now the Arctic and Atlantic Oceans with the Indo-west Pacific to the east. In the successive upheavals which have changed the shape of the land masses since then, the Tethys was reduced. The Mediterranean was formed from an area previously covered by part of it, and certain species which are found there today have descended from Arctic, Atlantic and Indo-west Pacific ancestors which moved into the Tethys first. They have been able to survive there because of the unique conditions which prevail. The surface waters of the Mediterranean, particularly in the south-eastern region, are warm and very saline so that in Summer, warm-water species can reproduce. The waters below 50m are cooler, however, and provide a satisfactory habitat for cold-water forms. In this book the Adriatic Sea is treated as part of the Mediterranean. The whole Mediterranean system does not house an isolated plant and animal community, although it contains many endemic (i.e. native) species. The neighbouring parts of the Atlantic provide habitats for a number of Mediterranean organisms. Some of these spread northwards with others of Atlantic origin from Gibraltar to the entrance to the English Channel, and are known as Lusitanian species. Beyond this point those which cannot survive without pure ocean water disappear, but so far as the plankton is concerned the Lusitanian effect may spread up the west coast of Ireland and north as far as Shetland and the northern North Sea in favourable years. The central and northern coasts of Britain and Ireland come under the influence of the North Atlantic Drift (colloquially called the Gulf Stream) which sweeps moderately warm Atlantic water around the north of Scotland. Some of this water extends into the northern North Sea so that the north-east coast of Scotland carries a greater diversity of Atlantic species than can be found further south in this sea, where the land cuts them off from the Atlantic, and the colder water inhibits their development. Generally the waters of the North Sea and the English Channel are slightly less saline than those of the Atlantic. Consequently a restricted Atlantic flora and fauna prevail, but a few Arctic species extend into these regions by virtue of currents from the north, in addition to running down the north-western coasts of Britain to reach Ireland and the Irish Sea. So far as regional distributions are concerned, the term *Atlantic* in the following text includes the entire western seaboard of Europe from Gibraltar to the Shetlands and Norway. It takes in the Bristol Channel and the Irish Sea, which are mentioned separately only when necessary.

The Baltic is surrounded by much colder land masses than the Mediterranean, and the influence of fresh water is far greater. Apart from the Kattegat and the Skagerrak which somewhat resemble the North Sea, the remainder of the Baltic shows peculiar physical conditions. In the north Baltic lies an area of really deep water, and this trench is filled with salt water over which floats less saline water. Here a number of fully marine organisms occur. The further one

Map showing the extent of the various regions mentioned in the book, also indicating the nature of the prevailing physical conditions.

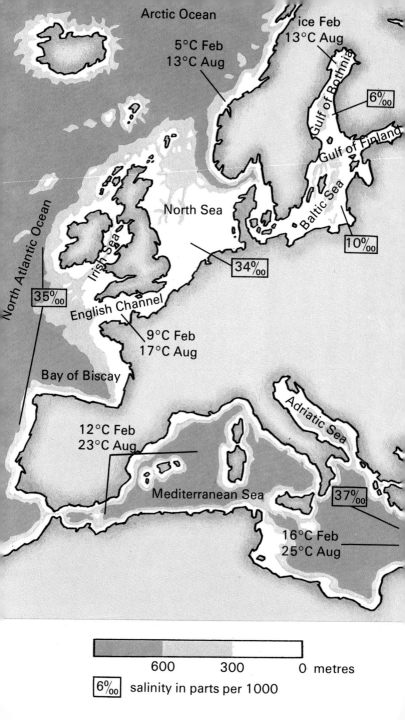

Arctic Ocean

5°C Feb
13°C Aug

ice Feb
13°C Aug

Gulf of Bothnia

6‰

Gulf of Finland

North Sea

Baltic Sea

10‰

North Atlantic Ocean

Irish Sea

34‰

35‰

English Channel

9°C Feb
17°C Aug

Bay of Biscay

Adriatic Sea

12°C Feb
23°C Aug

37‰

Mediterranean Sea

16°C Feb
25°C Aug

600   300   0 metres

6‰ salinity in parts per 1000

penetrates northwards the lower the salinity becomes. Consequently fewer marine species can survive here, although some freshwater species which can tolerate brackish conditions live here as well as genuinely brackish water species which cannot survive in either pure sea water or fresh water. Furthermore the Baltic is very cold and in the Gulfs of Bothnia and of Finland it may be frozen over for nearly half the year. Like the Mediterranean, it contains some species that were left behind after the decline of the Tethys Sea, but most of its marine inhabitants originate from the North Sea.

Life on the seashore

The seashore is that area of the coast which lies between the highest level to which the tides flow and the lowest level to which they ebb. All plant and animal life between these two points is subjected to the movement of the tides and the various side effects which they create. Tidal movement is brought about principally by the gravitational pull of the sun and the moon upon the vast masses of water in the oceans. Variations in ocean depth and the presence and shape of nearby land masses can modify the extent of the tides, and we see these effects particularly in the European area. The tidal range around much of Britain is between 2 and 5m, but in the Baltic Sea and the Mediterranean Sea there is frequently little or no tide, whilst in certain places, for instance the Bristol Channel, tides of 10m or more can occur. Normally the tidal cycle at any one place is repeated just over every 12 hours so that on successive days both the high and low waters appear on average about 50 minutes later than on the day before. In a few areas the form of the coastline is such that an extra tide is inserted between the main tides. Thus in the Solent and at other points in the English Channel there is an extra high tide phase in what is normally the low tide period.

Although the twelve-hourly rhythm of the tides is their most conspicuously variable feature, there are others. At new moon and at full moon the sun and the moon are pulling together almost in a straight line so that the tidal ranges at these times are greater. Such tides are known as *spring tides*. During the intervening periods the pull of the sun and the moon are less aligned and may be at right angles, thus reducing their combined effects, so that the tidal ranges are reduced. These are known as *neap tides*. Thus there is a monthly rhythm of spring and neap tides. In addition to this monthly rhythm there is also an annual rhythm, since at the equinoxes (March and September), the sun and the moon pull exactly in a straight line giving an exceptionally large tidal range at the spring tides. Conversely in December and June the spring tides are of a smaller range than at any other time of the year. Fig. 1 shows a diagrammatic representation of the range of the tide with the positions of the standard tidal levels which are used in technical descriptions of the shore. Fig. 2 shows the spring/neap tide cycles for 12 days at a given point on the coast.

The consequences of tidal movements on the shore are considerable. Whilst the greater area will be covered and uncovered by the sea once every 12 hours, the highest point of the shore may be completely covered for only a few days each month, i.e. during spring tides. When the tide is in, the temperature of the surface over which it passes is held more or less constant, there is no dehydration and the oxygen content of the rock pools and other areas of captive water will be upheld. When the tide ebbs the shore is exposed to fluctuating air temperatures and perhaps to the sun's radiation which may quickly heat rocks and sand. Water will be lost by evaporation on hot days with a consequent increase in salinity in rock pools and captive water; conversely when it rains the salinity in pools will fall. Temperature variations will also affect oxygen content. These are just some of the more important problems which face plants and animals living on the shore. Others include exposure and the mechanical effects of waves, which may exert colossal pressures on fixed organisms. There is also the problem of existing on a particular substrate. The type of shore determines the type of flora and fauna to be found. The organisms of an exposed rocky shore will be restricted to those that can withstand the effects of waves and wind, but on a sheltered rocky shore we shall find a much greater diversity of species, including those that cannot withstand these mechanical effects.

The manifestation of tidal movements is *zonation* of most plants and animals. Those organisms which can withstand exposure to air, with all its attendant variables, are to be found at the top of the shore where they may be covered by the tide for one or two hours of the day only. Those which can withstand exposure to air for only an hour or so each day will be found at the bottom of the shore. Between these two extremes lies a wealth of different species which can tolerate emersion or immersion to various degrees. Such organisms are zoned according to their requirements, and on a rocky shore or pier side it is usually easy to identify the zones. In each zone a particular type of plant or animal will dominate, and with a little practice they can be recognized easily. Zonation also occurs on sandy and muddy shores, but it is less easily recognized because most of the organisms burrow in the substrate rather than lie on its surface. It should be explained that on an exposed shore the various zones are broader than they are on a sheltered shore. This is because of the way in which wave and wind action serves to extend the influence of sea water up the shore beyond the point that it would have reached if the water were still. Fig. 3 shows the scheme of zonation that is recognized in this book.

The theory of zonation has been revised by J. R. Lewis. He divides the shore into three biologically defined zones (i.e. defined by the presence of particular species rather than by their height in relation to mean tide level), and they are technically named the littoral fringe, the eulittoral zone and the sublittoral zone. These zones are referred to in this book by the following names respectively: *upper shore, middle shore* and *lower shore*. Above the upper shore is a region of land that is to some extent under the influence of the sea. Apart from the most sheltered beaches the upper shore is wide, spray extended and above tidal reach, as fig. 2 shows. On rocky shores, it is defined as being above the barnacle or *Pelvetia* line and terminating at the upper limit of the periwinkles (*Littorina neritoides*) and lichens (e.g. *Verrucaria* species). The upper shore is the most difficult zone for marine organisms to live in and usually lacks a great diversity of species. The middle shore is generally a large region, and apart from the most exposed shores it is covered and uncovered by the tides every twelve hours or so. It provides a habitat for the most characteristic shore forms, and there is an abundance of species and individuals. The lower shore is that region extending down from the upper limit of the laminarians and is usually uncovered only at the lowest level of the spring tides. It is the most hospitable zone for marine animals to survive in and is the lowest zone we can recognize on the shore. Below the lower shore the shallow sea provides an entirely different set of conditions which are considered on pages 12 and 13.

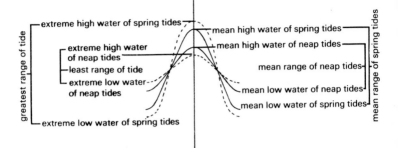

Fig. 1 Diagrammatic representation of the tidal range (After Lewis, 1964)

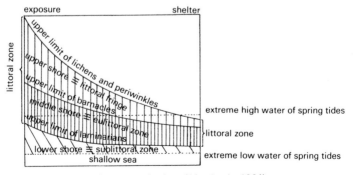

Fig. 2 Diagrammatic representation of the spring/neap tide cycle during 12 days at a given point (After Lewis, 1964)

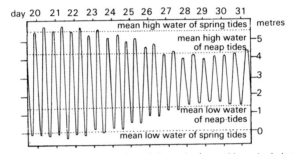

Fig. 3 Scheme of zonation on a rocky shore (After Lewis, 1964)

Types of seashore

The European area embraces a great variety of shores depending on the coastal geography and the form of the substrate. Most of these shores can, however, be related to one of four types: rocky, shingle, sandy or muddy. It should be emphasized that at any one point the local climatic conditions and geological formations will have a profoundly modifying effect upon the types of organism to be found. It should also be remembered that shores are rarely static. They are usually being eroded by the sea and the elements, or being built up either by the sea or by material washed down from the land by rivers. Although one is apt to consider different shore types separately, in practice they often grade into one another.

Rocky shores are the most variable type, their character depending on the prevailing rock. The profile of the rocky shore is usually related to the strata formation. If this is sloping there will usually be a variety of crevices and pools. If it is flat one will encounter rocky platforms and ledges. Rocky shores usually provide a great diversity of animals and plants because the number of ecological niches available is so great.

By comparison with rocky shores all other types of beach may at first sight appear barren and deserted. In practice this is true of shingle beaches where the pebbles are constantly being rolled about by the action of waves, so that most forms of life find it impossible to exist; also the spaces between the pebbles are too large to retain water by capillarity when the tide ebbs, so that virtually nothing can survive under or between the pebbles.

Sandy shores are made up of vast numbers of fine grains — usually quartz. The profile of a sandy shore depends to a great extent on the degree of exposure to wave action. Because the particles are so small water is usually retained by capillary action in the minute spaces between the grains. This water effectively lubricates the grains and also allows the animals to survive in the sand after the tide has fallen. The amount of water that is held depends upon the size of the particles, and can be tested by foot pressure. If there is little water in the sand, it appears to look slightly drier around the area of pressure, but if there is much, the sand becomes wet and slushy, especially if you tread up and down several times in one spot. Although the surface of the sand is affected by the fall of the tide, bringing about water loss, temperature and salinity changes, these effects do not appear to penetrate very deeply so that organisms several centimetres down can exist quite well. Providing the sandy shore is stable and not being moved by wave action, it provides a good environment for marine organisms. The diversity of species may not be as great as that on a rocky shore, but the density at which the individuals are disposed on a sandy shore is often very high.

Muddy shores are made of the finest particles of all. For the mud to accumulate the shore must be virtually flat. In addition to the silt (which is of mineral origin) there will also be a variety of organic debris accumulated here. The fine particles may cause difficulty for some animals since it can block delicate structures; some species benefit from the organic material included while others do not. Hence the number of species represented may be restricted to certain specialized ones, although their populations can be considerable. Estuaries with shores of fine sand and mud can be exceedingly productive, as the extent of some commercial cockle beds well demonstrates.

The shallow seas

For the purposes of this book the shallow sea is regarded as that area of the sea which stretches from the lowest point to which the tide ebbs, to the outer limit of the continental shelf. It will therefore include areas of quite deep water but will not comprise of the vast depths which one associates with the oceans beyond the continental shelf. The extent of the continental shelf is variable, but it takes the form of a gently sloping terrace running seaward. It terminates at the point where the seabed falls away steeply to the ocean depths, and this usually occurs from depths of between 200 and 300m. As the map on page 7 shows, the European land mass is fringed by the continental shelf.

By comparison with the seashore, the shallow sea provides a more constant environment. Organisms living there are not subjected to the changes associated with the ebb and flow of the tides as are those dwelling on the beaches. There is therefore no risk from desiccation, overheating or lack of oxygen. Consequently the shallow sea is populated by a greater diversity of animals including many species not specialized to withstand the rigours of shore life. Plants, on the other hand, are less in evidence because the sunlight upon which they depend for the synthesis of their nutrient materials cannot always penetrate sufficiently through the overlying water. The shallow sea also differs from the ocean. Apart from having far deeper water, the ocean is to a great extent free from the influences of land. Shallow seas are generally not. Their salinity may be affected by the outfalls of rivers, especially during wet weather, and their mineral content can be influenced by the land mass and water draining from it. Frequently the water is clouded by suspensions of silt swept out to sea near estuaries, and today, sadly, it is often polluted by sewage or chemical waste released from coastal towns and from river mouths.

Whilst diving as a technique has limitations in terms of depth, it alone permits any sort of balanced appreciation of the shallow sea as a habitat. If you cannot dive you cannot get more than a second-hand impression of what is to be found beneath the sea, and you are dependent on vessels equipped with trawls, dredges and underwater television. Essentially two kinds of life are to be found: the floating and swimming organisms which inhabit the waters above the continental shelf; and those animals which live in, or on, the seabed itself. Examples of the former include myriads of drifting, microscopical organisms forming the plankton, the jellyfishes and sea-gooseberries, a few types of worms and of course the fishes. The animals which live on or in the seabed are mainly invertebrates such as sponges, anemones, molluscs, hosts of worms and a great variety of crustaceans including the familiar crabs and lobsters. In addition, there will be starfishes, sea-urchins and some bottom-dwelling fishes.

Just as there are different types of shore, so there are different types of seabed. The texture of the substrate will to a large extent dictate what types of organism live on it, and to a lesser extent the species which live in the water above the substrate, since they may be dependent on the seabed for food, shelter and breeding grounds. Sandy bottoms are characterized by a variety of burrowing invertebrates and the well-known flatfishes. Rocks provide a variety of niches for different species, and shell-gravel and muddy bottoms will also have their characteristic animal life.

Conservation and collecting

The immediate reaction of many people when they find something of interest is to take it home to have a better look. If possible this should be avoided, and one of the objects of this book is that it should be taken into the field rather than permanently kept on the bookshelf, and it should help to make removal of specimens less necessary. Although many of the species that are described here are relatively abundant, others are not, and because they may take several years to reach maturity and perhaps have restricted breeding seasons, they can be particularly vulnerable to over collecting. If you must take specimens from the beach try to take as few examples as possible. It is very tempting for divers in particular to collect large numbers of attractive specimens which may at first sight appear abundant; this may not in reality be the case so the temptation should be resisted. If you must take something under water to shoot with take a camera rather than a spear gun. Large, territorial fishes have become severely threatened, particularly in the Mediterranean, due to the unsporting use of spear guns, and current opinion is moving against the use of such devices.

Normally the first sight of any shore gives relatively little impression of the wealth of animal life that may be found there. Most marine plants, on the other hand, are relatively conspicuous. The best time to begin exploring the shore is one hour before low tide is due. When you arrive, go immediately to the water's edge so as to make maximum use of the exposure provided by the ebb tide. You can then work back as the tide returns. On rocky shores you will have to work hard to find representatives of all the animal groups present. Apart from noticing the animals that are attached to the exposed rocks, for instance, barnacles, limpets and dogwhelks, examine all the crevices and holes for periwinkles, topshells and sea-anemones. Where there is a good covering of seaweeds notice their zonation patterns and turn them over to look for the variety of species that may be growing on or under them. You should find hydroids, sponges, sea-mats and periwinkles at least. If there are smaller rocks which are free, turn them over and look for sea-anemones, worms, crabs and other crustaceans below. The animals you have exposed have deliberately chosen the underside of rocks, so ensure that you *turn the rocks back again after examination*, otherwise they will probably die. Investigate all rock pools carefully. They frequently contain a variety of organisms including swimming forms such as prawns and small fishes. On sandy shores and on mud, signs of life may at first sight be less obvious. The experienced observer will soon recognize the various types of worm cast and burrow entrance, however. To find what lives within the sand or mud you will have to dig carefully and sometimes sieve the sand. Such shores house a wealth of burrowing worms and bivalves as well as a few burrowing sea-anemones, snails, crustaceans, brittle-stars and heart-urchins.

If you are collecting for a purpose, arrange to look after your specimens carefully. Prevent them from becoming overheated by placing your jars in a rock pool to keep the temperature down. Put the lids on only when actually carrying the jars, and add just sufficient water to cover the specimens or let them swim freely. Only take the animals away from the beach if you are certain that you can keep them alive. After you have examined them return them to the spot they came from, or to a similar place. Much of what has been said applies to the diver collecting in the shallow seas. If fishes are being collected from 10m or below, remember that they will have to be decompressed by gradually raising them to the surface. Polythene bags are useful for this and they also make good containers for small invertebrates; larger specimens can be carried in string bags.

Illustrated key

Plants

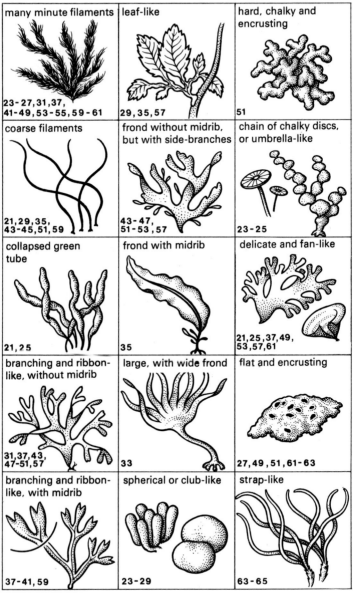

many minute filaments 23-27, 31, 37, 41-49, 53-55, 59-61	leaf-like 29, 35, 57	hard, chalky and encrusting 51
coarse filaments 21, 29, 35, 43-45, 51, 59	frond without midrib, but with side-branches 43-47, 51-53, 57	chain of chalky discs, or umbrella-like 23-25
collapsed green tube 21, 25	frond with midrib 35	delicate and fan-like 21, 25, 37, 49, 53, 57, 61
branching and ribbon-like, without midrib 31, 37, 43, 47-51, 57	large, with wide frond 33	flat and encrusting 27, 49, 51, 61-63
branching and ribbon-like, with midrib 37-41, 59	spherical or club-like 23-29	strap-like 63-65

Plant-like animals

Joint-legged animals

simple, branching or encrusting spongy growth	hard, branching growth; soft tentacles	small body; 6-8 legs
71-75	99-101	231
branching growths; tentacles cannot withdraw	fan-like growth	flat or compressed body; more than 8 legs
79	87, 95-97, 101	201-211
branching growths; tentacles can withdraw	free-living; 5 pairs of branching arms	rounded or compressed body; with pincers; more than 8 legs
81	241	211-213
soft body; tentacles surround mouth	branching colony; tentacles withdraw if disturbed	moderate – large, long body; with pincers; walking legs
87-95, 99	235-237, 305	201, 215-221
hard body; soft tentacles surround mouth	encrusting colony; tentacles withdraw if disturbed	small – large, ovoid or rounded body; with pincers; walking legs
99	235-237	219, 223-229

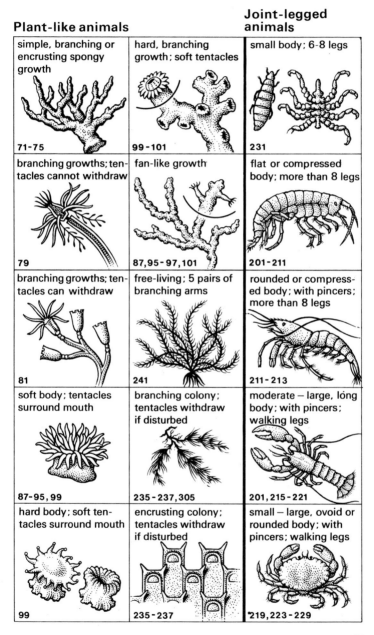

Animals with shells

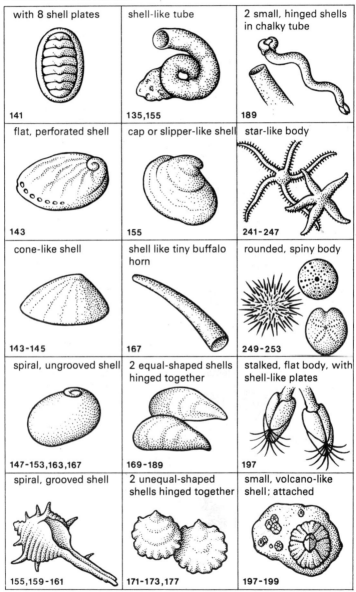

with 8 shell plates	shell-like tube	2 small, hinged shells in chalky tube
141	**135, 155**	**189**
flat, perforated shell	cap or slipper-like shell	star-like body
143	**155**	**241-247**
cone-like shell	shell like tiny buffalo horn	rounded, spiny body
143-145	**167**	**249-253**
spiral, ungrooved shell	2 equal-shaped shells hinged together	stalked, flat body, with shell-like plates
147-153, 163, 167	**169-189**	**197**
spiral, grooved shell	2 unequal-shaped shells hinged together	small, volcano-like shell; attached
155, 159-161	**171-173, 177**	**197-199**

Animals without shells

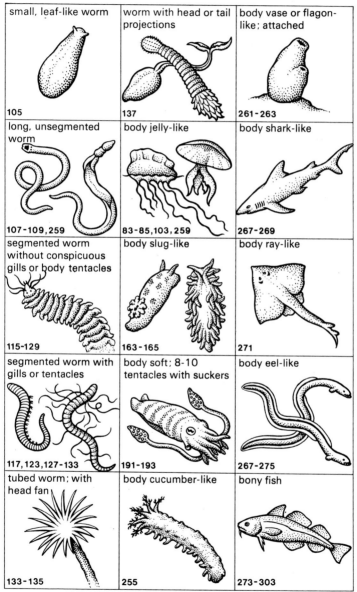

small, leaf-like worm 105	worm with head or tail projections 137	body vase or flagon-like; attached 261 - 263
long, unsegmented worm 107 - 109, 259	body jelly-like 83 - 85, 103, 259	body shark-like 267 - 269
segmented worm without conspicuous gills or body tentacles 115 - 129	body slug-like 163 - 165	body ray-like 271
segmented worm with gills or tentacles 117, 123, 127 - 133	body soft; 8-10 tentacles with suckers 191 - 193	body eel-like 267 - 275
tubed worm; with head fan 133 - 135	body cucumber-like 255	bony fish 273 - 303

Plant Kingdom

The plant kingdom is divided into a number of major groups which range from simple, unicellular organisms that can only be seen with the aid of the microscope, to the great trees which are so familiar on land. The sea provides a satisfactory environment for only a few groups of plants, however, and the majority of these belong to the lowest group of the plant kingdom, the Thallophyta. This group comprises the algae (including the seaweeds), the fungi and the lichens. The only other group that is significantly represented in the sea is the Angiospermae (flowering plants).

Green plants are anabolic organisms, that is, they elaborate organic material from inorganic sources with the aid of photosynthesis. No animal can do this; all animals depend either directly or indirectly on plants for their supply of food. Plants therefore form the first living stage of all *food chains* or *food webs*. (Food chains or food webs are terms used to describe the nutritional relationships existing between organisms and their consumers or predators in a community.)

The marine algae are divided into a number of subgroups of which three will be dealt with here. They are the Chlorophyceae (green algae), Phaeophyceae (brown algae) and Rhodophyceae (red algae). Whilst colour would appear to be their principal distinguishing characteristic, it must be remembered that colour may not only be variable, but it may change considerably if the plants have been removed from the sea for long periods, or if they are dying. Furthermore, many of the red and brown seaweeds are quite similar in colour. These facts make colour alone a rather unreliable criterion for the purposes of identification, and this also holds true for animals. The identification of marine algae is largely based on the form of the plant in question. Precise identification may depend on the accurate recognition of microscopic characters, and to a large extent such aspects of seaweed identification are beyond the scope of this book. Nevertheless with the gross descriptions of form, the colour plates and a little experience, it should be possible for the reader to succeed in what is quite a difficult area of seashore biology.

A typical seaweed is normally composed of a *holdfast* (or attachment organ) and a *frond*. The holdfast and frond together are termed the *thallus*. Many fronds become broken from their holdfasts and washed into positions where they are subsequently found. For this reason not all the illustrations show the holdfast. Unlike the higher plants, many algae show relatively little differentiation within their tissues, and only some, such as the laminarians, have any form of vascular system. Instead, most of the cells are developed in such a way that each can carry out many of the functions of the organism, and any specialized regions that do exist, such as holdfasts and reproductive organs, are reduced to a minimum. The form of the frond and the holdfast are important clues to identification. Holdfasts may be root-like, disc-like or may grow as a shaggy tangle of fine 'rootlets' – these are not roots in the strict sense, however, as they do not provide the seaweed with a special absorptive region. The frond may be rounded or cylindrical, flattened, flattened with a central rib or ribs, or intermediate, i.e. neither round nor flat. The style of branching is also important; it may be dichotomous, alternate, spiral or pinnate. Fig. 4 shows some of these features.

In some species, especially the brown and red algae, attention to the form and disposition of the reproductive organs will assist with identification. In the Phaeophyceae this is true of the order Fucales (e.g. *Fucus*). Here, the reproductive organs generally consist of small pits opening by minute pores. They are usually set in thickened portions of the frond near the tips of the branches. In other orders, such as the Ectocarpales (e.g. *Ectocarpus*), reproductive organs can be identified (with a hand lens) on the sides of the branches or in the angle of a junction between the stem and a side-branch. In some other genera (e.g. *Padina*), they occur on the surface of the frond arranged in groups. Some of the Rhodophyceae also have their reproductive organs set in pits. Other genera, like *Polysiphonia*, carry them on small branches of the frond, but they may be buried in the plant tissue itself, as in *Dilsea*. In some red algae the reproductive organs are extremely difficult to discern. The above descriptions do not take into account the various forms or functions of the reproductive organs, only their disposition. Where necessary this will be referred to further in the text. Fig. 4 also illustrates some reproductive organs.

The life histories of marine algae are, when first encountered, quite complicated. Essentially two generations alternate with each other. These are known as the *sporophyte* generation, which bears asexually produced spores and which, on the development of these spores, gives rise to the *gametophyte* or sexual generation. The gametophyte generation may consist of plants bearing both male and female organs, or of separate male and female plants. Sexual reproduction results in a new sporophyte generation. In some cases the sporophyte generation closely resembles the gametophyte. If the two generations are similar they are termed *isomorphic*. If they are dissimilar they are known as *heteromorphic*. In some cases the life cycles are less straightforward and a full account of them is beyond the scope of this book.

The occurrence of seaweeds is limited by light, which they require for photosynthesis. Thus they are restricted to depths where sufficient illumination exists. High turbidity in the sea will restrict illumination and thus plant growth, and only certain species will be able to exist in the reduced illumination characteristic of caves, etc. It must be realized that the European area provides a vast range of marine habitats both in terms of the physical conditions that prevail and in terms of the variety of substrates for plants to grow on. As has already been mentioned, zonation of organisms is a fundamental characteristic of the shore. Generally the green algae grow high on the rocky shore, either where they can be exposed as the tide ebbs, or in pools. The brown algae frequently form a characteristic order down the shore, i.e. *Pelvetia canaliculata, Fucus spiralis, Ascophyllum nodosum, F. vesiculosus, F. serratus* and *Laminaria* species. The red algae generally prefer less exposure to air and grow to the greatest depths in the sea. It must be remembered that the lists of descriptions of algae which follow are by no means exclusive. It has not been possible to include many of the smaller genera existing in the European area, and many that are mentioned are in fact represented by more species than can be described here. A very helpful check-list of British marine algae is given by Parke, M. and Dixon, P. S. 1968.

This account has paid little attention to the lichens or the marine angiosperms. However, more is said about them on pages 62–65. Here it should be noted that the former group dwell in the splash zone and are more characteristic of the terrestrial habitats. The sea-grasses are highly specialized angiosperms.

Fig. 4 Various patterns of thallus branching and reproductive organs: a = dichotomous; b = opposite; c = opposite with pinnate side-branches; d = alternate with alternate side-branches; e = spiral branching; f = sprig of *Fucus* with reproductive area shaded in black; g = magnified reproductive bodies of *Padina*; h = magnified reproductive body of *Polysiphonia*

Subkingdom Thallophyta
Group Algae

These mainly aquatic plants contain the green pigment chlorophyll. Their bodies are not differentiated into true roots, stems nor leaves, and they lack a vascular system. Reproduction is by spores.

Class Chlorophyceae Green algae

Algae in which the chlorophyll is not masked by brown or red pigment. Their structure ranges from minute, single-celled plants to larger thread- or frond-like plants composed of many cells.

Prasiola stipitata Suhr Frond 0.7–1.25 cm long; generally ovoid narrowing to a short stalk; edges often curled. **Colour** usually dark green. **Habitat** on rocks on the upper middle shore. **Distribution** Atlantic, English Channel and North Sea.

Monostroma grevillei Wittrock Frond 10–30 cm long; soft, delicate and funnel shaped with a split down one side when adult. **Colour** pale, translucent green. **Habitat** usually in rock pools on the lower shore or on rocks in shallow water. **Distribution** Atlantic, English Channel, North Sea and Baltic. N.B. about five other species also occur.

Blidingia minima (Kützing) Kylin *(=Enteromorpha minima)* Frond up to 10 cm long; may be unbranched or branched slightly; sometimes inflated. **Habitat** growing on rocks, pilings, etc., on the upper shore. **Distribution** Atlantic, English Channel and North Sea.

Enteromorpha intestinalis (Linnaeus) Link Frond 5 cm–1 m or more long; tubular and irregularly inflated and crinkled; generally not branched; may taper continuously along length. **Colour** pale green. **Habitat** in rock pools on upper shore, often in water with reduced salinity; sometimes washed up. **Distribution** Mediterranean, Atlantic, English Channel, North Sea and Baltic.

Enteromorpha compressa Greville Frond up to 30 cm long; tubular; main frond tapers only at the base and usually gives off a number of similar side-branches; not as soft and delicate as *B. minima* above. **Colour** dark to pale green. **Habitat** on rocks and pilings on upper, middle and lower shores; frequently in pools where the salinity is reduced; often washed up; sometimes in estuaries. **Distribution** Mediterranean, Atlantic, English Channel, North Sea and Baltic. N.B. this may be a branched form of *E. intestinalis*.

Enteromorpha linza (Linnaeus) J. Agardh *(=Ulva linza)* Frond 10–50 cm long; superficially flattened, but will be found to be hollow if a transverse section is carefully examined microscopically at the edges; unbranched, tapering slightly from middle towards apex and base; edges crinkled. **Colour** bright green. **Habitat** on rocks on upper, middle and lower shore; sometimes washed up. **Distribution** Mediterranean, Atlantic, English Channel, North Sea and Baltic. N.B. about eight other species also occur.

Ulva lactuca Linnaeus **Sea-lettuce** Frond 15–50 cm long; variably shaped, may be lobe-shaped, lance-shaped or perforated; generally wider at the top than at the base; stalk if present is solid. **Colour** translucent green. **Habitat** on rocks on upper, middle and lower shore; sometimes in pools; sometimes in shallow water; may float free or be washed up. **Distribution** Mediterranean, Atlantic, English Channel, North Sea and Baltic. N.B. about three other species also occur.

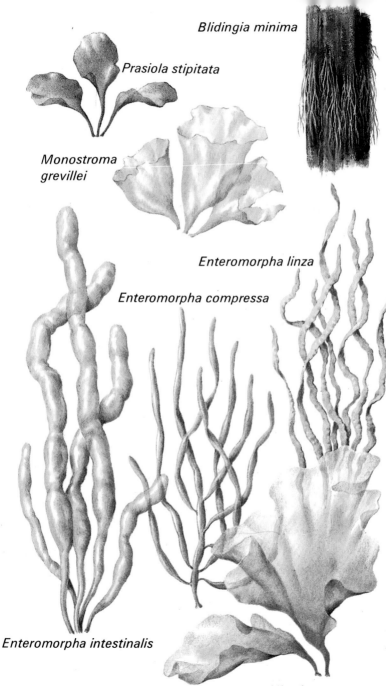

Blidingia minima

Prasiola stipitata

Monostroma grevillei

Enteromorpha linza

Enteromorpha compressa

Enteromorpha intestinalis

Ulva lactuca

Acrosiphonia arcta (Dillwyn) J. Agardh (= *Cladophora arcta*) Frond about 7 cm long; forms hemispherical tufted growths of many associated branching threads which are held together by minute coils and hooks; some branches grow down to assist with attachment. **Colour** usually deep green. **Habitat** on rocks and stones, middle and lower shore. **Distribution** Atlantic, English Channel, North Sea and Baltic. N.B. common in Spring and early Summer.

Spongomorpha aeruginosa (Linnaeus) Hoek (= *Cladophora lanosa*) Frond 1—3 cm long; forming growths of many woolly looking threads to give a spherical, tuft-like appearance. **Colour** light to dark green. **Habitat** attached to other seaweeds and the sea-grasses (e.g. *Zostera*, see page 65). **Distribution** Atlantic, English Channel, North Sea and Baltic.

Chaetomorpha linum (O. F. Müller) Frond 15—30 cm long; forming growths of many fine, almost cylindrical, unbranching threads which taper slightly at their bases (a hand lens will show that each filament is made of a chain of large cells); threads fixed by modified cell at base which often merges with that of neighbouring threads to form an attachment disc. **Colour** dark green. **Habitat** in pools on upper and middle shore, or attached to rocks covered by sand; often floating free and washed up. **Distribution** Mediterranean, Atlantic, English Channel, North Sea and Baltic.

Cladophora rupestris (Linnaeus) Kützing Frond 7—12 cm long; forming small to large coarse growths of many branching fronds; branching is usually irregular or opposite (see fig. 4); attachment area may send off runners to start new growths and so colonize large areas. **Habitat** on rocks on the middle and lower shore where it may grow underneath *Fucus serratus* (see page 39). **Distribution** Atlantic, English Channel, North Sea and Baltic. N.B. a closely related species occurs in the Mediterranean. About fifteen other species occur.

Valonia utricularis (Roth) C. Agardh Frond about 3 cm tall; often more bulbous or club-shaped than the specimens illustrated opposite; a number may arise from a communal holdfast. **Colour** iridescent green. **Habitat** on rocks down to 10 m. **Distribution** Mediterranean.

Dasycladus clavaeformis (Roth) C. Agardh Frond about 3 cm tall and tapering towards base; several may grow from one holdfast. **Colour** green with a felty texture. **Habitat** on rocks among sand and gravel in shallow and deeper water. **Distribution** Mediterranean.

Acetabularia mediterranea Lamouroux **Mermaid's Cup** Frond up to 8 cm long; stalk bears up to 100 leaf-like structures arranged segmentally so that they collectively resemble a disc; stalk is stiffened by a calcareous secretion. **Colour** greenish-white. **Habitat** on rocks and stones on middle and lower shore and in shallow water. **Distribution** Mediterranean.

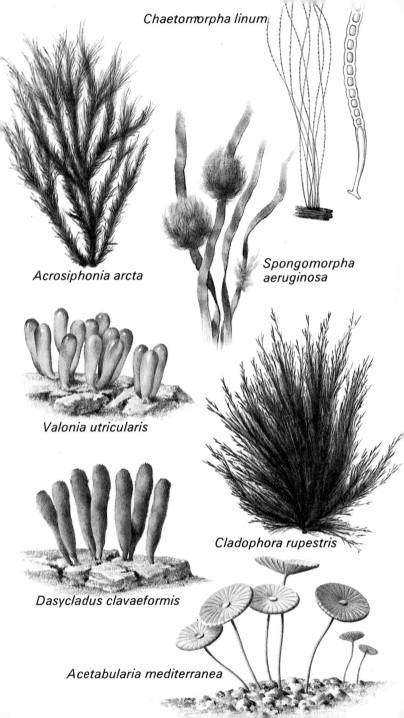

Chaetomorpha linum

Acrosiphonia arcta

Spongomorpha aeruginosa

Valonia utricularis

Cladophora rupestris

Dasycladus clavaeformis

Acetabularia mediterranea

Derbesia marina (Lyngbye) Solier Frond about 5cm long; usually forms a growth of fine filaments rising from a basal portion with occasional lateral branches; sometimes with ovoid reproductive bodies that can be seen with a hand lens. **Colour** bright green. **Habitat** on seaweed and mud on the upper, middle and lower shores. **Distribution** Atlantic and English Channel.

Derbesia lamourouxi (J. G. Agardh) Solier (Not illustrated) Similar to *D. marina*. **Distribution** Mediterranean, Atlantic north to Spain.

Bryopsis plumosa C. A. Agardh Frond up to 10cm long; feather-like, pinnate branches arranged more or less opposite on the main stem; branches are usually smaller towards the top. **Colour** yellow green in the male, and dark green in the female; glossy. **Habitat** on rocks and stones and on pool sides, middle and lower shore. **Distribution** Mediterranean, Atlantic, English Channel, North Sea and Baltic. N.B. common in Spring and Summer.

Udotea petiolata (Turra) Borgesen Frond about 6.5cm long; fan-like growths carried on a stalk; calcified; multiple growths of several fans may develop. **Habitat** among sand on stones and rocks down to 60m. **Distribution** Mediterranean.

Halimeda tuna (Ellis & Solander) Lamouroux **Calcareous Green Alga** Frond about 9cm; consists of a number of calcified, disc-like segments strung together in chains; some irregular branching. **Habitat** usually on hard substrates down to 20m. **Distribution** Mediterranean.

Codium tomentosum Stackhouse Frond 25–35cm long; tubular and dichotomously branching with a felt-like texture. **Holdfast** disc-like, consists of many entwined threads encrusting the substrate. **Colour** dark green. **Habitat** on mud, sand and rocks down to 20m. **Distribution** Mediterranean, Atlantic and English Channel.

Codium bursa (Linnaeus) C. A. Agardh Frond 3–20cm across; slender filaments entwine to form a soft, sponge-like, spherical growth; a mat of interwoven filaments attach it to the substrate. **Colour** dark green. **Habitat** attached to rocks in shallow water; sometimes washed up. **Distribution** Mediterranean and Atlantic. N.B. about three other species occur.

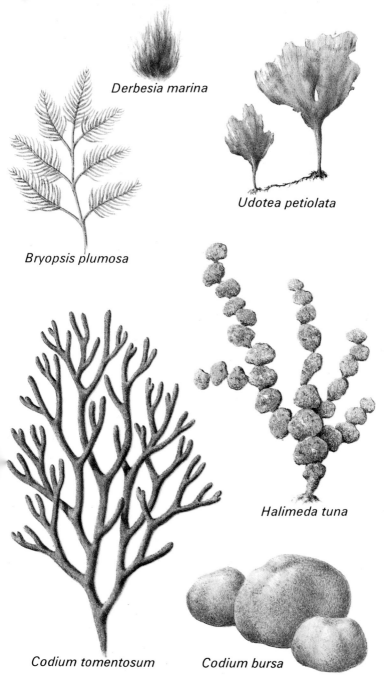

Derbesia marina

Udotea petiolata

Bryopsis plumosa

Halimeda tuna

Codium tomentosum

Codium bursa

Class Phaeophyceae Brown algae

Algae in which the chlorophyll is often masked by the brown pigment fucoxanthin. These are multicellular plants, often large, and are normally attached to the substrate. They do not generally flourish in warmer water, thus they are relatively scarce in the Mediterranean.

Ectocarpus siliculosus (Dillwyn) Lyngbye Frond 12–30cm long; tangled growth of fine, branching filaments which becomes free towards the tips; branches very variably arranged. **Holdfast** creeping and filamentous; a hand lens may reveal both club-shaped and more pointed reproductive bodies which are carried towards the tips of the branches, usually on short stems. **Colour** yellow-green-brown. **Habitat** attached to rocks and stones from the middle shore down to shallow water. **Distribution** Mediterranean, Atlantic, English Channel, North Sea and Baltic. N.B. this species represents an aggregation of several formerly separated species of *Ectocarpus*.

Spongonema tomentosum (Hudson) Kützing Frond 3–13cm long, but often less; similar to *E. siliculosus* above, but plants more entwined thus appearing as corded, woolly growths about 0.25cm wide. **Habitat** growing on larger seaweeds, e.g. *Fucus vesiculosus* or *Himanthalia* sp. (see pages 35 and 39), or on stones or shells on middle and lower shores. **Distribution** Atlantic, English Channel and North Sea.

Ralfsia verrucosa (Areschoug) J. Agardh Groups of individuals forming irregular encrustations 2–10cm across; individuals may be round and about 0.25cm thick; in the winter small, club-like reproductive bodies growing upwards may be seen with a hand lens; isomorphic generations (see page 19) follow each other in the life cycle. **Colour** dark brown-black. **Habitat** attached to rocks and shells, often in exposed places. **Distribution** Mediterranean, Atlantic, English Channel and North Sea. N.B. about four other species occur.

Leathesia difformis Areschoug Frond 2–5cm in diameter; globular or irregularly shaped, shiny, thick-walled growths which are solid when young but become more hollow with age; if the growths are cut across with a sharp knife and the inside examined with a hand lens it will be seen to be made of dichotomously branching filaments; the reproductive bodies are carried terminally on the outer extremities of these. **Colour** olive-brown. **Habitat** growing on rocks and smaller seaweeds. **Distribution** Atlantic, English Channel and North Sea in Spring and Summer. N.B. do not confuse with *Colpomenia* (see page 29).

Stilophora rhizodes J. G. Agardh Frond 15–60cm long; dichotomously branching frond (see page 19); branches taper near their tips and are covered in small spots; frond is solid when young but becomes tubular with age. **Habitat** on rocks or other seaweeds on the lower shore, often where the salinity is reduced, e.g. by streams. **Distribution** Atlantic and English Channel.

Stictyosiphon tortilis Reinke Frond 7–15cm long; much branched, alternately or opposite (see page 19). **Colour** yellow-brown. **Habitat** on stones, other seaweeds and shells on the lower shore and in shallow water. **Distribution** north Atlantic and northern North Sea.

Stictyosiphon adriaticus Kützing (Not illustrated) Similar to *S. tortilis* but up to 20cm long. **Distribution** Mediterranean.

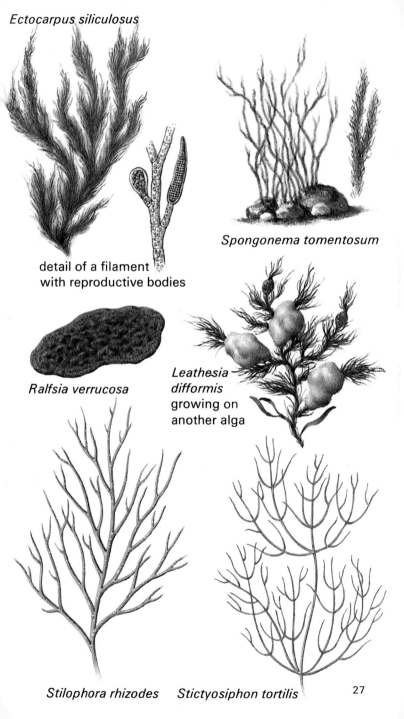

Ectocarpus siliculosus

Spongonema tomentosum

detail of a filament
with reproductive bodies

Ralfsia verrucosa

Leathesia difformis growing on another alga

Stilophora rhizodes *Stictyosiphon tortilis*

27

Asperococcus turneri (Smith) Hooker **(=*A. bullosus*)** Frond 15–30cm long; tubular growth carried on a narrow, short stalk. **Holdfast** small and disc-like. Often growing in groups; texture soft, slightly transparent and membranous, thickening with age. **Colour** olive green. **Habitat** attached to rocks and larger seaweeds on the middle and lower shore and in shallow water. **Distribution** Mediterranean, Atlantic, English Channel and North Sea in Summer.

Litosiphon pusillus (Hooker) **Harvey** Frond 5–10cm long; densely growing in clumps; texture soft and elastic; young specimens may be slightly hairy, older ones tubular. **Habitat** growing on *Chorda filum* (see page 35), which may thus resemble frayed ropes at the end of the growing season, on the extreme lower shore and in shallow water. **Distribution** Atlantic, English Channel and North Sea.

Scytosiphon lomentaria (Lyngbye) Link Frond 15–30cm long; tubular and resembling a miniature chain of sausages; not branched; tapers at the tip. **Colour** green-yellow. **Habitat** attached to rocks, stones and other seaweeds on the lower shore and in shallow water, often in exposed places. **Distribution** Mediterranean, Atlantic, English Channel, North Sea and Baltic.

Punctaria latifolia Greville Frond 20–40cm long and 7.5cm across; unbranched, leaf-like fronds borne on short stalk and dotted with small spots or hairs; may terminate in a wide- or narrow-angled point. **Habitat** on rocks, stones and shells (especially those of live limpets see pages 143 and 145) on middle and lower shores and in shallow water. **Distribution** Mediterranean, Atlantic, English Channel and North Sea. N.B. about three other species occur.

Petalonia fascia (O. F. Müller) Kuntze Frond may reach 30cm in length and 6cm across; edges may be frilled; the short stalk quickly widens to form the frond and is much shorter than that of the laminarians (see page 33). **Colour** glossy green-brown. **Habitat** on rocks, often those covered with sand, and in pools on the lower shore. **Distribution** Mediterranean, Atlantic, North Sea and Baltic. N.B. about two other species occur.

Colpomenia peregrina Sauvageau **Oyster Thief** Frond is a thin-walled, globular, hollow growth up to 20cm in diameter, although often the size of a table-tennis ball; covered all over with fine brown dots. **Habitat** in pools and attached to various seaweeds and shells on middle and lower shores and in shallow water. **Distribution** Atlantic, English Channel and North Sea. N.B. this species is easily distinguished from *Leathesia difformis*, since it is not gelatinous but is dry and papery.

Colpomenia sinuosa (Roth) **Derbes & Solier** (Not illustrated) Very similar to *C. peregrina*. **Distribution** Mediterranean.

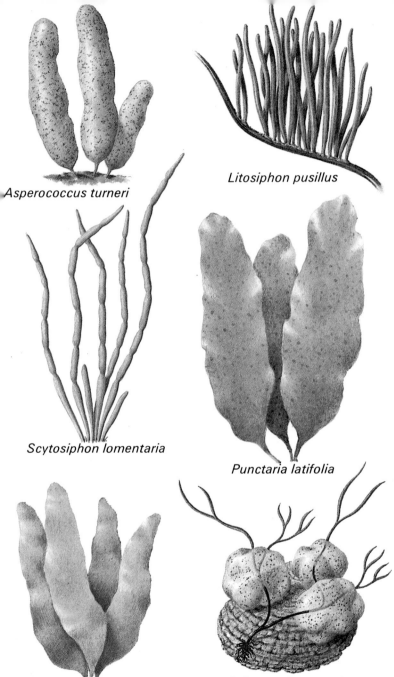

Asperococcus turneri

Litosiphon pusillus

Scytosiphon lomentaria

Punctaria latifolia

Petalonia fascia

Colpomenia peregrina

Cutleria multifida (Smith) Greville Frond 10–40cm long; forms flat, fan-like growths; dichotomously branched, tips of the branches divided; texture rather springy when fresh; usually spotted. **Holdfast** disc-like. **Colour** yellow-green. **Habitat** attached to rocks and shells, generally in shallow water; may be washed up. **Distribution** Mediterranean, Atlantic, English Channel and North Sea.

Sporochnus pedunculatus (Hudson) C. A. Agardh Frond 15–45cm long; filamentous growth of a central thread, bearing branches; each branch bears alternately arranged branchlets. **Colour** olive-green. **Habitat** on rocks on lower shore and in shallow water. **Distribution** Mediterranean, Atlantic, English Channel and North Sea.

Arthrocladia villosa (Hudson) Duby Frond 15–90cm long; consists of fine filaments with oppositely arranged branches; these in turn bear branchlets set in whorls (as shown by inset); branchlets may carry very fine, unbranching filaments which form part of the reproductive bodies and these impart a shaggy, green appearance. **Habitat** growing on rocks, stones and *Zostera* (see page 65). **Distribution** Mediterranean, Atlantic, English Channel and North Sea. N.B. distinguished from *Desmarestia* (see below) by the shaggy appearance resulting from the whorled branchlets.

Desmarestia aculeata Lamouroux Frond 30–180cm long; main stem is slightly compressed and pliable when young, becoming more rigid with age; main stem bears alternately arranged side-branches which have a thorny appearance; side-branches themselves are alternately pinnate (see page 19) and in Summer they bear very fine, branching filaments. **Holdfast** disc-like. **Habitat** attached to rocks on extreme lower shore and in shallow water; sometimes washed up. **Distribution** northern Atlantic and northern North Sea. N.B. other species of *Desmarestia* rot quickly when taken from the sea; *D. aculeata* only does so in Summer. Their colour changes from bright green (when young) or brown (when older) to verdigris.

Desmarestia ligulata (Lightfoot) Lamouroux Frond 60–180cm long; main stem somewhat flattened with a suggestion of a midrib, and bearing closely arranged, opposite branches; these branches themselves bear minute projections which may carry tufts of fine hairs. **Colour** olive-brown. **Habitat** attached to rocks in pools and in shallow water. **Distribution** Atlantic and English Channel. N.B. the pliable stem decomposes in the air to a flabby, green condition.

Desmarestia viridis O. F. Müller Lamouroux Frond about 30cm long, shorter and more delicate than *D. aculeata*; soft, pliable, slightly flattened stem carries oppositely arranged side-branches which are longer near the base and shorter away from it. These side-branches carry opposite sub-branches which give the plant a feathery appearance, and this opposite branching (see page 19) distinguishes this species from *D. aculeata* where the branching is alternate. **Colour** olive-green when young, red-brown when older. **Habitat** attached to stones and seaweed on the lower shore and in shallow water. **Distribution** Atlantic, English Channel and North Sea in Summer.

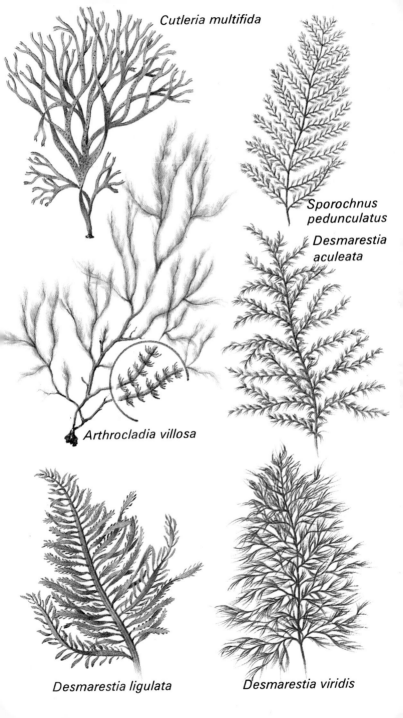

Cutleria multifida

Sporochnus pedunculatus

Desmarestia aculeata

Arthrocladia villosa

Desmarestia ligulata

Desmarestia viridis

Note on the family Laminariaceae The seaweeds illustrated on this plate are all members of an important family of brown algae, the Laminariaceae (kelps). This family includes some of the largest algae found in European waters. There is a characteristic alternation of heteromorphic generations (see page 19) and it is the asexual plant (sporophyte) which forms the typical kelp plant. The sexual phase (gametophyte) is microscopic and generally unfamiliar to the layman. Laminarians are characteristic of the extreme lower shore and of shallow, coastal water. They form a very characteristic zone on many rocky shores where they are usually uncovered only at the Spring tides. Laminarians provide an important habitat for a variety of other marine algae and animals. Some of these are specialized to live on the frond, but many more find food and shelter in the crevices and crannies provided by the massed branches of the holdfast. These holdfasts thus provide a rich hunting ground for the marine zoologist.

Laminaria digitata (Hudson) Lamouroux **Oarweed or Tangle** Frond usually about 1 m, but may be longer; thick, rounded, very flexible stipe broadening out into a wide, shiny blade; blade and stalk are about equal in length; the blade divides as it grows forming a number of strap-like fronds. **Holdfast** much branched. **Habitat** attached to rocks on the extreme lower shore and down to about 6 m; often washed up. **Distribution** Atlantic, English Channel, North Sea and Baltic. N.B. the brown weed fades to green and then white when washed up on the beach; this species usually occupies a slightly higher position on the extreme lower shore than does *L. hyperborea* (see below).

Laminaria hyperborea (Gunnerus) Foslie Frond up to 3.5 m long but often less; stiff, rough, rounded stalk tapers towards its upper part; blade is ovoid and split into a number of strap-like fronds. **Holdfast** much branched. **Habitat** attached to rocks and stones on the extreme lower shore and in shallow water. **Distribution** Atlantic, English Channel, North Sea and Baltic. N.B. the roughness of the stalk provides good anchorage for epiphytic and epizoic organisms; usually growing just below *L. digitata* (see above).

Laminaria ochroleuca De la Pylaie (Not illustrated) Similar to *L. hyperborea*, but blade yellowish and stem stiff and smooth. **Distribution** Atlantic north to English Channel approaches.

Laminaria saccharina Lamouroux **Sea Belt, Sugar Kelp or Poor Man's Weather Glass** Frond 20 cm–3 m long; relatively thin stalk which is usually about one quarter the blade length; blade somewhat like a crumpled ribbon. **Holdfast** of branching growths and two-tiered in appearance. **Habitat** attached to stones, rocks and shells from extreme lower shore down to about 20 m, especially in sheltered positions. **Distribution** Atlantic, English Channel and North Sea. N.B. avoid confusion with *Petalonia fascia* (see page 29).

Laminaria rodriguezi Bornet (Not illustrated) Somewhat similar to *L. saccharina* but usually about 40 cm long. **Frond** has a much shorter stalk and several may arise from a more simple, branching holdfast. **Habitat** on gravelly and harder substrates, sometimes in deep water. **Distribution** Mediterranean.

Saccorhiza polyschides (Lightfoot) Batters (=*S. bulbosa*) Frond 1.5—4.5 m long and nearly as broad across the blade; stalk or stipe is flat and twisted at the base, being wavy at the edges and quite stiff towards the upper part; blade widens suddenly from top of stipe and is almost semicircular; minute hairs borne in tufts on blade. **Holdfast** is collar-like with a number of attachment 'rootlets'. **Habitat** on rocks on extreme lower shore and in shallow water. **Distribution** Atlantic, English Channel and North Sea.

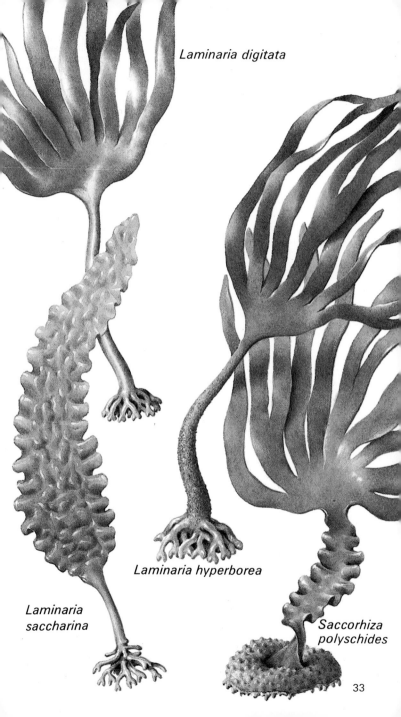

Laminaria digitata

Laminaria hyperborea

Laminaria saccharina

Saccorhiza polyschides

33

Sargassum vulgare J. G. Agardh Frond 15–30cm long; irregularly branching stem bears lance-like 'leaves' in addition to rounded bladders and branching reproductive bodies which are carried in clusters. **Colour** brown. **Habitat** on hard substrates down to about 30m. **Distribution** Mediterranean.

Sargassum hornschuchi C. A. Agardh Frond 30–40cm long; main stem bears irregular or alternate side-branches (see page 19) which are leaf-like; near the tip of the plant the side-branches also bear rounded bladders and clusters of tapering reproductive organs. **Colour** brown. **Habitat** on rocks from 10–100m. **Distribution** Mediterranean.

Chordaria flagelliformis (O. F. Müller) C. A. Agardh Frond 23–70cm long; growing singly or in groups; main stem rounded and solid, giving off a number of slippery, whip-like branches of various lengths. **Holdfast** disc-like. **Colour** dark brown. **Habitat** on stones, rocks and timbers on upper, middle and lower shores. **Distribution** Atlantic, English Channel, North Sea and west Baltic.

Chorda filum (Linnaeus) Stackhouse Frond up to 4.5m long; unbranched, slimy, whip-like stem which is hollow and air-filled when the plant is adult. **Holdfast** small and disc-like. **Colour** olive-brown. **Habitat** in shallow water from 2–20m, often in areas where the bottom is gravel. **Distribution** Atlantic, English Channel, North Sea and Baltic. N.B. there is an alteration of heteromorphic generations (see page 19); the plant described here is the sporophyte.

Alaria esculenta (Linnaeus) Greville **Dabberlocks** Frond 10–30cm long; consists of a short, rounded stalk or stipe with a distinguishable midrib which supports a long, thin 'leaf' or lamina; the midrib can be identified throughout the length of this and immediately distinguishes this species from the laminarians (see page 33) with which it might otherwise be confused. **Holdfast** branching. **Habitat** on rocks on the extreme lower shore and in shallow water, often in exposed places. **Distribution** northern Atlantic and North Sea.

Mesogloia vermiculata (Smith) S. F. Gray Frond about 6cm long; slimy, rounded stem bears numerous branches of various thicknesses and lengths giving them a tufted, fan-like, pyramidal appearance. **Colour** green-yellow-brown. **Habitat** on rocks often covered by sand on the middle and lower shores. **Distribution** northern Atlantic and North Sea.

Himanthalia elongata (Linnaeus) S. F. Gray (=*H. lorea*) **Sea-thong** Frond up to 2m long; strap-like, flattened and dichotomously branched; branches taper towards their tips; the 'main' portion of the plant grows up from a button-like structure; the buttons, which may often exist without the rest of the frond, develop just above the holdfast and are a useful distinguishing feature. **Colour** green-brown. **Habitat** growing in colonies in pools on the lower shore or in shallow water. **Distribution** Atlantic, and English Channel.

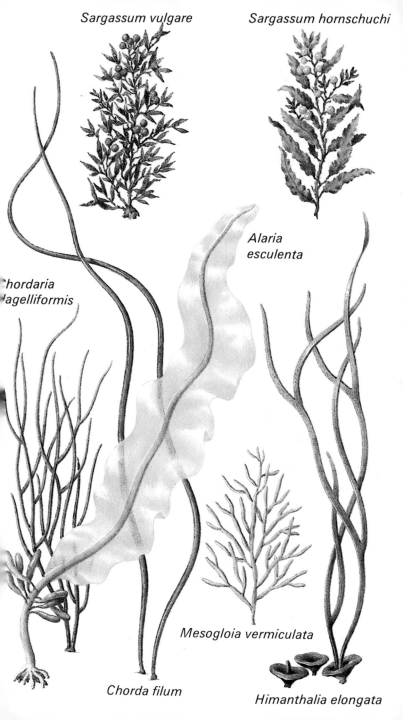

Sargassum vulgare

Sargassum hornschuchi

Alaria esculenta

Chordaria flagelliformis

Mesogloia vermiculata

Chorda filum

Himanthalia elongata

Halopteris scoparia (Linnaeus) Sauvageau (= *Stypocaulon scoparium*) Frond 8–15cm long; shaggy appearance in Summer, but less so in Winter; main stem branches alternately so that the tufted branches resemble a series of cones arranged upside-down on top of one another. **Colour** dark brown. **Habitat** attached to rocks on the lower shore, in rock pools and in shallow water. **Distribution** Mediterranean, Atlantic and English Channel.

Cladostephus verticillatus (Lightfoot) C. A. Agardh Frond 10–25cm long; main stem more or less dichotomously branching with branches bearing whorled, spiny branchlets; these may be lacking in the lower regions of the main stem and principal branches. **Holdfast** disc-like. **Colour** generally dull brown. **Habitat** on rocks, stones and red coralline seaweeds on the middle and lower shores. **Distribution** Mediterranean, Atlantic, English Channel and North Sea.

Halopteris filicina (Grattan) Kützing Frond 5–10cm long; main stem bears many alternately arranged side-branches which themselves carry pinnate branchlets (see page 19); usually the upper part of the stem bears more branches than the lower. **Holdfast** root-like. **Colour** green-brown. **Habitat** on rocks, larger seaweeds and shells on the lower shore. **Distribution** Mediterranean, Atlantic and English Channel.

Dictyopteris membranacea (Stackhouse) Batters Frond 10–30cm long; dichotomously branching, flattened; thinner than those of *Fucus* (see page 39); a conspicuous midrib may be the only part of the stem left in the lower regions of older specimens; membranous edges of fronds are dotted with groups of minute hairs; tips of branches are rounded and slightly split or notched. **Holdfast** disc-like and fibrous. **Colour** yellowish when juvenile, growing to darker brown. **Habitat** on rocks on the extreme lower shore and down to 80m. **Distribution** Mediterranean, Atlantic north to south-west Britain and Ireland, and western English Channel. N.B. when freshly collected it has a most unpleasant odour.

Dictyota dichotoma (Hudson) Lamouroux Frond about 13cm long; regularly dichotomous; transparent, delicate and flattened with rounded, notched tips; no midrib; fronds may be covered with groups of minute, hair-like reproductive bodies. **Colour** yellow-olive-brown-iridescent. **Habitat** on rocks and other seaweeds on middle and lower shores. **Distribution** Mediterranean, Atlantic, English Channel and North Sea.

Padina pavonia (Linnaeus) Lamouroux **Peacock's Tail** Frond about 10cm long; fan-shaped; narrow, rounded stalk or stipe gives rise to a rounded lamina; when young and smaller this is often quite thin and flat, but as it matures it develops into the characteristic concave fan. **Colour** outer surface has brown-green stripes; inner surface is lime-green. **Habitat** on stones and rocks in shallow water. **Distribution** Mediterranean, Atlantic and English Channel.

Taonia atomaria (Woodward) J. G. Agardh Frond 7–30cm long; membranous, translucent and shiny, broadening out sharply from the base and branching into wedge-shaped growths; presence of reproductive bodies and hairs imparts a striated appearance. **Colour** pale olive-green-brown above; darker below. **Habitat** usually on stones and rocks down to 20m. **Distribution** Mediterranean, Atlantic north to south-west Britain and Ireland, and English Channel.

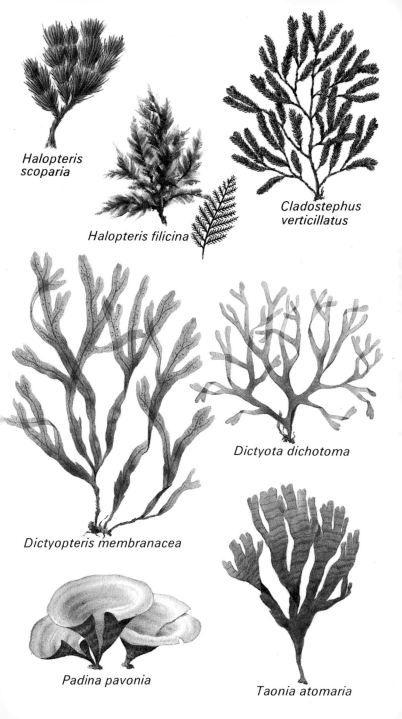

Halopteris scoparia

Halopteris filicina

Cladostephus verticillatus

Dictyota dichotoma

Dictyopteris membranacea

Padina pavonia

Taonia atomaria

Note on the wracks Members of the genera *Ascophyllum, Fucus* and *Pelvetia* are frequently found arranged in well-defined zones on the rocky shore where, together with the laminarians (see page 33), they are often the dominant algae. Although there may be some local variations, a typical zonation pattern would be *Pelvetia canaliculata* on the upper shore; *Fucus spiralis* on the middle upper shore; *Ascophyllum nodosum* and/or *Fucus vesiculosus* around the middle part of the middle shore; *Fucus serratus* on the lower middle shore.

Ascophyllum nodosum (Linnaeus) Le Jolis **Knotted Wrack** Frond 30–150cm long; tough, linear stem is rounded near the holdfast but flattened further along; main stem branches dichotomously several times and incorporates large air bladders spaced several centimetres apart; edge of main stem somewhat serrated, bearing many side-branches, many of which are slender and carry gold-yellow-olive reproductive bodies; lack of a midrib distinguishes these stems from those of *Fucus* (see below). **Habitat** attached to rocks on the upper and middle shores. **Distribution** Atlantic, English Channel and North Sea. N.B. this species is sometimes infected with the red tufts of *Polysiphonia* which are illustrated here growing on it.

Pelvetia canaliculata (Linnaeus) Decaisne & Thuret **Channelled Wrack** Frond 5–15cm long; conspicuously grooved or channelled on one side; dichotomously branched; midrib absent; no air bladders, but tips swollen to form reproductive bodies. **Habitat** on rocks on the upper shore where it forms a distinct zone. **Distribution** Atlantic, English Channel and North Sea.

Fucus serratus Linnaeus **Toothed Wrack** Frond about 60cm long but may be longer; short stalk or stipe develops into a tough, dichotomously branching frond; thick midrib; edge of frond conspicuously serrated with teeth pointing in the direction of growth; minute hairs arranged in clusters along the frond; no air bladders. **Colour** male plants may be more orange-brown than female plants. **Habitat** attached to rocks on lower middle shore, often forming a distinct zone. **Distribution** Atlantic, English Channel, North Sea and Baltic. N.B. often covered with epizoic animals, e.g. hydroids, bryozoans and spirorbid worms.

Fucus vesiculosus Linnaeus **Bladder Wrack** Frond 15–100cm long; tough, strap-like, dichotomously branching; margin not serrated; usually with conspicuous air bladders arranged in groups of two or three; olive-brown-yellow reproductive bodies at the tip of the frond; conspicuous midrib. **Habitat** on rocks on the middle shore except in very exposed places; forms a distinct zone. **Distribution** Atlantic, English Channel, North Sea and Baltic. N.B. a closely related species *F. virsoides*, which lacks the air bladders, occurs in the Mediterranean. About three other species occur.

Fucus ceranoides Linnaeus Frond 30–60cm long (generally smaller than other species of *Fucus*); delicate, dichotomously branching; prominent midrib which may lack the lamina near the holdfast; pointed reproductive bodies grouped terminally on the branches in fan-like clusters. **Habitat** growing on rocks and stones on the upper, middle and lower shores, usually where the salinity is reduced, e.g. in estuaries. **Distribution** Atlantic, English Channel and North Sea.

Fucus spiralis Linnaeus **Spiral Wrack** Frond 15–40cm long; tough, leathery; branches dichotomously and is usually twisted near the tips; margin not serrated; conspicuous midrib; conspicuous, rounded reproductive bodies borne on tips of branches; no air bladders. **Habitat** on rocks on the upper shore, but often absent from very exposed areas; may form a distinct zone. **Distribution** Atlantic, English Channel and North Sea.

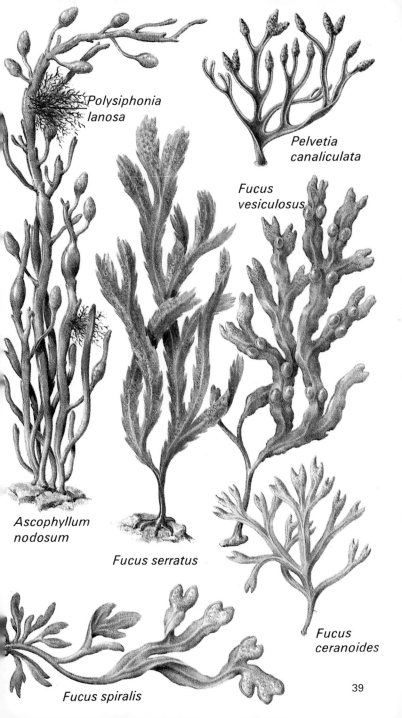

Polysiphonia lanosa

Pelvetia canaliculata

Fucus vesiculosus

Ascophyllum nodosum

Fucus serratus

Fucus ceranoides

Fucus spiralis

Bifurcaria bifurcata Ross (= *B. rotunda* = *B. tuberculata*) Frond 30—50cm long; main stem is rounded and unbranched for the lower quarter of its length, after which it bears alternately arranged branches; branches themselves fork irregularly or dichotomously, one sub-branch often being larger than the other; swollen reproductive bodies may occur at branch tips; air bladders may develop along the thallus. **Colour** brownish. **Habitat** on rocks in pools and shallow water, never exposed to the air. **Distribution** Atlantic north to Ireland, and English Channel.

Cystoseira baccata (Gmelin) Silva (= *C. fibrosa*) Frond 60—90cm long; main stem may be branched once or twice and bears many alternately arranged side-branches; the side-branches themselves bear many long, narrow branchlets which have a fine midrib and which taper at both the free end and at their bases; branchlets are often missing from the lower branches; air bladders present; bushy appearance overall. **Colour** black when dry. **Habitat** on rocks on the lower shore, in pools and shallow water. **Distribution** Atlantic north to Ireland, and English Channel.

Cystoseira tamariscifolia (Hudson) Papenfuss (= *C. ericoides*) Frond 30—45cm long; cylindrical main stem may be branched a few times and bears many alternately arranged branches; branchlets themselves carry many short spines along their length as well as tufted reproductive bodies near their tips; air bladders may occur singly or in groups; overall appearance bushy. **Colour** olive-brown; iridescent green-blue under water. **Habitat** attached to rocks on the lower shore, in pools and shallow water. **Distribution** Mediterranean, Atlantic and English Channel.

Cystoseira abrotanifolia J. G. Agardh Frond about 25cm long; main stem more or less straight, giving rise to alternately arranged side-branches; side-branches themselves shorter towards the apex of the plant, and bearing alternately arranged branchlets; reproductive bodies carried sub-terminally on branchlets. **Habitat** on stony bottoms down to about 30m. **Distribution** Mediterranean.

Halidrys siliquosa (Linnaeus) Lyngbye **Sea-oak** Frond 30—120cm long; main stem bears regular and alternately arranged side-branches; plant somewhat compressed; air bladders resemble the seed pods of some terrestrial plants and are divided internally into about ten compartments. **Holdfast** flattened and conical. **Habitat** on rocks on the middle and lower shore and in shallow water. **Distribution** Atlantic, English Channel and North Sea.

Cystoseira spicata Ercegovic Frond about 30 cm long; main stem divides near the holdfast into a few long branches which may carry alternately arranged, pinnate branchlets; reproductive bodies carried on branchlets. **Habitat** on hard substrates. **Distribution** Mediterranean.

As mentioned in the introduction to this section there is a number of genera of brown algae which may be found in the European area and which are not mentioned here. Dickinson, C. 1963 and Newton, L. 1931 describe many of these.

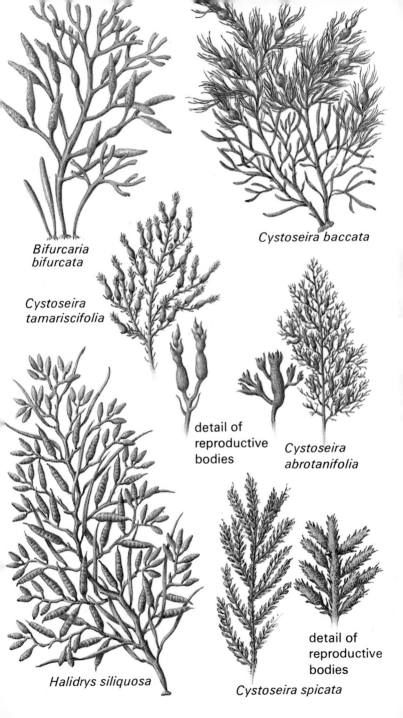

Bifurcaria bifurcata

Cystoseira baccata

Cystoseira tamariscifolia

detail of reproductive bodies

Cystoseira abrotanifolia

Halidrys siliquosa

detail of reproductive bodies

Cystoseira spicata

Class Rhodophyceae Red algae

Algae in which the chlorophyll is often masked by the red pigment phyco-erythrin. They are exclusively multicellular and usually of small to moderate size. The red algae occur in temperate and warm waters at almost all sites along the shore and at various depths in the sea.

Gelidium crinale (Turner) Lamouroux (=*G. aculeatum*) Frond about 5cm long; compressed main stem bears branches arranged in pinnate fashion; these bear small, awl-shaped branchlets particularly at the apex; texture cartilaginous. **Habitat** on sandy and rocky ground on the lower shore and in shallow water. **Distribution** Mediterranean and Atlantic. N.B. about three other species occur.

Gelidium latifolium (Greville) Bornet & Thuret Frond about 8cm long; main branches flat and ribbon-like and bearing fine, thin branchlets; texture cartilaginous. **Habitat** on rocks on the lower shore and in shallow water. **Distribution** Atlantic north to English Channel, south-west Britain and Ireland.

Gelidium sesquipedale Thuret Frond up to 20cm or more long; main stem slightly flattened bearing finer side-branches which taper towards their tips; texture more horny and less pliable than the two preceding species. **Habitat** on rocks on the upper, middle and lower shores, in pools sometimes under other seaweeds and in deeper water. **Distribution** Mediterranean, Atlantic as far as south-west England.

Nemalion helminthoides (Velley) Batters (=*N. elminthoides* =*N. multifidum*) Frond 10–25cm long; stems worm-like and branching, either just at the base or dichotomously at various points; although the branches taper towards their free ends, they are blunt at the tips themselves; texture gelatinous or cartilaginous. **Holdfast** minute and disc-like. **Colour** brown-red. **Habitat** middle shore on rocks and in pools, often in fairly exposed places. **Distribution** Atlantic (very rarely in North Sea and Baltic).

Scinaia furcellata (Turner) Bivona Frond 5–25cm long; arranged cylindrically, but occasionally flattened or compressed; dichotomous branch-ing repeated and regular with tips ending in a little blunt fork; texture slimy. **Holdfast** small and disc-like. **Colour** pink-brown-red. **Habitat** lower shore and shallow water. **Distribution** Atlantic north to south-west Britain and Ireland.

Pterocladia capillacea (Gmelin) Bornet & Thuret (=*P. pinnata*) Frond 5–15cm long; generally larger and stronger than most *Gelidium* species; somewhat compressed and with a tufted appearance; main stem may not bear as many oppositely arranged side-branches along its lower part as the specimen illustrated; branches often taper towards their bases and their free ends; frond hollow; texture cartilaginous. **Habitat** on rocks on the middle and lower shores and in shallow water, often in calm places. **Distribution** Mediterranean, Atlantic and English Channel.

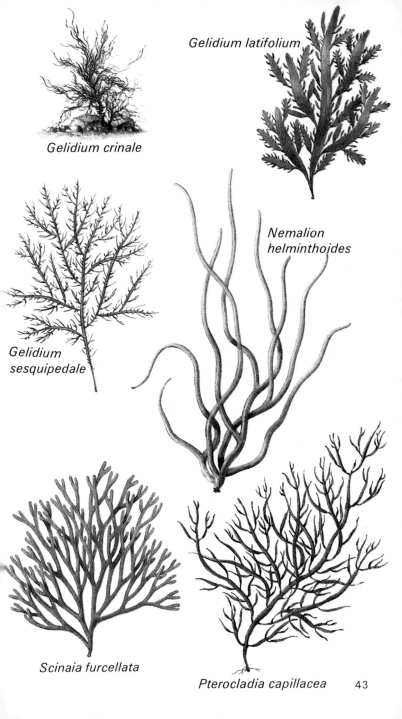

Gelidium latifolium

Gelidium crinale

Nemalion helminthoides

Gelidium sesquipedale

Scinaia furcellata

Pterocladia capillacea 43

Asparagopsis armata Harvey This is the gametophyte generation of ***Falkenbergia rufolanosa*** (Harvey) Smith (see below). When the two plants were named it was not appreciated that they were heteromorphic generations of the same species (see page 19). **Frond** 10–20cm long; slender, delicate, main stem bears irregularly placed branches; like the stem these branches are mainly covered with small, spirally distributed branchlets giving a tufted appearance; a few side-branches lack branchlets and bear alternate barbs or thorns; attached to substrate by a tangle of 'roots'. **Habitat** in shady pools on the lower shore. **Distribution** Mediterranean and Atlantic, especially near south-west Britain (Scilly Isles) and west Britain (Isle of Man). N.B. distribution is often very local and this species, which was originally described in Australia, is thought to have been introduced to European waters in about 1925.

Falkenbergia rufolanosa (Harvey) Smith This is the sporophyte generation of ***Asparagopsis armata*** Harvey (see above). **Frond** consists of small tufts of fine, tangled filaments attached to various other seaweeds. **Distribution** as for *A. armata*.

Bonnemaisonia asparagoides (Woodward) C. A. Agardh This is the gametophyte generation of ***Hymenoclonium serpens*** (Crouan frat) Batters (not described in this book). **Frond** 15–23cm long; rounded or compressed stem bearing alternate side-branches which are longest towards the base; the side-branches bear alternately arranged sub-branches and branchlets; branchlets are approximately the same length over the whole plant and arranged in the same plane. **Holdfast** small and disc-like. **Habitat** in shallow water. **Distribution** Mediterranean, Atlantic, English Channel and North Sea.

Furcellaria fastigiata (Linnaeus) Lamouroux **Frond** 10–20cm long; stiff, cylindrical, glossy stem branches regularly and equally; succeeding branches become regularly shorter towards the tips; in Summer the tips bear pod-like reproductive bodies, but these may be lacking at other times of the year so that the tips then appear more tapered. **Holdfast** is a mass of branching rootlets up to 2.5cm across. **Habitat** on rocks on the lower shore and in shallow water. **Distribution** Atlantic, English Channel, North Sea and Baltic. N.B. the genus *Polyides* (see page 51) is very similar, but may be differentiated from *F. fastigiata* by its rounded, discoidal holdfast.

Halarachnion ligulatum (Woodward) Kützing **Frond** 10–30cm long; strap-like, dichotomously branching stem bears many side-branches which are arranged irregularly or opposite; side-branches much narrower than the stem and often terminating in a notch; texture soft and gelatinous. **Colour** pink-red-yellow. **Habitat** on rocks and shells in shallow water; may be washed up. **Distribution** Mediterranean, Atlantic and English Channel.

Catenella repens (Lightfoot) Batters (*=C. opuntia*) **Frond** about 3cm long; moss-like growth of creeping fibres from which tiny, irregularly branching fronds arise; may grow in clumps about 5cm across. **Habitat** on upper shore on rocks and in crevices, sometimes among the holdfasts of *Fucus spiralis* and *Pelvetia canaliculata*. **Distribution** Atlantic, English Channel and North Sea.

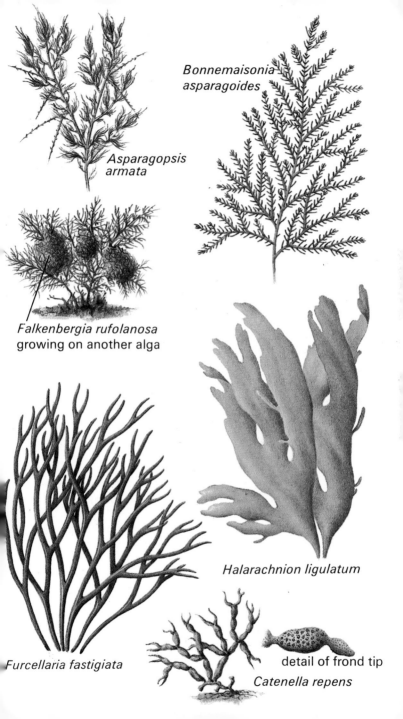

Bonnemaisonia asparagoides

Asparagopsis armata

Falkenbergia rufolanosa growing on another alga

Halarachnion ligulatum

Furcellaria fastigiata

detail of frond tip

Catenella repens

Calliblepharis ciliata (Hudson) Kützing Frond 15–30cm long; flat, strap-like main stem increases in width and branches irregularly; stem borne on a short, rounded stipe; short, awl-shaped side-branches occur all round the margin of the main stems and on their upper and lower surfaces. Holdfast consists of branching 'roots'. Habitat on rocks and in pools on middle and lower shores and in shallow water. Distribution Atlantic, north to south-west Britain and Ireland, and English Channel.

Cystoclonium purpureum (Hudson) Batters Frond 15–60cm long; rounded, succulent stems bear many irregularly disposed branches which themselves bear many branchlets; branches and branchlets taper towards their bases, often more so than in the specimen illustrated; branchlets noticeably finer than branches; rounded reproductive bodies may occur towards the tips of the branchlets. Holdfast root-like. Habitat on rocks and other seaweeds on the lower shore and in shallow water. Distribution Atlantic, English Channel, North Sea and Baltic.

Plocamium cartilagineum (Linnaeus) Dixon (*=P. coccineum* *=P. vulgare*) Frond 5–30cm long; tufted growth with strong main stems tending to have more irregularly arranged branches in the upper region and fewer or none at the base; branches bear branchlets whose terminal sub-divisions all occur on the same side (see inset illustration); almost globular reproductive bodies may occur over the plant. Habitat on rocks in shallow water; may be washed up. Distribution Mediterranean, Atlantic, English Channel and North Sea.

Phyllophora crispa (Hudson) Dixon (*=P. epiphyla* *=P. rubens*) Frond up to 25cm long; flat, ribbon-like stem borne on a very short, compressed or cylindrical stipe; branching may be dichotomous; branches generally have blunt tips; rigid, crisp texture. Holdfast very small and disc-like, but may coalesce with those of neighbours. Habitat usually attached to vertical rocks and pool sides on lower shore and in shallow water. Distribution Mediterranean and Atlantic. N.B. about three other species occur.

Hypnea musciformis (Wulfen) Lamouroux Frond 10–30cm long; upright stem bears a number of irregularly disposed, almost pinnate branches. Colour black-red-green. Habitat almost always growing entangled with other seaweed, generally in sheltered places. Distribution Mediterranean and Atlantic.

Ahnfeltia plicata (Hudson) Fries Frond 7–15cm long; forming stiff, springy tufts about 10cm wide with a texture reminiscent of fine wire. Holdfast is a thin, encrusting structure up to 2cm in diameter. Habitat in pools attached to rocks on the middle and lower shore. Distribution Atlantic, English Channel and North Sea.

Phyllophora membranifolia (Goodenough & Woodward) J. G. Agardh Frond 7–20cm long; generally fan-like, borne on a fairly long, cylindrical stipe or stalk, and branching into flattened, wedge-shaped 'leaves'; branching dichotomous; branches terminate in a notch. Holdfast small and disc-like. Colour usually brown-purple-red. Habitat usually attached to vertical rocks on pool sides, etc., on lower shore and in shallow water. Distribution Atlantic, English Channel, North Sea and Baltic.

Gracilaria verrucosa (Hudson) Papenfuss (*=G. confervoides*) Frond 7–50cm long; stringy stem grows up with a number of irregular branches which in turn may carry many slender branchlets; branchlets taper at their bases and at their free ends; reproductive bodies which resemble small, wart-like protuberances may be scattered over the plant; several stems may arise from the same fleshy discoidal holdfast. Habitat on rocks and gravel on the middle shore. Distribution Mediterranean, Atlantic and English Channel.

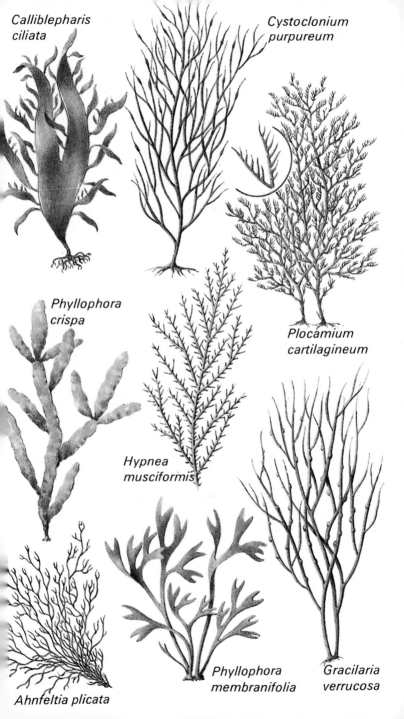

Calliblepharis ciliata

Cystoclonium purpureum

Phyllophora crispa

Plocamium cartilagineum

Hypnea musciformis

Ahnfeltia plicata

Phyllophora membranifolia

Gracilaria verrucosa

Chondrus crispus Stackhouse **Irish Moss or Carragheen** Frond
7–15cm long; basal part of stem is narrow and unbranched; upper stem
branches dichotomously; stem not channelled; branches form wedge-shaped
segments; somewhat variable in appearance with narrow and broader forms
existing; texture cartilaginous. **Holdfast** discoidal. **Colour** red-purple; may turn
green in strong light. **Habitat** on stones and rocks on the lower shore and in
pools, also in shallow water. **Distribution** Atlantic, English Channel, North Sea
and rarely in the Baltic. N.B. may be confused with *Gigartina stellata* (see
below).

Gigartina stellata (Stackhouse) Batters Frond 10–20cm long, but is
often shorter than *Chondrus crispus* (above); tufted appearance; flattish and
somewhat channelled or unrolled; narrow at base but becoming broader and
more strap-like towards the apex; dichotomously branched; older specimens
may be covered with small pimples which, in addition to the channelling,
further help to distinguish it from *Chondrus crispus*. **Habitat** on rocks on
extreme lower shore. **Distribution** Atlantic, English Channel and North Sea.

Gigartina acicularis (Wulfen) Lamouroux (Not illustrated) **Frond**
4–10cm; similar to *G. stellata* but rather more rounded, and slender. **Colour**
purple-red. **Distribution** Mediterranean and Atlantic north to south-west
Britain and Ireland where it is rare. N.B. about three other species occur.

Hildenbrandia prototypus Nardo Thallus about 3cm across, consisting
of a patch of thin tissue closely adhering to a stone or rock; with care it may be
peeled off; loses its sheen when dry. **Colour** pink or brown-red. **Habitat** on the
middle shore, often situated so that it keeps moist when the tide is out. **Distribution** Mediterranean, Atlantic, English Channel, North Sea and Baltic.

Peyssonnelia squamaria (Gmelin) Decaisne Thallus consisting of
leaf-like growths adhering to the substrate by 'roots' developing on their
undersides; growths may reach 10cm across or more; 'leaves' spread out,
upper surfaces marked with concentric rings of dark red and red-
brown. **Habitat** on rocks, shells and other seaweed on the extreme lower shore
and down to about 60m; may occur in caves and crevices. **Distribution**
Mediterranean. NB closely related species may occur in other areas.

Corallina officinalis Linnaeus Frond 5–12cm long; main stem bears
branches arranged exactly opposite; branches in their turn bear opposite
branchlets; plant appears to consist of a number of calcareous segments which
are longer than they are broad and which are linked by pliable joints to form the
frond; terminal reproductive bodies lack 'horns'. **Holdfast** chalky and
encrusting. **Colour** varies from purple-red-pink to yellow-white. **Habitat** on
rocks and in pools on the middle shore. **Distribution** Mediterranean, Atlantic,
English Channel, North Sea and rarely in the Baltic. N.B. avoid confusion with
the thecate hydroids (see page 81).

Corallina mediterranea Areschoug (*=C. elongata*) Frond up to
8cm long; similar to *C. officinalis*, but branches from base giving a tufted
appearance; branches bear pinnate branchlets; stem segments ovoid or slightly
triangular; terminal reproductive bodies bear horns. **Habitat** attached to rocks
in pools and in shallow water. **Distribution** Mediterranean, and Atlantic north
to English Channel'

Jania rubens (Linnaeus) Lamouroux (*=Corallina rubens*) Frond
2–5cm long; chalky and jointed as in *Corallina* but branching is dichotomous
and not opposite; often growing in dense tufts; in Spring there are conspicuous, rounded reproductive bodies. **Holdfast** minute and disc-like. **Colour**
rose-red. **Habitat** growing attached to other seaweeds especially on *Cladostephus* sp. (see page 37). **Distribution** Mediterranean, Atlantic, English Channel and rarely in North Sea.

Chondrus crispus
2 forms

Gigartina stellata

Hildenbrandia prototypus

Peyssonnelia squamaria

Corallina mediterranea

Corallina officinalis

Jania rubens

Lithophyllum incrustans Philippi Thallus consists of a patch of chalky tissue up to 4cm thick; growths may be irregular in outline and smooth or rather bumpy in appearance, sometimes lying on top of each other; adheres strongly to the substrate and may embrace small shells, etc.; the margin of the growth tends to be less differentiated from the rest in terms of colour or texture (c.f. *Lithothamnion calcareum* below). **Colour** mauve-purple-red-yellow, being darker in shady places. **Habitat** in rock pools on upper, middle and lower shores; appears to prefer exposed places. **Distribution** Mediterranean, Atlantic, English Channel and North Sea. N.B. about six other species occur. *Hildenbrandia prototypus* is extremely thin and is not calcareous (see previous page).

Melobesia farinosa Lamouroux Thallus circular or irregular, forming encrusting growths on the fronds of other seaweeds, *Zostera* (see page 65), hydroids and worm tubes. **Colour** pink. **Habitat** attached to hosts on the extreme lower shore and in shallow water. **Distribution** Mediterranean, Atlantic, English Channel and North Sea. N.B. about three other species occur.

Lithothamnion calcareum (Pallas) Areschoug Thallus somewhat similar to *Lithophyllum incrustans* (above) when young, and distinguished by slightly thicker margins; older specimens become somewhat erect with nodular branches and are reminiscent of red 'coral' (see page 101); growths may reach 8cm across. **Colour** violet-red. **Habitat** unattached, or occasionally encrusting pebbles on extreme lower shore and shallow water. **Distribution** Atlantic, English Channel and North Sea.

Lithothamnion fruticulosum (Kützing) Foslie Similar to *L. calcareum* **Thallus** consists of chalky growths up to 3cm thick and reaching 10cm across; upper surface with short branching processes which may be blunt or sharply terminated. **Habitat** on hard and softer substrates down to 80m. **Distribution** Mediterranean. N.B. about ten other species occur.

Polyides rotundus (Hudson) Greville (=*P. caprinus*) Frond 10–20cm long; rounded stem usually free of branches near the base, but dividing dichotomously about one-third of the way up the stem. **Holdfast** disc-like (not root-like as in *Furcellaria*, see page 45). **Colour** dull red, turning black when dry. **Habitat** on rocks and stones and in pools on lower shore and down to 20m. **Distribution** Atlantic, English Channel and North Sea.

Dilsea carnosa (Schmidel) Kuntze Frond 13–30cm long; short, rounded stipe gives way to a flattened, leaf-like frond; texture is gelatinous although plant looks tougher; the fronds may be split in older specimens; several fronds may develop from the discoidal holdfast. **Colour** usually dark red. **Habitat** attached to rocks on extreme lower shore and in shallow water. **Distribution** Atlantic, English Channel and North Sea.

Grateloupia filicina (Lamouroux) C. A. Agardh (=*G. minima*) Frond 5–12cm long; tufted, compressed growth; main stem tapers at free end and at base, and bears alternate or opposite branches; branches carry alternate or opposite branchlets. **Holdfast** discoidal. **Habitat** on stones and rocks on middle shore, usually near freshwater outfalls. **Distribution** Atlantic north to west Britain and Ireland, and English Channel.

Dumontia incrassata (O. F. Müller) Lamouroux Frond 2–50cm long; rounded stem is unbranched in lower regions, but higher up bears alternately or irregularly arranged branches; branches rounded and tapering towards bases and free ends; branchlets may be present; in young specimens the stem and branches are solid, but they may become hollow with age. **Colour** dull red in shady places, but becoming yellow-green-brown in strongly illuminated positions. **Habitat** on rocks and pebbles or on other seaweeds, often in pools on middle shore. **Distribution** Atlantic, English Channel and North Sea.

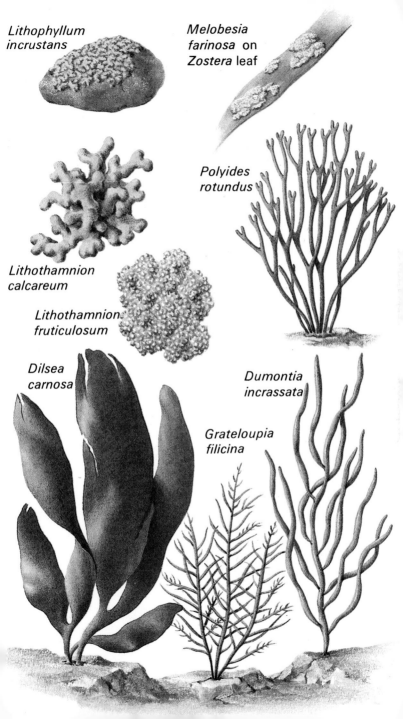

Lithophyllum incrustans

Melobesia farinosa on *Zostera* leaf

Polyides rotundus

Lithothamnion calcareum

Lithothamnion fruticulosum

Dilsea carnosa

Dumontia incrassata

Grateloupia filicina

Callophyllis laciniata (Hudson) Kützing Frond about 8cm long;
thickish, flat and quickly broadening out from the very short stipe; split up into a
number of wedge-shaped sections by a form of dichotomous branching;
branch tips blunt; reproductive bodies may appear as tiny leaflets arranged
around the periphery of frond in Summer, or as minute dots over the entire
surface. **Holdfast** small and disc-like. **Colour** opaque pink-red. **Habitat** on
rocks and stones in shallow water; may be washed up. **Distribution** Atlantic,
English Channel and North Sea.

Gastroclonium ovatum (Hudson) Papenfuss Frond 5–15cm long;
cartilaginous, round stem branches dichotomously or alternately; upper part of
plant bears small pip-like 'leaves'. **Holdfast** small and disc-like. **Habitat** on
rocks on the lower shore and in pools. **Distribution** Atlantic north to Scotland,
and English Channel.

Lomentaria articulata (Hudson) Lyngbye Frond 15–25cm long;
consists of a hollow stem and branches which are repeatedly constricted to give
a jointed or beaded effect; branches only occur at the joint between two
'beads'; main stem branches dichotomously from the base and thereafter the
pattern may be opposite; very small holdfast and attachment runners from the
stem; internally gelatinous. **Colour** dull purple-bright red; shiny, transparent
and iridescent under water. **Habitat** attached to rocks and other seaweeds on the
upper, middle and lower shores. **Distribution** Atlantic, English Channel and
North Sea.

Lomentaria clavellosa (Turner) Gaillon Frond 7–40cm long; undivided, rounded main stem bears opposite or alternate pinnate branches;
rounded branches and branchlets taper at bases and free ends; texture pliable
and gelatinous. **Colour** bright red-pink. **Habitat** on rocks and other seaweeds
on lower shore and in shallow water. **Distribution** Atlantic, English Channel
and North Sea.

Antithamnion cruciatum (C. A. Agardh) Nägeli Frond 2.5–5cm
long; main stem bears alternate branches and branchlets; tips of branches
tufted; under the microscope consists of many single, oblong cells joined end
to end, each cell bearing 2 opposite branchlets. **Habitat** on rocks in muddy
places on lower shore. **Distribution** Mediterranean, Atlantic and English
Channel. N.B. about four other species occur.

Callithamnion arbuscula (Dillwyn) Lyngbye Frond 5–15cm long;
bushy growth with short stipe; main stem zig-zags, bearing alternate branches
and branchlets; apices of branches tufted. **Holdfast** small, stout and
discoidal. **Habitat** on steep rocks on lower shore; often exposed. **Distribution**
Atlantic north from England and northern Ireland, and North Sea.

Callithamnion corymbosum (Smith) Lyngbye Frond 2–7cm long;
main stem bears alternately arranged branches which carry delicate, filamentous, alternate branchlets. **Habitat** on rocks and seaweed on lower shore and in
shallow and deeper water. **Distribution** Mediterranean, Atlantic, North Sea and
Baltic. N.B. about ten other species occur.

Rhodymenia   pseudopalmata (Lamouroux)   Silva   (= ***R.
palmetta***) Frond 4–10cm long; short stipe up to 2.5cm long, broadening
into a flattened, fan-like frond with dichotomous branching; more delicate and
membranous than *R. palmata*; never has peripheral 'leaflets'. **Holdfast** disc-
like. **Habitat** on rocks and laminarian stipes on lower shore and in shallow
water. **Distribution** Atlantic north to English Channel, and south-west Britain.

Rhodymenia palmata (Linnaeus) Greville **Dulse** Frond 10–30cm
long; no stipe; gradually expands from the wide, disc-like holdfast to form a
flattened, dichotomous 'fan'; younger parts are delicate, older parts are tougher
and darker and may bear small peripheral 'leaflets'. **Habitat** on rocks and
laminarian stipes (see page 33) on middle and lower shores and in shallow
water. **Distribution** Atlantic, English Channel and North Sea.

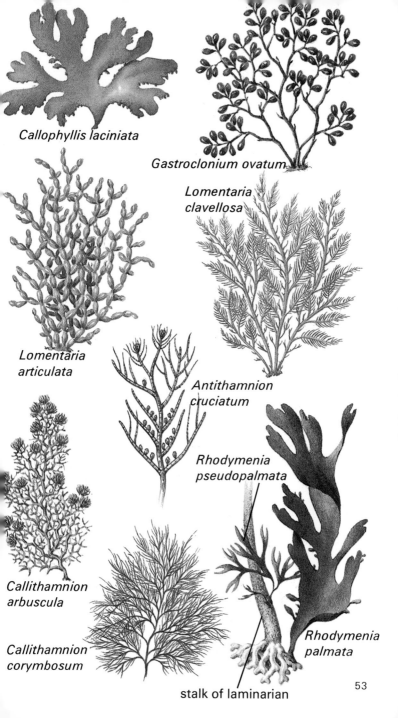

Callophyllis laciniata

Gastroclonium ovatum

Lomentaria clavellosa

Lomentaria articulata

Antithamnion cruciatum

Rhodymenia pseudopalmata

Callithamnion arbuscula

Rhodymenia palmata

Callithamnion corymbosum

stalk of laminarian

53

Ceramium rubrum (Hudson) C. A. Agardh Frond 2–30cm long; main stem branches dichotomously but unevenly; side-branches arranged likewise; terminal branchlets have tips which often point inwards like forceps; close inspection reveals a banded pigmentation effect on the stems and branches; overall appearance bushy; texture cartilaginous. **Holdfast** minute and cone-like. **Colour** variable; deep red-brown-yellowish. **Habitat** on rocks and other seaweed on upper middle and lower shores and in shallow and deeper water. **Distribution** Mediterranean, Atlantic, English Channel, North Sea and Baltic. N.B. about twenty-three other species occur. This is a very variable species.

Griffithsia flosculosa (Ellis) Batters Frond 7–20cm long; delicate, filamentous growth; main stem branches dichotomously but unevenly; filaments gradually taper towards the apex; reproductive bodies like minute spheres borne on small stalks may occur all over the filaments; texture when in the sea is stiff, but it quickly wilts when removed from water. **Holdfast** a tangle of 'rootlets'. **Colour** quickly lost if this species is placed in fresh water. **Habitat** attached to rocks in pools on the lower shore and in shallow water. **Distribution** Atlantic, English Channel and North Sea. N.B. about three other species occur.

Plumaria elegans (Bonnemaison) Schmitz Frond 5–10cm long, strong main stem branches dichotomously or alternately; branches usually bear alternate or opposite branchlets. **Holdfast** small and fibrous. **Colour** brown-purple. **Habitat** on shaded rocks and under overhangs, often hanging down in dingy clusters, on middle and lower shore. **Distribution** Atlantic, English Channel and North Sea. N.B. confusion with *Ptilota plumosa* (see below) can be avoided by examining the sub-terminal branchlets. In *Plumaria elegans* they are translucent. Also, in *Plumaria elegans* the main stem is covered with minute branchlets whereas these are lacking in *Ptilota plumosa*.

Ptilota plumosa (Hudson) C. A. Agardh Frond 10–30cm long; main stem rather stiff and irregularly branched in one plane; pinnate branchlets; subterminal branchlets are opaque and the main stem is smooth and free from minute branchlets (c.f. *Plumaria elegans* above). **Holdfast** a disc of matted fibres. **Habitat** generally on stipes of laminarians (see page 33) on extreme lower shore and in shallow water. **Distribution** Atlantic north from England and Ireland and North Sea.

Halurus equisetifolius (Lightfoot) Kützing **Sea-tail** Frond 7–22cm long; main stem branches irregularly in all planes around the vertical axis; the stiff stem and branches bear many whorls of small filaments each about 0.2cm long, thus giving the plant a bottle-brush appearance. **Colour** dark red. **Habitat** on rocks on the middle and lower shores, sometimes in pools. **Distribution** Atlantic and English Channel.

Sphondylothamnion multifidum (Hudson) Nägeli Frond 10–20cm long; main stem usually undivided and branching in one or two planes; branches arranged opposite or alternately; similar arrangement of sub-branches; whole plant covered in whorls of branchlets but these are much more separated than in *Halurus equisetifolius* (see above); texture crisp when fresh, wilts when collected. **Holdfast** well-developed and 'root-like'. **Colour** pink-red. **Habitat** on rocks on vertical sides of pools on lower shore. **Distribution** Atlantic and English Channel.

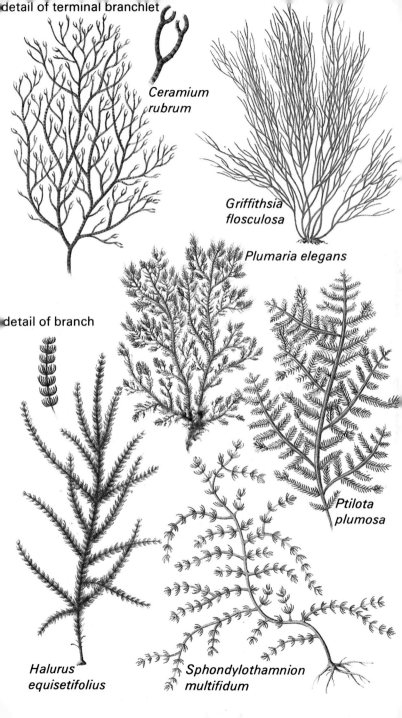

detail of terminal branchlet

Ceramium rubrum

Griffithsia flosculosa

Plumaria elegans

detail of branch

Ptilota plumosa

Halurus equisetifolius

Sphondylothamnion multifidum

Apoglossum ruscifolium (Turner) J. G. Agardh Frond 5–10cm long; broad, leafy main stem with midrib terminates in a rounded tip; edges waved; main stem bears alternately arranged branches and sub-branches which develop from the midrib; under a hand lens fresh specimens show wide-angled 'veins' diverging from the midrib; short stipe. **Habitat** on rocks and in pools as well as on laminarians on the middle and lower shore. **Distribution** Atlantic, English Channel and North Sea. N.B. avoid confusion with *Hypoglossum woodwardii* which occurs in similar habitats (see below).

Cryptopleura ramosa (Hudson) Newton Frond 10–20cm long; entwined, bushy growth generally as wide as it is long; leafy stem has a strong midrib; the lowermost region may lack the 'leaf', giving the midrib the appearance of a pliable stipe; edges of leafy stem waved and sometimes with small peripheral growths; stem bears irregular dichotomous branches which are somewhat wedge-shaped with rounded tips. **Holdfast** small and disc-like. **Colour** brown-red-purple. **Habitat** on rocks and laminarian stipes on the lower shore and in shallow water. **Distribution** Atlantic, English Channel and North Sea. N.B. avoid confusion with *Nitophyllum punctatum* (see below).

Delesseria sanguinea (Hudson) Lamouroux Frond up to 40cm overall; consists of a rounded, branching stalk or stipe (up to 15cm) and 'leaves' (10–25cm); 'leaves' are oval – lance-shaped, pointed at tip when young and rounded when older; 'leaves' show conspicuous midrib and 'veins'. **Habitat** attached to rocks or laminarians in deep pools on lower shore in shade, or in shallow water. **Distribution** Atlantic, English Channel, North Sea and rarely in the Baltic. N.B. avoid confusion with *Phycodrys rubens* (see below).

Hypoglossum woodwardii Kützing Frond 5–20cm long; main stem resembles a narrow leaf and bears alternately arranged branches and sub-branches which develop from the conspicuous midrib; under a hand lens, indistinct transverse veins may be seen; main stem and branches terminate with sharp points; several main stems may arise from disc-like holdfast. **Habitat** on rocks in pools and on laminarians on the middle and lower shores. **Distribution** Atlantic, English Channel and North Sea. N.B. avoid confusion with *Apoglossum ruscifolium* (see above).

Nitophyllum punctatum (Stackhouse) Greville Frond 10–50cm long; broad, wedge-shaped, membranous frond grows directly from the small, disc-like holdfast; one or more may develop from each attachment point; branching is fairly regular and dichotomous; the presence of many small, terminal branchlets may make the margins look frilly; no 'veins'; texture delicate. **Colour** red-pink, sometimes iridescent near the tips. **Habitat** on various seaweeds in pools on lower shore and in shallow water. **Distribution** Mediterranean, Atlantic and English Channel. N.B. avoid confusion with *Cryptopleura ramosa* (see above).

Membranoptera alata (Hudson) Stackhouse Frond 10–20cm long; flat main stem is like a narrow leaf with a conspicuous midrib, and under a hand lens shows distinct, fine 'veins'; irregular dichotomous branching; branches tapering towards the tips which are often notched. **Holdfast** small and discoidal. **Habitat** on rocks or on other red and brown seaweeds in shaded pools on middle and lower shore, and in shallow water. **Distribution** Atlantic, English Channel, North Sea and Baltic. N.B. can be distinguished from *Apoglossum* and *Hypoglossum* by the form of branching.

Phycodrys rubens (Linnaeus) Batters Frond 5–25cm long; consists of a branching stem and 'leaves'; these are much indented and 'veined' and resemble oak leaves; generally more branched and with shorter stems than *Delesseria* (above); colour is paler also. **Holdfast** small and disc-like. **Habitat** in shady places on rocks and on stipes of laminarians on lower shore; often washed up. **Distribution** Atlantic, English Channel, North Sea and west Baltic.

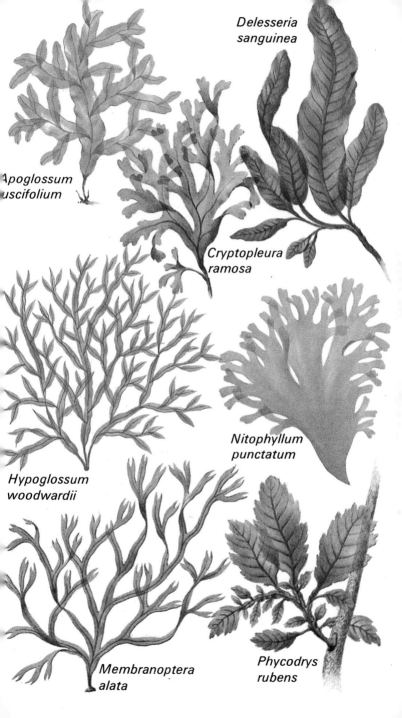

*Delesseria
sanguinea*

*Apoglossum
ruscifolium*

*Cryptopleura
ramosa*

*Hypoglossum
woodwardii*

*Nitophyllum
punctatum*

*Membranoptera
alata*

*Phycodrys
rubens*

Dasya hutchinsiae Harvey (=***D. arbuscula***) Frond 7–10cm long; main stem bears alternately arranged side-branches; these bear fine, filamentous branchlets; small, flask-shaped reproductive bodies may be carried on stalks by branchlets. **Holdfast** consists of 'rootlets'. **Colour** brown-crimson. **Habitat** on rocks on the lower shore and in shallow water. **Distribution** Mediterranean, and Atlantic northwards to west coast of Ireland.

Heterosiphonia plumosa (Ellis) Batters Frond 15–20cm long; flattened, somewhat feathery in appearance; main stem tapers towards free end; branches arranged alternately or irregularly, bearing sub-branches and branchlets. **Colour** red-deep crimson. **Habitat** on rocks or other seaweeds on extreme lower shore and in shallow water; may be washed up. **Distribution** Atlantic north to Ireland, English Channel and North Sea.

Bostrychia scorpioides (Hudson) Montagu Frond 5–10cm long; plant tufted or tangled; main stem irregularly or alternately branched; fine alternate branchlets; branches very often coiled towards the tips. **Holdfast** absent. **Colour** brownish. **Habitat** generally among the roots and stems of other plants (especially angiosperms) on the upper shore; very often in estuaries and salt marshes. **Distribution** Atlantic north to England and Ireland, English Channel and North Sea.

Laurencia pinnatifida (Hudson) Lamouroux **Pepper Dulse** Frond 2–30cm long; flattened, well-developed main stem alternately branched; branches subdivided into smaller branchlets; texture cartilaginous. **Holdfast** disc-like with 'rootlets'. **Colour** variable, depending on position on the shore, but often purple-brownish; may be green-yellow in the middle tide range. **Habitat** on rocks and in crevices from the middle shore down to shallow water. **Distribution** Mediterranean, Atlantic, English Channel and North Sea.

Laurencia obtusa (Hudson) Lamouroux Frond 7–15cm long; forms thick, globular growths; round main stems bears alternate or opposite branches which may be arranged spirally on the stem; branchlets similarly arranged; branches and branchlets become smaller towards the tips; cartilaginous texture. **Colour** variable; purple-pink-yellow. **Holdfast** small and disc-like, sometimes with 'rootlets'. **Habitat** usually on other seaweeds in pools on lower shore and in shallow water. **Distribution** Mediterranean, Atlantic, English Channel and North Sea. N.B. bleaches in strong light.

Odonthalia dentata (Linnaeus) Lyngbye Frond 7–30cm long; flattened plant with tufted appearance; midrib can be made out near the base; main stem bears alternate branches; sub-branches and branchlets alternately arranged; branches and branchlets have a toothed appearance. **Habitat** on rocks and, rarely, on other seaweeds such as laminarians on the lower shore and in shallow water. **Distribution** Atlantic north from England and Ireland, and North Sea.

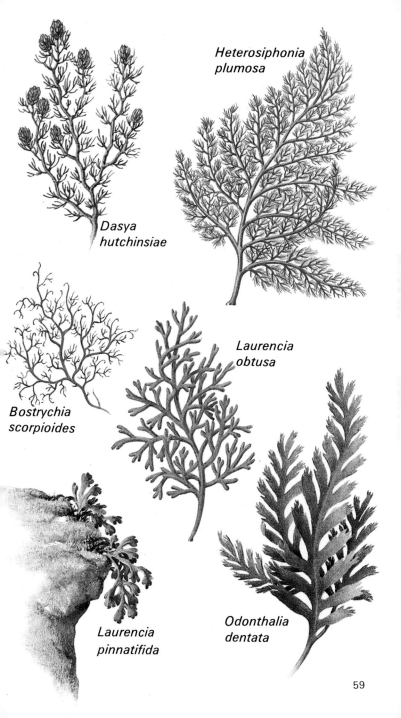

Heterosiphonia
plumosa

Dasya
hutchinsiae

Bostrychia
scorpioides

Laurencia
obtusa

Laurencia
pinnatifida

Odonthalia
dentata

59

Note on the genus Polysiphonia This large genus contains many poorly defined species. About thirty may be encountered in the European area of which the following four have been selected. A more complete coverage is provided by Newton, L. 1931.

Polysiphonia urceolata (Dillwyn) Greville Frond 15–25cm long; filamentous with a tufted appearance; main stems bear alternate branches in all planes around the long axis; several stems may develop from the creeping 'roots' which form the holdfast; may be found with characteristic urn-shaped, reproductive bodies. **Colour** purple-red-brown. **Habitat** on stones and other seaweeds and shells on the lower shore and down to 20m. **Distribution** Mediterranean, Atlantic, English Channel, North Sea and Baltic.

Polysiphonia elongata (Hudson) Sprengel Frond 15–30cm long; well-defined main stem; bushy appearance; branches develop about 2cm from base and are arranged alternately around the stem; sub-branches bear fine, clustered, terminal branchlets especially in Spring; texture gelatinous. **Holdfast** small, consists of 'rootlets'. **Colour** dark red-yellowish. **Habitat** on rocks, stones and shells as well as on some larger seaweeds on lower shore and in shallow water. **Distribution** Mediterranean, Atlantic, English Channel, North Sea and Baltic.

Polysiphonia lanosa (Linnaeus) Tandy (**=*P. fastigiata***) Frond up to 8cm long; a strong, filamentous plant growing in tufts on *Ascophyllum nodosum* and, rarely, on *Fucus* (see page 39); main stem bears alternate or dichotomous branches in all planes around the long axis; branches become shorter from the base; sub-branches similarly arranged; creeping 'rootlets' invade the host's tissue. **Habitat** on seaweeds and, rarely, on rocks. **Distribution** frequent wherever *Ascophyllum* is to be found; Atlantic, English Channel and North Sea. N.B. this species may in turn be affected by the small, cushion-like algal parasite *Choreocolax*.

Polysiphonia nigrescens (Hudson) Greville Frond 7–30cm long; growing in thick clusters; main stem may be much divided and bears alternate or irregular branches which in turn bear numbers of soft branchlets; some of the lower branches may be lost in older plants. **Holdfast** of branching 'rootlets'. **Colour** purple-brown; older plants become blackish. **Habitat** on rocks, stones and other seaweeds in pools on the middle shore. **Distribution** Atlantic, English Channel, North Sea and Baltic.

Rhodomela confervoides (Hudson) Silva (**=*R. subfusca***) Frond 7–30cm long; cylindrical main stem bears spirally arranged branches which are shorter from the base up; the branches may be divided and covered with fine, filamentous branchlets; plants which have over-wintered may show areas of softer growth in Spring; texture generally cartilaginous. **Holdfast** disc-like. **Colour** brown-red. **Habitat** on rocks and seaweeds from lower shore down to about 20m. **Distribution** Atlantic, English Channel, North Sea and Baltic. N.B. close examination with a hand lens reveals the lack of 'joints' in the tips of the branches which distinguishes this species from *Polysiphonia*.

Porphyra umbilicalis (Linnaeus) J. G. Agardh Frond 5–20cm long; irregular, gelatinous, membranous growth arranged in 'leaves', usually attached at one point. **Colour** red-purple-green, becoming black when dry. **Habitat** on stones and rocks especially when covered with sand. **Distribution** Mediterranean, Atlantic and North Sea. N.B. about five other species occur.

Vidalia volubilis (Linnaeus) J. G. Agardh Frond about 10cm long; flat, leaf-like stem slightly branched; edges of stem and branches toothed or serrated; midrib present. **Holdfast** disc-like. **Habitat** on stones and sandy and muddy substrates down to 80m. **Distribution** Mediterranean.

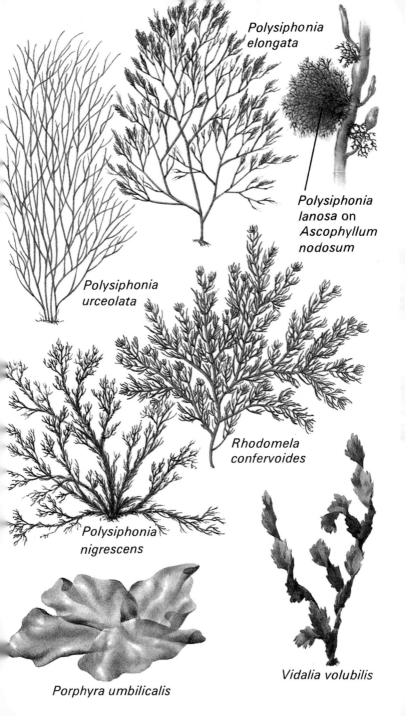

Polysiphonia elongata

Polysiphonia lanosa on *Ascophyllum nodosum*

Polysiphonia urceolata

Rhodomela confervoides

Polysiphonia nigrescens

Porphyra umbilicalis

Vidalia volubilis

Group Lichenes Lichens

Lichens have been less studied than the algae. They exist as dual plants, partly composed of fungal tissue and partly composed of algal tissue. Formerly they were classified as a discrete group, but recent work has shown that they should be classified with the fungi. Their life processes resemble both those of the algae and the fungi, but they also display particular properties of their own. Many botanical text books provide an excellent account of their structure and function. Here it may be said that the lichen thallus usually consists of flat or leafy outgrowths which encrust other plants, rocks or shells. The tissue may be brittle or soft, rough or smooth, tufted, branched or flat. Many lichens have fruiting structures which may assist with their identification. The precise identification of these organisms is in many cases a specialized operation, however, and reference should be made to Duncan, U. K. 1959 or Ferry, B. W. and Sheard, J. W. 1969. Unless otherwise stated the lichens described below will be found on the upper shore and on the rocks above it.

Roccella fuciformis (Linnaeus) Candolle Thallus strap-like; 5–20cm long; groups of flat, disc-like, fruiting bodies full of dusty, black spores. **Distribution** Atlantic north to south-west England and Ireland.

Ramalina siliquosa (Hudson) A. L. Smith Thallus strap-like; 2–5cm long; surface smooth and glossy; disc-like fruiting bodies coloured white-brown near tips of thallus. **Distribution** Atlantic, English Channel and North Sea.

Ochrolechia parella (Linnaeus) Massalongo Thallus encrusting; forms rounded patches 3–10cm in diameter; conspicuous, saucer-like fruiting bodies with grey, dusty spores. **Distribution** Atlantic, English Channel and North Sea.

Lichina pygmaea (Lightfoot) C. A. Agardh Thallus tufted, branching; about 1cm high resembling a minute seaweed. **Habitat** upper and middle shores. **Distribution** Atlantic, English Channel and North Sea. N.B. a related species occurs in the Mediterranean.

Verrucaria mucosa Wahlenberg Thallus smooth, closely attached to rocks; irregular shape up to 30cm across; texture may be jelly-like. **Habitat** middle shore. **Distribution** Atlantic and English Channel. N.B. a related species occurs in the Mediterranean.

Arthopyrenia sublittoralis (Leighton) Arnott Thallus growing in minute cavities in shells of barnacles, etc; a hand lens will reveal the lichen in its pit. **Habitat** upper and middle shores. **Distribution** Atlantic and English Channel, rarely in North Sea.

Xanthoria parietina (Linnaeus) T. A. Fries Thallus rough and leafy; 3–10cm across. **Habitat** often form a belt just below *Ramalina* on extreme upper shore. **Distribution** Atlantic, English Channel and North Sea.

Caloplaca marina Weddell Thallus flattish and encrusting with scattered, coarse granules forming patches up to 10cm across; not leafy. **Distribution** Atlantic, English Channel and North Sea. N.B. a related species occurs in the Mediterranean.

Lecanora atra (Hudson) Acharius Thallus encrusting; forms irregular patches from 2–8cm across; blackish fruiting bodies occur towards centre. **Distribution** Atlantic, English Channel and North Sea.

Anaptychia fusca (Hudson) Wainio Thallus thick and bushy, growing in close-set lobes; black fruiting bodies. **Distribution** Atlantic, English Channel and North Sea.

Verrucaria maura Acharius Thallus thin and encrusting, may cover extensive areas of rock; resembles oil spills. **Habitat** often associated with *Caloplaca* (see above). **Distribution** Atlantic, English Channel and North Sea.

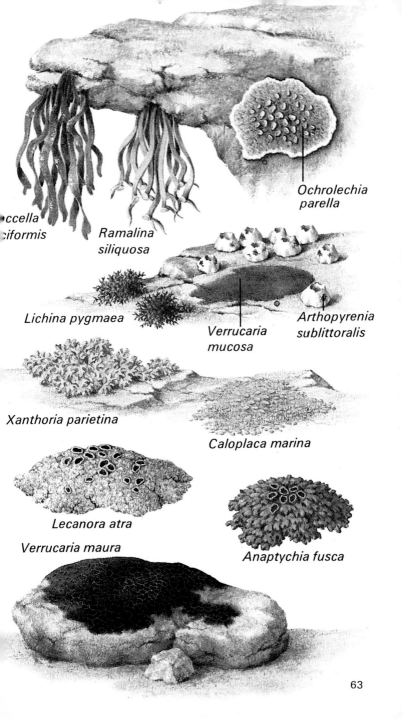

...ccella
...ciformis

Ramalina
siliquosa

Ochrolechia
parella

Lichina pygmaea

Verrucaria
mucosa

Arthopyrenia
sublittoralis

Xanthoria parietina

Caloplaca marina

Lecanora atra

Verrucaria maura

Anaptychia fusca

Subkingdom Angiospermae
Marine angiosperms (sea-grasses)

The angiosperms, or flowering plants, are the most familiar representatives of the plant kingdom on land, and they include the grasses, herbs, shrubs and trees. Although a number of species are adapted to live partly or wholly in fresh water, very few can tolerate life in the sea. However, the Baltic with its low salinity provides a habitat for a number of plants that are associated with freshwater habitats, but these are really beyond the scope of this book. Those that have been included will generally be met with in fully maritime conditions, such as prevail on the coasts of the North Sea, the Atlantic and the Mediterranean, although some of these specialized marine angiosperms also occur in the Baltic.

Zostera marina Linnaeus **Eel Grass, Sea-grass or Grasswrack** (Only section of leaf illustrated) Flat, long, narrow leaves rise for up to 1m, sometimes longer; between 0.5 and 1cm wide; veins of leaves as shown in illustration; inconspicuous flowers, to some extent resembling those of terrestrial grasses, may occur in Spring or Summer. **Colour** dark green or grass-green. **Habitat** usually on sheltered beaches or estuaries on gravel, sand and mud. **Distribution** Mediterranean, Atlantic, English Channel, North Sea and Baltic. N.B. as the number of cross-references in this book will show, *Zostera* often provides a habitat for other marine plants and animals.

Zostera nana Roth **Slender Eel Grass** (Only section of leaf illustrated) Very narrow leaves rise for up to 15cm, sometimes longer; about 0.1cm wide; veins of leaves as shown in illustration. **Habitat** on mud banks in estuaries, etc, on middle and lower shore. **Distribution** Mediterranean, Atlantic, North Sea and Baltic.

Posidonia oceanica (Linnaeus) **Neptune Grass** Flat, long, narrow leaves rise for up to 30cm, sometimes longer; about 1cm wide; base of leaves heavy and shaggy-looking; fairly conspicuous flowers may be found in Summer. **Colour** green-yellow. **Habitat** on soft substrates down to 100m. **Distribution** Mediterranean and Atlantic north to Biscay. N.B. broken leaves of this plant, when mixed with sand grains and rolled about by the waves, may form brownish soft balls sometimes known as 'sea-balls' (see illustration).

Cymodocea nodosa (Ucaria) Areschoug Narrow, flat leaves rise for up to 20cm from the thick, branching rootstock; base of leaves lack the shaggy appearance of *Posidonia oceanica* (above). **Habitat** often associated with *Zostera* (above) on mud and sand down to 10m. **Distribution** Mediterranean.

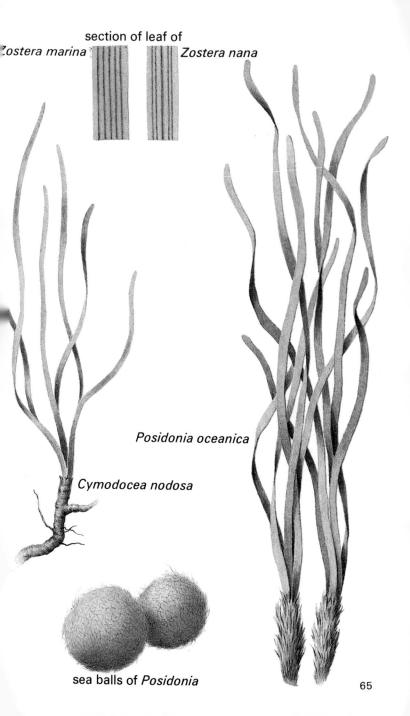

section of leaf of

Zostera marina   *Zostera nana*

Posidonia oceanica

Cymodocea nodosa

sea balls of *Posidonia*

Animal Kingdom

The animal kingdom comprises an immense variety of organisms ranging from simple, one-celled creatures to complex, multicellular mammals. Between these extremes lies a broad spectrum of forms showing immense diversity.

Animals differ from plants in several fundamental ways. Firstly they are irritable and may respond to stimuli by movements rather than by growth. Secondly they are catabolic rather than anabolic, in other words, for their nutrition they rely on breaking down organic material into its constituent parts rather than elaborating organic compounds from inorganic ones. In this respect animals form themselves into very complex food chains which are founded upon the plants or primary producers, but which themselves are often interrelated; for example, carnivores preying upon herbivores. In any community there may be a chain or web of energy relationships, and this is as true in the sea as on land. In the marine environment, there is not the diversity of plant life that characterizes terrestrial habitats. The function that is fulfilled by the lowly algae is just as important, however. Whether they are the vast kelps of the shallow sea or the unicellular plants of the ocean plankton, they provide food for the herbivorous animals. On the seashore we find weed-eating sea-snails like the periwinkles; in shallow water there are the herbivorous sea-urchins and grazing fishes. Next in the chain are the primary carnivores such as whelks, starfishes, sea-anemones and fishes which in their turn feed on the herbivorous animals. In the ocean, minute crustaceans like copepods form the primary converters of plant protein into animal protein. In addition to finding a food supply, either as large macroscopic seaweeds or minute, suspended food particles, animals need shelter to protect them from their enemies and to provide them with the facilities for reproduction. In this respect other factors are as important as the supply of food in determining whether or not a particular species of animal can survive in a particular location. Different species are able to withstand different circumstances in terms of both the physical and the biological conditions for life. Thus it is that the seashore and shallow sea permit such a diversity of life; for the movements of the tides and the consequent alternation of exposure to air and sea provide an almost infinitely graduated range of environments from the terrestrial region immediately above the highest point to which the tides flow, down to the shallow seabed which is never exposed to the air.

The seashore is probably the finest training ground for the zoologist. The principles of ecology, as well as other aspects of interrelationships between and within species, can be appreciated in almost every type of habitat, and also provide examples of the greatest evolutionary interest. Although fewer species are recognized in the sea than in other environments, all types of animal known are represented there. Whilst some groups have conquered fresh water and land with moderate or great success, many have prospered only in the sea. Furthermore some groups, such as the Ctenophora (comb-jellies or sea-gooseberries) and the Echinodermata (starfishes and sea-urchins), are exclusively marine.

The primary divisions or groups in the animal kingdom are known as *phyla* (singular phylum), and all the members of a phylum are considered by zoologists to be related to a common ancestral form by descent. When seeking to classify animals, zoologists must take into account their level of organization and style of organic architecture. In this respect, the following points are important. **1** Is the animal composed of one or many cells? **2** If many cells, are these arranged throughout the body as one type of tissue, or are they differentiated into various tissue types which can then form organs such as glands or muscles? **3** How are the tissues arranged throughout the body? **4** Is there a body cavity inside the animal in addition to the alimentary canal or gut? Another very important feature is the form of symmetry that an animal displays. Some are totally asymmetrical like a few of the sponges, but in fact such examples are rare. More frequent are radially symmetrical animals like the jellyfishes and sea-urchins (as adults, echinoderms display a very special type of radial symmetry based on five radial axes). The great majority of animals display bilateral symmetry (i.e. when divided in two from the head end towards the tail end they produce two halves which are mirror images of each other).

In the descriptions that follow, the text contains, as far as possible, details which complement the illustrations. A quick glance will show that in all cases the type of information that is provided is not exactly equivalent. Where this is the case it is largely a reflection of the state of the information currently available to scientists. In some cases it is known, for example, exactly how deep in the sea a particular species lives. In other cases this information is not known, and it is necessary to rely on a more general statement. It should also be remembered that the collector or beachcomber may find juveniles which are not as large as the adults generally encountered for the species.

Finally, as has already been pointed out, it is not possible in a book of this size to provide details of all the animals which might be encountered on the shore or in the shallow sea. However, as far as possible, references have been provided in the text and in the bibliography which should enable the reader to pursue the line of enquiry for a particular species a good deal further than is possible here.

Phylum Porifera Sponges

These are sessile animals whose bodies consist of a single cavity with a major exhalent opening, and many smaller inhalent openings which are partly lined by special cells called choanocytes. The bodies also contain calcareous or siliceous spicules, or horny fibres, which provide support.

Sponges are the simplest animals treated in this book, yet for all their simplicity they are among the most difficult to describe carefully and scientifically. They are arranged in three classes: the Calcarea, with calcareous spicules; the Hexactinellida or Triaxonida, with siliceous spicules each of which has a six-rayed pattern; and the Demospongiae, with siliceous spicules which are never six-rayed, and/or horny fibres made of material known as spongin. It will be realized from these divisions that the nature and shape of the sponge spicules are of great importance when classifying and identifying sponges. Unfortunately these spicules cannot be seen without the aid of a microscope and the facilities for making the necessary microscopical preparations. However, it is possible to identify sponges to some degree by examining their gross form, texture and coloration, as well as by considering their habitat and distribution. Identifications based on these characters only can be provided here.

Sponges occur on almost all types of seabed from the lower shore down to the ocean depths. The form of their bodies depends to a great degree on the amount of exposure they have to face. Thus, in very exposed conditions sponges will be rounded or flattened against the substrate. In sheltered places they often assume a plant-like growth pattern with erect and delicate branching stems and shoots.

The basic body form of the sponge is illustrated in fig. 5. This diagram also indicates the movement of sea water through the sponge. Water supplies the animal with oxygen and food in the form of minute, suspended particles. This water enters the body by a number of pores and passes along the cavity or *paragaster* to leave by the large exhalent pore or *osculum*. Other sponges are more complex in their organization. Fig. 5 also shows how a compound arrangement may be formed from a number of units which become arranged round a communal paragaster and which share a central osculum. There are many variations on sponge architecture which are beyond the scope of this book, although most general text books on zoology provide good accounts. At first sight the paragaster may be compared with the gut of a higher animal, but it cannot strictly be regarded as such, for it lacks the specializations of tissues associated with a digestive tract. The cells which compose the sponge body are of very few types only, and those which line the paragaster absorb their own

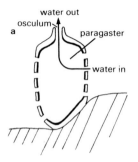
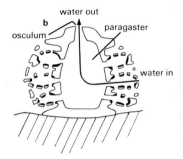

Fig. 5 Diagrammatic sections through (a) simple, and (b) complex sponges to show water currents and position of choanocytes (shown in heavy black)

food requirements by directly ingesting suitable particles. Because of their level of organization, no organs can be identified within the sponge body which is thus regarded as being developed at the cellular grade. This lack of differentiation of cells into a number of tissue types making up organs means that sponges are capable of regenerating themselves from broken fragments. Despite their simple level of organization, sponges are able to undergo sexual reproduction with the formation of eggs and sperms which, after fertilization, give rise to a free-swimming larva. If the larva settles on a suitable substrate, it will develop into a new sponge.

An interesting feature of sponges is the extent to which they become associated with other organisms. If a large sponge is broken open, a number of other animals such as worms and crabs may be found residing in the cavity. Some sponges are associated with hermit crabs, giving camouflage and protection to the crab which in turn transports the sponge to new feeding areas.

Although a great number of sponge species are known, very few are of commercial importance. One exception is the Mediterranean species *Spongia officinalis*, the bath sponge, which is extensively collected from some of the Greek island waters.

The sponges are a notoriously difficult group to work on, and there are relatively few books available which help with their identification. The classification of calcareous sponges has recently been brought up to date by Burton, M. 1963. Vosmeyer, G. C. J. 1935 describes the sponge fauna of Naples and the adjacent Mediterranean. This work is beautifully illustrated.

Class Calcarea

Sponges which contain calcareous spicules only. Their bodies are generally small and vase- or cup-shaped. They are generally pale in colour and grow away from light.

Leucosolenia complicata (Montagu) **Form** tubular, branching, up to about 2 cm high; an osculum is found at the end of each branch; roughish texture but branches fragile. **Colour** grey-white. **Habitat** attached to seaweeds, hydroids, shells and ectoprocts from middle shore down to about 100 m. **Distribution** Atlantic, English Channel, North Sea and west Baltic.

Leucosolenia botryoides (Ellis & Solander) (Not illustrated) **Form** similar to *L. complicata*, tubular but generally not branching, rising to about 2 cm from a branching, root-like system of canals which adhere to the substrate; oscula large. **Colour** whitish. **Habitat** attached to seaweeds on the extreme lower shore and in shallow water. **Distribution** Mediterranean, Atlantic, English Channel, North Sea and west Baltic.

Leucosolenia coriacea (Montagu) **Form** branching, encrusting, up to about 3 cm high and 10 cm wide as growths of twisted tubes; 1 osculum may suffice for several tubes where they join together. **Colour** white-grey-yellow-brown-red. **Habitat** under stones, rocks and shells from lower shore down to about 100 m. **Distribution** Atlantic, English Channel and North Sea.

Sycon ciliatum (Fabricius) and *Sycon coronatum* (Ellis & Solander) **Form** tubular, erect, up to 3 cm high; outer surface has a shaggy appearance under a hand lens; crown of longer, stiff spicules may be visible round the osculum at the apex. **Colour** cream-yellow. **Habitat** on rocks and shells from lower shore down to about 100 m. *S. ciliatum* generally grows in clumps of several individuals, while *S. coronatum* is usually solitary. Some authorities believe there is only one species. **Distribution** Mediterranean, Atlantic, English Channel and North Sea.

Sycon raphanus (Schmidt) **Form** tubular, barrel-shaped, up to 2 cm high with prominent ring of spicules showing up like bristles around the osculum, and a 'hairy' texture around the body caused by more spicules; sponge usually carried on a short stalk which attaches it to the substrate. **Colour** white-brown. **Habitat** often attached to seaweeds and eel-grasses in shallow water. **Distribution** Mediterranean.

Grantia compressa (Fabricius) **Purse Sponge** **Form** growths may reach 5 cm and are rounded and inflated under water; often collapses when taken out of water to form a flat, purse-like object with an opening which is the large terminal osculum. **Colour** white-grey-yellow. **Habitat** in groups, often under rocky overhangs and among red seaweeds on the lower shore and in shallow water. **Distribution** Mediterranean, Atlantic, English Channel and North Sea.

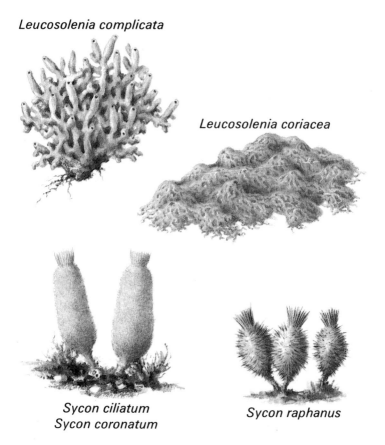

Leucosolenia complicata

Leucosolenia coriacea

Sycon ciliatum
Sycon coronatum

Sycon raphanus

Grantia compressa

Class Demospongiae

Sponges with siliceous spicules (never six-rayed) and/or horny fibres of spongin. Their bodies may be variously shaped, sometimes quite large. They are often brightly coloured and grow in well-illuminated places.

Oscarella lobularis (Schmidt) **Form** encrusting, usually about 0.5 cm thick and covering an area about 10 cm wide; growth arranged in thick 'lobules' or lobes. **Colour** pink-brown-yellow, occasionally blue-violet. **Habitat** on stones, rocks and seaweeds from middle shore down to shallow water. **Distribution** Mediterranean, Atlantic, English Channel and North Sea.

Suberites domuncula (Olivi) (=*Ficulina ficus*) **Sulphur Sponge** or **Sea-orange Form** rounded, globular growth, up to 30 cm in diameter but frequently less; texture fleshy; occasionally it is less round and encrusts rocks and piles, etc. **Colour** orange-yellow. **Habitat** from shallow water down to about 200 m; frequently associated with whelk shells occupied by hermit crabs — the sponge may gradually dissolve away the whelk shell to provide the crab with shelter directly. **Distribution** Mediterranean, Atlantic, English Channel and North Sea. N.B. avoid confusion with *Myxilla* (see page 75).

Cliona celata Grant **Boring Sponge Form** smooth surfaced, branching, net-like. **Colour** yellow-green-blue. **Habitat** may occur on the surface of soft rocks and shells as well as boring into them so that they become penetrated by a network of canals filled with the sponge body; the outer surfaces of the affected rocks and shells are easily recognized by the many holes (each about 0.2 cm in diameter) from which a small portion of the sponge may project; also frequently attacking dead *Ostrea* and *Venus* shells (see pages 173 and 181), from the lower shore down to about 100 m. **Distribution** Mediterranean, Atlantic, English Channel, North Sea and west Baltic.

Tethya aurantia (Pallas) **Form** rounded, globular, up to 10 cm in diameter; outer surface covered with conspicuous warts; osculum and pores about the same size. **Colour** pale gold. **Habitat** growing singly or in colonies on stones, rocks and in caves from shallow water down to about 130 m. **Distribution** Mediterranean, Atlantic, English Channel and North Sea.

Axinella verrucosa (Esper) **Form** erect, branching, up to about 25 cm high; form may be very variable. **Colour** pink-gold-orange. **Habitat** generally on hard substrates between 10 and 100 m. **Distribution** Mediterranean and Atlantic.

Hymeniacidon sanguinea (Grant) (=*H. perleve*) **Form** encrusting, with growths up to 50 cm wide; many small oscula randomly placed; surface furrowed or smooth; form may be very variable. **Colour** orange-scarlet-deep red. **Habitat** on rocks from middle shore down to shallow water. **Distribution** Atlantic, English Channel, North Sea and west Baltic.

Spongilla fluviatilis (Pallas) (=*Ephydatia fluviatilis*) **Freshwater Sponge Form** branching, with irregular growths up to about 20 cm; surface 'fuzzy' when seen in detail. **Colour** green; small, rounded, brown-orange overwintering bodies may be visible in the tissue at certain times of the year. **Habitat** attached to tree roots and stones, etc., in fresh water. **Distribution** in many European rivers and in the Baltic Sea where the salinity is sufficiently low to allow it to grow.

Oscarella lobularis

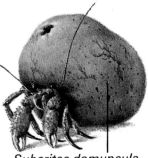
Suberites domuncula

Cliona celata

Axinella verrucosa

Tethya aurantia

Hymeniacidon sanguinea

Spongilla fluviatilis

73

Halichondria panicea (Pallas) **Breadcrumb Sponge** Form often growing in large encrustations up to 20cm across and about 2cm thick; the many oscular openings resemble craters set in minute volcanic cones; surface texture fairly smooth; form may be variable. **Colour** white-orange-yellow-green-brown. **Habitat** on stones, seaweeds and shells from middle shore down to quite deep water. **Distribution** Mediterranean, Atlantic, English Channel, North Sea and west Baltic.

Mycale massa (Schmidt) **Form** massive, round encrusting, up to 5cm across or more. **Colour** yellow-grey-pale orange. **Habitat** sometimes attached to shells and coralline algae which may occur on muddy and sandy substrates from 15m down. **Distribution** Mediterranean.

Myxilla incrustans (Esper) **Form** encrusting, forming thick, cushion-like growths up to 15cm across and 5cm thick; the large oscula are arranged unevenly over the furrowed surface. **Colour** yellow-brown-orange. **Habitat** on rocks, or sometimes on hydroids or spider crabs from lower shore down to about 130m. **Distribution** Mediterranean, Atlantic, English Channel and North Sea. N.B. avoid confusion with *Suberites domuncula* (see page 73).

Spongia officinalis Linnaeus (=*Euspongia officinalis*) **Bath Sponge** Form moderately large, growing in massive, irregular or globular shapes, up to 20cm across — occasionally they may be more than twice as large as this; relatively few oscula which are raised from the surface and slightly crater-like; there are no siliceous spicules and the skeleton consists entirely of spongin fibres (these remain after the sponge has been cleaned and cured and they constitute the 'sponge' of the bathroom). **Colour** red-brown-green. **Habitat** on rocks from shallow water down to 50m or more. **Distribution** Mediterranean.

Verongia aerophoba (Schmidt) (=*Aplysina aerophoba*) **Form** erect, pillar-like and cylindrical, up to 15cm high; the flattened tips, in which lie the terminal oscula, have the appearance of being 'sawn off'; individuals join at base; the skeleton lacks spicules and consists of spongin fibres; hard nodules may be embedded in the tissue. **Colour** yellow-green-black. **Habitat** generally on rocks in shallow water. **Distribution** Mediterranean, and Atlantic north to Biscay.

Ircinia fasciculata (Pallas) (=*Hircinia fasciculata*) **Form** irregular, massive, forming growths up to 15cm across; oscula are slightly raised. **Colour** violet-brown. **Habitat** generally under stones and in crevices in shallow water. **Distribution** Mediterranean. N.B. a number of closely related species occur in the same area.

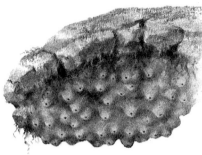

Halichondria panicea

Mycale massa

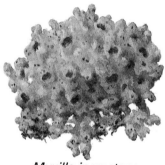

Myxilla incrustans

Spongia officinalis

Verongia aerophoba

Ircinia fasciculata

75

Phylum Cnidaria

This phylum is composed of generally soft-bodied, flower-like animals, often with a jellyfish stage in the life cycle.

The Cnidaria includes some of the most beautiful and abundant marine animals. They are of simple form, having sac-like bodies composed of an inner layer of cells (endoderm) surrounded by an outer layer (ectoderm). These two layers are separated by a jelly-like layer called the mesoglea. The interior of the sac acts as a stomach and opens to the outside via the mouth which also serves for an anus. Around the mouth are rings of tentacles armed with stinging cells. These tentacles grasp the prey and, after it has been immobilized by the stinging cells, force it into the mouth. There are no circulatory nor excretory systems, and the nervous system is very simple. Each animal is termed a *polyp*, unless it is a jellyfish when it is usually called a *medusa*.

Three classes are recognized. Members of the class Hydrozoa (sea-firs) are hydroids which occur in most habitats from the shore to the deep sea, and they are the simplest cnidarians. The polyps often grow close together and are interconnected by tubular extensions of the stomach (see fig. 6). This arrangement frequently leads to the formation of colonies in which some of the polyps are specialized for feeding, whilst others are responsible for reproduction or defence. The form and growth pattern of the colony are important guides to its identification. In some types the tubular inter-gastric connections are surrounded by a protective skeletal sleeve (the perisarc) — these are the order of *athecate* hydroids. Elsewhere the perisarc extends up around the gastric region and provides a protective cup (the theca) which houses the whole polyp and into which the tentacles can be withdrawn. Such hydroids are known as *thecate*, and are placed in another order. Hydroid life cycles are complicated. Adult colonies which may grow on stones, shells or seaweeds, can develop non-feeding, reproductive polyps from which free-swimming medusae bud off. These are swept away by tides and currents and can only swim upwards and float downwards. The umbrella-shaped bell (see fig. 7) contracts rhythmically, lifting the medusa in the water. Sex organs are developed by the medusae and when the sperms and eggs are ripe, they are released into the sea where fertilization occurs. A larva is formed which eventually settles on the seabed to form a new colony. Early naturalists did not understand this life cycle and so they gave the hydroids different names from their respective medusae. Both hydroids and medusae generally feed on small organisms which collide with their sting-celled tentacles. A third order in the class Hydrozoa is the Siphonophora. These are large, floating, colonial hydrozoans which differ from other members of the class because they are free-living for the whole of their life cycle. One specialized polyp forms the *float* and is surrounded by many others developed for feeding, reproduction or defence. Many siphonophores are surface animals relying on wind and water currents for movement. They prey on fishes which they catch with their long, trailing tentacles, and usually appear in European waters when strong south-westerly winds sweep them in from the Atlantic. Their long tentacles may be broken off when they are cast up on the shore. The order Chondrophora is very similar to the order Siphonophora.

In the class Scyphozoa (jellyfishes) the medusa stage dominates, and individuals spent most of their lives as floating predators catching their prey with their long, trailing tentacles equipped with stinging cells. The ripe gonads of the jellyfish release sperms and eggs and, after fertilization, a small larva forms which settles on the seabed to develop a small, hydroid-like organism (the *scyphistoma*). This stage buds repeatedly, giving rise to miniature jellyfishes which then develop into the characteristic adults. In one group (stalked jellyfishes) the small, trumpet-shaped adults are not free swimming, but live attached to the fronds of seaweeds and stones. Scyphozoans occur at most depths in the shallow seas.

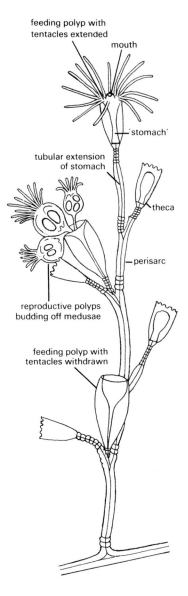

feeding polyp with tentacles extended

mouth

'stomach'

tubular extension of stomach

theca

perisarc

reproductive polyps budding off medusae

feeding polyp with tentacles withdrawn

The class Anthozoa (sea-anemones and their allies) is a diverse group with no medusa stage. The polyps are more sophisticated than the hydrozoan type and can either burrow in soft substrates or live attached to rocks and shells. The best-known anthozoans are the sea-anemones which belong to the order Actinaria. Examples are to be found on the shore as well as in deeper water. Like other cnidarians they are carnivorous, catching their food with tentacles. They can reproduce asexually by division, or sexually when a fertilized egg develops into another polyp — usually via a larval stage. The order Antipatharia comprises the black corals. These have colonial polyps spread out over a hard, horny, tree-like skeleton. The Ceriantharia and Zoantharia resemble sea-anemones. The former are rather worm-like, and live in slimy tubes buried in mud or sand where their long tentacles can protrude ; the latter are small and colonial, and are usually found encrusting rocks and stones. The true corals (order Madreporaria) are represented by a few species in the European seas. They differ from anemones because they have hard, chalky skeletons which support and protect the lower regions of the polyp, and into which the tentacles can usually be drawn. Many are colonial, unlike the European representatives of the closely related Corallimorpharia which, although they resemble coral polyps in many ways, lack the characteristic skeleton of limestone. The orders Alcyonacea, Gorgonacea and Pennatulacea are closely related and usually have polyps with branching tentacles. They are always colonial and have a variety of growth forms.

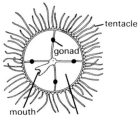

tentacle

gonad

mouth

underside of bell or umbrella

Fig. 6 Branch of *Gonothyraea loveni* to show the form of feeding and reproductive polyps

Fig. 7 Medusa of *Obelia geniculata*

Class Hydrozoa
Order Athecata
Hydroids in which the horny perisarc does not surround the polyps. The polyps can always be seen even when disturbed.

Protohydra leuckarti Greef Solitary; up to 0.2 cm high; lacking perisarc and tentacles. **Habitat** brackish water; often attached to dead seaweeds in muddy areas. **Distribution** Baltic.

Hydra **species** Solitary; up to 2 cm high; possessing tentacles but no perisarc. **Colour** brown-white-green according to species. **Habitat** on water plants in sheltered places; characteristic of fresh water. **Distribution** Baltic where salinity is low.

Coryne pusilla Gaertner Colonial with creeping 'roots' and irregularly branching stems; 1 cm high or more; terminal, cylindrical-shaped, pink-coloured polyps bear club-shaped tentacles; occasionally found with spherical reproductive bodies. **Habitat** in rock pools on lower shore growing on seaweeds, and in deeper water on rocks. **Distribution** Mediterranean, Atlantic, English Channel and North Sea.

Tubularia indivisa Linnaeus Colonial with creeping 'roots' and erect, seldom branching stems often tightly plaited; up to 18 cm high; terminal, flask-shaped, red-pink polyps bear an outer ring of drooping white tentacles and a shorter, stiffer, inner ring; occasionally with reproductive bodies resembling miniature bunches of grapes; perisarc often striped longitudinally and yellowish. **Habitat** in rock pools on the lower shore and attached to rocks and wrecks in deeper water. **Distribution** Atlantic, English Channel and North Sea. N.B. a number of closely related species occur in these areas and in the Mediterranean.

Clava multicornis (Forskål) Colonial with an open network of 'roots'; short, unbranching stems rising to 1.3 cm; terminal, elongated, pink polyps with tapering tentacles; occasionally found with spherical reproductive bodies. **Habitat** in rock pools on lower shore and on stones and seaweeds in shallow water. **Distribution** Atlantic, English Channel, North Sea and Baltic.

Clava squamata (O. F. Müller) (Not illustrated) Similar to *C. multicornis* (above), but with a densely packed network of 'roots' and crowded groups of club-shaped polyps on short stems reaching 2.5 cm high. **Habitat** on seaweeds from lower middle shore down to shallow water. **Distribution** Atlantic and English Channel.

Hydractinia echinata (Flemming) Colonial; densely growing with an encrusting perisarc; spindle-shaped, white-brown-red polyps rising on stems up to 1.5 cm high. **Habitat** on *Buccinum* shells (see page 161) inhabited by hermit crabs, and sometimes on stones in shallow water. **Distribution** Mediterranean, Atlantic, English Channel, North Sea and occasionally in the Baltic.

Eudendrium rameum (Pallas) Colonial and bush-like; up to 15 cm high with creeping roots; strong stem with brown perisarc; flask-shaped pink polyps. **Habitat** in water usually deeper than 10 m., on rocks and in caves. **Distribution** Mediterranean, Atlantic, English Channel and rarely in the North Sea and Baltic.

Bougainvillia ramosa (Van Beneden) **Medusa generation** rounded and bell-shaped; up to 0.4 cm high; 4 groups of 4–9 tentacles; mouth stalk and gonads (when ripe) green-brown. **Habitat** pelagic. **Hydroid generation** colony reaching up to about 5 cm high, spindle-shaped polyps with up to 12 pale tentacles; perisarc yellow-brown. **Habitat** on stones and other hydroids from lower shore down to 30 m. **Distribution** Mediterranean, Atlantic, English Channel, North Sea and west Baltic.

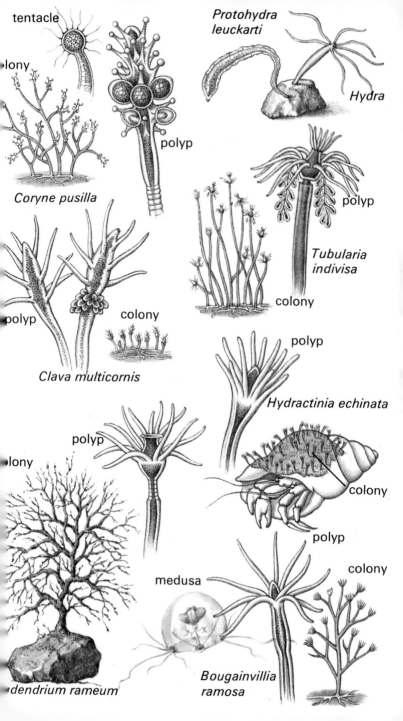

tentacle

lony

Coryne pusilla

polyp

Protohydra leuckarti

Hydra

polyp

Tubularia indivisa

colony

polyp

colony

Clava multicornis

polyp

Hydractinia echinata

colony

polyp

colony

lony

polyp

medusa

polyp

dendrium rameum

Bougainvillia ramosa

Rathkea octopunctata (M. Sars) Medusa of the hydroid **R. octopunctata** (Hydroid not illustrated). Blunt, cone-shaped umbrella reaching about 0.5cm high; generally with 8 clusters of 4 tentacles arranged round the bottom of the umbrella. **Habitat** pelagic. **Distribution** Atlantic, English Channel, North Sea and Baltic.

Order Thecata

Hydroids in which the horny perisarc extends around the polyps, so providing a cup into which they can be withdrawn from view when disturbed. Most species have a characteristic growth pattern (avoid confusion with some of the Ectoprocta, see pages 232–237).

Obelia geniculata (Linnaeus) Colonial with creeping 'roots' and erect, zig-zag, branching stems reaching 4cm high; bell-shaped polyp cups supported on a red-brown perisarc which is characteristically ringed at branch points; polyps borne on alternate sides of stem. **Habitat** on seaweeds on the lower middle shore and lower shore, and in shallow water. **Distribution** Mediterranean, Atlantic, English Channel, North Sea and Baltic.

Gonothyraea loveni (Allman) Colonial with creeping 'roots' and erect stems which reach up to 3cm high; polyp cups narrower than in *Obelia* and fringed with small teeth. **Habitat** on seaweeds, e.g. *Fucus*, on the lower middle shore and lower shore, and in shallow water. **Distribution** Mediterranean, Atlantic, English Channel, North Sea and Baltic.

Aequorea aequorea (Forskål) Probably the medusa of **A. paracuminata** (Not illustrated). Cap-shaped medusa reaching up to 10cm in diameter, occasionally much larger; up to 400 long, pale tentacles; mouth with red lips; gonads blue-pink when mature. **Habitat** pelagic. **Distribution** Mediterranean, Atlantic and North Sea.

Sertularia cupressina (Linnaeus) **White Weed** Colonial with creeping 'roots' and relatively large branching colonies reaching up to 45cm high; main stem often twisted and frequently branched so that polyps occur in tufts arranged in 2 rows with longish, cylindrical cups; colonies white or pink. **Habitat** on stones, shells (e.g. *Chlamys opercularis*, see page 165) and sometimes on crabs, in shallow and deeper water. **Distribution** Atlantic, English Channel, North Sea and west Baltic.

Plumularia catharina Johnston Colonial with creeping 'roots' and branching stems which reach up to 10 high; clear identifying character is the arrangement of the side-branches which are exactly opposite; polyp cups are quite deep with an even, untoothed margin and are borne on the main stem as well as on the side-branches. **Habitat** on stones, shells and the tunics of seasquirts (see pages 261 and 263). **Distribution** Atlantic, English Channel and North Sea.

Campanularia hincksi Alder Colonial with conspicuous, elongated polyp cups which are castellated round the margin and supported on a long branch; up to 0.5cm high from the base stem which creeps over the substrate; long, elongated reproductive polyps may arise directly from the base stem, being ringed and tapering towards the opening at the top (not illustrated here). **Habitat** on shells, other hydroids and ectoprocts from about 10–60m deep. **Distribution** Mediterranean, Atlantic, English Channel and North Sea.

For identification of other hydroids see Hincks, T. 1868.

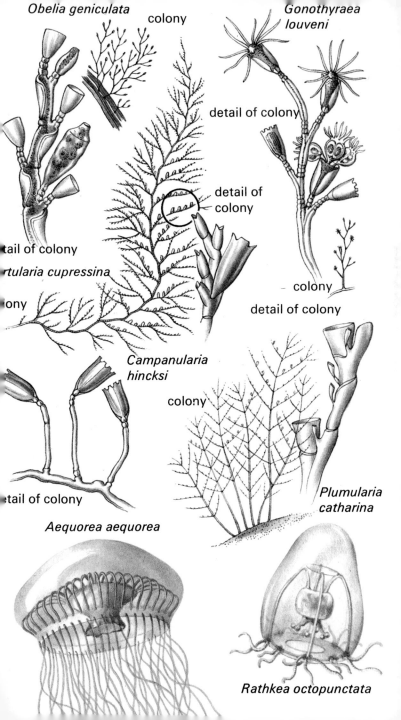

Obelia geniculata

colony

Gonothyraea louveni

detail of colony

detail of colony

tail of colony

rtularia cupressina

ony

detail of colony

colony

detail of colony

Campanularia hincksi

colony

tail of colony

Plumularia catharina

Aequorea aequorea

Rathkea octopunctata

Order Siphonophora

Colonial, free-floating or swimming hydrozoans with many individuals variously modified to provide floats, stems linking the polyps, and feeding, defensive and reproductive individuals. Some species float on the surface, others swim in deeper water. They are generally oceanic but are occasionally washed into coastal areas by rough weather.

Physalia physalis (Linnaeus) **Portuguese Man-o'-war** Large and conspicuous float or *pneumatophore* reaching up to 30cm long by 10cm wide; below this the other individuals are suspended in a complex association and in great numbers; a very short stem is attached to the base of the float from which are suspended several large, fishing and defensive tentacle-like polyps known as *dactylozooids*, smaller dactylozooids, bunches of feeding or *gastrozooids* without tentacles but with mouths, and many branched reproductive individuals or *gonodendra*; gonodendra may release medusae which form part of the life cycle like the medusae of the other hydroids. **Colour** pneumatophore silver blue with red tinging; rest of colony blue-purple. **Habitat** pelagic; surface dweller. **Distribution** Mediterranean and Atlantic. N.B. when rarely cast ashore the pneumatophore may be broken from the remaining part of the colony which thus appears missing. Beware dangerous stinging cells.

Muggiaea atlantica Cunningham Helmet-shaped swimming bell up to 2cm long; transparent; retractile stem hangs from the bell and supports a great number of combinations of individuals; each group is known as a *cormidium* and consists of a feeding zooid equipped with 1 tentacle, a reproductive zooid and a small swimming bract (like a medusa) which enables the reproductive zooids to lead a free existence. **Habitat** found swimming at various depths. **Distribution** Mediterranean and Atlantic.

Galeolaria truncata (M. Sars) (Not illustrated) Similar to *Muggiaea atlantica* but equipped with 2 swimming bells each about 1 cm long; front bell is slightly larger than the rear; retractile stem bears numerous cormidia. **Habitat** found swimming at various depths; often in shoals. **Distribution** Mediterranean, Atlantic and North Sea.

Physophora hydrostatica Forskål Small, apical float or pneumatophore below which hangs a stem polyp about 6cm in length supporting 2 rows of swimming bells; below these trail feeding, defensive, fishing and reproductive polyps. **Colour** predominantly yellow-pink-red. **Habitat** found swimming at various depths. **Distribution** Mediterranean, Atlantic, very occasionally English Channel and North Sea.

Halistemma rubra Vogt (Not illustrated) Similar to *Physophora hydrostatica* but overall length 20cm or more; 9 pairs of swimming bells on the stem polyp. **Colour** red. **Habitat** found swimming at various depths. **Distribution** Mediterranean.

Order Chondrophora

Close relative of the siphonophores.

Velella velella (Linnaeus) **By-the-wind-sailor** Modified siphonophore with a bluish, round or oval disc reaching 8cm in diameter, which encloses the float and contains a horny skeleton equipped with a sail; when alive the sail is covered with soft tissue and projects above the surface of the water to catch the wind and aid dispersal; large feeding zooid under the disc is encircled by a ring of reproductive zooids; at the periphery is a larger ring of tentacle-like fishing zooids. **Habitat** pelagic; surface dweller; sometimes in shoals. **Distribution** Mediterranean and Atlantic.

Porpita umbella Otto (Not illustrated) Similar to *Velella velella* but without the characteristic sail; blue-green disc reaching up to 8cm in diameter. **Habitat** pelagic; surface dweller; often in shoals. **Distribution** Mediterranean and Atlantic.

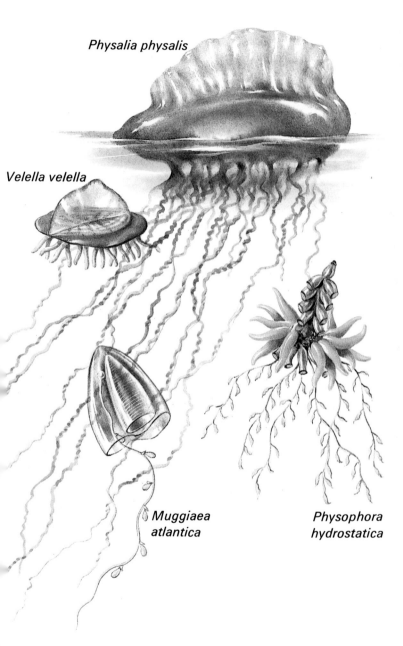

Physalia physalis

Velella velella

Muggiaea atlantica

Physophora hydrostatica

Class Scyphozoa Jellyfishes

Cnidarians in which the medusa stage is dominant, but which normally pass through a small polyp phase during the life cycle; this polyp is termed the *scyphistoma*. The medusae are mostly pelagic, but a few are sessile.

Haliclystus auricula (Rathke) **Stalked Jellyfish** or **Sessile Jelly-fish** Trumpet-shaped body; up to 5cm high; 'bell' drawn out into 8 lobes each bearing tentacles; mouth with 4 corners; conspicuous, wart-like 'anchor' arranged between each lobe (these are used for temporary attachment). **Habitat** attached by means of adhesive stalk to seaweeds or sea-grasses in rock pools on lower shore and in shallow water. **Distribution** Atlantic, English Channel and, rarely, North Sea and west Baltic. N.B. a closely related species *Lucernariopsis campanulata* may be found; this lacks the wart-like anchors.

Charybdea marsupialis (Linnaeus) **Mediterranean Sea-wasp** (Not illustrated) Transparent, yellow-red, box-shaped 'umbrella' up to 6cm high; trailing 4 long tentacles reaching 30cm or more. **Habitat** pelagic. **Distribution** Mediterranean. N.B. can inflict painful stings.

Pelagia noctiluca (Forskål) 'Umbrella' mushroom-shaped; transparent, but tinted yellow-red; up to 10cm in diameter; 4 arms around mouth; 8 slender trailing tentacles around periphery; tentacles longer than mouth arms when fully extended; 8 small, wart-like sense organs alternate with tentacles. **Habitat** pelagic. **Distribution** Mediterranean, Atlantic and English Channel. N.B. can inflict severe and painful stings. Luminescent when disturbed at night.

Chrysaora hysoscella (Linnaeus) **Compass Jellyfish** 'Umbrella' saucer-shaped; up to 30cm in diameter and drawn out into 32 lobes at periphery, and bearing 24 tentacles alternating with 8 sense organs; 4 mouth arms longer than tentacles. **Habitat** pelagic. **Distribution** Atlantic, English Channel and North Sea.

Cyanea lamarckii Péron & Lesueur 'Umbrella' saucer-shaped; up to 15cm in diameter, sometimes more; drawn out into 32 lobes at periphery and bearing numerous tentacles (not all illustrated for simplicity) arranged in 8 clusters; 4 frilly mouth arms shorter than tentacles. **Colour** blue-white. **Habitat** pelagic. **Distribution** Atlantic north from Biscay, English Channel and North Sea. N.B. can inflict severe stings.

Cyanea capillata (Linnaeus) (Not illustrated) Similar to *C. lamarckii*. Up to 50cm in diameter, but occasionally more. **Colour** brick-red-yellow. **Habitat** pelagic. **Distribution** Atlantic north from Biscay, English Channel, North Sea and west Baltic.

Aurelia aurita (Linnaeus) **Common Jellyfish** 'Umbrella' saucer-shaped; up to 25cm in diameter; frilly mouth arms longer than the numerous short tentacles; 8 sense organs; 4 conspicuous purple-violet reproductive organs which are horseshoe-shaped when seen from above. **Colour** transparent; tinged blue-white. **Habitat** pelagic. **Distribution** Mediterranean, Atlantic, English Channel, North Sea and Baltic. N.B. inset illustration shows *scyphistoma* (see above) which is found attached to rocks and seaweeds in pools and shallow water; from this the small larvae with bilobed arms bud off; they are known as *ephyrae*.

Rhizostoma pulmo (Macri) **(= *R. octopus*)** 'Umbrella' dome-shaped; up to 90cm in diameter; no peripheral tentacles; 96 edge lobes and 16 sense organs; 8 fused mouth arms. **Colour** blue-white-yellow, with yellow or blue-red mouth arms. **Habitat** pelagic. **Distribution** Mediterranean, Atlantic, North Sea and west Baltic.

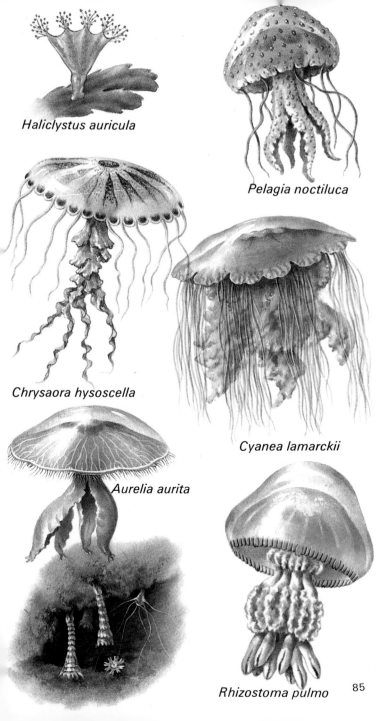

Haliclystus auricula

Pelagia noctiluca

Chrysaora hysoscella

Cyanea lamarckii

Aurelia aurita

Rhizostoma pulmo

85

Class Anthozoa Sea-anemones and their allies

Cnidarians which lack a medusa stage in their life cycle. The polyps may be solitary or colonial, and are often large and conspicuous; a chalky skeleton may or may not be present.

Order Antipatharia Black corals
The thorny, black branching is skeleton surrounded by softer tissues bearing polyps which cannot retract their tentacles; the tentacles are unbranched.

Antipathes subpinnata (Ellis & Solander) **Black Coral** Colonial, with a black-brown skeleton up to 1m high; white-grey outer tissue with small, bilaterally symmetrical polyps up to 0.1cm high. **Habitat** on muddy substrates with stones between 10 and 250m. **Distribution** Mediterranean and Atlantic as far north as English Channel approaches.

Order Ceriantharia
Solitary polyps living in thick, mucuous tubes buried in the seabed so that the crown of unbranched tentacles, which are arranged in 2 whorls, can protrude. There is no adhesive basal disc as in true anemones.

Cerianthus lloydi Gosse Polyp up to 20cm high, often less; long, yellow body bearing about 60 brown, peripheral tentacles reaching up to 4cm; similar number of shorter, inner tentacles; animal characteristically withdraws into its slimy tube with a rapid jerk if disturbed. **Habitat** burrowing in muddy sand from 1—35m. **Distribution** Atlantic, English Channel and North Sea.

Cerianthus membranaceus (Spallanzini) (Not illustrated) Similar to *C. lloydi*, but with about 130 peripheral tentacles reaching 20cm in length; violet-brown body may be 35cm high. **Distribution** Mediterranean.

Order Zoantharia Encrusting 'anemones'
These polyps are usually colonial, and are linked by a stolon which may or may not be easily seen. They encrust existing surfaces such as rocks and shells, and have smooth, slender tentacles which sometimes appear to have minute terminal expansions.

Epizoanthus couchi (Johnston) Colonial, with the stolons rather obscure; grey-brown polyps up to 1cm high; about 35 slender tentacles reaching 0.5cm long. **Habitat** on rocks, stones and pebbles from extreme lower shore down to deep water. **Distribution** Atlantic, English Channel and North Sea.

Epizoanthus incrustatus (Düben & Koren) (Not illustrated) Similar to *E. couchi*, but usually found on shells inhabited by the hermit crab *Anapagurus laevis* (see page 221) from 10—100m. **Distribution** Atlantic, English Channel and North Sea.

Epizoanthus arenaceus (Delle Chiaje) (Not illustrated) Similar to *E. couchi*, but with about 24 white tentacles per polyp; often on shells of *Aporrhais* sp. and *Murex* sp. (see pages 155 and 159) from 10m downward. **Distribution** Mediterranean.

Parazoanthus dixoni Haddon & Shackleton Colonial, with stolons as thin lamellae connecting yellowish polyps which reach 2cm high; about 40 tentacles. **Habitat** on stones and other organisms, e.g. sponges, from 10m downward. **Distribution** Atlantic, English Channel and North Sea.

Parazoanthus axinellae (O. Schmidt) (Not illustrated) Similar to *P. dixoni* but with polyps up to 1cm high and bearing about 36 golden-yellow tentacles. **Habitat** on cave walls, rock faces, sponges and sea-squirts from 1m downward. **Distribution** Mediterranean and Atlantic as far north as English Channel approaches.

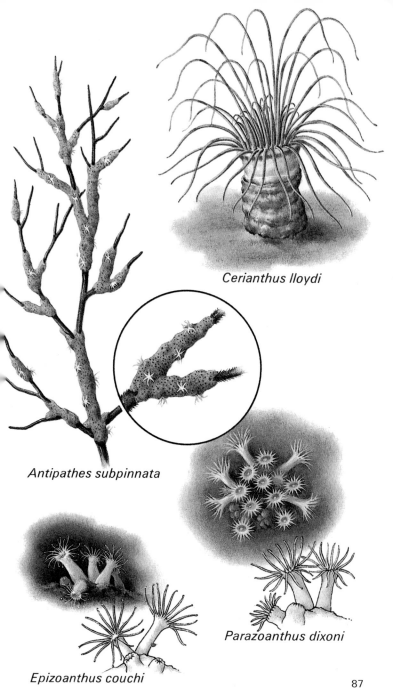

Cerianthus lloydi

Antipathes subpinnata

Parazoanthus dixoni

Epizoanthus couchi

Order Actinaria Sea-anemones

Solitary, often conspicuous anthozoans with no calcareous, hard skeleton. They are sedentary, with the polyp base modified either for burrowing, or for adhering to rocks and shells by means of an adhesive, sucker-like disc. The tentacles are simple and unbranched.

Fagesia carnea (Gosse) **(** = ***Milne-Edwardsia carnea*)** No adhesive basal disc; not more than 2cm high when extended; worm-like translucent pink body; 27 delicate tentacles. **Habitat** occupies small holes (made by other organisms) in rocks, overhangs, cave walls, etc. on extreme lower shore. **Distribution** Atlantic, English Channel and North Sea; usually very local.

Edwardsia callimorpha (Gosse) No adhesive basal disc; not more than 10cm high when fully extended; worm-like, translucent pink body; 16 delicate tentacles, transparent and marked with fine dots; diameter across tentacles when expanded 3.5cm. **Habitat** burrowing in muddy sand and gravels (often around *Zostera* beds, see page 65) on extreme lower shore and down to 10m. **Distribution** Mediterranean, Atlantic, English Channel and North Sea.

Halcampa chrysanthellum (Peach) No adhesive basal disc; not more than 5cm when fully extended; worm-like, translucent buff-coloured body, tinged yellow above; 12 short, stout tentacles with a red-brown horseshoe mark at the base. **Habitat** in sandbanks and among *Zostera* beds (see page 65), sometimes under stones or in pools from lower shore down to 100m. **Distribution** Atlantic, English Channel, North Sea and Baltic.

Peachia hastata Gosse No adhesive basal disc; worm-like anemone up to 10cm high when fully extended; translucent brown-pink column with 12 fine, vertical lines and 4 minute, adhesive warts; usually about 12 translucent tentacles, with characteristic arrow-shaped marks at their bases; diameter across tentacles up to 4cm when expanded. **Habitat** in sandy mud, sand, and shell gravel from lower shore down to 30m. **Distribution** Mediterranean, Atlantic, English Channel and North Sea.

Condylactis aurantiaca (Delle Chiaje) Base adhesive and sucker-like; body up to 40cm high when fully expanded and 7cm across the column; white body with orange-red longitudinal stripes and white, wart-like suckers; green-white tentacles have violet tips and may be the only conspicuous part of the animal. **Habitat** often attached to stones or rocks which are themselves buried in sand or gravel from 0.5m down to 10m. **Distribution** Mediterranean.

Fagesia carnea

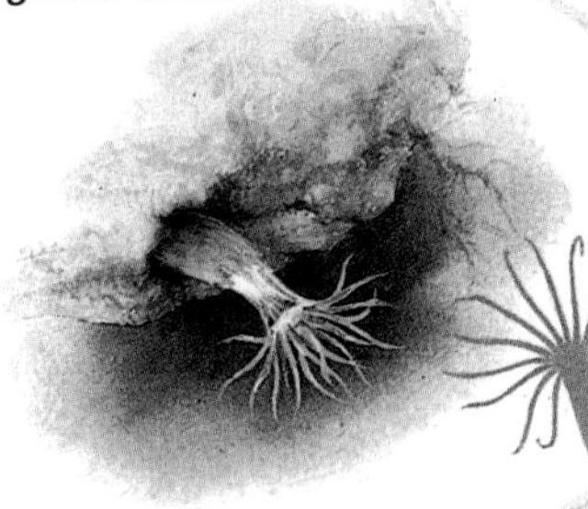

Edwardsia callimorpha

whole animal

Halcampa chrysanthellum

Condylactis aurantiaca

whole animal

Peachia hastata

89

Actinia equina Linnaeus **Beadlet Anemone** Base adhesive and
sucker-like; smooth column up to 7cm high and 6cm across when fully
expanded; about 200 densely packed retractile tentacles which can reach 2cm
in length and are arranged in 5—6 circlets; they fold in quickly when the animal
is disturbed; 24 relatively conspicuous blue spots arranged on the periphery of
the oral disc outside the tentacles; when the tide is out it may appear as a blob of
jelly up to 3cm high. **Colour** variable; brown, red, orange or green; sometimes
red with green-yellow spots (strawberry variety). **Habitat** common on rocks
and in crevices from the middle shore down to 8m. **Distribution** Mediterranean,
Atlantic, English Channel and North Sea.

Actinia cari Delle Chiaje Base adhesive and sucker-like; cone-shaped
column up to 5cm high and 7cm in diameter at the base; about 190 retractile
tentacles reaching 2cm in length; they fold in when the animal is disturbed (as
illustrated). **Colour** clear blue or green peripheral spots outside the tentacles as
in *A. equina* (above); body brown, blue-green, green or yellow with encircling
lines. **Habitat** on rocks, stones and piers from 0.5—1.5m. **Distribution** Mediterranean.

Anemonia sulcata (Pennant) **Oplet** Base lightly adhesive and sucker-
like; smooth column reaching up to 10cm high, but often squat with base
spread out; about 170 wavy tentacles which may reach 15cm in length, and
arranged in up to 6 circlets; tentacles cannot be fully retracted. **Colour** column
brown, grey or green; tentacles similar with or without purple tips; characteristically 2 white lines run from opposite sides of the disc to the mouth. **Habitat**
on the lower shore and down to 23m on rocks and, occasionally, seaweeds;
generally prefers strong light. **Distribution** Mediterranean, Atlantic north to
west Scotland, and English Channel east to the Solent.

Tealia felina (Linnaeus) Base strongly adhesive and sucker-like; warty
column reaching up to 15cm when large specimens are fully expanded;
characteristically with pieces of shells and gravel adhering to the column so that
when closed the animal may be quite inconspicuous; 80—160 stout, retractile
tentacles. **Colour** body grey, blue or green with irregular red bands or patches;
mouth and oral disc olive-green, pink or blue; coloration very variable and some
combinations may be outstandingly beautiful; tentacles translucent and
banded with white, grey, green, blue or red shades. **Habitat** on hard substrates
often in crevices and fairly shaded from strong light. **Distribution** Atlantic,
English Channel, North Sea and west Baltic. N.B. four varieties have been
identified of which two are mentioned here.
1. Variety *coriacea* Warts conspicuous on column; base up to 5.5cm in
diameter. **Habitat** common shore form; may also be found in shallow or deeper
water. **Distribution** round all British and Irish coasts, and from the English
Channel approaches to Norway, and in the Baltic.
2. Variety *loftensis* Warts relatively inconspicuous on column; base up to
12cm or more in diameter; large tentacles reaching up to 6cm long; column
usually higher than wide and not usually encrusted with gravel, etc. **Habitat** on
rocky substrates from 10—600m. **Distribution** widespread and common; not
recorded from the English Channel.

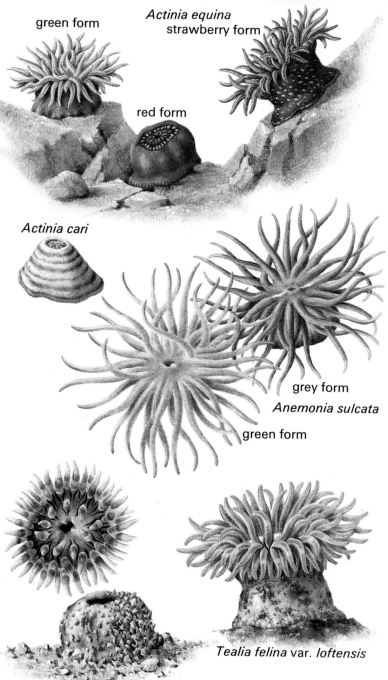

green form

Actinia equina
strawberry form

red form

Actinia cari

grey form
Anemonia sulcata

green form

Tealia felina var. *coriacea*

Tealia felina var. *loftensis*

91

Aiptasia couchi (Cocks) **Trumpet Anemone** Base lightly adhesive and sucker-like; orange-brown column with minute warts, broadening out towards the oral region and reaching 6 cm high; sometimes column is patterned with cream-brown; 82 large tentacles, stout at the base and tapering to fine points, may be 3 cm long and rarely retracted fully; could be confused with *Anemonia sulcata* brown variety (see page 91) but characteristically has many pale lines running from the tentacle bases to the mouth, rather than the 2 white lines of *A. sulcata*. **Habitat** on rocks, extreme lower shore and shallow water; often local. **Distribution** Mediterranean, Atlantic north to the English Channel approaches, Channel Islands, south Devon and Cornwall.

Aiptasia mutabilis (Gravenhorst) Base adhesive and sucker-like; smooth column reaches up to 20 cm and is yellow-brown, occasionally with violet tinges; about 190 transparent tentacles with irregular brown spottings or rings. **Habitat** on rocks and shells on lower shore and in shallow water. **Distribution** Mediterranean.

Diadumene cincta Stephenson Base adhesive; smooth, orange-coloured column with characteristic collar at its upper limit (may not be seen when fully expanded), reaching to 3 cm in height and 0.35 cm in diameter; slender, light orange tentacles do not taper quickly, but are fully retractable; may be confused with the young of *Metridium senile*, orange variety (see page 95) but the tentacles of the latter species are less rapidly retracted. **Habitat** on rocks and shells on lower shore and in shallow water. **Distribution** local and rare in English Channel and southern North Sea.

Haliplanella luciae (Verrill) **(=***Diadume luciae***) Orange-striped Anemone** (Not illustrated) Base adhesive; column wrinkled when retracted, smooth and pillar-like when extended to 1 cm; collar similar to *Diadumene cincta*; tentacles 1 cm long; retractile and delicate. **Colour** dark green with up to 20 vertical, orange stripes; tentacles green-grey. **Habitat** on stones and pebbles among mud and sand, on extreme lower shore and down to 4 m. **Distribution** Mediterranean, Atlantic, English Channel, North Sea and west Baltic. N.B. some small specimens of *Actinia equina* (see page 91) have similar coloration. Check to see whether or not the specimen in question has blue spots on the periphery of the oral disc outside the tentacles; these are characteristic of *Actinia equina*.

Bunodactis verrucosa (Pennant) **Gem Anemone** Base adhesive, up to 3 cm in diameter when the animal is closed; conical column reaches 3 cm high and carries 6 rows of white warts interspersed with many more rows of blue-grey warts; about 48 transparent tentacles up to 1.5 cm long. **Colour** translucent and mottled green, grey or pink. **Habitat** in rock pools on lower shore and in shallow water, frequently in small crevices well exposed to light and sometimes surrounded by sand. **Distribution** Mediterranean, Atlantic, English Channel east to the Solent.

Anthopleura balli (Cocks) Base adhesive and sucker-like; warty column reaching to 5 cm or more; warts largest near the top; column pink-orange or yellow-green which are the principal varieties of this variably coloured species (as illustrated); tentacles not readily retractile and translucent with grey, pink or brown mottlings and sometimes green tinges. **Habitat** shuns strong light and occurs on rocks, particularly in holes or on the sides or undersides of crevices, on middle and lower shores and occasionally deeper. **Distribution** Mediterranean, Atlantic north to the Irish Sea, English Channel east to Sussex and North Sea; often rare and local.

Anthopleura thallia (Gosse) Base lightly adhesive; column reaching up to 4 cm with warts which are more pronounced near the top; column green-grey fading to the base; about 60 translucent, pale, tapering tentacles up to 2.5 cm long. **Habitat** middle and lower shore in pools on rocks, often in strong illumination (unlike *A. balli*); sometimes gregarious. **Distribution** Atlantic north to south-west Scotland, English Channel east to Devon; rare.

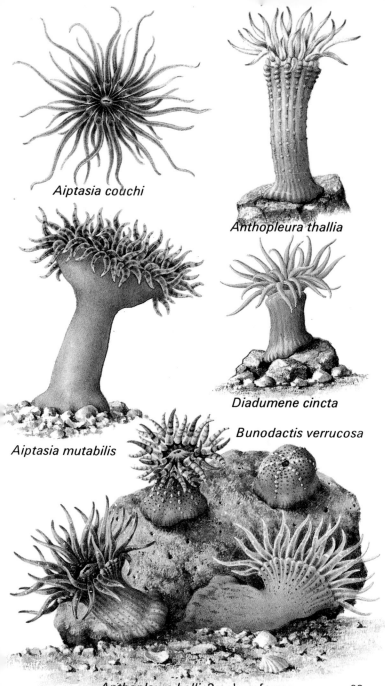

Aiptasia couchi

Anthopleura thallia

Diadumene cincta

Aiptasia mutabilis

Bunodactis verrucosa

Anthopleura balli 2 colour forms

93

Metridium senile (Linnaeus) Base adhesive; column smooth, reaching up to 8cm or more; well-developed collar visible below the crown of fine, slender tentacles; tentacles are more crowded and numerous, giving a 'feather duster' effect; tentacles generally more translucent than the column; form and shape of the individuals may be extremely variable, and the juveniles do not necessarily resemble the adults and can be difficult to identify. **Colour** there are several colour varieties of which 2 are shown; others include brown, cream and orange. **Habitat** on rocks, wrecks and piers from 0.5—3m. **Distribution** Mediterranean, Atlantic, English Channel and North Sea.

Amphianthus dohrni (von Koch) Base elongated; about 2cm wide and modified to wrap around the stem of other organisms, e.g. the gorgonian *Eunicella verrucosa* (as shown here) or certain hydroids; individuals are sometimes closely grouped, thus giving a colonial effect, although they are really solitary; low, pillar-shaped column may be buff, pink or red and reaches up to 1.2cm in height; about 48 translucent, buff-white tentacles. **Habitat** on rocky substrates from 20—600m wherever a suitable supporting organism can grow; this species cannot easily be confused with any other in the European area because of its habits. **Distribution** Mediterranean, Atlantic north to the English Channel approaches and south-west Ireland.

Calliactis parasitica (Couch) **'Parasitic' Anemone** Base firmly adhesive; column stout and pillar-like, reaching up to 8cm; numerous tentacles in the adult, which may reach 3cm in length. **Colour** column dark grey or brown with white or longitudinal stripes; tentacles translucent yellow-grey. **Habitat** on muddy substrates from 3—100m. **Distribution** Mediterranean, Atlantic north to the west of Ireland and the Irish Sea, and English Channel. N.B. this is not a true parasite, but a commensal of the hermit crab. The anemone is frequently found attached to an empty shell of *Buccinum undatum* (see page 161). Several species of hermit crab may take up residence in the shell; the anemone protects the crab from the attacks of predators such as *Octopus*, and also obtains food from the crabs' feeding activities. Several anemones may be associated with 1 crab, but both crab and anemone can occur separately.

Adamsia palliata (Bohadsch) Commensal anemone almost always associated with the hermit crab *Eupagurus prideauxi* (see page 221). Base and column highly modified to form an adhesive investment around the crab's body which itself is usually contained inside the shell of a small gastropod; as the crab grows the base of the anemone secretes a horny substance which effectively extends the shell; base may reach 7cm across if measured free from the crab; column is squat, giving way to tentacle disc almost immediately; about 500 tentacles. **Colour** base brown to yellow, usually with red spots or blotches; tentacle disc and tentacles white and translucent; when disturbed the anemone may eject fine, lilac-purple threads (called *acontia*); may be immediately distinguished from *Calliactis parasitica* by the way the base is folded round the shell, as well as by the different colouring. **Habitat** on sandy and muddy substrates from 4—100m. **Distribution** Mediterranean, Atlantic, English Channel and North Sea.

Amphianthus dohrni
on *Eunicella verrucosa*

Metridium senile

pink form

white form

Calliactis parasitica
on shell occupied by
Eupagurus bernhardus

Adamsia palliata
on shell occupied by
Eupagurus prideauxi

Sagartia elegans (Dalyell) Base strongly adhesive, up to 4 cm in diameter but often less; red-brown column bearing wart-like suckers and reaching up to 6 cm; up to 200 tentacles which may reach up to 1.5 cm long. **Habitat** on rocks and in crevices from the lower shore down to 50 m; when disturbed the animal ejects white threads (*acontia*). N.B. there are several colour variants of which three are illustrated.

1. Variety *venusta*   Tentacles and oral disc with no patterns; disc orange; tentacles white. **Distribution** widely distributed around Ireland and the south-west of Britain.

2. Variety *rosea* (Not illustrated)   As above but disc orange, white or drab; tentacles rose or magenta. **Distribution** limited distribution in Ireland and south-west Britain.

3. Variety *nivea* (Not illustrated)   As above, disc and tentacles white. **Distribution** widely distributed around Ireland and the south and west of Britain.

4. Variety *miniata*   Tentacles and mouth disc with well-marked pattern usually in shades of brown. **Distribution** Atlantic, English Channel and North Sea. N.B. these varieties were formerly described as species in their own right by P. H. Gosse in his classical work of 1860, *Actinologia Britannica*.

Sagartia troglodytes (Price) Base firmly adhesive, diameter up to 3.5 cm depending on the variety; column with warty suckers reaching up to 4 cm high; 100–200 tentacles, each up to 0.75 cm long. **Habitat** generally under stones or partly buried in gravel or sand. N.B. there are two well-established varieties:

1. Variety *decorata*   Column yellowish, becoming paler and greyer above with vertical lines; mouth disc and tentacles intricately patterned. **Habitat** on the lower shore and down to 50 m in very dirty and muddy conditions, as well as in sand. **Distribution** Atlantic, English Channel and North Sea north to Norway.

2. Variety *ornata*   Column dark olive-green with slightly paler vertical lines and spots; mouth disc and tentacles intricately patterned; base of disc generally about 1 cm in diameter. **Habitat** essentially a shore form inhabiting areas with cleaner sand than variety *decorata*. **Distribution** the same, but commoner on south-west English Channel coasts.

Cereus pedunculatus (Pennant) **Daisy Anemone** Base firmly adhesive, reaching 3.3 cm in diameter; variably shaped, smooth column with grey suckers near the top, often trumpet-shaped when fully extended, and generally orange to buff-grey in colour; mouth disc often puckered and generally brown with darker markings; sometimes beautifully patterned; up to about 750 short tentacles of brown colour dotted and patterned with cream. **Habitat** typically a shore species, in clean rock pools or in crevices as well as on stones and shells buried in mud (sometimes in great numbers); occasionally in estuaries. **Distribution** Mediterranean, Atlantic north to Scottish borders and English Channel; not confirmed from the North Sea.

Actinothoë sphyrodeta (Gosse) Base adhesive, reaching up to 1 cm in diameter; grey-white, pillar-like column up to 3 cm high; mouth disc sometimes coloured; may eject fine white threads when disturbed; may have over 100 grey-white tentacles. **Habitat** on the undersides of pebbles or vertical and overhanging rock faces and cave walls where the water is clean; on lower shore and in shallow water. **Distribution** Atlantic to south-west Ireland and English Channel east to Dorset.

Sagartiogeton undata (Müller) Base firmly adhesive, reaching up to 4 cm in diameter; column may contract to a flat mound with the upper part introverted, but in full expansion forms a tall pillar reaching up to 6 cm; drab colour, yellower above with vertical, brown-grey stripes; may eject fine white threads when disturbed; oral disc light brown, bearing 100 slender, transparent tentacles. **Habitat** normally attached to stones or shells buried in sandy mud on the extreme lower shore and down to 50 m. **Distribution** Mediterranean, Atlantic, English Channel and North Sea to Norway and west Baltic.

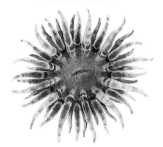

Sagartia elegans var. *miniata*

Sagartia elegans var. *venusta*

Sagartia troglodytes var. *decorata*

Sagartia troglodytes var. *ornata*

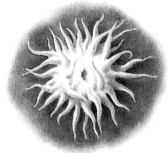

Actinothoë sphyrodeta

Cereus pedunculatus

Sagartiogeton undata

Order Madreporaria True corals

Anthozoans with hard, calcareous skeletons into which the polyps can almost, if not completely, withdraw when disturbed. Often colonial. N.B. avoid confusion with calcified ectoprocts (see pages 235 and 237).

Caryophyllia smithi Stokes **Devonshire Cup Coral** Solitary, with stout, brown-white skeleton up to 1.5cm high and with conspicuous ridges (septa); polyps variable in colour — white, pink, brown or green, often with contrasting lips, e.g. red or green; tentacles variable in colour terminating in a small knob. **Habitat** on rocks or stones from the extreme lower shore to 100m. **Distribution** Atlantic, English Channel and northern North Sea (Scotland, Sweden, etc.). N.B. sometimes associated with the small barnacle *Pyrgoma anglicum* (see page 199) which may be found growing on the periphery of the coral cup, resembling a small wart 1–2mm high.

Caryophyllia clavus Sacchi (Not illustrated) This may prove to be a variety of *C. smithii*. As above, but with skeleton somewhat like an inverted bullet, and up to 2cm high; polyps pink to brown. **Habitat** from 1–200m. **Distribution** Mediterranean.

Balanophyllia regia Gosse **Scarlet-and-gold Star Coral** Solitary, with cylindrical skeleton up to 1cm high; perforated septa not visible in life because polyps cannot withdraw entirely; brilliant orange or scarlet body; tentacles transparent with yellow flecks *lacking a knob on the tip*. **Habitat** on extreme lower shore and in shallow water. **Distribution** Atlantic, Bristol Channel and west English Channel; rare and local.

Balanophyllia italica Michelin **(=** *Balanophyllia verrucaria***)** (Not illustrated) As *B. regia*, but skeleton like an inverted cone reaching 2.5cm and being oval at the top, not round; sides of septa may be spiny or granulated; polyps iridescent, colourless — yellow-brown. **Habitat** on rocks and stones from 1–100m, often crowded together or associated with *Cladocora* (see below). **Distribution** Mediterranean and Atlantic.

Cladocora cespitosa (Linnaeus) Bushy colonies with branching tubular skeletons reaching up to 10cm high, with 'stems' 2–5cm in diameter; polyps brown. **Habitat** on rocks and shells from 1–70m. **Distribution** Mediterranean.

Lophelia pertusa (Pallas) Colonial, with irregularly branching, yellow-white skeletons reaching up to 50cm in height; pinkish polyps loosely scattered over the skeleton. **Habitat** on rocky substrates in water from 60–600m. **Distribution** Mediterranean (Adriatic), Atlantic (west coast of Scotland) and northern North Sea (west coasts of Sweden and Norway).

Dendrophyllia ramea (Linnaeus) Tree-like colonies up to 50cm high, with side-branches and polyps arranged in 2 rows; thin-walled skeleton outwardly ribbed; polyps light yellow colour. **Habitat** on rocks from 30m downward. **Distribution** Mediterranean.

Order Corallimorpharia

Anthozoans without a hard skeleton. The polyps have tentacles which terminate in a small knob.

Corynactis viridis Allman **Jewel 'Anemone'** Solitary, small polyp with brilliant colours (which may fade in the aquarium); body 0.25–0.5cm in diameter; broad, adhesive base; tentacles arranged in 3 circlets; mouth borne on a minute cone. **Habitat** on rocks on extreme lower shore and down to 100m. **Distribution** Atlantic north to west English Channel and south-west Ireland.

Cladocora cespitosa

Dendrophyllia ramea

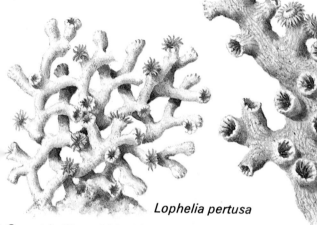

Lophelia pertusa

Caryophyllia smithi with *Pyrgoma anglicum*

Balanophyllia regia

Corynactis viridis

skeleton of *Caryophyllia smithi*
with *Pyrgoma anglicum*

99

Order Alcyonacea Soft corals

Colonial anthozoans whose retractable polyps have 8 branching (pinnate) tentacles; polyps embedded in the body mass which has a skeleton made of a great number of free calcareous ossicles which makes these colonies soft and flexible. They are usually attached to rocks and stones.

Alcyonium digitatum (Linnaeus) **Dead Man's Fingers** Erect, stout, branching colonies up to 20cm high; white, yellow, orange or pink colour varieties; frequently branching in one plane and bearing a great number of white, retractable polyps which withdraw when disturbed; each polyp can extend up to 1 cm; tentacles with about 16 branchlets on either side. **Habitat** on rocks or stones on the lower shore and down to 100m. **Distribution** Atlantic from Biscay northward, English Channel and North Sea.

Alcyonium palmatum Pallas (Not illustrated) Similar to *A. digitatum* but more branched and larger, reaching 50cm; colonies white, pink, brown or red with translucent white polyps; tentacles with 11–13 branchlets on either side. **Habitat** attached to stones or shells on muddy substrates, or standing freely, in shallow water down to 20m. **Distribution** Mediterranean, Atlantic to English Channel approaches, and south-west Britain.

Parerythropodium coralloides (Pallas) Encrusting red colonies growing over branching stems of seaweeds or dead gorgonians (see below); polyps with white tentacles. **Habitat** on rocky substrates where suitable supporting organisms grow, from 8–90m. **Distribution** Mediterranean and Atlantic north to Biscay.

Order Gorgonacea Sea-fans and their allies

Colonial anthozoans in which the polyps have 8 branching tentacles. The polyps are retractable, and embedded in tissue supported by a branching, central skeleton of calcium carbonate bound with a horn-like substance called *gorgonin*. They are anchored at the base by a holdfast.

Corallium rubrum (Linnaeus) **Red 'Coral'** or **Precious 'Coral'** Colonial, branching in all planes, reaching 50cm in height; outer surface of main skeleton grooved; small polyps with white tentacles cover whole colony. **Colour** red, pink or white, or occasionally brown or black. **Habitat** on hard substrates with poor illumination, from 50–200m. **Distribution** Mediterranean. N.B. do not confuse with calcified ectoprocts (see pages 235 and 237).

Eunicella verrucosa (Pallas) **Sea-fan** (Illustrated on page 95) Colonial, branching in one plane only, reaching 30cm in height; soft, pink outer tissue surrounds a brown horny skeletal support; numerous pink polyps borne in slight swellings reaching up to 0.3cm when fully expanded. **Habitat** attached by holdfast to rocks, usually from 15m downward. **Distribution** Mediterranean, Atlantic north to west English Channel.

Paramuricea chamaeleon (Koch) Colonial, branching in one plane only, reaching up to 30cm in height; red or violet outer tissue, often brown at tips of branches, surrounds the horny skeletal support; polyps may reach up to 0.6cm in full extension, being crowded near the tips of the branches. **Habitat** on rocky substrates from 15m downward. **Distribution** Mediterranean.

Order Pennatulacea Sea-pens

Feather-shaped anthozoan colonies with a horny or chalky skeleton supporting the central column. The polyps are divided laterally, sometimes on branches.

Pennatula phosphorea Linnaeus **Phosphorescent Sea-pen** Feather-like colony with central column up to 40cm high; area bearing polyps roughly as long as that which does not. **Colour** red; white polyps about 0.1cm long. **Habitat** on sand and clay from 20m downward. **Distribution** Mediterranean, Atlantic, North Sea and west Baltic.

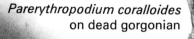

Parerythropodium coralloides
on dead gorgonian

lcyonium digitatum

*Corallium
rubrum*

*Pennatula
phosphorea*

*aramuricea
amaeleon*

101

Phylum Ctenophora Sea-gooseberries

These animals differ in several respects from the cnidarians and thus are often separately classified. The body is usually gooseberry-shaped and composed of two thin layers of cells separated by a volume of transparent, iridescent or luminous jelly which constitutes the animal's main bulk. The mouth is situated at the bottom of the body and leads into a series of digestive canals which open by one or two minute pores at the top. Radiating from the body are a series of up to eight swimming structures called *comb-rows*. Each comb-row is made up of a number of plates consisting of fused cilia. These beat up and down rhythmically, so driving the animal through the water.

Ctenophores are highly predatory and feed on other floating animals. Many have tentacles which can be protruded from pits on either side of the body and trailed along like fishing lines. These tentacles carry cells which cannot sting the prey, but lasso it, thus securing it until it is passed to the mouth.

Class Tentaculata Ctenophores with retractile tentacles

Pleurobrachia pileus (O. F. Müller) **Sea-gooseberry** Rounded, oval body up to 3cm in length with conspicuous comb-rows running from the apex, but terminating short of the bottom of the animal; relatively long, branching tentacles. **Colour** white-orange gut. **Habitat** common in open water and occasionally found in rock pools; may be in shoals. **Distribution** Mediterranean, Atlantic, English Channel, North Sea and Baltic.

Bolinopsis infundibulum (O. F. Müller) Oval body reaching up to 15cm in length; 2 conspicuous comb-rows at either side of the mouth which may be half the length of the rest of the body; branched tentacles. **Habitat** open water; sometimes in shoals. **Distribution** Mediterranean, Atlantic, English Channel, North Sea and west Baltic.

Hormiphora plumosa Agassiz Similar to *Pleurobrachia pileus*. Pear-shaped body with conspicuous comb-rows. **Colour** gut brown; tentacles with brown and yellow branches. **Habitat** open water. **Distribution** Mediterranean.

Cestus veneris Lesueur Ribbon-like body, 8cm long and 1.5cm high; 4 transparent comb-rows; main tentacles reduced, but secondary tentacles lie in 2 grooves near the mouth. **Colour** transparent; sometimes green-violet. **Habitat** open water. **Distribution** Mediterranean and Atlantic usually south of Britain; extremely rare in North Sea.

Class Nuda Ctenophores lacking tentacles

Beroë cucumis Fabricius Mitre-shaped body up to 10cm or more long; comb-rows run from the apex to the base; branched inner canals visible. **Colour** transparent; occasionally pinkish. **Habitat** open water. **Distribution** Mediterranean, Atlantic, North Sea and Baltic.

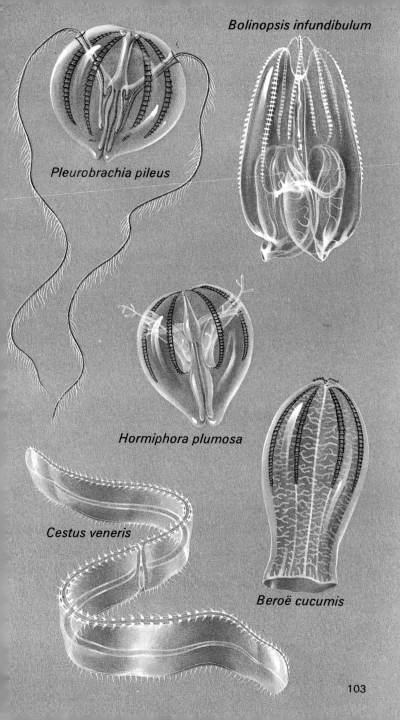

Bolinopsis infundibulum

Pleurobrachia pileus

Hormiphora plumosa

Cestus veneris

Beroë cucumis

103

Marine worms

The animal kingdom includes many different types of worms. The different types cover a range of body plans and life styles and are grouped as follows: phylum Platyhelminthes (the flatworms); phylum Nemertina (the ribbon worms); phylum Nematoda (the round worms); phylum Annelida (the segmented worms); and phylum Priapuloidea, phylum Echiuroidea, phylum Sipunculoidea (these last three phyla are generally regarded as minor groups).

Apart from their bilateral symmetry, bodies composed of three cell layers, and the fact that they all require a moist if not aquatic environment, these groups have relatively little in common. Disposition of appendages, presence or absence of segmentation, number of body openings, habit and the pattern of locomotion should all be of assistance when seeking to distinguish between these various phyla.

Phylum Platyhelminthes Flatworms
Class Turbellaria

Generally free-living, leaf-shaped worms. They lack a body cavity separating the gut from the remaining tissues. The mouth opens on the underside, and the pharynx is often everted for feeding. The gut is simple or branched, and sometimes visible through the skin; there is no anus. Rudimentary sense organs at the anterior end include eye spots and tentacles. Locomotion is with a characteristic, gliding movement effected by the combined action of thousands of cilia on the underside, although the animals can change their shape by muscle contraction. A further account of Baltic turbellarians may be obtained from Forsman, B. 1972.

Convoluta convoluta (Abildgaard) **Length** up to 0.6 cm. **Head** broader than tail and lacking distinct tentacles. **Body** flattened and leaf-like, often turned up at the edges; gut lacking. **Colour** green, due to symbiotic algae. **Habitat** among seaweeds from lower shore down to 15 m. **Distribution** Mediterranean, Atlantic, English Channel, North Sea and Baltic.

Monocelis lineata (O. F. Müller) **Length** up to 0.2 cm. **Head** not readily discernible from body and lacking distinct tentacles. **Body** slightly pointed at the head end; gut simple. **Colour** opaque white gut visible through skin. **Habitat** among seaweeds (e.g. *Ulva* see page 21) from middle shore downward. **Distribution** Mediterranean, Atlantic, English Channel and North Sea.

Procerodes ulvae (Oersted) **Length** up to 0.5 cm. **Head** bears triangular tentacles and 2 eyes. **Body** rounded at the rear and tapering towards the head; gut with 3 branches. **Habitat** under stones, often near freshwater outlets, from upper shore downward. **Distribution** Atlantic, English Channel, North Sea and Baltic.

Oligocladus sanguinolentus (Quatrefages) **Length** up to 1.3 cm. **Head** rounded, bears 2 tentacles and many eyes. **Body** flattened and leaf-shaped with rounded tail; gut visible and with a number of branches. **Colour** transparent body, white above with brown-red spots. **Habitat** under stones and seaweeds from middle shore downward. **Distribution** Atlantic, English Channel and North Sea.

Prostheceraeus vittatus (Montagu) **Length** up to 3 cm or more. **Head** bluntish, bears 2 conspicuous tentacles. **Body** flat, leaf-shaped, with edges thrown into folds and tapering to a point at the tail. **Habitat** under stones in mud. **Distribution** Atlantic, western English Channel and North Sea.

Thysanozoon brocchii Grube **Length** up to 5 cm. **Head** blunt, bears 2 tentacles; dorsal surface carries papillae. **Body** less flat than some species, being thicker along the middle with a blunt tail; edge sometimes thrown into folds. **Colour** generally brown and pink. **Habitat** among seaweeds and mussel banks from the lower shore downward. **Distribution** Mediterranean.

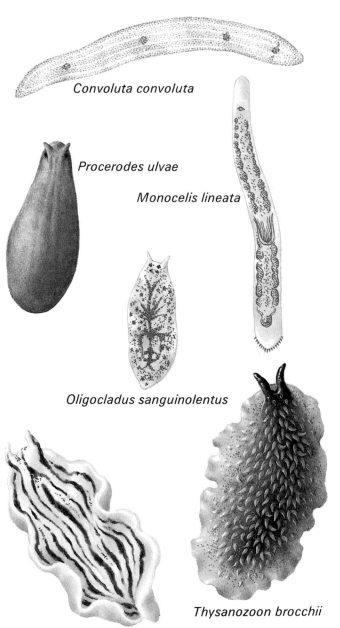

Convoluta convoluta

Procerodes ulvae

Monocelis lineata

Oligocladus sanguinolentus

Prostheceraeus vittatus

Thysanozoon brocchii

105

Phylum Nemertina Ribbon worms

These ribbon-shaped worms are often extremely long. The unsegmented body is composed of three cell layers and there is no body cavity separating the gut from the other tissues. The mouth is anterior and the anus posterior, with a characteristic proboscis opening via the mouth to capture and handle prey. Rudimentary sense organs including eyespots are present.

Nemertines are frequently abundant animals but because they are fragile and often burrow in sand and mud, they may be overlooked. The extension of the proboscis may greatly increase the apparent length of the animal. The form and disposition of the eyes, together with the shape of the head, are most helpful in assisting identification, and there is generally a slit along each side of the head which should also be looked for with the assistance of a hand lens. For this reason the heads of the animals have been illustrated approximately one and a half times larger than their bodies.

Tubulanus annulatus (Montagu) Length up to 12cm, occasionally 70cm. Body flat below, rounded above, narrowing behind the head and tapering towards the tail; no eyes visible, but head slits open just behind the snout. Colour head usually paler than patterned body. Habitat in sand under stones, in rocky clefts or in disused annelid worm tubes from lower shore down to 10m and beyond. Distribution Mediterranean, Atlantic, English Channel and North Sea.

Cephalothrix rufifrons (Johnston) Length up to 8cm, occasionally more. Body shape variable, according to state of extension, generally tapering towards head and tail; adult bears no eyes or other marks on head. Colour generally pale yellow with red-orange head; often a distinct line runs part way down the centre of the body. Habitat in mud under stones and among shells from the lower shore downward. Distribution Atlantic, English Channel and North Sea.

Cerebratulus fuscus (McIntosh) Length up to 10cm. Head bears 4–8 eyes with deep slits. Body flattened and tapering towards head and tail; tail bearing a thin, terminal filament. Colour varies from skin colour to grey-brown. Habitat among coralline seaweeds, shells or pebbles associated with *Laminaria* holdfasts (see page 33), or in mud, from lower shore down to 100m or more. Distribution Mediterranean, Atlantic and English Channel.

Lineus longissimus (Gunnerus) Length up to 5m, but much larger specimens have been recorded. Head bears a dense group of eyes on each side, and deep slits behind. Body rounded, narrowed behind the head and tapering for the last part only. Colour brown-ivory. Habitat under stones and among rocks from lower shore and in shallow water. Distribution Atlantic, English Channel, North Sea and west Baltic.

Lineus bilineatus (Renier) Length up to about 30cm. Head broad, lacks eyes but bears deep slits. Body tapering towards tail. Colour shades of brown, with white line down the middle of the back. Habitat in deeper water among coralline seaweeds and shells, occasionally under shells on lower shore. Distribution Mediterranean, Atlantic, English Channel and North Sea.

Lineus ruber (O. F. Müller) **Red Ribbon Worm** Length up to 16cm. Head spatulate, fractionally wider than the adjoining part of the body with shallow slits; 3 or 4 eyes in a row on each side. Body flattened, the latter part tapering towards the tail. Colour red-brown; ventral surface paler than dorsal surface. Habitat under stones among muddy gravel from middle to lower shore down to deep water. Distribution Mediterranean, Atlantic, English Channel, North Sea and Baltic.

Micrura aurantiaca (Grube) Length up to 10cm. Head bears short, white snout which lacks eyes; mouth has shallow slits. Body flat below and rounded above. Colour brick-red with white proboscis. Habitat under stones in

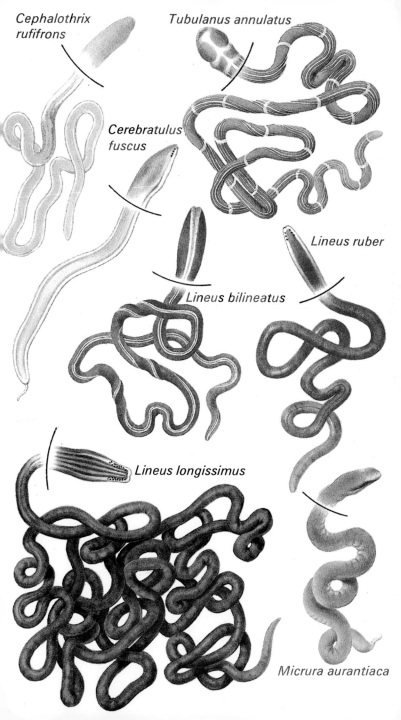

Cephalothrix rufifrons

Tubulanus annulatus

Cerebratulus fuscus

Lineus ruber

Lineus bilineatus

Lineus longissimus

Micrura aurantiaca

rock pools and in deeper water. **Distribution** Mediterranean, Atlantic and English Channel.

Prosorhochmus claparèdi Keferstein Length up to 3.5cm. **Head** broad and spatulate, often slightly wider than the body and with a conspicuous central notch from which a pale streak leads beyond the grey ganglia; 4 eyes situated well back, the anterior pair larger than the posterior pair and the left eyes widely separated from the right; 1 pair of slits. **Body** flattened, with a slight constriction behind the head, tapering in the region of the tail. **Colour** pale yellow but occasionally orange. **Habitat** in crevices and among fissures in rocks on upper and middle shore. **Distribution** Atlantic and English Channel.

Oerstedia dorsalis (Abildgaard) Length up to 2.5cm but often less. **Head** slightly notched in front; 4 eyes arranged in a square; 1 pair of slits. **Body** almost circular in cross section and slightly tapering at each end. **Colour** dorsal surface brown-red with either yellow granules or a yellow dorsal stripe, and ventral surface paler; or green-brown with brown annular markings and a white stripe. **Habitat** among laminarians and other growths down to 20m or more; seldom on the shore. **Distribution** Mediterranean, Atlantic, English Channel, North Sea and west Baltic.

Amphiporus lactifloreus (Johnston) Length up to 8cm but often less. **Head** flat and spatulate; several groups of eyes arranged in a marginal row on each side, and in groups over or close to the conspicuous pink ganglia, giving an overall near-triangle of eyes; 2 sets of slits run obliquely. **Body** flattened ventrally and rounded dorsally, and not tapering towards the blunt tail. **Colour** various shades from pink to white, but pink predominates; translucent line along dorsal surface indicates the position of the retracted proboscis. **Habitat** under stones on the lower shore and associated with laminarians, and in deeper water. **Distribution** Mediterranean, Atlantic, English Channel, North Sea and west Baltic.

Prostomatella obscurum (Schultze) (= *Prostoma obscurum*) Length up to 3cm. **Head** bears 4 eyes. **Body** relatively short. **Colour** grey-green with a longitudinal green stripe down the middle of the back. **Habitat** among seaweeds and mud in areas of reduced salinity, generally in shallow water; this is a brackish water species. **Distribution** Baltic.

Tetrastemma melanocephalum (Johnston) Length up to 3.5cm. **Head** flattened and generally slightly wider than the body, with a conspicuous frontal notch; 4 eyes, the first pair of which lie within the conspicuous patch of black skin so that they are not readily distinguished, while the second pair lie behind the pigment patch and are conspicuous; 1 pair of obliquely set slits. **Body** flattened when extended but more rounded when contracted, slightly constricted behind the head and not tapering until near the tail. **Colour** dull yellow-green, with a squarish black patch on the head. **Habitat** on seaweeds and under stones on the lower shore and down to 60m. **Distribution** Mediterranean, Atlantic, English Channel, North Sea and west Baltic.

Drepanophorus spectabilis (Quatrefages) Length up to 8cm. **Head** conical or diamond-shaped; many eyes situated dorsally and laterally; oblique slits with accessory furrows. **Body** flattened, thickening suddenly behind the head. **Colour** red-yellow with 5 conspicuous, ivory, longitudinal stripes. **Habitat** under stones, in rock crevices and among shells down to 40m. **Distribution** Mediterranean, Atlantic and English Channel.

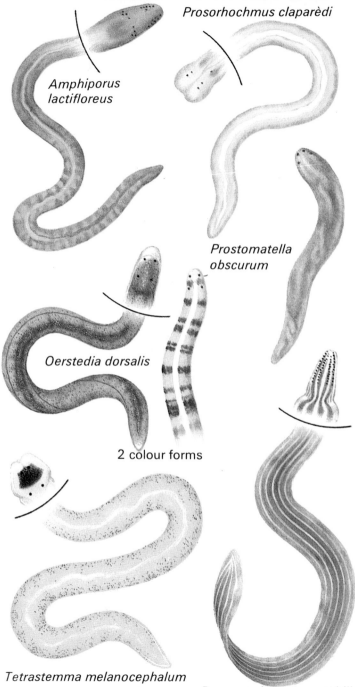

Prosorhochmus claparèdi

Amphiporus lactifloreus

Prostomatella obscurum

Oerstedia dorsalis

2 colour forms

Tetrastemma melanocephalum

Drepanophorus spectabilis

Phylum Annelida Segmented worms

A very important group of worms of between seven and eight thousand species. The body is composed of three cell layers, with the middle layer divided into two by a true, fluid-filled body cavity (the coelom). The body is divided lengthwise into a number of recognizable segments, each one of which usually carries bristles known as *chaetae* as well as other structures. The head is often well developed, bearing sense organs and a simple brain, and the mouth opens by the second segment (the first segment is the prostomium or preoral segment). The anus opens on the terminal segment. Well-developed longitudinal and circular muscles of the body wall allow extension and contraction of the body, and are often associated with locomotory segmental appendages.

This phylum is divided into three large classes: the bristle worms (Polychaeta), the earthworms and their allies (Oligochaeta) and the leeches (Hirudinea). Of these, the polychaetes have representatives in almost all marine environments, but they rarely occur in fresh water and only very rarely in damp terrestrial habitats. The other classes have a few marine representatives, but are more significant in fresh water or on land. This brief account cannot do justice to the evolutionary and ecological significance of the annelids in general, but something of the importance of the polychaetes will be appreciated by readers exploring the sea and the shore because of their abundance, diversity and their exceptionally wide geographical distribution.

Throughout the accompanying line diagrams, the following key letters have been applied: ac=aciculum (rod which supports the parapodium); an= antenna; c=cirrus (small outgrowth of head or parapodium); ch=chaeta, bristle or seta; d=dorsal surface; e=eye; ft=free tooth; g=gill; lo=lateral organ (small structure on parapodium of some species); j=jaw; mi=marginal membrane of head of some species which is incised at the edge; mm=marginal membrane of head of some species which has a scalloped edge; p=palp; pr=prostomial process; pro=proboscis; s=scale; t=tooth; tc=tentacular cirrus of head; v=ventral surface.

Class Polychaeta Bristle worms

Annelids with a preoral segment or prostomium. The head is formed from several highly modified segments fused together and carries a variety of specialized structures such as antennae, eyes, palps, jaws and tentacular cirri (see fig. 8). The rest of the body is composed of a relatively large number of similar segments, most of which bear a pair of locomotory appendages called parapodia; these sometimes have a respiratory function also. The parapodia are composed of several structures which are important in the identification of the various species (see fig. 9). The sexes are usually separate, and fertilization takes place in the sea; a pelagic larva is often formed. Habits and habitats are very variable.

This diverse group of worms cannot be divided satisfactorily into orders, but falls into a number of families of which twenty-six are treated in this book. The basic body plan has been described, but it is modified in the various groups. The polychaetes may be described loosely as errant (free-living and predacious) or sedentary (burrowing or tube-dwelling); yet within these groupings many variations of form occur. Three characteristics in particular help to identify the worms correctly. The presence or absence of a tube and the form of

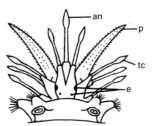

Fig. 8 Head of *Lepidonotus clava*

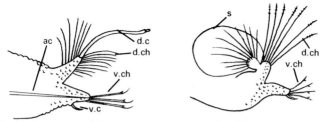

Fig. 9 Cirrus-bearing (left), and scale-bearing parapodia of *Hermione hystrix*

the tube itself is a clue to a number of families. A hard, calcareous tube occurs in the Serpulidae; in the Amphictenidae and Terebellidae it consists of grains of sand cemented into an organic matrix; and in the Sabellidae the tube is built of mud. If the worm is a burrowing variety then the shape and form of the burrow should be considered. Next, the form of the head and the disposition of the appendages should be examined. These are shown in fig. 8 and in a number of other cases on the following pages. Finally, the form of the parapodia should be investigated. A hand lens may be essential, and mounting parapodia on a slide and examining them with a microscope will often assist further. Fig. 10 shows the arrangement of bristles or chaetae as well as the dorsal and ventral parapodial cirri and other structures in a typical polychaete.

When examining an unidentified worm it should be remembered that errant polychaetes generally have well-developed eyes and tentacles for receiving information from the environment and for seeking prey. They often have a protrusible proboscis which may be armed with powerful jaws, and their parapodia are powerfully built for crawling or swimming. Generally the form of the proboscis may be discerned only when it has been everted. Pressing the pharyngeal region of such worms either when they are alive or narcotized may cause the proboscis to be everted. In other proboscis-bearing species the shape of the organ can sometimes be made out through the relatively transparent body wall of the anterior region. Fig. 11 shows the general characters of an errant polychaete's anterior end. Sedentary polychaetes usually have reduced sensory structures and reduced parapodia, but their gills may be large and conspicuous, and are often also used to filter food from the water as well as to extract oxygen.

Fauvel, P. 1923 and 1927 provides a detailed identification for most of the European polychaetes.

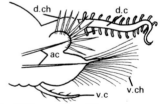

Fig. 10 Parapodium of *Harmothoë impar*

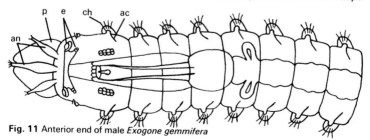

Fig. 11 Anterior end of male *Exogone gemmifera*

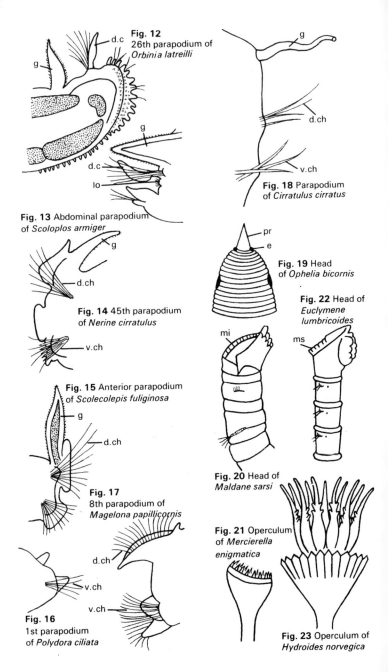

Fig. 12 26th parapodium of *Orbinia latreilli*

Fig. 13 Abdominal parapodium of *Scoloplos armiger*

Fig. 14 45th parapodium of *Nerine cirratulus*

Fig. 15 Anterior parapodium of *Scolecolepis fuliginosa*

Fig. 16 1st parapodium of *Polydora ciliata*

Fig. 17 8th parapodium of *Magelona papillicornis*

Fig. 18 Parapodium of *Cirratulus cirratus*

Fig. 19 Head of *Ophelia bicornis*

Fig. 20 Head of *Maldane sarsi*

Fig. 21 Operculum of *Mercierella enigmatica*

Fig. 22 Head of *Euclymene lumbricoides*

Fig. 23 Operculum of *Hydroides norvegica*

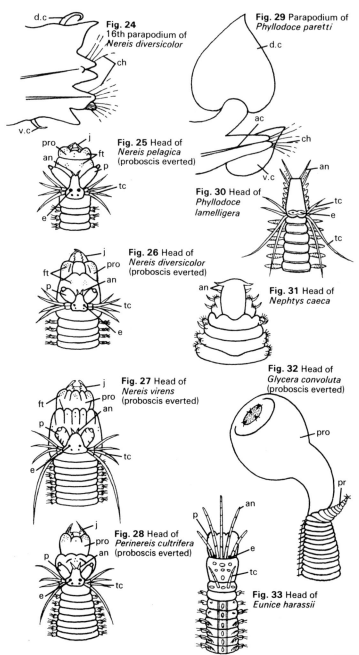

Fig. 24 16th parapodium of *Nereis diversicolor*

Fig. 25 Head of *Nereis pelagica* (proboscis everted)

Fig. 26 Head of *Nereis diversicolor* (proboscis everted)

Fig. 27 Head of *Nereis virens* (proboscis everted)

Fig. 28 Head of *Perinereis cultrifera* (proboscis everted)

Fig. 29 Parapodium of *Phyllodoce paretti*

Fig. 30 Head of *Phyllodoce lamelligera*

Fig. 31 Head of *Nephtys caeca*

Fig. 32 Head of *Glycera convoluta* (proboscis everted)

Fig. 33 Head of *Eunice harassii*

113

Family Aphroditidae Scale worms

Free-living polychaetes whose dorsal surface is partly or entirely covered by interfolded scales. N.B. handling may dislodge these so giving a false impression of their numbers.

Aphrodite aculeata Linnaeus **Sea-mouse** Length 10–20cm. Readily distinguished from other members of the family by its large bulk and mat of grey-brown hairs masking the scales on the dorsal surface. **Body** oval shaped; convex above, flat and sole-like below; about 40 segments bear conspicuous, gold-brown or iridescent chaetae on the ventral surface. **Habitat** on soft substrates in shallow and deeper water. **Distribution** Mediterranean, Atlantic, English Channel, North Sea and west Baltic.

Hermione hystrix (Savigny) **Length** up to 6cm. **Head** hidden from above, bears 2 eyes, 1 long antenna, 2 long palps and 2 pairs of tentacular cirri. **Body** flat and oval shaped; dorsal surface bears scales which overlap left and right; 32–34 segments bear chaetae; parapodia of two types, bearing cirri or scales (see fig. 9) alternating with each other. **Colour** red-brown above. **Habitat** in gravel, sand and mud, and among bivalves such as scallops and oysters down to about 100m. **Distribution** Mediterranean, Atlantic, English Channel and North Sea.

Lepidonotus clava (Montagu) **Length** up to 3cm. **Head** partly hidden from above, bears appendages as shown in fig. 8. **Body**, covered for most of its length by rounded non-overlapping scales; 26 segments bear chaetae arranged in two groups per parapodium; alternate parapodia bear scales; dorsal cirrus recurved. **Colour** brown. **Habitat** under rocks and stones on the lower shore. **Distribution** Mediterranean, Atlantic and English Channel.

Harmothoë impar (Johnston) **Length** up to 2.5cm. **Head** hidden from above, bears 4 eyes, 1 median and 2 lateral antennae, 2 stout palps and 2 pairs of tentacular cirri. **Body** flat, completely covered by 15 pairs of overlapping scales which carry papillae on their lateral edges; 35–40 segments bear chaetae; form of parapodia shown in fig. 10; alternate parapodia bear scales. **Colour** brown-green scales with a yellow-grey central spot. **Habitat** under stones, rocks and seaweeds on the lower shore and in shallow water. **Distribution** Mediterranean, Atlantic, English Channel, North Sea and west Baltic.

Scalisetosus assimilis (McIntosh) (Not illustrated) **Length** up to 2cm. **Head** not entirely covered by 15 pairs of transparent scales. **Habitat** among the spines of *Echinus esculentus* (see page 251). **Distribution** Atlantic, English Channel and North Sea.

Polynoë scolopendrina (Savigny) **Length** up to 12cm. **Body** has 15 pairs of overlapping scales which cover about half the length of the body; 80–100 segments bear chaetae; alternate parapodia from segment 2 to 32 carry scales. **Colour** variable; head is often red, as may be the body below the metallic-sheened scales. **Habitat** in other worm tubes, cracks in rock and in sand. **Distribution** Mediterranean, Atlantic, English Channel and North Sea.

Acholoë astericola (Delle Chiaje) (Not illustrated) **Length** up to 5cm. **Colour** male opaque white and female orange-red. **Habitat** always in the ambulacral groove of the starfishes *Astropecten irregularis* and *Luidia ciliaris* (see page 241). **Distribution** Mediterranean, Atlantic and English Channel.

Aphrodite aculeata

Hermione hystrix

Harmothoë impar

Lepidonotus clava

Polynoë scolopendrina

Family Syllidae

Small, delicate, free-living polychaetes with thread-like bodies, often beautifully coloured. The head generally possesses 4 eyes, 3 antennae, 2 palps, and 2 pairs of tentacular cirri. The eversible proboscis is divided into two parts, of which the anterior appears cylindrical, chitinous and armed with 1 or more teeth. Parapodia are not bilobed, and dorsal and ventral cirri are usually present (the dorsal cirri are often long, 'jointed' and conspicuous); 2 anal cirri are present. Reproduction is sometimes by budding, so that stolons of several individuals arranged in a chain may be encountered. This is a large family which includes many genera and species, of which only a very few can be included here.

Syllis prolifera Krohn Length 1–2.5cm. **Head** bears proboscis with 1 tooth; 4 eyes; 2 minute ocelli; middle antenna longer than lateral antennae; palps slightly triangular. **Body** dorsal cirri of parapodia long, and composed of 20–40 'joints'. **Colour** body very variable, greyish to reddish, anterior region sometimes with brown, pink or orange markings. **Habitat** on the lower shore and in shallow water among seaweeds and stones. **Distribution** Mediterranean, Atlantic, English Channel and North Sea.

Exogone gemmifera (Pagenstecher) (See fig. 11) **Length** up to 0.4cm. **Head** bears 4 large eyes; 3 antennae arranged in a line in front of the eyes, with the middle antenna longer than the lateral antennae; 1 pair of tentacular cirri reduced to small, button-like processes; form of head shown in fig. 11. **Body** 24–33 segments bear chaetae; dorsal cirri ovoid and shorter than the parapodium which bears them, ventral cirri very small, 2 long anal cirri. **Habitat** on the lower shore and in shallow water among seaweeds, bryozoans and ascidians. **Distribution** Mediterranean, Atlantic, English Channel, North Sea and west Baltic. N.B. eggs and embryos may be found attached to the underside of the female; eggs reddish in colour.

Autolytus pictus (Ehlers) **Length** up to 2.5cm. **Head** bears proboscis with 10 large teeth, alternating with 10 smaller teeth; if withdrawn, proboscis may be seen as an S-shaped organ; longest tentacular cirri almost as long as lateral antennae. **Body** 60–100 segments bear chaetae; form of parapodia varies along the body according to function; dorsal cirri of 1st chaeta-bearing segment are very long and conspicuous while those on the 2nd are much shorter; 2 thick anal cirri. **Colour** variable; pale-pink below, violet markings above. **Habitat** among laminarian holdfasts (see page 33), sponges and stones. **Distribution** Mediterranean, Atlantic, English Channel and North Sea.

Family Hesionidae

Free-living polychaetes with cylindrical bodies, and segmentation weakly marked. The eversible proboscis may bear jaws. Parapodia bear long dorsal cirri.

Kefersteinia cirrata (Keferstein) **Length** up to 7.5cm. **Head** bears a short, thick, eversible proboscis without jaws, which has a large opening surrounded by many papillae; 4 eyes; 2 palps thicker than the 2 smaller antennae; 8 pairs of tentacular cirri. **Body** fragile; 36–65 segments bear chaetae, arranged in one group per parapodium; dorsal cirri long, ventral cirri short. **Colour** varies with sex and maturity; green-brown-yellow. **Habitat** among worm tubes, shells and seaweeds on lower shore and in shallow water. **Distribution** Mediterranean, Atlantic, North Sea and west Baltic.

Castalia punctata (O. F. Mülier) **Length** up to 2.5cm. **Head** bears eversible proboscis; 4 eyes, anterior larger than posterior; 2 lateral antennae are thinner than the 2 palps; 6 pairs of long tentacular cirri. **Body** 40–50 segments bear chaetae; dorsal cirri much longer than ventral cirri. **Habitat** among stones, shells and seaweeds from lower shore downward. **Distribution** Atlantic and North Sea.

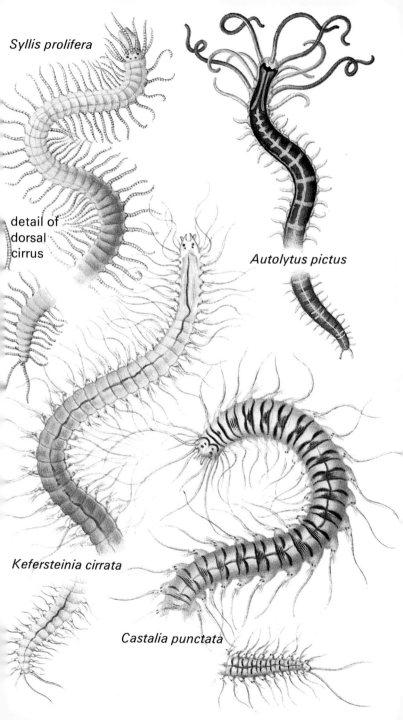

Syllis prolifera

detail of
dorsal
cirrus

Autolytus pictus

Kefersteinia cirrata

Castalia punctata

Family Nereidae

Often large, active, free-living polychaetes. The head bears an eversible proboscis with large, black jaws, 4 eyes, 2 antennae, 2 ovoid palps terminating with small button-like structures and 4 pairs of tentacular cirri. The bodies possess many segments bearing chaetae on well-developed parapodia (see fig. 24).

Nereis pelagica Linnaeus Length up to 12 cm. **Head** proboscis carries free teeth as well as the 5—7 teeth on each of the jaws; form of head shown in fig. 25. **Body** cylindrical, tapering posteriorly; 80—100 segments bear chaetae; dorsal cirrus of parapodia long and fairly conspicuous. **Colour** adult normally red-brown-yellow with a distinct dorsal blood vessel. **Habitat** among rocks, shells and seaweeds on lower shore, and in shallow water. **Distribution** Mediterranean, Atlantic, English Channel, North Sea and west Baltic. N.B. a pelagic, reproductive variety (known as the *epitoke*) may be encountered, whose posterior segments carry parapodia modified for swimming.

Nereis diversicolor (O. F. Müller) **Rag Worm** Length up to 12 cm. **Head** bears a proboscis carrying free teeth as well as the 5—8 teeth on each of the jaws; posterior tentacular cirri extend back as far as the 5th or 7th chaeta-bearing segments; form of head shown in fig. 26. **Body** 90—120 segments bear chaetae. **Colour** very variable, but often green-yellow with tints of orange and red; distinct dorsal blood vessel makes a red line all the way down the back. **Habitat** from the middle shore down to shallow water, burrowing in sand or mud, often in brackish conditions. **Distribution** Mediterranean, Atlantic, English Channel, North Sea and west Baltic.

Nereis virens M. Sars **King Rag Worm** Length usually up to 20 cm, may occasionally reach 40 cm. **Head** bears proboscis carrying free teeth as well as the 6—10 teeth on each of the jaws; posterior tentacular cirri reach back as far as the 5th or 8th chaeta-bearing segment; form of head shown in fig. 27. **Body** large, may be as thick as the average finger; 100—175 segments bear chaetae; parapodia of complex form with many appendages varying in proportion along the body. **Colour** adult green with iridescent purple, edges of parapodia bordered with yellow. **Habitat** on lower shore and in shallow water, often burrowing in sand. **Distribution** Atlantic around the north and west coasts of Britain and Ireland, North Sea and west Baltic. N.B. a pelagic epitoke with a slightly modified body may be encountered.

Nereis fucata (Savigny) Length up to 20 cm. **Head** posterior tentacular cirri extend back as far as the 3rd or 5th chaeta-bearing segment. **Body** 90—120 segments bear chaetae. **Colour** adult brown-yellow with white markings in the middle of each segment. **Habitat** the adults are found inside whelk shells (often of *Buccinum undatum*, see page 161) which are occupied by hermit crabs (e.g. *Eupagurus bernhardus* and *E. prideauxi*, see page 221). **Distribution** Mediterranean, Atlantic, English Channel and North Sea. N.B. a pelagic epitoke may be encountered.

Perinereis cultrifera (Grube) Length up to 25 cm. **Head** posterior tentacular cirri extend back as far as the 5th or 6th chaeta-bearing segment; form of head shown in fig. 28. **Body** somewhat flattened and tapering towards the tail; 100—125 segments bear chaetae. **Colour** adult brown-green with parapodia reddish above. **Habitat** on gravel, sand or mud on lower shore and in pools and shallow water. **Distribution** Atlantic, English Channel and North Sea. N.B. a pelagic epitoke may be encountered.

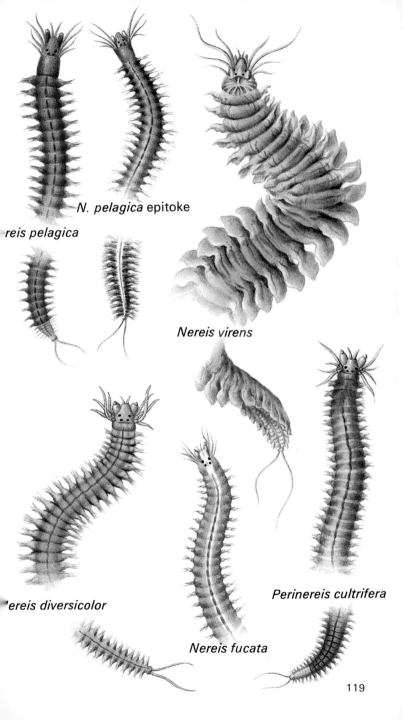

N. pelagica epitoke

reis pelagica

Nereis virens

Nereis diversicolor

Nereis fucata

Perinereis cultrifera

Family Phyllodocidae Paddle worms

Free-living polychaetes with parapodia whose dorsal cirri are typically large, conspicuous and leaf-like, so giving the appearance of paddles. The ventral cirri are similar but smaller, and the chaetae are generally arranged in one group per parapodium (see fig. 29) ; 2 anal cirri.

Phyllodoce lamelligera (Gmelin) **Length** from 6—60 cm. **Head** bears an eversible proboscis which lacks jaws; 2 black eyes; 4 antennae; 4 pairs of tentacular cirri; form of head shown in fig. 30. **Body** 300—400 segments; parapodia bear conspicuous, lance-shaped olive or green dorsal cirri. **Colour** blue-brown. **Habitat** under rocks and stones from the lower shore downward, often among laminarians. **Distribution** Mediterranean, Atlantic and English Channel.

Phyllodoce paretti (Blainville) **Paddle Worm** Length 15—30 cm. Head bears an eversible proboscis which lacks jaws; 2 large eyes; 4 short antennae; 4 tentacular cirri which may not all be readily visible from above. **Body** long and tapering at either end; about 200 segments; form of parapodia shown in fig. 29. **Colour** variable; often dark blue above, with black, green or yellow markings on parapodia. **Habitat** under stones and rocks by day, often in sandy and muddy places, from the lower shore downward. **Distribution** Mediterranean, Atlantic, English Channel and North Sea.

Phyllodoce maculata (Linnaeus) Generally similar to *P. paretti*. **Length** up to 10 cm. **Head** bears eversible proboscis which lacks jaws. **Body** about 250 segments with chaetae; conspicuous, brown-grey, leaf-like dorsal cirrus on parapodia. **Colour** green-yellow with three or four brown patches on the back of each segment. **Habitat** in sand and mud under pebbles, lower shore downward. **Distribution** Atlantic, English Channel, North Sea and west Baltic.

Eulalia viridis (O. F. Müller) **Green Leaf Worm** Length 5—15 cm. **Head** small, rounded, clearly visible and bears long, eversible proboscis which lacks jaws; 2 conspicuous eyes; 5 antennae; 4 pairs of tentacular cirri. **Body** 60—200 segments; parapodia with large, green, triangular dorsal cirri and small, ovoid ventral cirri. **Colour** grass-green, sometimes with blacker or bluer shades. **Habitat** in rock crevices in shallow water and on the lower shore where it sometimes creeps about over the rocks when the tide is out. **Distribution** Mediterranean, Atlantic, English Channel, North Sea and west Baltic. N.B. the gelatinous, green egg cases of this worm may be found on the lower shore on sand or rocks, usually attached to seaweeds or pebbles.

Eulalia sanguinea Oersted (Not illustrated) **Length** up to 6 cm. **Body** 60—140 segments; parapodia with leaf-shaped, grey-green dorsal cirri. **Colour** very variable; white-pale green or brown, sometimes with paler dorsal line. **Habitat** among seaweeds and stones from lower shore downward. **Distribution** Mediterranean, Atlantic, English Channel and North Sea.

Family Tomopteridae

Free-living, planktonic polychaetes whose bodies are transparent and bear large parapodia which lack chaetae and acicula.

Tomopteris helgolandica (Greeff) **Length** up to 1.7 cm. **Head** bears 2 conspicuous palps and eyes; behind this are a pair of very short chaeta-bearing appendages, followed by another pair whose length is about two-thirds that of the body. **Body** bilobed parapodia lack chaetae. **Colour** transparent and colourless. **Habitat** planktonic. **Distribution** western Mediterranean, Atlantic and English Channel. N.B. various related species occur in all areas except the Baltic.

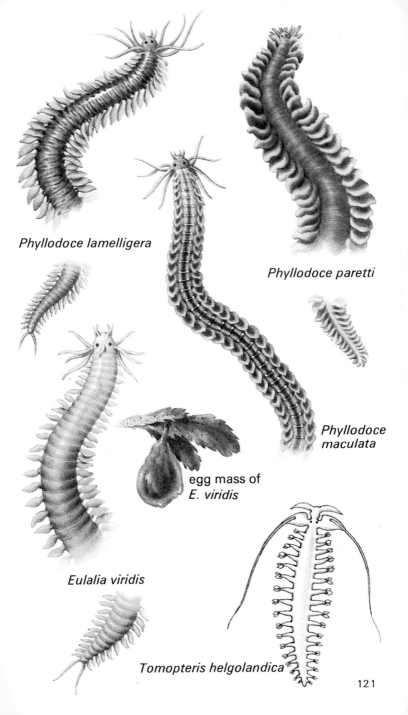

Phyllodoce lamelligera

Phyllodoce paretti

Phyllodoce maculata

egg mass of
E. viridis

Eulalia viridis

Tomopteris helgolandica

121

Family Nephtydidae

Medium to large, free-living polychaetes with flattened bodies. A small head bears an eversible proboscis, carries papillae and horny jaws, and 4 short antennae. Movement is by a characteristic rapid wriggling of the body.

Nephtys caeca (O. F. Müller) **Length** up to 25cm. **Head** eyes not visible; form of head shown in fig. 31. **Body** 90–150 segments; parapodia distinctly bilobed; dorsal cirrus very small, ventral cirrus conical; from the 4th chaeta-bearing segment back, the parapodia bear a gill situated between the two groups of chaetae; characteristic thread at tail. **Colour** various body colours (2 forms are shown); generally pearly grey with other shades. **Habitat** burrowing in sand from the middle shore downward. **Distribution** Atlantic, English Channel, North Sea and west Baltic.

Family Glyceridae

Small to medium free-living polychaetes whose bodies taper at both ends. An eversible proboscis carries papillae and several, often 4, jaws. Antennae are minute.

Glycera convoluta Keferstein **Length** up to 10cm. **Head** anterior end reduced to small prostomial process with 4 minute antennae; bulbous, eversible proboscis with 4 jaws and many fine cylindrical papillae; form of head shown in fig. 32. **Body** round and transparent; 120–180 segments each marked by 2 annular rings. **Colour** tinted red-pink. **Habitat** in sand or mud, often among seaweeds. **Distribution** Mediterranean, Atlantic, English Channel and North Sea.

Family Eunicidae

Large, free-living polychaetes. The head has 2 eyes, 5 antennae, 2 bilobed palps and 1 pair of tentacular cirri (see fig. 33). The first two apparent body segments lack parapodia and chaetae. Large gills are present.

Eunice harassii Audouin & Milne-Edwards **Length** up to 25cm. **Head** form shown in fig. 33. **Body** parapodia with comb-like gills from about the 4th segment back. **Habitat** lower shore downward under stones and rocks. **Distribution** Mediterranean, Atlantic and English Channel.

Marphysa bellii (Audouin & Milne-Edwards) **Length** up to 20cm. **Head** eyes small; antennae weakly annulated. **Body** long and filiform; 200–300 segments with chaetae; comb-like gills between about segments 12–35. **Colour** body pink; gills red. **Habitat** lower shore in sand and mud, and in shallow water. **Distribution** Mediterranean, Atlantic and English Channel.

Marphysa sanguinea (Montagu) Similar to *Eunice harassii*. **Length** 30 to 60cm. **Head** antennae very short and not conspicuous. **Body** flattened; about 300 segments bear chaetae; gills not comb-like, but arise as a bunch of about 7 filaments. **Habitat** in rock crevices and sometimes among seaweeds from lower shore downward. **Distribution** Mediterranean, Atlantic and English Channel.

Ophryotrocha puerilis Claparède & Mecznikow **Length** up to 1 cm. **Head** bears 2 eyes, 2 small antennae and 2 small palps. **Body** quite short and stubby, tapering slightly towards the extremities; 20–30 segments; parapodia bilobed without gills and with chaetae arranged in 2 groups. **Colour** whitish and transparent, so that the jaws can be seen within. **Habitat** among other invertebrates, e.g. bryozoans, ascidians and echinoderms. **Distribution** Mediterranean, Atlantic, English Channel and North Sea.

Nephtys caeca

Glycera convoluta

Eunice harassii

Marphysa sanguinea

arphysa bellii

Ophryotrocha puerilis

Family Orbiniidae

Polychaetes which usually burrow in mud or sand. The head generally lacks appendages but possesses 2 eyes. The body bears numerous segments and is divided into two regions, of which the thoracic half is flattened and enlarged, and the abdominal half is long and half cylindrical. Parapodia bear simple gills on the dorsal surface.

Orbinia latreilli (Audouin & Milne-Edwards) **Length** up to 40cm. **Head** lacks eyes and appendages. **Body** flat above, rounded below; very long and fragile; 400 segments bear chaetae, of which 35 may be in the thoracic region; gills borne on 5th chaeta-bearing segment back; two terminal threads on tail; form of 26th parapodium shown in fig. 12. **Colour** generally pink anteriorly and yellowish posteriorly. **Habitat** on seabed in sand and mud. **Distribution** Atlantic, English Channel and North Sea.

Scoloplos armiger (O. F. Müller) **Length** up to 15cm. **Head** no appendages are visible, but 2 eyes may be seen sunk deeply in the head. **Body** long; up to 200 segments bearing chaetae, of which up to 20 may be in the flattened thoracic region; gills are generally borne anywhere from the 9th chaeta-bearing segment backward; form of abdominal parapodia is shown in fig. 13. **Colour** generally pink or orange. **Habitat** on the seabed in sand or mud and among *Zostera* (see page 65). **Distribution** Atlantic, English Channel, North Sea and west Baltic.

Family Spionidae

Polychaetes which usually burrow in sand or in mud. The head is often characterized by 2 frontal horns, 4 eyes and 2 palps. The dorsal and ventral parapodial cirri are often lamella-like; gills are carried dorsally on a number of parapodia. The body is not apparently regionalized.

Scolecolepis fuliginosa (Claparède) (Not illustrated) **Length** up to 6cm. **Head** bears 2 frontal horns, 4 eyes and 2 banded palps. **Body** long and slender; about 150 segments; gills borne on the first chaeta-bearing segment and backwards from it; form of anterior parapodia is shown in fig. 15. **Colour** variable; often reddish. **Habitat** on the seabed burrowing in tubes in sand and mud; sometimes under pebbles; occasionally in colonies. **Distribution** Mediterranean, Atlantic, English Channel and North Sea.

Nerine cirratulus (Delle Chiaje) **Length** up to 8cm. **Head** bears 4 small eyes disposed in a square, and 2 long palps which can reach back as far as the 24th chaeta-bearing segment when straightened out. **Body** long, slender; about 200 chaeta-bearing segments; gills developed from about the 2nd segment back, but a few may be absent around the 10th segment; form of 45th parapodium shown in fig. 14. **Colour** variable, but mainly blue-green; male whiter and female very green. **Habitat** on the seabed in sand or mud. **Distribution** Mediterranean, Atlantic, English Channel and North Sea.

Polydora ciliata (Johnston) **Length** up to 3cm. **Head** bears 4 eyes arranged in a square and 2 long, thin palps. **Body** relatively thin; up to 180 chaeta-bearing segments; parapodia from the 7th as far back as the 10th before the last bear gills; fan-shaped tail appendage; form of 1st parapodium is shown in fig. 16. **Colour** variable; usually brown-yellow. **Habitat** found boring into oysters. **Distribution** Mediterranean, Atlantic, English Channel, North Sea and west Baltic. N.B. only the palps may at first be visible as minute, fine threads protruding from the holes in the shell.

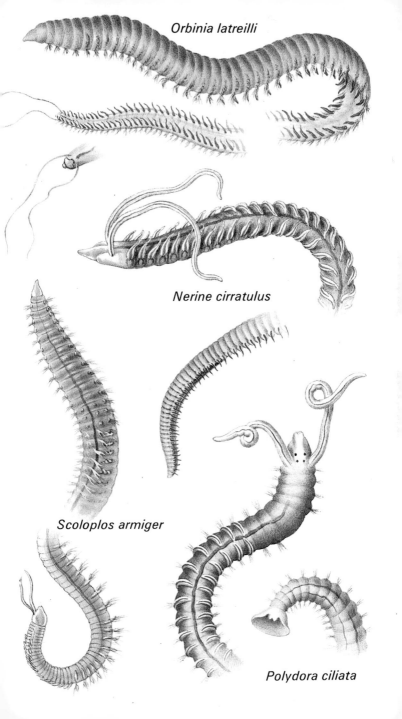

Orbinia latreilli

Nerine cirratulus

Scoloplos armiger

Polydora ciliata

Family Magelonidae

Burrowing polychaetes, with an oval, flattened 1st segment. A large proboscis is present, but no antennae nor eyes. They possess 2 long palps with papillae. The body is divided into two regions; gills are lacking and parapodia have 2 lobes. Lamellae-shaped dorsal and ventral cirri. One genus is known.

Magelona papillicornis O. F. Müller **Length** up to 17 cm. **Head** typical; proboscis large. **Body** 150 segments bear chaetae, of which the first 8 differ from the remainer; remaining parapodia have large dorsal, and small ventral, lamellae; form of 8th parapodium shown in fig. 17. **Colour** palps and anterior end pale pink; posterior grey or greenish with white on sides. **Habitat** in sand in shallow and deeper water. **Distribution** Mediterranean, Atlantic, English Channel and North Sea.

Family Chaetopteridae

Tube-dwelling polychaetes with soft bodies divided into three regions. No eversible proboscis, but 2 eyes and 2 or 4 palps are present on the head. The anterior region of the body has few segments; the middle section has very few, highly modified segments bearing conspicuous, bilobed parapodia; posterior segments numerous.

Chaetopterus variopedatus (Renier) **Length** up to 25 cm. **Head** broad, bears 2 palps and a large, terminal mouth. **Body** first 9 or so body segments bear chaetae; middle region characterized by a 'waist', and segments bearing 3 flap-like paddles ventrally; posterior part has bristled parapodia. **Habitat** in parchment-like, u-shaped tubes up to 40 cm long; often buried in mud or sand in shallow and deeper water. **Distribution** Mediterranean, Atlantic, English Channel and North Sea.

Family Cirratulidae

Sedentary polychaetes with cylindrical, tapering bodies. The head sometimes has eyes but lacks appendages. One anterior segment bears either distinct palps, or several tentacular filaments. The parapodia are bilobed, lack dorsal and ventral cirri, and bear simple, long, contractile gill filaments which show 2 conspicuous blood vessels (see fig. 18).

Cirriformia tentaculata (Montagu) **Length** up to 20 cm. **Head** indistinct; no eyes, but several pigment spots. **Body** swollen dorsally and flattened or concave ventrally; about 300 compressed segments; gills on all chaeta-bearing segments except the last few. **Habitat** in sand, mud and under pebbles from lower shore downward; often only the blood-red tentacles apparent. **Distribution** Atlantic, English Channel and North Sea.

Cirratulus cirratus (O. F. Müller) **Length** up to 12 cm. **Head** indistinct; bears 4—8 eyes arranged in rows on both sides of 1st segment. **Body** up to 130 segments; gills carried on all chaeta-bearing segments; form of parapodia shown in fig. 18. **Habitat** and **Distribution** similar to *Cirriformia tentaculata*, but sometimes found in cracks of rocks.

Family Chlorhaemidae

Burrowing polychaetes. The chaetae of anterior segments surround the head which has a retractile mouth siphon, eyes, 2 large palps and retractable gills. Parapodia are bilobed, and the blood is green.

Flabelligera affinis M. Sars **Length** up to 6 cm. **Body** up to 50 segments. **Habitat** under pebbles and on seaweeds in mud, and on sea-urchins. **Distribution** Atlantic, English Channel, North Sea and west Baltic.

Stylarioides plumosa (O. F. Müller) **Length** up to 6 cm. **Head** bears 4 eyes, 2 fat palps and 8 cylindrical gills. **Body** 60—70 segments bear chaetae. **Habitat** in cracks of rock and in mud from lower shore downward. **Distribution** Atlantic, English Channel and North Sea.

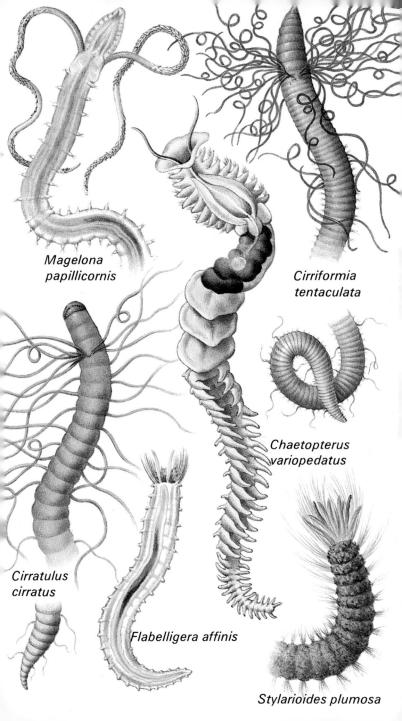

Magelona papillicornis

Cirriformia tentaculata

Cirratulus cirratus

Chaetopterus variopedatus

Flabelligera affinis

Stylarioides plumosa

Family Opheliidae

Polychaetes with a conical preoral segment. The head has an unarmed proboscis; the main eyes are hidden by the skin, but lateral eyes are sometimes visible. Other head appendages are lacking. The body is short, convex dorsally and concave ventrally for all or part of its length. Bilobed parapodia are generally reduced and lack dorsal cirri, but ventral cirri are occasionally present.

Ophelia bicornis Savigny Length up to 6cm. **Head** form shown in fig. 19. **Body** about 32 segments bear chaetae; conspicuous ventral gutter runs from the 10th chaeta-bearing segment to the tail; 15 pairs of gills. **Habitat** on the seabed, often in loose sand. **Distribution** Atlantic and English Channel.

Family Capitellidae

Polychaetes with a conical, retractile preoral segment. The head has a large, unarmed proboscis, and the mouth opens ventrally; 2 eyes are present. The body is earthworm-like, divided into two, with the anterior part short and often slightly swollen. The posterior region is thinner, much longer, and bears small, often twisted, gills and bilobed parapodia.

Capitella capitata (Fabricius) Length up to 10cm. **Head** bears 2 small eyes ventrally. **Body** tapers towards both ends, very variable, and not a typical example of the family; fragile; 90 or more segments bear chaetae. **Habitat** often in dirty sand or under pebbles on lower shore and in shallow water. **Distribution** Mediterranean, Atlantic, English Channel, North Sea and west Baltic.

Family Arenicolidae

Body composed of two or three distinct regions with many short segments. The head bears an unarmed proboscis but lacks antennae and palps. The parapodia are bilobed, with a conical dorsal lobe and a twisted ventral lobe.

Arenicola marina (Linnaeus) **Lugworm** Length up to 20cm. **Head** bears eversible proboscis covered by papillae. **Body** cylindrical; 6 swollen anterior segments without gills are followed by 13 segments with gills; posterior part of body less swollen. **Habitat** burrowing in sand from middle shore downward. **Distribution** Mediterranean (rarely), Atlantic, English Channel, North Sea and west Baltic.

Arenicolides ecaudata (Johnston) Length up to 25cm. **Head** lacks eyes and appendages. **Body** tapers slightly at both ends; 40–60 segments bear chaetae; gills on all segments from about the 15th back. **Habitat** in twisting burrows in sand or mud from the lower shore downward. **Distribution** Atlantic, English Channel and North Sea.

Family Maldanidae Bamboo worms

Cylindrical bodies with a trunk at both ends. The body is not divided into distinct regions, and there are relatively few, long segments. Shape slightly bamboo-like.

Euclymene lumbricoides (Quatrefages) Length up to 15cm. **Head** eyes rarely visible; form of head shown in fig. 22. **Body** thin, with 19 segments bearing chaetae, tapering slightly after the 15th segment; preoral segment is conical. **Habitat** burrowing in sand from lower shore downward. **Distribution** Mediterranean, Atlantic and English Channel.

Maldane sarsi Malmgren Length up to 10cm. **Head** oval, keel-shaped, of complex form, being convex and bordered by a membrane cut into, but not scalloped (as in *Euclymene lumbricoides*); the segment bearing the mouth and the next 3 are all similar and glandular; no eyes; form of head shown in fig. 20. **Body** 19 segments bear chaetae which occur in three forms: bent, barbed and straight. **Habitat** on muddy substrates often in deep water. **Distribution** Atlantic and North Sea.

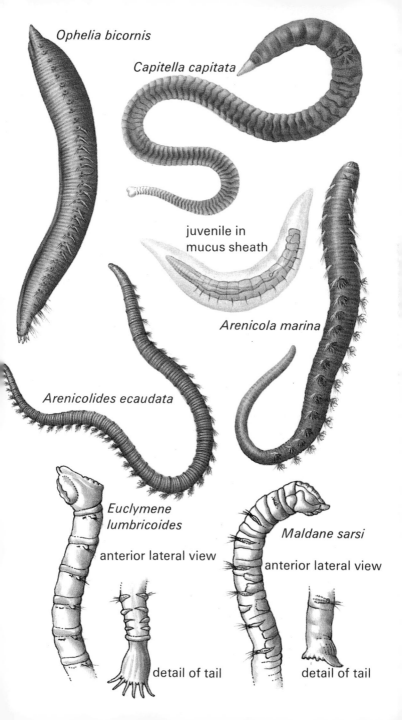

Ophelia bicornis

Capitella capitata

juvenile in
mucus sheath

Arenicola marina

Arenicolides ecaudata

*Euclymene
lumbricoides*

anterior lateral view

detail of tail

Maldane sarsi

anterior lateral view

detail of tail

Family Oweniidae

Tube-dwelling polychaetes with cylindrical bodies. They possess few segments, the anterior segments being longer than the posterior segments. The head lacks appendages and is capped by a small, folded membrane. All members of the family inhabit tubes attached generally to shells or stones.

Owenia fusiformis Delle Chiaje Length up to 10cm. **Head** typical and with 6 branched gills. **Body** 20–30 segments; 3 short segments follow head, then 5–7 long segments after which the remainder are shorter. **Colour** green-yellow. **Habitat** in membranous tube with grains of sand or shell debris attached; generally on muddy sand from lower shore downward; part of the tube usually apparent. **Distribution** Mediterranean, Atlantic, English Channel and North Sea.

Family Sternaspididae

Polychaetes with short bodies and short segments. The anterior chaetae are short and robust. Posterior segments bear filamentous gills and long chaetae.

Sternaspis scutata (Ranzani) Typical of family **Length** up to 3cm. **Head** reduced, lacks appendages; mouth ventral. **Body** 20–22 body segments; first 3 segments bear chaetae arranged in arcs each side; 2 conspicuous genital papillae on 7th segment. **Colour** white-grey-yellow. **Habitat** in sand and mud. **Distribution** Mediterranean, Atlantic, and English Channel.

Family Sabellariidae

Tube-dwelling polychaetes with cylindrical bodies divided into three parts. The head end has modified chaetae set in up to 3 concentric rings to form a stopper for the tube; this is followed by 2 segments with reduced chaetae plus 3–4 other segments; the abdominal region is composed of about 30 segments with parapodia. A slender terminal region is present.

Sabellaria alveolata (Linnaeus) Typical of family **Length** up to 4cm. **Body** has 32–37 segments. **Habitat** in tubes arranged in colonies and made of large sand grains; encrusting rocks and shells from lower shore downward. **Distribution** Mediterranean, Atlantic, English Channel and North Sea.

Family Amphictenidae

Short, stumpy, tube-dwelling polychaetes whose bodies are divided into three parts. The thoracic part carries modified head with gills and includes the first three segments with chaetae; the abdomen has bilobed parapodia; the short tail region is concave dorsally.

Pectinaria koreni (Malmgren) (=*Lagis koreni*) Length up to 5cm. **Head** shielded dorsally by chaetae; bears many club-like papillae. **Body** typical of family. **Habitat** in tubes made of medium-sized sand grains, lying in sand with worm upside down. **Habitat** lower shore downward. **Distribution** Mediterranean, Atlantic, English Channel, North Sea and west Baltic.

Family Terebellidae

Tube-dwelling polychaetes whose bodies are divided into two regions. The swollen thorax bears a reduced head with eyes and modified segments bearing many tentacles and blood-red branching gills. The abdomen tapers with reduced appendages. The tubes are membranous and covered with mud, sand, etc., and are buried or fixed to stones or plants.

Amphitrite gracilis (Grube) Length up to 12cm. **Body** long and gelatinous; 100–200 segments; 2 pairs of gills. **Habitat** in twisted burrows in sand or mud from lower shore downward. **Distribution** Mediterranean, Atlantic, English Channel and North Sea.

Amphitrite johnstoni Malmgren Length up to 25cm. **Body** has 90–100 segments; 3 pairs of gills. **Habitat** and **Distribution** similar to *A. gracilis*.

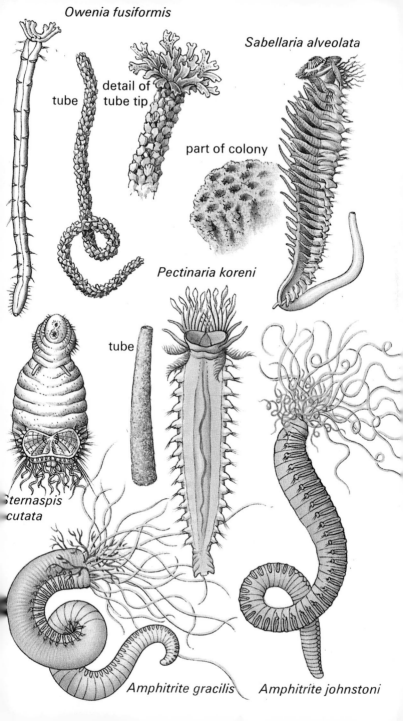

Owenia fusiformis

tube

detail of
tube tip

Sabellaria alveolata

part of colony

Pectinaria koreni

tube

*Sternaspis
cutata*

Amphitrite gracilis

Amphitrite johnstoni

Lanice conchilega (Pallas) **Sand Mason** Typical of family **Length** up to 30cm. **Head** mouth-bearing segment has 2 triangular lobes; short 2nd segment lacks appendages; 2 leaf-like lobes on 3rd segment; eyes may be visible; 3 pairs of gills. **Body** 150–300 segments; swollen thoracic region consists of 7 chaeta-bearing segments; abdomen thin and fragile. **Tube** composed of moderate to large sand grains with characteristic frayed appearance at the top; top projects from sand. **Habitat** from middle shore downward. **Distribution** Mediterranean, Atlantic, English Channel and North Sea.

Family Sabellidae

Tube-dwelling polychaetes whose bodies are divided into two regions; often flattened, with a short thoracic part, and a long abdomen. The head is reduced and the eyes bear a crown of flower-like gills borne on the 1st segment so as to surround the mouth. The tube is mucoid, with particles of sand and mud usually embedded in it.

Sabella pavonina Savigny **Peacock Worm Length** up to 25cm. **Head** reduced; bears 1 pair of palps and 2 semicircular clusters of variably patterned gills each consisting of 8–45 filaments and which may superficially appear united to form a single crown. **Body** rounded above and flattened below; 100–600 segments; thorax has 6–12 segments bearing chaetae. **Colour** variable. **Habitat** in membranous tubes standing free from substrate; in mud and sand in shallow water. **Distribution** Mediterranean, Atlantic, English Channel and North Sea.

Potamilla reniformis (O. F. Müller) **Length** up to 10cm. **Head** reduced; 2 pointed palps; 2 gill clusters each of 10–15 filaments which carry the eyes (up to 8 on each filament); 2 leaf-shaped lobes at the base of the gills on the dorsal side. **Body** 60–200 segments; thoracic region consists of 9–12 chaeta-bearing segments. **Tube** transparent, horn-like; more or less covered in mud. **Habitat** on seabed among cracks of rocks, old shells, etc. **Distribution** Mediterranean, Atlantic, English Channel and North Sea.

Bispira volutacornis (Montagu) **Length** up to 15cm. **Head** reduced, bears 2 short palps; 2 gill clusters which are twisted and which consist of a number of filaments; about 2–3 pairs of eyes borne on each filament. **Body** almost round but slightly flattened on ventral surface, about 100 segments bear chaetae; about 8 segments on the thorax bear chaetae. **Tube** short, membranous and supple; covered with fine mud and grey coloured at the opening, elsewhere it is colourless and transparent. **Habitat** often in colonies attached to the undersides of rocks in shallow and deeper water. **Distribution** Mediterranean, Atlantic and English Channel.

Myxicola infundibulum (Renier) **Length** up to 20cm. **Head** reduced; 2 dark, half-moon-shaped palps; 2 groups of gill filaments, each arranged in a semi-circle and consisting of 20–40 lance-like filaments which are more or less linked up by side-branches; gills often dark violet colour and 2–3cm long. **Body** flattened, can contract quickly and powerfully; about 130 double-ringed chaeta-bearing segments; 7 or 8 chaeta-bearing segments form the thoracic region. **Tube** composed of transparent jelly and up to 3cm thick. **Habitat** on seabed in sand or mud with tube just protruding. **Distribution** Mediterranean, Atlantic, English Channel and North Sea.

Family Serpulidae

Tube-dwelling polychaetes whose bodies are generally cylindrical and divided into a thoracic region with a few segments, and an abdominal region with many segments. A reduced head bears conspicuous gills arranged in two groups to form a crown; eyes are borne on the gills. Palps are absent or poorly developed. A conspicuous membrane or collar which sheaths the thoracic membrane, but does not quite meet on either side of the dorsal surface, is present. There is a characteristic stopper or operculum which looks rather like a small trumpet and

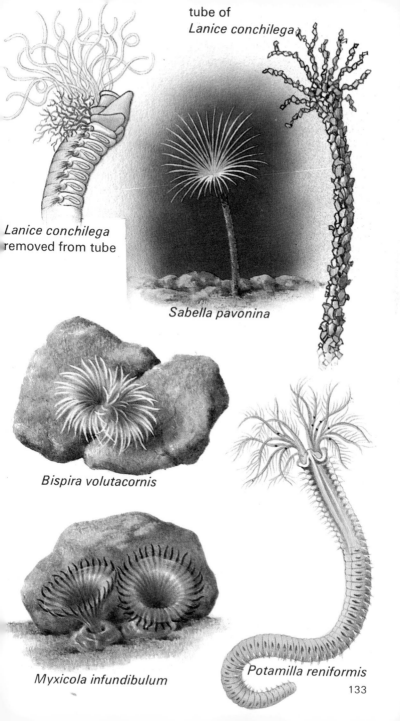

tube of
Lanice conchilega

Lanice conchilega
removed from tube

Sabella pavonina

Bispira volutacornis

Myxicola infundibulum

Potamilla reniformis

133

which, by using special opercular muscles, is pulled down to close the hard, chalky tube.

Serpula vermicularis Linnaeus **Length** up to 7 cm. **Head** bears 2 gills each with 30–40 filaments, united at the base; stopper trumpet-shaped and bearing small teeth. **Body** 200 segments bear chaetae, of which 7 are thoracic. **Colour** very variable. **Tube** normally fixed at the base only, the rest stands free and is often twisted. **Habitat** tubes fixed to stones, rocks and old shells on the lower shore and in shallow water. **Distribution** Mediterranean, Atlantic, English Channel and North Sea.

Hydroides norvegica (Gunnerus) **Length** up to 3 cm. **Head** bears 2 gills each with 15–20 filaments, united at the base; stopper of complicated shape (see fig. 23) and slightly reminiscent of a thistle crown. **Body** about 100 segments bear chaetae, of which 7 are thoracic. **Tube** white in colour; cylindrical and often twisted, sometimes spiral, ridged or keeled. **Habitat** fixed to stones, shells and bottoms of boats. **Distribution** Mediterranean, Atlantic, English Channel, North Sea and west Baltic.

Mercierella enigmatica Fauvel **Length** up to 2.5 cm. **Head** bears 2 gills each with 6–10 thick, short filaments, not apparently united at their bases by a membrane; stopper bears small spines (shape shown in fig. 21). **Body** between 70–120 segments bearing chaetae, of which 7 are thoracic. **Tube** white in colour; thin, ringed by successive collars, and only the terminal part occupied by the animal. **Habitat** grow in enormous colonies and may form a reef. **Distribution** Mediterranean, Atlantic and English Channel; local, often in brackish water such as lagoons and river mouths, etc. N.B. colonies begin by individuals attaching themselves to reeds, stones and jetsam. Not reported north of London.

Pomatoceros triqueter (Linnaeus) **Length** up to 2.5 cm. **Head** bears 2 gills each with 18–20 thick, short filaments bound at the base by a membrane; stopper of variable form often with a cone mounted like the mute in a trumpet, may or may not carry a few small spines. **Body** 80–100 segments bear chaetae, of which 7 are thoracic. **Tube** characteristically much looped and encrusting pebbles, rocks or shells; tapering gradually towards the rear; conspicuous spine over the entrance; outside triangular in section. **Colour** very variable. **Habitat** very common in many places on the lower shore and in shallow water. **Distribution** Mediterranean, Atlantic, English Channel and North Sea.

Filograna implexa Berkeley **Length** up to 0.5 cm. **Head** bears 2 gills each bearing 4 filaments; stopper transparent and scoop-shaped. **Body** sharply divided into thoracic and abdominal regions by a waisted segment; 25–35 segments bear chaetae of which 6–9 may form the thorax. **Tube** minute white calcareous structure, the mouth being sometimes slightly bell-shaped. **Habitat** on the seabed among pebbles and shells. **Distribution** Mediterranean, Atlantic, English Channel and North Sea.

Protula tubularia (Montagu) **Length** up to 5 cm. **Head** bears 2 slightly spiralled gills, each of which carries 30–45 filaments; no operculum. **Body** 100–125 segments bear chaetae, of which 7 are thoracic. **Tube** cylindrical, white and almost smooth. **Habitat** fixed at the bottom to rocks, stones and shells, down to 100 m. **Distribution** Mediterranean, Atlantic and English Channel.

Spirorbis borealis Daudin **Length** up to 0.35 cm. **Head** bears 2 gills each with 4–5 filaments; operculum calcareous. **Body** coiled in coiled shell so that it is asymmetrical; 21–35 segments bear chaetae of which 3 are thoracic. **Tube** very easily recognized encrusting seaweeds, shells and rocks. **Habitat** middle and lower shore, and in shallow water. **Distribution** Mediterranean, Atlantic, English Channel and North Sea. N.B. many other species are known.

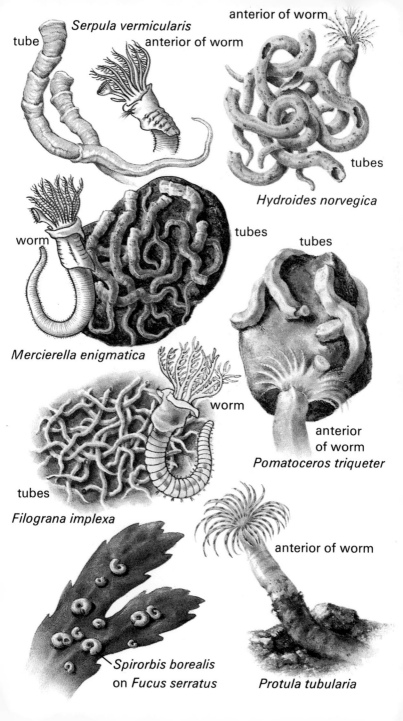

Serpula vermicularis

tube

anterior of worm

anterior of worm

tubes

Hydroides norvegica

worm

tubes

Mercierella enigmatica

tubes

worm

anterior of worm

Pomatoceros triqueter

tubes

worm

Filograna implexa

anterior of worm

Spirorbis borealis on Fucus serratus

Protula tubularia

Phylum Priapuloidea

The Priapuloidea are gherkin-shaped worms with active, eversible probosces. Their bodies are apparently segmented (although not internally) and are composed of three cell layers. A true coelom is present. The tail appendages resemble a tassel.

Priapulus caudatus Lamark **Length** about 8cm. **Body** plump and cylindrical; anterior end has a club-like proboscis armed with spines, bearing a mouth at the tip; single tail appendage. **Habitat** burrowing in sand or mud from the lower shore downward. **Distribution** Atlantic, North Sea and west Baltic.

Phylum Echiuroidea

The pear- or carrot-shaped female bears a long, retractile proboscis. The mouth is ventral and the anus terminal. The body is composed of three cell layers and has a coelom. The female feeds on small animals and organic deposits; the male is small and parasitic on the female.

Thalassema neptuni Gaertner **Length** up to 7cm. **Body** slimy and sausage-shaped, tapering at both ends; covered with small papillae; anterior end has an unbranched, grooved, tongue-like proboscis adjacent to the mouth which is associated with a conspicuous pair of bristles; anterior end very contractile. **Colour** anterior yellow-blue; middle grey-pink; posterior white. **Habitat** among stones and rocks on lower shore and in shallow water. **Distribution** Atlantic north to English Channel approaches.

Bonellia viridis Rolando **Length** female up to 15cm; male up to 2mm. **Body** anterior end bears a very long proboscis reaching up to 1m, with a forked tip and characteristic gutter leading to the mouth. **Habitat** in holes in rocks from depths of 1—100m. **Distribution** Mediterranean and Atlantic.

Echiurus echiurus (Pallas) **Length** up to 15cm. **Body** cylindrical or carrot-shaped; covered with rows of small warts; anterior end bears a shovel-like proboscis up to 4cm long, associated with 2 conspicuous bristles; posterior end bears 2 rows of bristles. **Colour** yellow-grey-orange. **Habitat** in U-shaped burrows in sand from middle shore downward. **Distribution** north Atlantic, North Sea and English Channel.

Phylum Sipunculoidea

These are cylindrical-shaped worms with an anterior mouth borne on a protrusible proboscis and surrounded by small, frilly tentacles. The anus is situated on the upper side of the body.

Phascolion strombi (Montagu) The shells of *Aporrhais pespelecani*, *Turritella communis* and *Dentalium entalis*, as well as the tubes of *Pectinaria koreni* (see pages 131, 155 and 167) may be filled with mud, perforated by a small hole. The worm-like object in the centre is the proboscis of *P. strombi*.

Sipunculus nudus Linnaeus **Length** up to 20cm. **Body** tough-skinned and elongated with latticed surface texture; papillae only on proboscis which bears the mouth beset by 4 tentacles. **Habitat** in sand and mud from middle shore downward. **Distribution** Mediterranean, Atlantic and North Sea.

Golfingia elongata (Keferstein) **Length** up to 10cm. **Body** highly contractile, slender and cylindrical and tapering at both ends, although shape may appear variable due to movement; no papillae; proboscis at anterior end may reach 5cm in length when fully everted, and carries the mouth at its tip, surrounded by up to 24 small tentacles. **Colour** pale and straw-like. **Habitat** burrowing in mud from lower shore downward. **Distribution** Mediterranean, Atlantic, English Channel and North Sea.

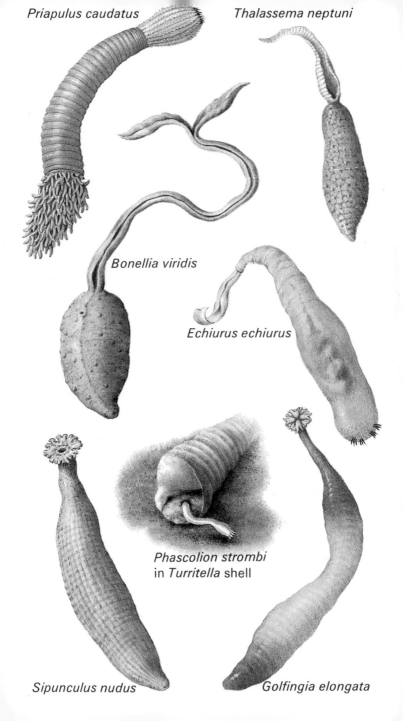

Priapulus caudatus

Thalassema neptuni

Bonellia viridis

Echiurus echiurus

Phascolion strombi
in *Turritella* shell

Sipunculus nudus

Golfingia elongata

Phylum Mollusca

The molluscs are usually bilaterally symmetrical animals with an unsegmented body composed of three layers of cells, and possessing a body cavity (coelom) which is very much reduced. The head is often well developed, and a chitinous, toothed ribbon called the *radula* is frequently found in the pharynx (this is used for scraping algae from rocks or for drilling into the shells of prey, etc.). The muscular foot is used for many different functions. The dorsal visceral hump is covered by a mantle which secretes the shell (when present), and which also encloses the mantle cavity where the gills lie and into which the anus and other ducts discharge. Sexes are sometimes separate, and there is generally a pelagic larva in marine species.

This important group of invertebrates is probably the second largest phylum in the animal kingdom, the arthropods being the largest. Most molluscs are aquatic, and many of them are marine, but a few species (the terrestrial snails and slugs), have conquered land. This phylum shows a very characteristic type of body plan, but each of its seven constituent classes has pursued a particular variation of this, so that when viewed overall the group appears diverse. Of the seven classes, five are discussed in this book. These are the *Polyplacophora* (chitons), *Gastropoda* (snails and slugs), *Scaphopoda* (tusk shells), *Bivalvia* (bivalves) and *Cephalopoda* (squids and octopuses). The remaining two classes are of great evolutionary importance, but their members are relatively small and obscure; one class is very restricted in its distribution.

The molluscs have led with great success various life styles in the sea. In many cases they show a remarkable level of evolutionary development, and this is often evident in the range of sensory and locomotory structures they display. Consequently in a number of species, notably within the Cephalopoda, complex and sophisticated behaviour patterns occur. Because of their hard shells many molluscs have fossilized well, therefore more is known of their evolutionary history than is the case with many other types of invertebrate.

The most characteristic feature of the molluscs is their shell, although in some groups it is internal or lacking. It provides support and protection for the soft parts of the body and often performs other functions such as regulating buoyancy in floating or swimming species. The symmetry of the shell is dictated by that of the animal which occupies it. Most molluscs are bilateral, but many of the gastropods are assymetrical as adults. This is due to a peculiar phenomenon known as *torsion*, which results from the unequal development of the left and right sides of the body and leads to an apparent twisting of the visceral hump. The effects of this are that the anus and gills, which originally developed behind the hump, now come to lie in front of it. Torsion first appeared in the evolution of the gastropods, and these evolutionary origins are reflected in the larval development of most gastropods, where it occurs at about the time of metamorphosis. Torsion should not be confused with spiralization of the visceral hump — that part of the body which encloses most of the internal organs — and the shell, which is a different phenomenon allowing an increase in the volume of the viscera. The shell is essentially arranged in several layers, of which the outermost is normally the horny periostracum. In some cases this is rubbed away. Beneath this lies the ostracum or prismatic layer, made up of layers of calcium carbonate laid down on an organic framework; sometimes this is followed by another layer (the nacreous layer), which resembles mother-of-pearl. The secretion and maintenance of the shell is the function of the mantle. Unlike the arthropod exoskeleton, which must be moulted to permit growth, the molluscan shell grows by the addition of new shell material. The newest part of the shell is that adjacent to the actively secreting part of the mantle. The gastropod shell can be regarded as a coiled tube. If it is held upright so that the mouth faces the observer and the tip points up, the coil is right-handed (dextral) if the mouth is on the right; and left-handed (sinistral) if the mouth is on the left. As the animal grows, the tube is made longer and wider so that the newest part is that nearest the mouth.

The mantle is generally active at secreting the shell at one point along its length, that being near to the opening or periphery of the shell. In bivalves there are two valves hinged together. Sometimes these valves are equal, and sometimes they are not. The bivalve shell grows peripherally due to mantle activity, and the point of mantle attachment to the shell is marked by the pallial line. The form and symmetry of the shells are indicated in figs. 34 and 35.

The forms and habits of the various classes of molluscs vary greatly. The chitons (Polyplacophora) are relatively inconspicuous and creep slowly over rocks and shells in search of their algal food. They number about 1000 species.

The Gastropoda is the largest class, comprising roughly 90 000 known species. It is divided into three subclasses, all of which move on a flattened foot. The first of these is the Prosobranchia (limpets, winkles, whelks, etc.). These are familiar seashore animals and, although not swiftly moving, they search actively for their food which is taken with the help of the radula. The subclass Opisthobranchia includes the sea-slugs. The adults have undergone detortion of their bodies and are frequently colourful and attractive, unlike their terrestrial namesakes. They are usually carnivorous. In the third subclass (the Pulmonata) the mantle cavity has developed into a lung which breathes air. Very few pulmonates are marine, but some freshwater species are found in the Baltic, and elsewhere if the water is brackish.

The Scaphopoda is a small class of about 350 species. The head is reduced and these animals live partly buried in sand and mud.

The class Bivalvia numbers about 15 000 species. Most of these are marine, and many are burrowers. They all filter sea water with their gills to collect particles of food. The foot is frequently developed to form an efficient digging organ.

In the class Cephalopoda the foot has been greatly modified to form eight or ten suckered tentacles. The head merges with these and houses the highly developed brain and sensory organs. These animals are active predators and rapid movers. There are about 750 species.

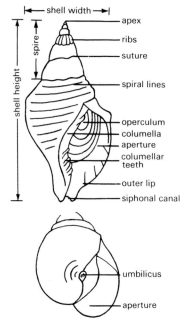

Fig. 34 External features of a gastropod shell

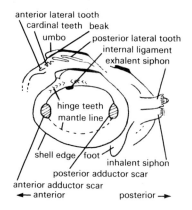

Fig. 35 Internal organs of a bivalve (shell removed)

Class Polyplacophora Chitons or coat-of-mail shells

Bilaterally symmetrical molluscs in which the mantle forms 8 transverse, calcareous plates containing spicules; these plates are surrounded by a fleshy girdle. The ventral surface is formed entirely by the foot. The body is ringed by a row of gills lying in the mantle groove on the underside. N.B. the precise classification of chitons is often a difficult process, and may involve the removal and detailed examination of one or more dorsal plates. The values given below are an *approximate* ratio for apparent shell width to total width. Further descriptions of many of the European chitons are given by Matthews, G., 1953.

Lepidopleurus asellus (Gmelin) **Coat-of-mail Chiton** Length up to 2 cm. **Dorsal plates** almost smooth and ash coloured; ratio about 4 : 5. **Fleshy edge** of one colour. **Gills** 8–13 pairs in the mantle groove on the underside. **Habitat** on shells and rocks and sometimes on coarse sand, on lower shore down to about 150 m. **Distribution** Atlantic, English Channel and North Sea.

Tonicella rubra (Linnaeus) **Length** up to 1.25 cm. **Dorsal plates** smooth, with spines and usually shining red; ratio about 3 : 4. **Fleshy edge** spotted red and white, granular and with spines. **Gills** 10–15 pairs. **Habitat** on rocks on lower shore and in shallow water. **Distribution** Atlantic and English Channel.

Chitona squamosus Linnaeus (Not illustrated) **Length** up to 2.5 cm. **Dorsal plates** slightly ridged, grey with black or brown spots and uneven brown lines; ratio about 7 : 9. **Fleshy edge** with pale and dark stripes. **Habitat** on lower shore rocks. **Distribution** Mediterranean.

Lepidochitona cinereus (Linnaeus) **Length** up to 2 cm; less flattened than many other species. **Dorsal plates** slightly granular and variously coloured olive-grey-dull red; ratio about 3 : 4. **Fleshy edge** red-brown-green with minute granules. **Gills** 16–19 pairs. **Habitat** on rocks and under stones, on upper and lower shores. **Distribution** Mediterranean, Atlantic, English Channel, North Sea and south-west Baltic. N.B. generally regarded as the commonest chiton on most shores.

Callochiton achatinus (Brown) **Length** about 2 cm. **Dorsal plates** smooth and shiny; ratio 3 : 5. **Fleshy edge** broad with rounded granules; characteristic red-brown spots on 1st and last plates, and also occasionally on other plates. **Gills** 20–25 pairs. **Habitat** on rocks and under stones on lower shore. **Distribution** Mediterranean, Atlantic, English Channel, North Sea and south-west Baltic.

Acanthochitona crinatus (Pennant) **Length** up to 1.25 cm. **Dorsal plates** rough, with well-defined granules arranged on either side of the central crest, usually brown-yellow; ratio about 2 : 5. **Fleshy edge** relatively broad; 18 conspicuous groups of bristles arranged round the edge of the shell plates. **Gills** 10–15 pairs. **Habitat** among rocks on lower shore. **Distribution** Atlantic, English Channel and North Sea.

Ischnochiton albus (Linnaeus) (Not illustrated) **Length** about 1 cm. **Dorsal plates** often shiny, with conspicuous central crest and very fine ridges; ratio about 2 : 3. **Fleshy edge** covered by large, smooth granules and edged with small spines; slightly separated from the shell plates. **Gills** 12–16 pairs. **Habitat** among rocks on lower shore and in shallow water. **Distribution** Mediterranean and Atlantic.

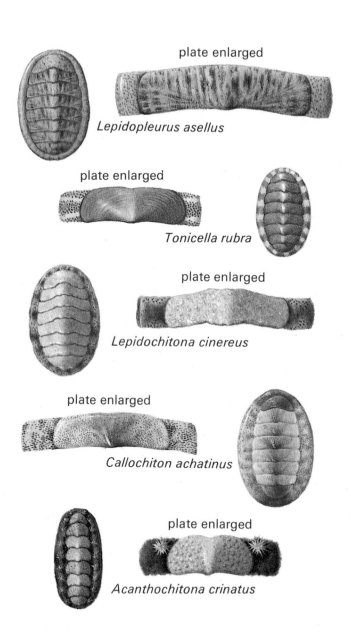

plate enlarged

Lepidopleurus asellus

plate enlarged

Tonicella rubra

plate enlarged

Lepidochitona cinereus

plate enlarged

Callochiton achatinus

plate enlarged

Acanthochitona crinatus

Class Gastropoda Snails and slugs

Asymmetrical molluscs with a well-developed head and a broad, flattened foot.
The shell is normally single and coiled in a helix; this coiling is not associated
with the twisting of the visceral mass known as torsion. The larval phase is
sometimes passed in the egg case.

Subclass Prosobranchia Sea-snails

Adults show torsion. The prosobranchs are generally marine and breathe by
gills. Fig. 34 sets out some of the important features of the morphology of the
shell. The shell is made up of a series of whorls. The first is at the apex and the
last is the broadest, known as the *body whorl*. The line where one whorl joins its
neighbour is the *suture*, and the central column around which the whorls
appear wrapped is the *columella*. The columella may be solid or hollow. If
hollow, the pore by which it opens is known as the *umbilicus*. Graham, A. 1971
provides a detailed account of many of the European prosobranchs.

Order Archaeogastropoda Limpets, ormers, topshells, etc.

Algae browsers, usually lacking an operculum for closing the shell. The shell is
usually lined with mother-of-pearl.

Haliotis lamellosa Lamarck **Common Ormer** Shell up to 7cm long;
flattened with a series of openings on the top; outer surface has a folded or
creased appearance and may be encrusted with calcareous algae. **Colour**
brown-red-green. **Habitat** among rocks and under stones on lower shore and
in shallow water. **Distribution** Mediterranean.

Haliotis tuberculata Linnaeus **Green Ormer** Similar to *H. lamellosa*
though not usually encrusted. **Shell** up to 8cm long. **Colour** green-brown-red;
there is a thick lining of mother-of-pearl inside the shell. **Habitat** among rocks
and under stones on the lower shore and in shallow water. **Distribution**
Mediterranean and Atlantic north to Channel Isles.

Eumarginula elongata da Costa **Slit Limpet** Shell up to 0.8cm long;
conical with a characteristic slit on the front border; apex of shell turned over
(view sideways). **Colour** white-yellow. **Habitat** on rocks and under stones on
the lower shore. **Distribution** Mediterranean.

Eumarginula reticulata Sowerby **Slit Limpet** (Not illustrated) Shell
up to 2cm long; ribbed and with characteristic slit at front; apex slightly turned
over. **Colour** white-grey-green or yellow. **Habitat** on rocks on the lower shore
and down to 60m. **Distribution** Mediterranean, Atlantic, English Channel and
North Sea.

Diodora apertura (Montagu) (*= D. graeca*) **Keyhole
Limpet** Shell up to 4cm long; conical and ribbed with characteristic keyhole
at apex (when alive a small siphon protrudes here); no trace of coiling; animal's
mantle may expand around the base of the shell. **Colour** greyish. **Habitat** on
rocks on lower shore and down to 20m. **Distribution** Atlantic, English Channel
and North Sea.

Diodora italica (Defrance) **Keyhole Limpet** Shell up to 4.5cm long;
sturdy, with clearly sculptured radial ribs. **Colour** white-grey with grey-violet
ribs. **Habitat** on rocks down to 10m. **Distribution** Mediterranean.

Acmaea virginea (O. F. Müller) **White Tortoiseshell
Limpet** Shell up to 1.25cm long; flattened, smooth, delicate cone shape with
the apex offset towards the front of the shell. **Colour** white-pinkish. **Habitat** on
lower shore and down to 10m, especially associated with *Laminaria* (see page
33). **Distribution** Mediterranean, Atlantic, English Channel, North Sea and
west Baltic.

Acmaea tessulata (O. F. Müller) **Tortoiseshell Limpet** Similar to *A.
virginea*, but markings are reminiscent of tortoiseshell. **Shell** up to 2.5cm

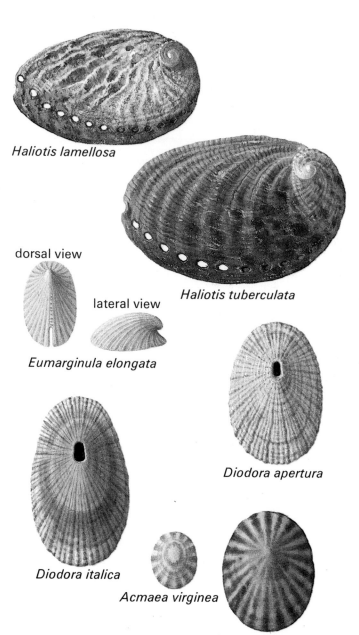

Haliotis lamellosa

Haliotis tuberculata

dorsal view

lateral view

Eumarginula elongata

Diodora apertura

Diodora italica

Acmaea virginea

Acmaea tessulata

long. **Habitat** on rocks, etc., on lower shore and in shallow water. **Distribution** Atlantic, North Sea and west Baltic.

Note on the genus Patella A number of species of this genus occur in the European area, of which five are treated here. They are all characterized by a conical, rough, ribbed shell whose apex lies towards the front of the animal rather than centrally. There is no opening in the apex as there is in the keyhole limpets. The shell fits tightly and exactly against the substratum. A careful examination of the mantle tentacles (which may be visible protruding from the periphery of the body under the lip of the shell when the animal crawls in a dish of sea water) and of the interior of the shell, may be necessary to distinguish the species. All five species of *Patella* illustrated have been painted with the front of the shell uppermost. Only the interiors are shown for *Patella*, but for *Patina* the exterior is shown. Several species of limpet often occur on the same rocky shore at different levels.

Patella vulgata Linnaeus **Common limpet** Shell up to 7 cm long; tall and often with a blunt tip; ribs irregular. **Colour** exterior greenish blue or grey, often encrusted with barnacles (see pages 197 and 199); interior white or yellow, with a white-brown scar left by the animal inside the shell apex; marginal mantle tentacles transparent. **Habitat** on rocks on upper and middle shore; the shells becoming less tall the further down they occur, and individuals less numerous where seaweeds are thick; often found in exposed places. **Distribution** Atlantic, English Channel and North Sea.

Patella aspera Lamarck (=*P. athletica*) Shell up to 7 cm long; quite flattened; exterior lacking contrasting rays. **Colour** interior white, sometimes with blue iridescence; foot orange; marginal mantle tentacles cream. **Habitat** on rocks from about the centre of the middle shore down to the bottom of the lower shore; generally in exposed places. **Distribution** Atlantic north to south-west Britain, and North Sea (Scotland to Norway).

Patella intermedia Jeffreys (=*P. depressa*) Shell up to 4 cm long; less tall than *P. vulgata*, ribs finer; exterior and interior margins may show dark rays. **Colour** interior with orange-cream scar; foot dark; marginal mantle tentacles opaque. **Habitat** on rocks on the middle shore often in exposed places. **Distribution** Atlantic north to Anglesey (North Wales), English Channel east to Isle of Wight; generally absent from Ireland.

Patella coerulea Linnaeus Shell up to 4.5 cm long; with fine ridges and an irregular wavy margin. **Colour** exterior green, brown, red or violet; interior has dark stripes with a blue mother-of-pearl scar. **Habitat** on rocks, usually on relatively horizontal surfaces, on lower half of the middle shore. **Distribution** Mediterranean.

Patella lusitanica (Gmelin) Shell up to 4 cm long; less long, narrower, but taller than *P. coerulea*. **Colour** outer surface of shell spotted black; interior with dark rays running a little way in; pale scar. **Habitat** on rocks, usually on relatively vertical surfaces on upper half of the middle shore. **Distribution** Mediterranean and Atlantic north to Biscay.

Patina pellucida Linnaeus **Blue-rayed Limpet** Shell about 1.5 cm long; smooth and semi-transparent. **Colour** rows of beautiful, bright blue spots running from the top to the margin; these may fade with age. **Habitat** generally attached to the fronds and holdfasts of *Laminaria* (see page 33) on the lower shore and in shallow water. **Distribution** Atlantic, English Channel and North Sea. N.B. younger animals sometimes occur on the fronds and may appear brighter than older individuals located more often on the holdfasts.

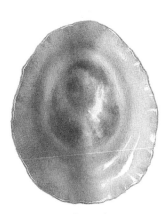

Patella vulgata

Patella aspera

Patella intermedia

Patella coerulea

Patella lusitanica

young specimen

older specimen

Patina pellucida

Note on the genera Gibbula and Monodonta These topshells are conical in shape and circular in section. The inner layer is mother-of-pearl and may show through if the shell is worn. A horny or calcareous operculum closes the mouth of the shell when the snail's foot is withdrawn.

Gibbula divaricata (Linnaeus) Shell up to 2.3cm high but less wide; whorls (sometimes more); upper surface of the whorls is bumpy, suture between whorls pronounced; umbilicus conspicuous. **Colour** yellow-white with red or purple marks. **Habitat** buried in sand down to about 10m. **Distribution** Mediterranean, Atlantic and English Channel.

Gibbula umbilicalis (da Costa) **Purple Topshell** Shell about 1.25cm high; rather wider than high; generally like a compressed cone with slightly convex outline; there may be 7 whorls; umbilicus conspicuous. **Colour** green-grey with conspicuous purple stripes. **Habitat** on rocks on the middle shore and the upper part of the lower shore. **Distribution** Atlantic and English Channel.

Gibbula cineraria (Linnaeus) **Grey Topshell** Shell about 1.25cm high and of similar width; up to 7 whorls which may appear somewhat compressed; umbilicus small. **Colour** greyish shell with darker grey-red markings in the form of very narrow bands which may be somewhat faded. **Habitat** under stones and on seaweeds on the lower shore and down to about 20m. **Distribution** Atlantic, English Channel and North Sea.

Gibbula divaricata (Linnaeus) Shell up to 2.3cm high but not as wide; about 6 whorls which are not compressed so that the shell resembles a coil rather than a cone; umbilicus lacking; mouth wide. **Colour** grey-green with red spots. **Habitat** under stones and among seaweeds from lower shore downward. **Distribution** Mediterranean.

Gibbula adansoni (Payraudeau) Shell about 1.3cm high and not as wide; a fairly tall cone shape with quite well-defined whorls numbering about 6. **Colour** red-brown with white markings. **Habitat** on rocks and stones on the lower shore. **Distribution** Mediterranean.

Monodonta lineata (da Costa) (= *Gibbula lineata*) **Toothed Winkle** or **Thick Topshell** Shell about 2.5cm high and of similar width; quite conical with about 6 poorly defined whorls and slight umbilicus (in some specimens this may be obscured by growth); mouth shows mother-of-pearl which usually stretches to the umbilical region. **Colour** grey-green with purple zig-zags; top of shell may be worn away and appear pearly yellow. **Habitat** on rocks on the middle shore. **Distribution** Atlantic north to Anglesey and west English Channel. N.B. 'tooth' on the inside of the mouth opening easily distinguishes this shell from *Littorina littorea* (see page 151).

Monodonta turbinata (Born) (= *Gibbula turbinata)* Shell about 2.5cm high and of similar width; quite conical with about 6 whorls; slight 'tooth' on the inside of the mouth opening. **Colour** white-yellow with dark oblong markings arranged in parallel rows coiled around the spire; mouth is white. **Habitat** on rocks, usually on the lower shore. **Distribution** Mediterranean.

Several other species of *Gibbula* and *Monodonta* have been recorded from the European area.

Gibbula magus

Gibbula umbilicalis

Gibbula cineraria

Gibbula divaricata

Gibbula adansoni

tooth

Monodonta lineata

Monodonta turbinata

147

Clanculus corallinus (Gmelin) **Shell** about 1 cm wide and not quite as high; about 6 whorls covered in small knobs arranged in spirals; 2 'teeth' on inside of mouth opening. **Colour** coral red-brown; sometimes patterned. **Habitat** on rocks on lower shore down to about 10 m. **Distribution** Mediterranean.

Cantharidus striatus (Linnaeus) **Grooved Topshell** Shell about 1 cm high, but less wide; steep cone shape with almost straight sides; bottom whorl has about 6 spiral ridges of which the basal one is most developed and gives a keel effect; umbilicus lacking. **Colour** grey-white with brown-red vertical markings. **Habitat** on rocks on substrates from extreme lower shore down to about 100 m. **Distribution** Mediterranean, Atlantic north to the south-west of the British Isles and west English Channel.

Calliostoma zizyphinum (Linnaeus) **Common Topshell** or **Painted Topshell** Shell about 2.5 cm high and of similar width; strongly conical with straight sides; about 9 whorls which are relatively shallow; umbilicus lacking. **Colour** yellow-pink mottling with brown or red stripes. **Habitat** on rocks and under stones on lower shore and down to 100 m. **Distribution** Mediterranean, Atlantic, English Channel and North Sea.

Astraea rugosa (Linnaeus) **Rough Star-shell** Shell about 5 cm high and of similar width; thick and heavy with about 7 whorls which are moulded into bumps on their upper surface and have thorny, spiral lines on their sides; foot of snail carries a calcareous operculum with spiral markings (here shown stopping the aperture). **Colour** usually red-brown. **Habitat** on rocks from the lower shore downward. **Distribution** Mediterranean and Atlantic coasts of Spain and Portugal.

Leptothyra sanguinea (Linnaeus) **Shell** about 0.9 cm wide but less high; about 5 whorls with conspicuous, spiral grooves cut into them; foot of snail carries a calcareous operculum. **Colour** blood-red (but may be encrusted as shown here). **Habitat** among seaweeds and rocks on lower shore and in shallow water. **Distribution** Mediterranean.

Tricolia pullus (Linnaeus) **Pheasant Shell** Shell about 0.8 cm high but less wide; generally about 4 whorls, of which the last takes up more than half the total height; foot of snail bears conspicuous white calcareous operculum. **Colour** white and glossy with irregular brown-red markings. **Habitat** in rock pools on the extreme lower shore, especially among red seaweeds; sometimes found on sandy substrates. **Distribution** Mediterranean, Atlantic and English Channel.

Theodoxus fluviatilis (Linnaeus) **Shell** about 1 cm wide, but less high and of unusual shape — being flattened; mouth partly blocked by columellar growth; outer lip usually thickened; foot of snail bears calcareous operculum. **Colour** speckled. **Habitat** freshwater and estuarine regions where the salinity does not exceed 0.6 % and where the calcium content is high; in situations where the animal may be protected from water currents and strong light, e.g. under stones and wood. **Distribution** may be common in areas bordering the Atlantic region where the right conditions prevail; in the Baltic it is found on brown seaweeds and stones, occurring with increasing frequency in more open, turbulent water, providing the salinity is low.

Calliostoma zizyphinum

Clanculus corallinus

Cantharidus striatus

Astraea rugosa

Leptothyra sanguinea

Theodoxus fluviatilis

Tricolia pullus

Order Mesogastropoda Periwinkles, tower shells, worm shells, etc.

Algae eaters, deposit feeders and predators. The inner shell lacks mother-of-pearl but often has a horny operculum.

Lacuna vincta (Montagu) **Banded Chink Shell** Shell about 0.8cm high, sometimes more, but less wide; generally of conical shape with about 5 smooth whorls; apex pointed; mouth oval; small but deep umbilicus. **Colour** green-yellow and semi-transparent with red-brown banding. **Habitat** lower shore and in shallow water on seaweeds (e.g. *Ceramium* and *Polysiphonia*, see pages 55 and 61). **Distribution** Atlantic, English Channel, North Sea and west Baltic.

Note on the genus Littorina The following four species are all characterized by solid shells lacking an umbilicus, but possessing smooth columellas. The foot of the snail carries a horny operculum. These species are generally common on rocky shores where they have each evolved to fit a particular niche. They can variously withstand exposure to air, desiccation and lowered salinity and their respiratory and reproductive processes show adaptations to the particular position they have taken up on the shore. Heller, J. 1975 recently revised the taxonomy of some British littorinids.

Littorina littoralis (Linnaeus) (=*L. obtusata*) **Flat Periwinkle** Shell up to 1 cm high, occasionally larger; spire very compressed so that the mouth and the last whorl comprise virtually all the height; shell apparently smooth but if examined with a hand lens, very fine sculpturing can be seen. **Colour** variable; brown, red, green, orange and yellow, sometimes banded. **Habitat** on seaweeds (especially *Fucus vesiculosus* and *Ascophyllum nodosum* see page 39) on the lower middle, and upper parts of lower shores. **Distribution** Atlantic, English Channel, North Sea and west Baltic. N.B. this winkle is a gill breather and feeds on seaweeds.

Littorina saxatilis (Olivi) (=*L. rudis*) **Rough Periwinkle** Shell about 0.8cm high; 6–9 whorls separated by deep sutures; each whorl has ridges and grooves which make the shell rough to the touch; outer lip of the opening meets the spire almost at right angles. **Colour** variable; red-black. **Habitat** in cracks and crevices, and on stones on the upper shore and on the upper part of the middle shore. **Distribution** Atlantic, English Channel, North Sea and west Baltic. N.B. mantle cavity is modified to form a lung for breathing air; feeds on seaweeds.

Littorina neritoides (Linnaeus) **Small Periwinkle** Shell about 0.5cm high; sharply conical with pointed apex; smooth surface and fragile appearance; outer lip of the opening roughly parallel to the spire where the two meet. **Colour** blue-black. **Habitat** on extreme upper shore, usually in crevices; generally more plentiful where the beach is exposed. **Distribution** Mediterranean, Atlantic, English Channel and North Sea. N.B. lung breather which feeds on lichens. Do not confuse it with small examples of *L. saxatilis* which occur lower on the shore and are rough to the touch.

Littorina littorea (Linnaeus) **Edible Periwinkle** Shell about 2.5cm high; sharply conical with pointed apex and surface sculpturing; outer lip of opening is more or less parallel to the spire where the two meet. **Colour** grey-black-brown-red and always patterned with concentric darker lines; columella white. **Habitat** on rocks, stones and seaweeds on the middle and lower shores. **Distribution** Mediterranean, Atlantic, English Channel, North Sea and west Baltic. N.B. a gill breather which feeds on seaweed. It may migrate up or down the shore during the breeding seasons. Do not confuse small specimens with *L. saxatilis* (see above) where the outer lip of the shell opening meets the spire at right angles, or with *Monodonta lineata* (see page 147). The black banded tentacles of *L. littorea* may also be seen.

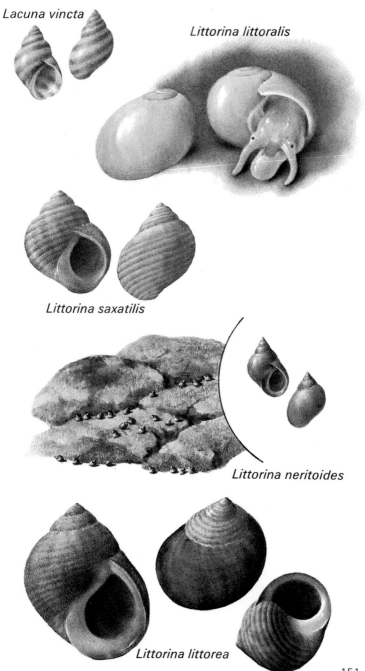

Lacuna vincta

Littorina littoralis

Littorina saxatilis

Littorina neritoides

Littorina littorea

151

Truncatella subcylindrica (Linnaeus) **Looping Snail** Shell about
0.5 cm high; conspicuous because of the lack of apical whorls on the adult shell
(these break off from the young shell when it reaches maturity); adult has about
3 whorls remaining; mouth ear-shaped. **Colour** yellow-brown, with the shell
surface finely ribbed. **Habitat** in muddy places on the upper shore usually
associated with seaweeds or stones. **Distribution** Mediterranean and Atlantic.
N.B. it moves by looping like a leech.

Hydrobia ulvae (Pennant) **Laver Spire Shell** Shell about 0.6 cm high
and complete (possessing all apical whorls) as adult; conical shape terminates
in blunt apex; whorls do not appear swollen; outer lip of opening is more or less
straight edged where it joins the spire at an acute angle. **Colour** brown to
yellow; diamond-shaped area of pigment on the head between the eyes. **Habitat** on mud in estuaries, normally on the middle shore and in other places where
the water is brackish. **Distribution** Atlantic, English Channel, North Sea and
Baltic. N.B. the left tentacle is thicker than the right tentacle.

Hydrobia ventrosa (Montagu) Shell about 0.6 cm high and complete
(possessing all apical whorls) as adult; conical shape often terminates in a
sharper point than *H. ulvae*; whorls appear swollen; outer lip opening is curved
and joins the spire at a right angle. **Colour** brownish; v-shaped area of pigment
on the head between the eyes. **Habitat** often in lagoons without direct
communication with sea water and where the water is brackish; in the Baltic it
may be found associated with seaweeds and also on gravel substrates where
there is some wave action. **Distribution** Atlantic, English Channel, North Sea
and Baltic.

Paludestrina jenkinsi (Smith) (*=Potamopyrgus jenkinsi*) Shell
about 0.5 cm high; last whorl takes up about two-thirds total shell height and
may be keeled or bear bristles. **Colour** yellowish, but often blackened by
deposits. **Habitat** in muddy conditions among stones and seaweeds where the
water is brackish and running; sometimes in lagoons on sand. **Distribution**
Atlantic, English Channel, North Sea and Baltic.

Graham, A. 1971 provides more information on the identification of *Hydrobia*
and *Paludestrina* species.

Bithynia tentaculata (Linnaeus) Shell about 1 cm high; conical and
smooth; umbilicus minute; about 6 whorls with conspicuous growth lines
showing previous positions of the mouth; mouth wide. **Colour** brown, with
dark growth lines. **Habitat** in fresh water, on vegetation in Summer and on mud
in Winter. **Distribution** Baltic; may occur elsewhere in ponds, canals and rivers.

Alvania cancellata (da Costa) Shell about 0.3 cm high; spiral and
longitudinal lines mark the surface. **Colour** brown-pink-grey. **Habitat** on rocks
and gravel and among other organisms on the extreme lower shore and in
shallow water. **Distribution** Atlantic, English Channel and North Sea; related
species occur in the Mediterranean and in the foregoing areas.

Rissoa parva (da Costa) Shell about 0.7 cm high; slight ribs; the lips of the
aperture are somewhat turned out. **Colour** generally white-grey-brown.
Habitat extreme lower shore and shallow water, usually associated with
coraline seaweeds and under stones; sometimes in pools. **Distribution**
Atlantic, west English Channel, North Sea and west Baltic. N.B. many other
related species and varieties are known from the European area. One such is
Cingula cingillus (Montagu) (not illustrated) which is a minute, conical,
banded shell occurring in crevices and under stones especially in silty places on
the middle and lower shore and in shallow water.

Truncatella subcylindrica

Hydrobia ulvae

Hydrobia ventrosa

Paludestrina jenkinsi

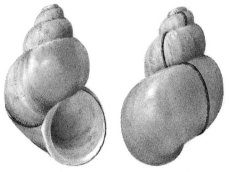

Bithynia tentaculata

Rissoa parva

Alvania cancellata

Turritella communis Risso **Tower Shell** Shell 4—6 cm high; many conspicuous whorls; relatively narrow for its height; spiral ridges on the whorls; mouth relatively small. **Colour** variable; red-brown-yellow-white. **Habitat** lies partly buried in sand or mud, sometimes associated with other organisms, generally down to about 80m. **Distribution** Mediterranean, Atlantic, English Channel and North Sea.

Turritella triplicata (Brocchi) **Tower Shell** (Not illustrated) Similar to *T. communis.* **Shell** about 5 cm high; straight-sided so that the whorls are not conspicuous. **Colour** pale, with red-brown markings. **Distribution** Mediterranean.

Vermetus gigas Bivone **Giant Worm Shell** Shell up to 20 cm long; irregularly coiled tube. **Colour** grey-white. **Habitat** on soft and hard substrates, stones and shells. **Distribution** Mediterranean. N.B. several other related species are found in Europe.

Bittium reticulatum (da Costa) **Needle Shell** Shell up to 1.5 cm high and relatively narrow; many finely latticed whorls with minute tubercles. **Colour** brownish. **Habitat** under stones and among rocks on the lower shore and in shallow water. **Distribution** Atlantic, English Channel, North Sea and west Baltic.

Cerithium vulgatum Bruguière **Common Cerith** Shell about 4.5 cm high; many sculptured whorls; mouth oval and outer lip slightly frilled. **Colour** white-brown. **Habitat** on stones, sand and mud down to about 10m. **Distribution** Mediterranean.

Aporrhais pespelecani (Linnaeus) **Pelican's Foot Shell** Shell about 3.5 cm; many whorls with conspicuous tubercles; last whorl bears a flared outer lip which is ribbed and produced into about 4 points, although this may not be apparent in juvenile specimens; the fluted lip generally shields the animal's head. **Colour** greyish. **Habitat** burrows in mud, sand or gravel down to about 80m. **Distribution** Mediterranean, Atlantic, English Channel and North Sea.

Capulus ungaricus (Linnaeus) **Bonnet Limpet** or **Hungarian Cap Shell** Shell about 5 cm wide; bonnet-shaped; apex turned backwards and slightly coiled; periostracum provides a fringe to the opening. **Colour** white-yellow marked by spiral ridges; interior white; periostracum brown. **Habitat** attached to other shells, usually bivalves, from which it steals food by means of its long proboscis; normally in deep water around 100m. **Distribution** Mediterranean, Atlantic, English Channel and North Sea.

Crepidula fornicata (Linnaeus) **Slipper Limpet** Shell up to 2.5 cm wide; oval-shaped; apex shows some coiling; outer surface shows growth lines. **Colour** yellow, white, green-brown, sometimes with red markings; underside usually white. **Habitat** usually attached to others of the same species and to bivalves, e.g. mussels and oysters in shallow water. **Distribution** Atlantic, English Channel and North Sea. N.B. this species normally lives in groups and forms a chain of individuals. In such cases the animals at the bottom of the chain are the oldest and are females. Those at the top start life as males and as they age, become females. This species is a serious pest in oyster beds, and was introduced from America with imported oysters. It has now spread from East Anglia along the east coast to Scotland and around the south coast to Wales.

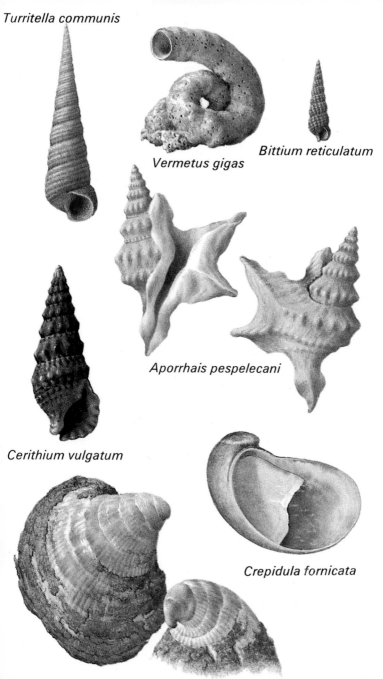

Turritella communis

Vermetus gigas

Bittium reticulatum

Aporrhais pespelecani

Cerithium vulgatum

Crepidula fornicata

Capulus ungaricus

155

Velutina velutina (O. F. Müller) **Velvet Shell** Shell up to 2 cm long; about 3 whorls of which the last is the largest and has a wide opening; covered by a velvet-like periostracum and partly enclosed by the thick yellow mantle of the snail in life. **Colour** brownish. **Habitat** among *Alcyonium* and sea-squirts (see pages 101, 261 and 263) from the lower shore down to about 50 m. **Distribution** Atlantic, English Channel and North Sea.

Trivia monacha (da Costa) (=*Cypraea europaea*) **European Cowrie** Shell about 1.2 cm when measured along the slit-like opening; spire very short; polished surface traversed by about 20 delicate ribs. **Colour** pink-purple-brown above and pale below; characteristically bearing about 3 conspicuous, dark brown spots above; in life the shell may be partly covered by the variously coloured mantle folds of the animal. **Habitat** among rocks and compound ascidians on which it feeds and deposits its eggs on the lower shore and in shallow water. **Distribution** Mediterranean, Atlantic, English Channel and North Sea.

Trivia arctica (Montagu) (Not illustrated) Similar in all respects to *T. monacha*, but generally slightly smaller and lacking the conspicuous dark brown spots on the upper part of the shell. **Habitat** rarely found between the tidemarks, usually down to 100 m. **Distribution** Atlantic, English Channel and North Sea.

Pseudosimnia carnea (Poiret) Shell about 1.5 cm when measured along the slit-like opening; relatively slender for its length; outer lip toothed; small spire. **Colour** outer lip pale. **Habitat** in deep water, often among gorgonians (see page 101). **Distribution** Mediterranean.

Erronea pirum (Linnaeus) **Pear Cowrie** Shell up to 5 cm when measured along slit-like opening; outer and inner lip toothed. **Colour** red-brown above with irregular darker markings; light red below. **Habitat** on hard substrates in deep water and associated with seaweeds. **Distribution** Mediterranean and Atlantic north to Portugal.

Natica alderi Forbes **Common Necklace Shell** Shell about 1.5 cm high; globular and with a low spire; last whorl expanded; umbilicus half occluded by growth of shell; ear-shaped operculum. **Foot** of snail appears large and may be partly reflected over the shell when the animal is active. **Colour** shiny and white-yellow with light, red-brown patterns. **Habitat** burrowing in sand where it hunts for bivalve prey, on lower shore and down to about 70 m. **Distribution** Mediterranean, Atlantic, English Channel and North Sea.

Clathrus clathrus (Linnaeus) **Common Wentletrap** Shell up to 4 cm high, often less; a number of whorls bearing conspicuous diagonal stripes; mouth round; operculum horny. **Colour** varies from colourless to brown-red. **Habitat** generally in water down to 80 m, but migrates to rocks on the shore near sand and mud to spawn. **Distribution** Mediterranean, Atlantic, English Channel, North Sea and west Baltic. N.B. animal has long proboscis.

Dolium galea (Linnaeus) **Giant Tun shell** Shell up to 15 cm high; characteristic spiral ridges and a low spire. **Colour** white-brown-yellow. **Habitat** in deep water. **Distribution** Mediterranean and Atlantic coasts of Portugal and Spain.

Ianthina exigua Lamarck **Violet Sea Snail** Shell about 1.5 cm high; thin-walled and with about 5 whorls; delicate, v-shaped markings. **Colour** violet (violet pigment may also be released). **Habitat** a pelagic snail floating by means of a raft of trapped air bubbles and feeding on siphonophores; shells may occasionally be washed up after periods of westerly gales. **Distribution** Atlantic.

Cassidaria echinophora (Linnaeus) **Knobbed Helmet Shell** Shell up to 10 cm across and higher than it is wide; bears large tubercles

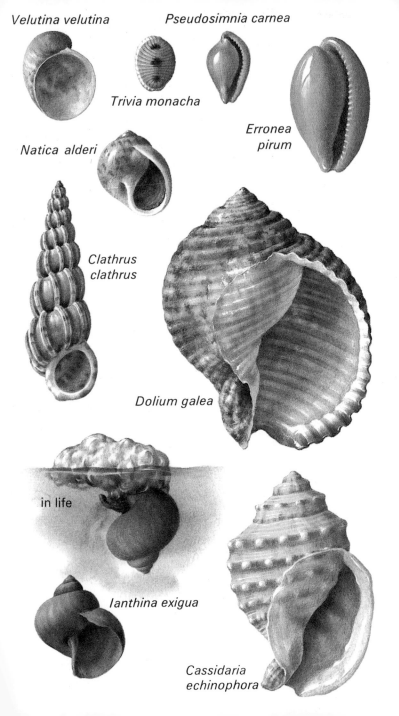

Velutina velutina

Pseudosimnia carnea

Trivia monacha

Erronea pirum

Natica alderi

Clathrus clathrus

Dolium galea

in life

Ianthina exigua

Cassidaria echinophora

arranged in spirals; siphonal canal present; horny operculum. **Colour** reddish-brown-grey. **Habitat** on sandy substrates in both shallow and deep water. **Distribution** Mediterranean and neighbouring Atlantic.

Order Neogastropoda Whelks, etc.

Deposit feeders and predators. The inner shell lacks mother-of-pearl and an operculum is present. The snails have well-developed siphons which are often supported by a siphonal groove or canal in the shell.

Murex brandaris Linnaeus **Shell** about 8cm high with long, straight siphonal canals which may take up half the total height of the shell; quite robust and bearing conspicuous spines arranged in rows along it; about 6 whorls, the last being much the largest; snail bears horny operculum on its foot. **Colour** yellow-grey. **Habitat** on mud and stones in shallow water. **Distribution** Mediterranean.

Murex trunculus Linnaeus **Shell** about 7cm high with shorter siphonal canal which occupies about a quarter of the total height of the shell; robust, but with swellings and tubercles arranged in rows rather than as conspicuous spines as in *M. brandaris*. **Colour** grey-white, with violet-brown bands. **Habitat** both soft and hard substrates from the lower shore downward. **Distribution** Mediterranean.

Nucella lapillus (Linnaeus) **(=*Thais lapillus*) Dogwhelk** **Shell** about 3cm high with short siphonal canal; heavy with about 5 whorls which are marked with spiral lines; the last whorl being the largest; outer lip of the opening is thick and toothed in adults. **Colour** varies, but is basically ash-grey to cream, often marked or patterned with dark brown spirals; snail itself cream coloured. **Habitat** on rocky shores, except those which are very exposed, in crevices and among barnacles (on which it preys) in the middle shore region. **Distribution** Atlantic, English Channel and North Sea. N.B. egg capsules resembling grains of barley may be found (see page 305).

Ocenebra erinacea (Linnaeus) **Sting Winkle** or **Oyster Drill** **Shell** up to 6cm high, sometimes smaller; siphonal canal open in juvenile specimens, but closed in for the greater part of its length in older specimens so that it is tubular; unevenly sculptured; about 5 ribbed whorls of which the last is the largest; whorls have spiral lines or ridges; outer lip of opening toothed and thick. **Colour** yellow-white with dark brown marks. **Habitat** on muddy gravel, sand and rocks from the lower shore down to deep water (possibly to 100m), but migrating inshore to spawn. **Distribution** Mediterranean, Atlantic, English Channel and North Sea. N.B. a notable pest in oyster beds, attacking the oysters by means of the radula which functions like a drill, and then sucking out the oyster's flesh.

Tritonalia aciculata (Lamarck) **Shell** up to 2cm high; about 6 ribbed whorls; opening of shell toothed on the outer lip. **Colour** brownish; interior of opening brown. **Habitat** on rocks and sand from about 10m downward. **Distribution** Mediterranean and neighbouring Atlantic coasts.

Pyrene scripta (Linnaeus) **Shell** about 2cm high; a steep cone with relatively straight sides and about 7 whorls; outer lip of opening toothed. **Colour** white with brown-orange markings. **Habitat** on rocks down to about 10m. **Distribution** Mediterranean.

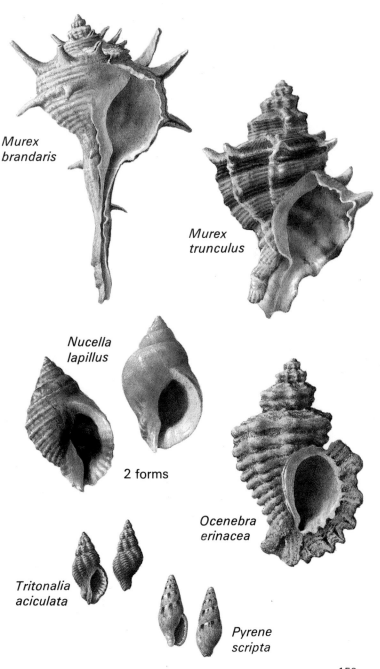

Murex brandaris

Murex trunculus

Nucella lapillus

2 forms

Ocenebra erinacea

Tritonalia aciculata

Pyrene scripta

159

Fusus rostratus (Olivi) **Shell** about 4cm high; conspicuous siphonal canal, open with smooth edges, up to about a third total shell length; sharply pointed spire with 9 whorls; well-developed ribs; outer lip slightly crenulate. **Colour** red-brown. **Habitat** on muddy and sandy substrates. **Distribution** Mediterranean.

Mitra ebenus Lamarck **Mitre-shell Shell** about 2cm high; pointed spire of about 9 whorls which are sculptured and have a narrow, whitish spiral line; aperture narrow with smooth outer lip and with several ridges on the columellar edge. **Colour** dark brown. **Habitat** on rocky and stony substrates. **Distribution** Mediterranean.

Persicula miliaris (Linnaeus) **Shell** about 0.7cm high; very compressed spire; long, narrow aperture. **Colour** whitish to yellowish, usually with red markings. **Habitat** on stony and sandy substrates. **Distribution** Mediterranean.

Buccinum undatum Linnaeus **Buckie** or **Common Whelk Shell** up to 8cm high, sometimes more; short siphonal canal; spire pointed with well-defined whorls which are lined and ribbed; aperture large with smooth outer edge. **Colour** pale brown. **Habitat** on sand and mud from shallow water down to about 100m. **Distribution** Atlantic, English Channel, North Sea and west Baltic. N.B. empty shells of this species are often inhabited by hermit crabs (see page 221). They are also sometimes covered with sponges, hydroids and anemones. The large, rounded, spongy egg masses of *Buccinum undatum* are often washed up on the shore, each hollow cell being an individual egg-case (see page 305).

Nassarius reticulatus (Linnaeus) **Netted Dogwhelk Shell** up to 3cm high; short siphonal canal; conical; about 7 whorls which are not well defined and which are patterned in small squares due to the crossing of lines and ribs; oval aperture with thick, toothed outer lip. **Colour** brown. **Habitat** under stones and in crevices, often in muddy areas on the lower shore and in shallow water. **Distribution** Mediterranean, Atlantic, English Channel, North Sea and west Baltic.

Nassarius incrassatus (Ström) (Not illustrated) **Thick-lipped Dogwhelk Shell** up to 1.5cm high; conical; short siphonal canal; about 7 well-defined, convex whorls which are sculptured with lines and ribs; oval aperture with thick outer lip. **Colour** brownish with dark bands. **Habitat** under stones and in crevices, often in muddy places on the lower shore and in shallow water. **Distribution** Mediterranean, Atlantic, English Channel and North Sea.

Conus mediterraneus Brugière **Mediterranean Cone Shell** Shell up to 5cm high; short siphonal canal; spire very compressed; long, slit-like aperture with smooth edges. **Colour** yellow, brown and green. **Habitat** on sandy bottoms often in shallow water. **Distribution** Mediterranean. N.B. this species is not as poisonous as its tropical relatives, but it has a hollow venom tooth used for injecting its prey, and can cause pain and irritation to humans.

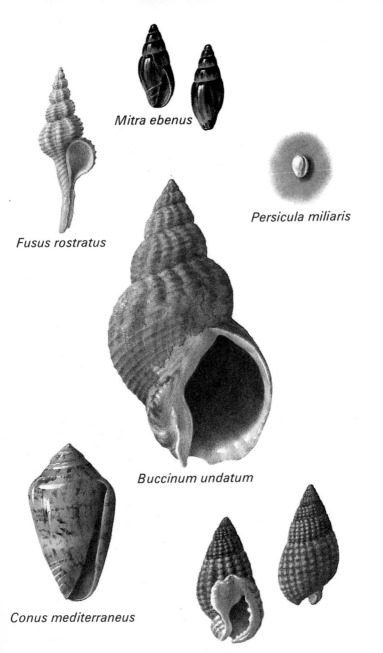

Mitra ebenus

Fusus rostratus

Persicula miliaris

Buccinum undatum

Conus mediterraneus

Nassarius reticulatus

161

Subclass Opisthobranchia

Gastropods which undergo torsion followed by de-torsion. The shell is reduced or absent. These animals often have conspicuous external gills and are brightly coloured.

Order Tectibranchia Sea-slugs

Internal gills. Although present, the shell is usually reduced and often enfolded by the mantle.

Actaeon tornatilis (Linnaeus) Shell about 2 cm long and barrel-like with up to 7 whorls; resembles a prosobranch (see pages 143–161). **Colour** pink-grey-yellow. **Habitat** burrowing in sand or mud, generally on the lower shore and in shallow water. **Distribution** Mediterranean, Atlantic, English Channel and North Sea.

Bullaria striata (Brugière) (Not illustrated) **Body** up to 6 cm long and unable to withdraw into the shell. **Shell** about half as long as body; spire reduced. **Colour** shell brownish, patterned. **Habitat** on sand and mud, often among seaweeds on the lower shore and in shallow water. **Distribution** Mediterranean, and Atlantic.

Scaphander lignarius (Linnaeus) **Body** may reach 14 cm long and is unable to withdraw into the shell. **Shell** about half as long as body; aperture tapers towards the apex. **Colour** shell yellow-white. **Habitat** on sandy and muddy substrates. **Distribution** Mediterranean and Atlantic north to English Channel.

Philine aperta (Linnaeus) **Body** up to 2 cm long; enclosing the shell. **Shell** thin, reduced. **Colour** body grey-white and translucent; shell white. **Habitat** on sand on the extreme lower shore and in shallow water. **Distribution** Mediterranean, Atlantic, English Channel, North Sea and west Baltic.

Aplysia punctata Cuvier **Sea-hare** **Body** up to 14 cm long; almost enclosing shell; 4 head tentacles. **Shell** about 1.5 cm wide; delicate. **Colour** younger individuals reddish; older individuals brown-green. **Habitat** among seaweeds in shallow water and occasionally swimming. **Distribution** Atlantic, English Channel and North Sea. N.B. may eject purple dye when disturbed. Two closely related species, *A. depilans* and *A. fasciata*, occur in the Mediterranean. They reach about 25 cm long and are similar to *A. punctata*. *A. fasciata* has an orange border to its mantle.

Order Sacoglossa

A shell is lacking in most species. These animals are often highly coloured.

Elysia viridis (Montagu) **Body** about 3 cm long; flattened and soft; 2 head tentacles; no gills. **Colour** green. **Habitat** on green seaweeds such as *Codium* (see page 25) from the middle shore downward. **Distribution** Mediterranean, Atlantic, English Channel, North Sea and west Baltic.

Order Pleurobranchomorpha

The shell is internal or lacking, and the body is covered dorsally by a membranous shield.

Pleurobranchus membranaceus Montagu **Body** up to 12 cm long; dorsal shield from under which protrudes broad red foot, 2 head tentacles and a gill on the right side. **Colour** orange-yellow-white. **Habitat** on mud and gravel in shallow water. **Distribution** Mediterranean, Atlantic and English Channel.

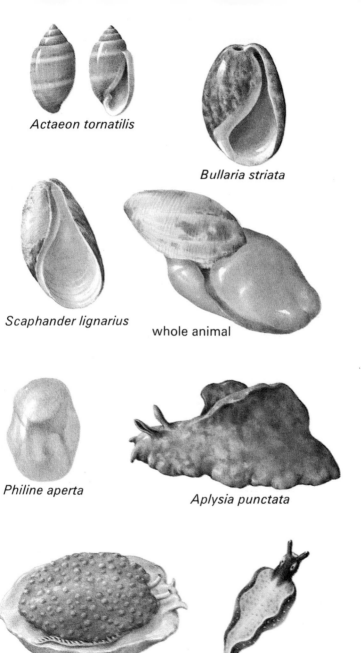

Actaeon tornatilis

Bullaria striata

Scaphander lignarius

whole animal

Philine aperta

Aplysia punctata

Pleurobranchus membranaceus

Elysia viridis

Order Nudibranchia

Opisthobranchs lacking a shell, and often highly coloured. The position of the external gills and other appendages is important in identification.

Archidoris pseudoargus (Rapp) **Sea-lemon** Body up to 7cm long; 2 unbranched head tentacles; back covered with small warts and bearing anus towards rear; 9 branching gills in a ring on the back. **Colour** yellowish with brown-green-pink markings. **Habitat** moves up to the lower shore in Summer to spawn, otherwise in deeper water, generally among rocks. **Distribution** Atlantic, English Channel and North Sea.

Jorunna tomentosa (Cuvier) Similar to *A. pseudoargus*. **Body** up to 4cm long; small warts on the back; 2 brownish unbranched head tentacles and 15 whitish branching gills in a ring on back. **Colour** yellowish with brown markings. **Habitat** among rocks on the lower shore in Summer and in deeper water at other times. **Distribution** Mediterranean, Atlantic, English Channel and North Sea.

Peltodoris atromaculata Bergh Body up to 6cm long; 2 unbranched head tentacles and 9 branching gills in a ring on the back. **Colour** whitish with dark brown markings. **Habitat** among rocks on the lower shore in Summer and in deeper water at other times. **Distribution** Mediterranean.

Cadlina laevis (Linnaeus) Body about 2cm long; small warts; 2 unbranched head tentacles and 5 branching gills in a ring on the back. **Colour** pure white with pale yellow spots on the sides. **Habitat** in pools on the lower shore and in shallow and deeper water. **Distribution** Atlantic north from Scotland and North Sea.

Limacia clavigera (O. F. Müller) Body about 2cm long; flat with over 20 appendages of varying sizes; these appendages are difficult to distinguish from the head tentacles; 3 branched gills around the anus. **Colour** body white, appendages usually have orange-red tips. **Habitat** usually in shallow water. **Distribution** Mediterranean, Atlantic, English Channel and North Sea.

Dendronotus frondosus (Ascanius) Body about 5cm long; head tentacles are branched and there are many branched appendages arranged in pairs along the back. **Colour** yellow-pink-white with darker markings on back. **Habitat** among rocks and on sand in shallow water and down to about 100m. **Distribution** Atlantic, English Channel, North Sea and west Baltic.

Spurilla neapolitana (Della Chiaje) Body about 6cm long; 2 pairs of unbranched head tentacles and many pairs of branched appendages on the back. **Colour** brownish. **Habitat** in shallow water. **Distribution** Mediterranean and neighbouring Atlantic.

Facelina auriculata (O. F. Müller) Body up to 2.5cm long; thin; 2 dissimilar pairs of unbranched head tentacles and about 6 groups of appendages on the back. **Colour** pale; appendages dark red with white tips. **Habitat** among rocks on the lower shore and in shallow water. **Distribution** Atlantic and English Channel.

Aeolidia papillosa (Linnaeus) **Common Grey Sea-slug** Body may be 8cm long; 2 pairs of unbranched head tentacles; many appendages carried on the back which are 'parted' in the middle. **Colour** grey-brown. **Habitat** on stony and rocky shores, between high and low water marks. **Distribution** Atlantic, English Channel and North Sea.

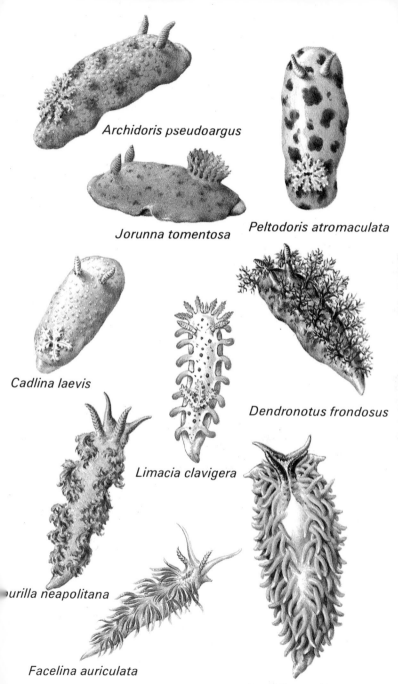

Archidoris pseudoargus

Jorunna tomentosa

Peltodoris atromaculata

Cadlina laevis

Limacia clavigera

Dendronotus frondosus

...urilla neapolitana

Facelina auriculata

Aeolidia papillosa

Subclass Pulmonata

Gastropods which undergo torsion and bear a shell. The operculum is lacking. The mantle cavity is modified to form a lung for breathing air, and may be further adapted to permit respiration under water. Although the pulmonates are generally terrestrial or freshwater animals, several species fall within the scope of this book.

Limnaea stagnalis Linnaeus **Great Pond Snail** Shell up to 5 cm high, but not as wide; high spire with about 6 quite well-defined whorls; horn-like. **Colour** pale-midbrown. **Habitat** in fresh water, in ponds and ditches among weeds throughout Europe; in marine areas where the salinity is very low, usually in sheltered places among seaweeds. **Distribution** Baltic.

Limnaea peregra O. F. Müller **Wandering Pond Snail** Shell up to 2 cm high, but not as wide; spire not sharply pointed and with about 5 quite well-defined whorls. **Colour** pale-midbrown. **Habitat** in fresh water, dwelling in swamps and bogs in many parts of Europe; seldom found in rivers; in marine areas where the salinity is very low, usually in sheltered and exposed areas among stones and seaweeds. **Distribution** Baltic. N.B. this species is very variable in appearance.

Physa fontinalis Linnaeus **Bladder Snail** Shell up to 1.2 cm high, but not as wide; short spire with about 4 quite well-defined whorls; when crawling, 2 mantle lobes show outside the shell, the anterior lobe with 9 finger-like projections and the posterior one with 6; horn-like, transparent and delicate. **Habitat** in fresh water, often associated with water weeds such as *Potamogeton* sp.; more abundant in northern Europe; in marine areas where the salinity is very low. **Distribution** Baltic.

Gadinia garnoti Payraudeau Shell about 0.5 cm high and twice as wide; limpet-like; apex curves towards posterior; solid, marked with rays and concentric spiral lines. **Colour** white-yellow. **Habitat** among rocks on the shore. **Distribution** Mediterranean.

Phytia myosotis Draparnaud (=*Alexia myosotis*) Shell about 0.9 cm high and about half as wide; about 7 whorls; aperture may show 3 ridges on the inner lip and 1 on the outer. **Colour** grey-yellow-brown. **Habitat** in estuaries, salt marshes and under stones on the upper shore. **Distribution** Mediterranean, Atlantic and English Channel.

Leucophytia bidentata (Montagu) Shell about 0.9 cm high and about half as wide; conical spire; about 6 whorls; aperture shows 2 ridges on the inner wall. **Colour** grey-white. **Habitat** in crevices and among seaweed debris on the upper shore and in salt marshes. **Distribution** Atlantic and English Channel.

Otina ovata (Brown) (=*Otina otis*) Shell up to 0.5 cm high and about half as wide; ear-shaped; about 2 whorls; animal and shell slightly resemble a minute ormer when creeping over rocks. **Colour** red-brown-purple. **Habitat** in crevices and old barnacle shells on the upper shore. **Distribution** Atlantic and English Channel.

Class Scaphopoda

Bilaterally symmetrical molluscs. The three-lobed foot is somewhat reduced and projects from the wider end. It is used for burrowing. The shell is tubular and tapering.

Dentalium entalis Linnaeus **Tusk Shell** Shell up to 5 cm long. **Colour** yellow-white. **Habitat** sand and mud in deeper water. **Distribution** Atlantic, English Channel and North Sea. N.B. related forms occur in the Mediterranean.

Limnaea peregra

Limnaea stagnalis

Gadinia garnoti

Physa fontinalis

Leucophytia bidentata

Phytia myosotis

Otina ovata

Dentalium entalis

167

Class Bivalvia (= Lamellibranchia or Pelecypoda)

These molluscs are bilaterally symmetrical. The body is compressed laterally and enclosed by a shell of two valves, which are linked dorsally by a ligament and hinge. The head is rudimentary or missing, and tentacles and a radula are lacking. The foot is ventral and without a crawling surface. Bivalves are filter and deposit feeders, with the sexes usually separate, and the larva frequently free-living and planktonic.

Some important features of bivalve shells are shown in fig. 35. The two valves may be massive and strong or fine and delicate. The elastic ligament can be inside the shell, outside it, or both. It forces the valves open, but in life its action is opposed by the contractions of the closing or adductor muscles whose attachment scars can often be seen inside the shell. The hinge prevents the two valves slipping out of alignment with each other, yet allows them to open and close. It may be smooth, crenulate or toothed. Each valve develops from the beak above which lies the convex *umbo* (pleural umbones). The margin or free shell edge may also be smooth, crenulate or toothed, and the outer surface of the valves can be of many textures. Sometimes part of the periostracum (see page 138) persists over it. In many burrowing species the mantle (also discussed on page 138) is extended posteriorly via a gap in the valves as two siphons which enable the animal to draw in fresh sea water bearing food and oxygen, even though it may be buried in sand itself. The foot is often used for burrowing, but sometimes secretes threads (byssus) which are used for sticking the animal to rocks. In the illustrations that follow almost all the bivalves are shown with their anterior ends pointing towards the right-hand side, and their dorsal surfaces uppermost. For a more detailed account of many European bivalves, see Tebble, N. 1966.

Nucula nucleus (Linnaeus) **Common Nut-shell** Shell up to 1.25cm long; valves similar; edge crenulate; hinge with more anterior teeth than posterior teeth; adductor scars equal. **Colour** periostracum brown-green-yellow; dark brown internal ligament. **Habitat** in clay, gravel and sand from shallow water down to about 150m. **Distribution** Mediterranean, Atlantic, English Channel, North Sea and west Baltic. N.B. animal lacks siphons.

Arca noae Linnaeus **Noah's Ark Shell** Shell up to 8cm long; valves similar; edge smooth, apart from crenulate posterior; straight hinge with many small, equal teeth; external ligament; adductor scars equal; dorsal view shows umbones far apart; outer surface ribbed and sometimes covered with short-haired periostracum. **Colour** dark brown with lighter marks; periostracum brownish. **Habitat** attached to rocks and stones by byssus threads, usually offshore. **Distribution** Mediterranean and Atlantic.

Arca tetragona Poli **Cornered Ark Shell** Shell up to 5cm long; similar to *A. noae* but valves more rectangular and finely sculptured; may be encrusted with other organisms. **Colour** periostracum brown; exterior white-yellow; interior white with darker patches. **Habitat** on stones and rocks (to which it is attached by a green byssus) on lower shore and down to about 100m. **Distribution** Mediterranean, Atlantic and English Channel.

Glycymeris glycymeris (Linnaeus) **Dog Cockle** Shell up to 6.5cm long and nearly circular; valves similar; edge crenulate; 2 rows of up to 12 teeth on each hinge; external ligament; umbones separated but not so greatly as in the above shells; outer surface finely sculptured. **Colour** typical brown markings on exterior; interior white or brown. **Habitat** burrowing just below the surface of mud, sand or gravel from shallow water down to about 80m. **Distribution** Mediterranean, Atlantic, English Channel and Baltic.

Glycymeris pilosa (Linnaeus) Shell up to 7cm long; similar to *G. glycymeris* but with hairy periostracum. **Colour** violet. **Habitat** burrowing in sand or mud down to deep water. **Distribution** Mediterranean.

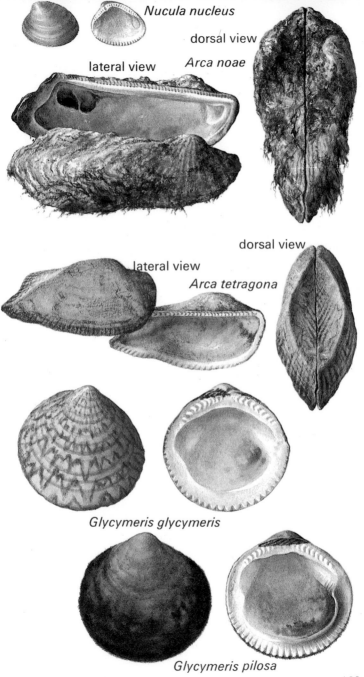

Nucula nucleus

dorsal view

Arca noae

lateral view

dorsal view

lateral view

Arca tetragona

Glycymeris glycymeris

Glycymeris pilosa

Anomia ephippium Linnaeus **Common Saddle Oyster** Shell up to 6cm long; thin, flat, lower (right) shell with aperture; thicker, domed, upper (left) valve; 1 adductor and 2 byssus muscle scars on upper valve, 1 adductor scar on lower; upper valve with scaly outer surface often covered with other organisms. **Colour** white-pale brown. **Habitat** attached to rocks and other shells (to whose shapes it often conforms), from middle shore downward. **Distribution** Mediterranean, Atlantic, English Channel and North Sea. N.B. calcified byssus connects the upper valve to the substrate via the aperture in the lower valve. Animal almost circular in outline.

Mytilus edulis Linnaeus **Common Mussel** Shell varies in length from 1–10cm; typical mussel shape with similar valves; edge smooth; hinge lacks conspicuous teeth but has up to 12 crenulations near the umbones; beaks terminal; ligament external; anterior adductor scar small, posterior scar large. **Colour** exterior brown-blue-black, sometimes with brown markings; periostracum thin and dark brownish; periphery of mantle white-yellowish; interior pearly with dark border. **Habitat** on stones and rocks in estuaries and on rocks on more exposed shores often in extensive beds and associated with barnacles, from middle shore downward. **Distribution** Mediterranean, Atlantic, English Channel, North Sea and Baltic.

Mytilus galloprovincialis Lamarck **Mediterranean Mussel** For a long time this has been regarded as a separate species, but it is probably a race of *M. edulis* which it closely resembles apart from the following differences. **Shell** umbones more pointed and turned down; broader and less angular dorsally. **Colour** periphery of mantle dark. **Habitat** not found in estuaries. **Distribution** Mediterranean and Atlantic north to English Channel.

Modiolus modiolus (Linnaeus) **Horse Mussel** Shell up to 14cm long, but may reach 20cm; valves similar; edge smooth; hinge without teeth; beaks not terminal, but a little way from the anterior; anterior adductor scar small, posterior scar large; mantle margin not frilled; shell thick with horny periostracum which may have spines in young individuals. **Colour** animal usually dark orange; exterior of shell purplish; interior pale. **Habitat** extreme lower shore down to about 150m, often associated with laminarians (see page 33). **Distribution** Atlantic from Biscay northward, English Channel and North Sea.

Modiolus barbatus (Linnaeus) **Bearded Horse Mussel** Shell up to 6cm long, but usually smaller; similar to *M. modiolus* but thick, horny periostracum persists over posterior part and it is arranged in the form of many semicircular rows of serrated whiskers. **Colour** similar to *M. modiolus*. **Habitat** on rocks and shells from the lower shore down to about 100m. **Distribution** Mediterranean, Atlantic, English Channel and North Sea.

Musculus discors (Linnaeus) **Shell** up to 1.25cm long; valves similar; edge smooth except where the ribs meet it; up to about 12 anterior ribs, about three times as many posterior, often smaller; beaks not quite terminal. **Colour** shell paler than preceding species. **Habitat** under rocks and among seaweeds and other invertebrates from the middle shore downward. **Distribution** Mediterranean, Atlantic, English Channel and North Sea.

Brachyodontes minimus (Poli) **Dwarf Mussel** Shell up to 1cm long; valves similar and very thin; edge smooth; hinge with minute teeth; terminal umbones sometimes worn away; horny periostracum. **Colour** exterior dark brown with violet marks; interior pearly. **Habitat** usually in shallow water attached by byssus threads to rocks, etc. **Distribution** Mediterranean and Atlantic.

Lithophaga lithophaga (Linnaeus) **Date Mussel** Shell up to 7cm long; edge smooth; cigar-shaped with fine sculptured lines; hinge without teeth. **Colour** exterior bluish; interior white-blue. **Habitat** boring into limestone and coral skeletons, etc., in shallow water. **Distribution** Mediterranean.

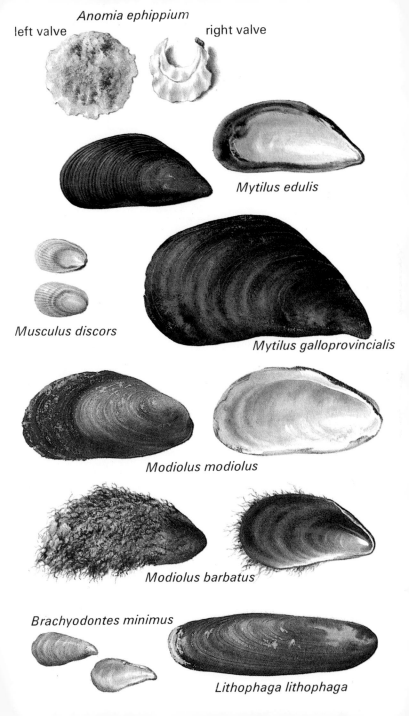

Anomia ephippium

left valve   right valve

Mytilus edulis

Musculus discors

Mytilus galloprovincialis

Modiolus modiolus

Modiolus barbatus

Brachyodontes minimus

Lithophaga lithophaga

Pteria hirundo (Linnaeus) **Wing Oyster** Shell up to 7.5cm long; unusual asymmetrical shape; valves dissimilar; edge smooth; dorsal region drawn out at each end to form 2 ears, posterior ear up to six times longer than the anterior ear. **Colour** periostracum brown; exterior grey-brown; interior pearly white. **Habitat** attached to stones in mud, clay and gravel, sometimes in quite deep water. **Distribution** Mediterranean and Atlantic north to the British Isles. N.B. several related species occur in these regions.

Pinna fragilis Pennant **Fan Mussel** Shell up to 30cm long; fan-shaped; similar valves; edge smooth, though sometimes broken; hinge lacks teeth; external ligament; anterior adductor scar small, posterior scar larger; outer surface has concentric lines and ribs, occasionally with spines. **Colour** exterior brownish; interior brownish and glassy. **Habitat** standing upright in muddy sand and gravel attached to a sunken stone or pebble by byssus threads, often in quite deep water. **Distribution** Atlantic and English Channel.

Pinna nobilis Linnaeus **Fan Mussel** (Not illustrated) Similar to *P. fragilis*. Shell up to 45cm long; outer surface of shell has prominent over-lapping scales. **Colour** exterior red-brown; interior violet-blue-grey. **Habitat** as for *P. fragilis*. **Distribution** Mediterranean and Atlantic.

Pinna rudis Linnaeus **Fan Mussel** (Not illustrated) Similar to *P. fragilis*. Shell up to 25cm long; thin and bears about 8 rows of teeth arranged concentrically at the wider end. **Colour** exterior yellow-brown. **Habitat** as for *P. fragilis* **Distribution** Mediterranean.

Ostrea edulis Linnaeus **Common European Oyster** or **Flat Oyster** Shell up to 10cm long; shape rounded and very variable; valves dissimilar; lower valve (left) saucer-like, prominently sculptured and often attached to rocks and stones; upper (right) flat and sculptured; margin often crenulate; hinge lacks teeth; internal ligament; single adductor scar; periostracum very thin. **Colour** grey-brown. **Habitat** from shallow water down to about 80m where there is a suitable substrate, and in commercial beds. **Distribution** Mediterranean, Atlantic, English Channel and North Sea.

Crassostrea angulata (Lamarck) **Portuguese Oyster** Shell up to 15cm wide and about half as long; sculptured valves dissimilar; lower valve (left) trough-like; upper (right) flattish; edges usually interfold; hinge lacks teeth; internal ligament. **Colour** periostracum dirty brown; exterior dirty white; interior white-purple. **Habitat** in shallow water on rocks and stones and in commercial beds. **Distribution** Atlantic, English Channel and North Sea.

Pecten maximus (Linnaeus) **Great Scallop** or **St James' Shell** Shell up to 15cm long; upper (left) valve flat; conspicuous ribs are rounded in section. **Colour** upper valve red-brown; lower (right) is white-brown with brownish markings. **Habitat** on sand and gravel, usually in quite deep water. **Distribution** Atlantic, English Channel and North Sea. N.B. the illustration shows the interior of the upper valve and the exterior of the lower one.

Pecten jacobaeus Linnaeus **Fan-shell** (Not illustrated) Shell up to 13cm long; typical scallop-shape with conspicuous ribs and ears; upper (left) valve is flat; lower (right) is saucer-like and ribs on shell are not rounded but more square in section. **Colour** upper valve red-brown and occasionally spotted, lower valve pinkish. **Habitat** on sand and gravel, usually in quite deep water. **Distribution** Mediterranean.

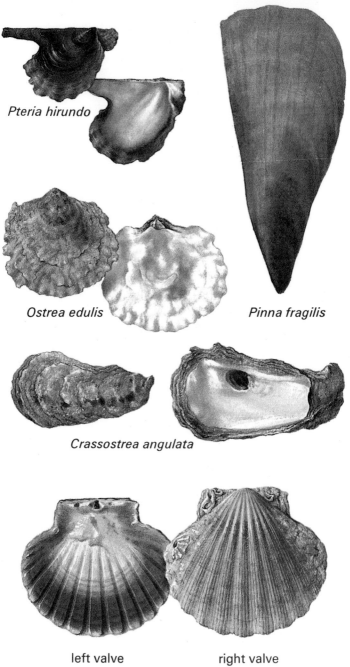

Pteria hirundo

Ostrea edulis

Pinna fragilis

Crassostrea angulata

left valve   right valve
Pecten maximus

Chlamys varia (Linnaeus) **Variegated Scallop** Shell up to 6cm long, slightly wider; oval; both valves convex but not exactly similar; about 28 ribs bearing scale-like teeth which are usually abraded near the umbones and may be rubbed from most of the shell; edge indented by ribs; hinge lacks teeth in adult, hinge length is about half shell width; one adductor scar towards posterior; posterior 'ear' half to one-third length of anterior. **Colour** very variable; purple-red-white-yellow-brown, sometimes patterned. **Habitat** living free or attached by byssus threads to the substrate, extreme lower shore down to 80m. **Distribution** Mediterranean, Atlantic, English Channel and North Sea.

Chlamys opercularis (Linnaeus) **Queen Scallop** Shell up to 9cm long; rounded; similar to *C. varia* but lower (right) valve less convex than upper (left); about 20 ribs; anterior ear slightly longer than posterior one. **Colour** very variable as in *C. varia*; sometimes spotted or striped. **Habitat** attached to substrate by byssus threads when young, usually on gravel and sand, occasionally on extreme lower shore and down to about 200m. **Distribution** Mediterranean, Atlantic, English Channel and North Sea. N.B. this scallop can swim very actively by flapping its shells.

Chlamys tigerina (O. F. Müller) **Tiger Scallop** Shell up to 2.5cm long; rounded; valves almost similar, lower (right) fractionally less convex than upper (left); sometimes smooth, sometimes with many fine ribs and sometimes with a few prominent ones; posterior ear very much smaller than anterior one. **Colour** brown-yellow-white, being variable and sometimes patterned. **Habitat** on sand, gravel and stones from extreme lower shore down to about 100m. **Distribution** Atlantic, English Channel and North Sea.

Chlamys glabra (Linnaeus) **Smooth Scallop** Shell about 5cm long; rounded; valves convex but not exactly equal; about 11 finely lined ribs; ears almost equal. **Colour** variable; brown-red-white with patterns. **Habitat** attached to rocks by byssus threads or living free on sand, usually offshore. **Distribution** Mediterranean.

Spondylus gaederopus Linnaeus **Thorny Oyster** Shell up to 10cm long and rather wider; oval; lower valve convex with variably wide spines; upper valve flatter with sharper spines and many delicate ribs; outer surface of shell often encrusted with other invertebrates. **Colour** exterior brownish or violet; interior pale white. **Habitat** attached to rocks on the seabed. **Distribution** Mediterranean.

Lima lima (Linnaeus) **Spiny Lima** or **File-shell** Shell up to 5cm long and somewhat wider; asymmetrical; valves similar; shell edge indented by ribs; about 20 equal ribs bearing scales which are more conspicuous away from the umbones; hinge without teeth in the adult; ligament internal in a pit; single adductor muscle scar; anterior ear larger. **Colour** white. **Habitat** in crevices and beneath stones in shallow water. **Distribution** Mediterranean.

Lima hians (Gmelin) **Gaping File-shell** Shell up to 2.5cm long; asymmetrical; similar to *L. lima* but with about 50 spiny ribs; when viewed from the front there is a very conspicuous gape between the valves. **Colour** delicate white, becoming dirtier and browner in older specimens. **Habitat** from extreme lower-shore down to about 100m, sometimes in a 'nest' made from stones constructed by using its byssus threads, and among holdfasts of *Laminaria* (see page 33). **Distribution** Mediterranean, Atlantic and English Channel. N.B. very conspicuous, non-retractile, orange-coloured tentacles around the shell edge. This species can swim.

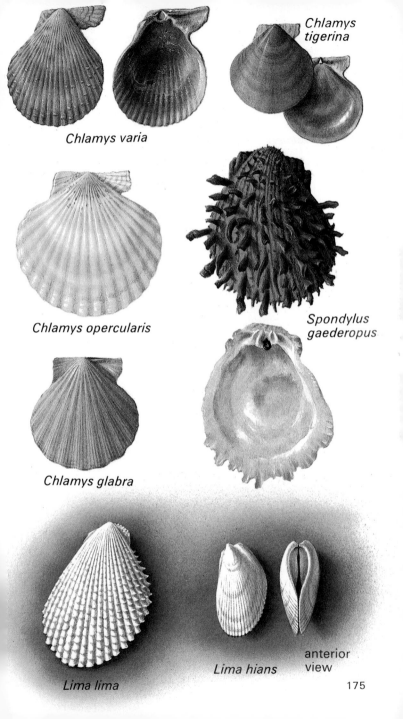

Chlamys varia

Chlamys tigerina

Chlamys opercularis

Spondylus gaederopus

Chlamys glabra

Lima lima

Lima hians

anterior view

175

Astarte borealis (Schumacher) Shell up to 4.5 cm long but not as wide; solid and heavy; valves similar; edge smooth; hinge with apparently 2 cardinal teeth on each valve; beaks slightly anterior of centre; umbones facing forward; external ligament; anterior and posterior adductor scars similar. **Colour** black-brown periostracum covers white, finely and concentrically lined exterior; interior pale brown-white. **Habitat** burrowing in muddy seabeds. **Distribution** Atlantic and North Sea, north of the British Isles. N.B. animal lacks siphons and has a very long foot which may be extended if left undisturbed. Other related species are known in British and Mediterranean waters.

Loripes lucinalis (Lamarck) Shell up to about 2 cm long; rather thin, rounded; valves similar; edge smooth; hinge with 2 small cardinal teeth and 2 minute lateral teeth per valve; umbones roughly central and pointing anteriorly; external ligament; posterior adductor shorter and rounder than anterior; periostracum reduced; outer surface has five concentric lines. **Colour** exterior yellow-white; interior white. **Habitat** burrowing in clay, sand and gravel from extreme lower shore down to about 150 m. **Distribution** Mediterranean, Atlantic, English Channel and North Sea.

Myrtea spinifera (Montagu) Shell up to 2.5 cm long but not as wide; oval; valves similar; edge smooth; left valve with 2 cardinal and 2 lateral teeth (1 on either side), right valve with 1 cardinal tooth and similar lateral ones; beaks slightly anterior of centre; posterior adductor scar smaller than anterior; periostracum reduced; fine lines on outer surface concentrically arranged. **Colour** exterior white-cream; interior white. **Habitat** in silt or muddy gravel on the seabed from about 10 m to 100 m. **Distribution** Mediterranean, Atlantic and English Channel.

Montacuta ferruginosa (Montagu) Shell up to 0.8 cm long but considerably less wide; oval; valves similar; edge smooth. **Colour** thin, reddish periostracum; interior white-purple. **Habitat** a common commensal of *Echinocardium cordatum* (see page 253) which burrows in sand on the lower shore and in shallow water. **Distribution** Mediterranean, Atlantic, English Channel and North Sea.

Arctica islandica (Linnaeus) (*= Cyprina islandica*) Shell up to 12.5 cm long but not as wide; solid, heavy, oval-shaped; valves similar; edge smooth; hinge with 3 cardinal teeth and 1 lateral tooth behind; umbones anterior to middle of shell and pointing forward; external ligament; anterior adductor scar a little smaller than posterior; thick periostracum; outer surface concentrically and finely lined. **Colour** periostracum yellow-red-brown and shiny; interior white. **Habitat** burrowing in sand and mud from extreme lower shore downward. **Distribution** Atlantic, English Channel, North Sea and west Baltic.

Glossus humanus (Linnaeus) (*= Isocardia cor*) **Heart Shell** Shell up to 10 cm long; plump, solid; circular in outline and easy to identify because of the spirally coiled umbones which incline anteriorly and away from the hinge; valves equal; external ligament. **Colour** dark brown periostracum. **Habitat** in sand and mud on the seabed from about 10 m downward. **Distribution** Mediterranean and Atlantic.

Cardita trapezia (Linnaeus) Shell up to 0.6 cm long; trapezium-shaped; valves similar; edge smooth, not indented by the ribs; hinge with 2 cardinal teeth on left valve, 1 on right valve; umbones anterior to middle; outer surface with about 12 ribs. **Colour** exterior white-brown; interior white. **Habitat** on seabed attached to rocks. **Distribution** Mediterranean.

Chama gryphoides Linnaeus **Mediterranean Jewel-box** Shell up to 4 cm long; valves dissimilar; left valve cup-like, and attached to substrate; right valve acts as lid and is free; growth lines show as layers of shell. **Colour** exterior white; interior brown-violet. **Habitat** attached to rocks from shallow water downward. **Distribution** Mediterranean.

Astarte borealis

Loripes lucinalis

Glossus humanus

Myrtea spinifera

Montacuta ferruginosa

Arctica islandica

Cardita trapezia

Chama gryphoides

Acanthocardia aculeata (Linnaeus) **Spiny Cockle** or **Red Nose** Shell up to 10cm long; plump; valves similar; edge strongly toothed corresponding to conspicuous furrows on inside and outside of shell; hinge with 2 cardinal teeth in each valve; 1 posterior and 1 anterior lateral tooth in left valve, anterior cardinal tooth of this valve bigger than posterior tooth; right valve with 1 posterior and 2 anterior lateral teeth; umbones forward from the middle of the shell; external ligament; 2 adductor muscle scars; about 22 ribs on each valve, each rib bearing a line of spines; spines more developed posteriorly and ventrally, anteriorly they are blunter and bend towards the posterior; outer shell with fine concentric markings. **Colour** exterior yellow-white; interior white. **Habitat** in sand, from about 10m downward. **Distribution** Mediterranean, Atlantic, English Channel and North Sea.

Acanthocardia echinata (Linnaeus) **Prickly Cockle** Shell up to 7.5cm long; similar to *A. aculeata* but in the left valve the cardinal teeth are similar in size; rib spines of outer shell have bases which are broad and usually anastomose with those of their neighbours. **Colour, Habitat** and **Distribution** as for *A. aculeata*.

Parvicardium papillosum (Poli) Shell up to 1.25cm long; rounded; valves similar; edge deeply crenulated; hinge, teeth and adductor scars much as for *A. aculeata*; beaks just anterior of centre; external ligament; about 25 tuberculated ribs on each valve. **Colour** periostracum pale brown; exterior white-grey-yellow, often with red-brown patterns; interior white-pink, smooth not grooved. **Habitat** soft substrates. **Distribution** Mediterranean and Atlantic.

Parvicardium exiguum (Gmelin) **Little Cockle** Shell up to 1.25cm long; less rounded than *P. papillosum*, but edge and hinge are alike; beaks well forward; periostracum thicker; about 21 ribs which show tubercles only anteriorly and ventrally when adult. **Colour** periostracum brown; exterior brown; interior of shell white-green and smooth. **Habitat** extreme lower shore down to about 60m on sand and mud, sometimes in estuaries and brackish water. **Distribution** Mediterranean, Atlantic, English Channel and North Sea.

Cerastoderma edule (Linnaeus) (=*Cardium edule*) **Common Cockle** Shell up to 5cm long; oval; valves similar; edge crenulate all round, corresponding to grooves which run for a short way inside the shell; external ligament which is as long as about one-third of the shell height; umbones slightly anterior to middle; right valve has 2 cardinal teeth, and 2 anterior and 2 posterior lateral teeth; periostracum reduced. **Colour** exterior brown; interior white with brown marks. **Habitat** on lower shore downward burrowing in mud, sand or gravel, in estuaries and in commercial beds; tolerates salinities between 34‰ and 20‰. **Distribution** Mediterranean, Atlantic, English Channel and North Sea.

Cerastoderma glaucum (Poiret) (=*Cardium glaucum = Cardium lamarcki*) **Lagoon Cockle** Shell usually 3–5cm long; more triangular in outline than *C. edule*; valves similar; edge crenulate anteriorly, smooth posteriorly and with interior grooves which run nearly to the umbones (i.e. much further in than for *C. edule*); length of external ligament about a quarter of shell height (i.e. relatively shorter than in *C. edule*); umbones slightly anterior of middle; periostracum well developed. **Colour** exterior pale brown-grey; interior dark-light brown. **Habitat** usually in brackish water and lagoons and permanently submerged; burrows in soft sand and mud; will tolerate salinities down to 4‰. Distribution Mediterranean, Atlantic, English Channel, North Sea and Baltic to the Gulf of Finland.

Cerastoderma hauniense Petersen & Russell Shell 0.8–2cm long; similar to *C. glaucum* but with 1 anterior lateral tooth on right valve (*C. glaucum* has 2). **Habitat** normally not burrowing, usually attached to seaweeds by byssus threads. **Distribution** Baltic north to Stockholm skärgård.

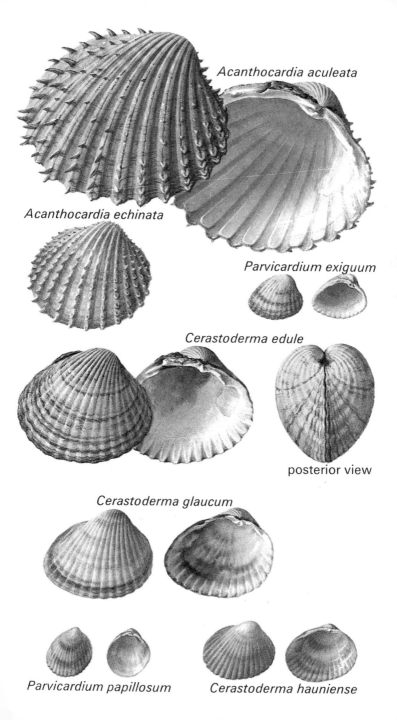

Acanthocardia aculeata

Acanthocardia echinata

Parvicardium exiguum

Cerastoderma edule

posterior view

Cerastoderma glaucum

Parvicardium papillosum

Cerastoderma hauniense

Dosinia lupinus (Linnaeus) Shell up to 3.75cm long; rounded; valves similar; edge smooth; hinge with 3 cardinal teeth on both valves, the left valve bearing an extra small tooth anteriorly; umbones anterior to middle; beaks pointing forward and bordering on a heart-shaped depression called the *lunule* (seen in the illustration of the anterior end); external ligament; adductor scars roughly equal; fine concentric lines on outer surface of valves. Siphons lack horny coating, can reach up to three times shell length and are united apart from the tip. Colour periostracum yellowish; interior white. Habitat burrowing in sand and shell gravel from extreme lower shore down to about 125m. Distribution Mediterranean, Atlantic, English Channel and North Sea.

Venus verrucosa Linnaeus **Warty Venus** Shell up to 6.25cm long; heavy, rounded; valves similar; inside edge crenulate except posteriorly, and sometimes toothed outside; hinge with 3 cardinal teeth on both valves; umbones forward from centre; beaks bordering lunule (see above); external ligament; adductor scars similar; brown periostracum may be present; outer surface of shell strongly marked with concentric ridges which break up into tubercles towards the posterior. Siphons lack horny coating and are united apart from the tip. Colour exterior yellow-white-grey with brown markings; interior white. Habitat just burrowing in sand or gravel from extreme lower shore down to about 100m. Distribution Mediterranean, Atlantic and English Channel.

Venus ovata Pennant **Oval Venus** Shell up to 2cm long; triangular, rounded; valves similar; edge crenulate apart from opposite the extreme ligament which is rather hidden; hinge with 3 cardinal teeth on both valves, no lateral teeth; umbones anterior and beaks pointing forward to border the lunule (see *Dosinia lupinus*, above); adductor scars about equal; up to 50 ribs run up the shell and are intersected by concentric lines. Siphons united. Colour exterior white-pale brown; interior white-orange-purple. Habitat just burrowing in sand or gravel between 3–180m. Distribution Mediterranean, English Channel and North Sea.

Venus fasciata (da Costa) **Banded Venus** Shell about 2.5cm long; valves similar; edge smooth apart from posterior part; hinge with 3 cardinal teeth on both valves; umbones, beaks, lunule and adductor scars all similar to *V. verrucosa*; external ligament; exterior with a few pronounced, heavy, concentric ridges, between which are many finer lines. Siphons united. Colour exterior white, yellow or pink with darker rays; interior white-purple. Habitat just burrowing in sand or gravel from 3–100m. Distribution Mediterranean, Atlantic, English Channel and North Sea.

Venus striatula (da Costa) **Striped Venus** Shell up to 4.5cm long; triangular, rounded; similar to *V. fasciata* but without the broad, heavy, concentric ridges, and with many finer ridges which are closer together ventrally; posterior of shell more elongated. Siphons united. Colour exterior dirty white, cream or yellow with brown marks. Habitat burrowing in sand from lower shore down to about 55m. Distribution Mediterranean, Atlantic, English Channel and North Sea.

Venerupis rhomboides (Pennant) **Banded Carpet Shell** Shell up to 6cm long; more oval than in *Venus*; valves similar; edge smooth; umbones and beaks well forward; no lunule; external ligament; outer shell with many concentric, but no radiating, lines. Colour pigment arranged in 4 radiating areas; exterior pink-brown with red-brown marks; interior shiny white. Habitat burrowing in sand and gravel from extreme lower shore down to about 180m. Distribution Mediterranean, Atlantic, English Channel and North Sea.

Venerupis pullastra (Montagu) **Pullet Carpet Shell** Shell up to 5cm long; similar shape to *V. rhomboides*; outer shell with concentric lines crossed by fine, radiating lines which are more developed posteriorly. Colour exterior cream-grey with patterns; interior shiny white, sometimes with purple marks. Habitat and Distribution similar to *V. rhomboides*.

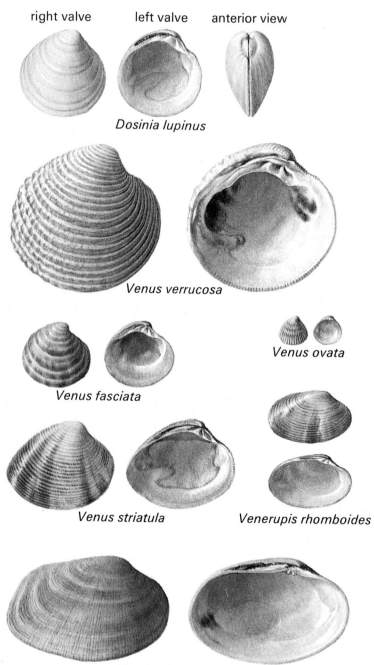

right valve   left valve   anterior view

Dosinia lupinus

Venus verrucosa

Venus ovata

Venus fasciata

Venus striatula   *Venerupis rhomboides*

Venerupis pullastra

181

Notirus irus (Linnaeus) **(=*Irus irus*)** Shell up to 2.5cm long; valves similar and longer than their width; edge smooth; umbones well forward; no lunule; inset external ligament; thin periostracum; outer shell surface bears about 15 concentric ridges with finer radiating markings showing between. **Colour** exterior dirty white; interior white-yellow. **Habitat** in holes and crevices of rock and among the holdfasts of *Laminaria* (see page 33), on extreme lower shore and in shallow water. **Distribution** Mediterranean, Atlantic north to south-west Ireland and west English Channel.

Petricola lithophaga Retzius Shell up to 3cm long; valves similar and longer than their width; outer edge marked by the limits of the conspicuous radiating ribs, inner margin smooth; hinge with 2 cardinal teeth on each valve; umbones well forward; ribs of shell better developed at the front and intersected by fine concentric markings. **Colour** grey-white. **Habitat** boring in soft rock and mud in shallow water. **Distribution** Mediterranean.

Mactra corallina (Linnaeus) **Rayed Trough Shell** Shell up to 5cm long; quite light, triangular; valves similar; edge smooth; hinge complex; umbones almost central; thin external ligament behind umbones, internal ligament as a triangular structure slightly posterior and ventral to the beaks; 2 adductor scars almost equal; fine periostracum; outer shell marked with fine concentric lines. **Siphons** short and enclosed in a horny sheath. **Foot** white and pointed. **Colour** brownish rays run from umbones to shell edge; periostracum brown-green; interior purple-white. **Habitat** burrowing in sand and gravel, from extreme lower shore down to about 100m. **Distribution** Mediterranean, Atlantic, English Channel and North Sea.

Spisula solida (Linnaeus) **Thick Trough Shell** Similar to *M. corallina*. Shell up to 4.5cm long; more solid; under a hand lens the cardinal teeth can be seen to be finely milled or ridged whereas those of *M. corallina* are smooth. **Colour** periostracum light brown; exterior yellow-white with concentric lines and grooves. **Habitat** similar to *M. corallina*. **Distribution** Atlantic, English Channel and North Sea.

Spisula elliptica (Brown) **Elliptical Trough Shell** (Not illustrated) Shell up to 4.5cm long; similar to *S. solida* but lighter and less wide in relation to its length; elliptical; surface almost smooth. **Habitat** burrowing in sand on lower shore and in shallow water. **Distribution** Atlantic north from southern Britain, English Channel and North Sea.

Lutraria lutraria (Linnaeus) **Common Otter Shell** Shell up to 12.5cm long; oval; valves equal and nearly twice as long as they are wide, and not meeting at either end; edge smooth; hinge complex with 2 cardinal teeth on the left valve forming a conspicuous projection like an inverted v which fits into a similar-shaped socket on the right valve; external and internal ligaments; siphons may extend to more than twice shell length. **Colour** periostracum brown-green; exterior marked with concentric lines; covered by a transparent sheath which may have brownish markings; interior white. **Habitat** burrowing in mud, sand and gravel from the extreme lower shore down to about 100m. **Distribution** Mediterranean, Atlantic, English Channel and North Sea. N.B. do not confuse this shell with *Mya* (see page 187), where the form of the teeth is different.

Donax vittatus (da Costa) **Banded Wedge Shell** Shell up to 3.75cm long and half as wide; valves equal; shell edge strongly toothed; umbones placed well back; external ligament; shining, polished periostracum; very fine lines radiate from the umbones. **Siphons** 2; short. **Colour** exterior white-yellow-brown-purple, pigment of outer shell concentrated into bands; interior white-yellow. **Habitat** burrowing in sand from middle shore down to about 20m. **Distribution** Mediterranean, Atlantic, English Channel and North Sea.

Notirus irus

Petricola lithophaga

Mactra corallina

Spisula solida

Donax vittatus

Lutraria lutraria

183

Tellina tenuis da Costa **Thin Tellin** Shell up to 2cm long; delicate, flattened, valves almost equal; edge smooth; beaks and umbones slightly posterior; 2 cardinal teeth on each valve, lateral teeth clearly seen on right valve; external ligament; posterior adductor muscle scar shorter than anterior and a little thicker; shiny periostracum; outer surface with very fine concentric lines. **Siphons** 2; not united, and may be several times as long as the shell. **Colour** variable; exterior yellow-orange-pink-white with pigment often banded; similar colours inside. **Habitat** burrowing in sand from the middle shore down to shallow water. **Distribution** Mediterranean, Atlantic, English Channel, North Sea and Baltic. N.B. owing to the strength of the ligament the 2 valves often remain connected long after the death of the animal, as illustrated. May be present in great numbers.

Tellina fabula (Gmelin) Shell up to 2cm long; similar to *T. tenuis* but more pointed posteriorly; fine concentric lines and, on the right valve only, very fine diagonal lines and grooves run from left ventral to right dorsal (a hand lens will help here). **Colour** exterior white-yellow-orange; interior usually white. **Habitat** burrowing in sand from extreme lower shore down to about 55m, so that its local distribution hardly overlaps *T. tenuis*. **Distribution** Mediterranean, Atlantic, English Channel, North Sea and Baltic.

Tellina crassa Pennant **Blunt Tellin** Shell up to 6.25cm long; oval; larger, heavier and plumper than either *T. tenuis* or *T. fabula*; valves almost equal, left not as convex as right; edge smooth; hinge with 2 cardinal teeth and 1 anterior lateral tooth and 1 posterior lateral tooth on each valve; umbones posterior from centre; external ligament; narrow lunule; posterior adductor scar shorter and thicker than anterior; outer serface with conspicuous concentric lines. **Colour** periostracum ochre; interior red-yellow with white margin. **Habitat** burrowing in mud, sand and gravel from 1–150m. **Distribution** Atlantic, English Channel and North Sea.

Tellina distorta (Poli) Similar to *T. tenuis*. Shell up to 2cm long; beaks in posterior half. **Colour** white-grey with pink stripes. **Habitat** on soft substrates. **Distribution** Mediterranean.

Gastrana fragilis (Linnaeus) Shell up to 4.5cm long; valves similar; edge smooth; 2 cardinal teeth on both valves, lateral teeth lacking; umbones anterior of mid-line; posterior of shell extended and more pointed than anterior; conspicuous external ligament; posterior adductor scar thicker than anterior; outer shell with irregular concentric lines. **Colour** white to grey-yellow; periostracum pale brown. **Habitat** burrowing in mud, clay and sand in shallow water, sometimes in estuaries. **Distribution** Mediterranean and Atlantic north to Norway.

Macoma balthica (Linnaeus) **Baltic Tellin** Shell up to 2.5cm long; similar to *T. tenuis* but plumper and heavier; valves almost similar; edge smooth; hinge with 2 small cardinal teeth but lacking lateral ones; umbones about central; external ligament; posterior adductor scar thicker than anterior one; outer shell with fine concentric lines. **Colour** variable; exterior white-pink-purple and banded; interior pink-purple; periostracum often colourless. **Habitat** burrowing in mud and sand in shallow brackish water, e.g. estuaries. **Distribution** Atlantic north from Spain, English Channel, North Sea and Baltic.

Scrobicularia plana (da Costa) **Peppery Furrow Shell** Shell up to 6.25cm long; light, oval and flattened; valves similar; hinge with 2 cardinal teeth on left valve and 1 on right; posterior adductor scar shorter than anterior; periostracum on periphery of valves; outer surface with concentric lines. **Siphons** very long. **Colour** periostracum brown; exterior grey-pale yellow; interior white. **Habitat** burrowing in mud and sand between the tidemarks, often in salinities lower than *Macoma balthica*. **Distribution** Mediterranean, Atlantic, English Channel, North Sea and Baltic.

Tellina tenuis

Tellina fabula

Tellina crassa

Tellina distorta

Gastrana fragilis

Macoma balthica

Scrobicularia plana

185

Gari depressa (Pennant) **Large Sunset Shell** Shell up to 6.25cm long; oval; valves almost equal; conspicuous posterior gape between valves; edge smooth; 2 diverging cardinal teeth on right valve, 1 diverging tooth and 1 simple cardinal tooth on left valve, no lateral teeth; umbones slightly forward; external ligament; stout periostracum; outer shell has rayed markings and with fine concentric lines and ridges. **Siphons** 2; relatively short and separate. **Colour** exterior pink; interior white-purple; periostracum green-brown. **Habitat** burrowing in sand from extreme lower shore down to about 50m. **Distribution** Mediterranean, Atlantic, English Channel and North Sea.

Solenocurtus strigillatus (Linnaeus) **(=*Solecurtus strigillatus*)** Shell up to 8cm long; oblong with rounded ends; valves equal; 1 cardinal tooth on left valve and 2 on right; beaks and umbones slightly forward of mid-line; external ligaments. **Colour** exterior pinkish with 2 conspicuous paler rays; yellow-green periostracum. **Habitat** burrowing in sand and sandy gravel in shallow water. **Distribution** Mediterranean.

Pharus legumen (Linnaeus) Shell up to 12.5cm long; long and narrow; valves similar; long edges (dorsal and ventral) not parallel; beaks and umbones reduced and a little forward from the mid-line in front of conspicuous, black external ligament. **Colour** exterior whitish with fine concentric lines; yellow-green-brown periostracum. **Habitat** burrowing in sand on extreme lower shore and in shallow water. **Distribution** Mediterranean and Atlantic north to southwest Britain and Ireland.

Ensis ensis (Linnaeus) Shell up to 12.5cm long; long, narrow and curved; valves similar; beaks and umbones reduced and positioned at anterior; shell tapers towards posterior; dark external ligament. **Siphons** short and united, except at the tip. **Colour** exterior whitish with red and brown patterns; yellow-green periostracum. **Habitat** burrowing in sand on extreme lower shore and in shallow water. **Distribution** Mediterranean, Atlantic, English Channel and North Sea.

Ensis siliqua (Linnaeus) **Pod Razor Shell** Shell up to 20cm long; long, narrow; valves similar; dorsal and ventral edges almost parallel; beaks and umbones reduced and at the anterior; not tapering posteriorly; dark external ligament. **Siphons** similar to *E. ensis*. **Colour** exterior whitish and finely lined vertically and horizontally, being patterned with red; glossy yellow-green periostracum. **Habitat** burrowing in sand on extreme lower shore and down to about 35m. **Distribution** Mediterranean, Atlantic, English Channel and North Sea.

Solen marginatus Montagu **Grooved Razor Shell** Shell up to 12.5cm long; long, narrow; similar to *E. siliqua*, but with a conspicuous, almost vertical groove or constriction just behind the anterior edge in front of the reduced beaks and umbones. **Colour** exterior pale yellow with fine lines; pale brown periostracum. **Habitat** burrowing in sand on the lower shore and in shallow water. **Distribution** Mediterranean, Atlantic, English Channel and North Sea.

Mya truncata Linnaeus **Blunt Gaper** Shell up to 7.5cm long; solid; left valve not as convex as right and bearing spoon-shaped process which projects towards the right valve and to which the internal ligament is attached; equivalent process in the right valve does not project; external ligament; conspicuous gape at posterior of shell as shown. **Colour** dirty white-cream. **Habitat** burrowing in mud and sand from middle shore down to 70m. **Distribution** Atlantic, English Channel and North Sea.

Mya arenaria Linnaeus **Sand Gaper** Shell up to 15cm long; more oval than *M. truncata* but has a similar arrangement of valves and hinge processes. **Colour** exterior dirty white-white; interior brown. **Habitat** burrowing in mud and sand from the lower shore down to 70m, and in estuaries. **Distribution** Atlantic, English Channel, North Sea and Baltic.

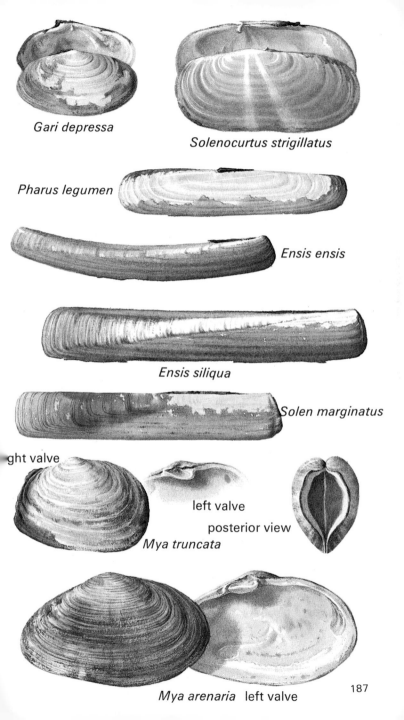

Gari depressa

Solenocurtus strigillatus

Pharus legumen

Ensis ensis

Ensis siliqua

Solen marginatus

ght valve

left valve

posterior view

Mya truncata

Mya arenaria left valve

187

Hiatella arctica (Linnaeus) Shell up to 3.75cm long; irregularly shaped (frequently individuals are different shapes); edge smooth; hinge teeth usually worn away in adults; beaks and umbones well forward; external ligament; round anterior adductor scar slightly smaller than posterior one; shell with uneven concentric lines. **Colour** exterior white-yellow; interior white; yellow-brown periostracum. **Habitat** boring into soft rock or occupying holes already there, being anchored by byssus threads, on lower shore and in shallow water. **Distribution** Mediterranean, Atlantic, English Channel and North Sea.

Gastrochaena dubia (Pennant) **Flask Shell** Shell up to 2.5cm long; smooth; valves similar; hinge lacks teeth; beaks and umbones well forward; external ligament; posterior scar longer than anterior; conspicuous ventral gape at front (as illustrated). **Siphons** united. **Colour** exterior white-pale brown; interior white. **Habitat** boring into soft rocks or firm sand on the extreme lower shore and in shallow water; a characteristic flask-like cavity is formed which is lined with particles of shell and secretion from the animal. **Distribution** Mediterranean, Atlantic north to south-west Britain and Ireland.

Pholas dactylus Linnaeus **Common Piddock** Shell up to 15cm long; light; valves similar; edge smooth except anteriorly where it may be crenulate; umbones forward and reflected back on the shell; 4 accessory shell plates are situated dorsally; wide anterior ventral gape (as illustrated); periostracum covers the sculptured outer shell which bears concentric and radiating ribs which are roughest in front where they assist with drilling; interior of shell with 2 free teeth or apophyses (1 per valve); long, united siphons covered by horny sheath. **Colour** pale yellow periostracum; exterior white-grey; interior white. **Habitat** boring into soft rock, wood, firm sand or peat on lower shore and in shallow water. **Distribution** Mediterranean, Atlantic north to south-west Britain and Ireland and English Channel.

Zirfaea crispata (Linnaeus) **Oval Piddock** Shorter and stubbier than *Pholas dactylas*. Shell up to 9cm long; valves similar; edge smooth apart from anterior; valves hardly meet, apart from the forward umbones, and at one point ventrally; outer shell with concentric ridges, rougher at front; inner shell with 1 strong tooth or hypophysis per valve. **Siphons** long and united; covered in horny sheath. **Colour** interior white; brown periostracum. **Habitat** boring in clay and soft rock on lower shore and in shallow water. **Distribution** Atlantic north from Biscay, English Channel and North Sea.

Teredo navalis Linnaeus **Ship Worm** Shell reduced; each valve has an inner tooth or hypophysis, shell functions as a drill and encloses only part of the worm-like animal; mantle secretes a hard, chalky tube up to 20cm long which follows the course of the animal as it bores through wood; a pair of special, hard pallets can close off the open end of the tube when the siphons have been withdrawn; the pallets are up to 0.5cm long. **Colour** white. **Habitat** boring in submerged wooden structures such as pilings and boats. **Distribution** Mediterranean, Atlantic, English Channel, North Sea and west Baltic. N.B. several related species occur in the region.

Thracia papyracea (Poli) **Paper Thracia** Shell up to 3.5cm long; fragile; left valve smaller than right; beaks and umbones back from mid-line; hinge lacks teeth; internal ligament and external ligament; outer shell surface with concentric lines. **Colour** white. **Habitat** on sand from the extreme lower shore downward. **Distribution** Mediterranean, Atlantic, English Channel and North Sea.

Pandora albida (Röding) **Pandora Shell** Shell up to 3.75cm long; asymmetrical valves not equal; left valve trough-like, right valve flat; beaks and umbones well forward; internal ligament; adductor scars about equal. **Colour** exterior white with fine concentric lines; pale brownish periostracum. **Habitat** on sand and mud usually in shallow water. **Distribution** Atlantic, English Channel and North Sea.

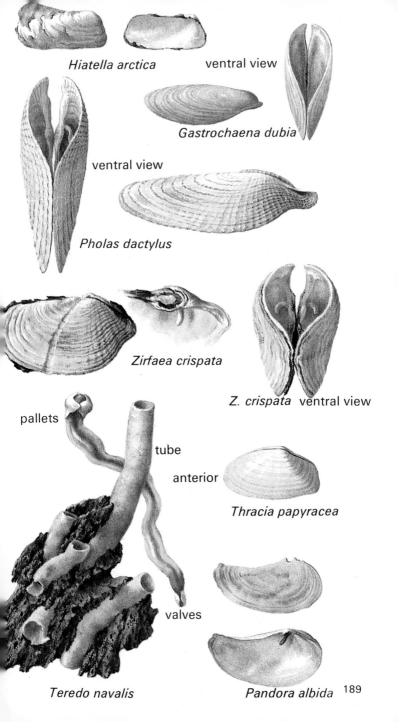

Hiatella arctica

ventral view

Gastrochaena dubia

ventral view

Pholas dactylus

Zirfaea crispata

Z. crispata ventral view

pallets

tube

anterior

Thracia papyracea

valves

Teredo navalis

Pandora albida 189

Class **Cephalopoda** Cuttlefishes, squids and octopuses

Uncoiled, cylinder- or sac-shaped molluscs. The foot is divided into a number of suckered tentacles surrounding the mouth and joining the head. The head bears conspicuous eyes and is immediately connected with the abdomen (visceral region). A shell is sometimes present internally, but rarely externally, and is sometimes lacking. The mouth leads to a pair of horny jaws resembling a parrot's beak; the radula is like a tongue. The sexes are separate.

Order **Decapoda** Cuttlefishes and squids

Cephalopods with cylinder-shaped bodies bearing lateral fins. There is an internal shell or cuttlebone. The mouth is surrounded by 10 tentacles of which 2 are usually much longer than the remaining 8, and may be extended or retracted.

Sepia officinalis (Linnaeus) **Common Cuttlefish** Length up to 30 cm. **Body** relatively broad and somewhat flattened so as to be oval in cross-section; conspicuous funnel on the underside near the head; paired fins run from behind the head to the tip of the body. **Colour** very variable; may be black-brown striped or mottled above, paler to white below, but individuals are capable of rapid colour change, especially when threatened; the animal may also take the colour or patterning of its background. **Habitat** over sand and in bays and estuaries, sometimes among eel-grass (*Zostera* sp. see page 65). **Distribution** Mediterranean, Atlantic, English Channel and North Sea. N.B. the cuttlebone is often washed ashore.

Sepia elegans d'Orbigny (Not illustrated) **Length** up to 12 cm. **Body** similar to *S. officinalis* but not so broad. **Colour** red-brown above. **Habitat** as for *S. officinalis*. **Distribution** Mediterranean and Atlantic.

Sepiola atlantica d'Orbigny **Length** up to 5 cm. **Body** relatively short and cup-shaped, and bearing a pair of flap-like fins which do not run along its entire length. **Colour** very variable; black-brown to pale above, usually pale below. **Habitat** swimming over or burrowing in sand in shallow water. **Distribution** Atlantic and English Channel.

Loligo vulgaris Lamarck **Long-finned Squid** Length up to 50 cm. **Body** torpedo-shaped, with paired fins running about half way along, and joining together at the tip; viewed from above these fins have a diamond-shaped appearance; a small, shield-like part of body projects slightly over the head; shell horny and somewhat pen-like. **Colour** variable; often pink-white with purple-brown mottling above. **Habitat** seldom found close to the shore. **Distribution** Mediterranean, Atlantic, English Channel and occasionally in the North Sea and west Baltic.

Loligo forbesi Seenstrup **Common Squid** (Not illustrated) **Length** up to 60 cm. **Body** similar to *L. vulgaris*. **Colour** variable, but pink, red and brown predominate. **Habitat** seldom found close to the shore. **Distribution** Atlantic, English Channel, North Sea and occasionally in the west Baltic.

Alloteuthis subulata (Lamarck) **Length** up to 15 cm. **Body** similar to *Loligo*, but much smaller; paired narrow fins do not give a diamond-shaped appearance when viewed from above but are more lance-shaped; small, shield-like part of body projects a little over the head. **Colour** pale grey with brown-purple spots. **Habitat** seldom found close to the shore. **Distribution** Atlantic, English Channel and North Sea.

Ommastrephes sagittatus Lamarck **Sagittal Squid** Length up to 60 cm. **Body** torpedo-shaped, bearing paired fins running about one-third of the way along and joining at the tip; no small shield-like part of the body projecting over part of the head; the 2 long tentacles are not retractile and can

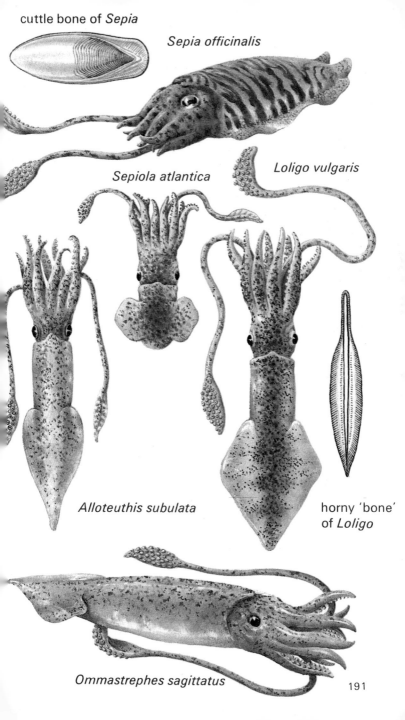

cuttle bone of *Sepia*

Sepia officinalis

Sepiola atlantica

Loligo vulgaris

Alloteuthis subulata

horny 'bone' of *Loligo*

Ommastrephes sagittatus

191

always be seen. **Habitat** often found in surface waters at night. **Distribution** Mediterranean, Atlantic, rarely in North Sea and west Baltic.

Order Octopoda Octopuses and their allies

Cephalopods with bag-like bodies and no internal shell. An external shell is rarely present. There are no fins, although the 8 arms which carry suckers may be linked at their base by a web of skin.

Argonauta argo Linnaeus **Paper Nautilus** Length adult females up to about 20cm; adult males up to 1cm. **Body** female largely encased in a white, very thin, paper-like shell; 2 of the 8 arms are specialized for holding the shell so they fold back over the body and are usually appressed to the shell; male body dwarf, lacking a shell. **Colour** highly variable; can change quickly according to situation, as can the form of patterning; ranges from silver-white-green-grey-red-blue with and without spots. **Habitat** may creep on the bottom, but often found swimming. **Distribution** Mediterranean and Atlantic.

Octopus vulgaris Lamarck **Common Octopus** Length up to 100cm overall but often no more than 60cm. **Body** strong arms bear 2 rows of suckers; upper side of body often covered in warts. **Colour** variable; grey-yellow-brown-green according to situation. **Habitat** among rocks and stones and often in a lair where stones have been arranged for camouflage and protection. **Distribution** Mediterranean, Atlantic north to English Channel.

Eledone cirrhosa (Lamarck) **Lesser Octopus** Length up to 50cm. **Body** arms bear 1 row of suckers; may be smooth or warty. **Colour** predominently red-brown above and white below. **Habitat** among rocks and stones, occasionally at extreme lower shore. **Distribution** Atlantic, English Channel and northern North Sea.

Eledone moschata Lamarck **(=*Ozaena moschata*)** (Not illustrated) **Length** up to 40cm overall. **Body** very similar to *E. cirrosa*. **Colour** yellow-grey with darker spots. **Habitat** among stones and rocks. **Distribution** Mediterranean.

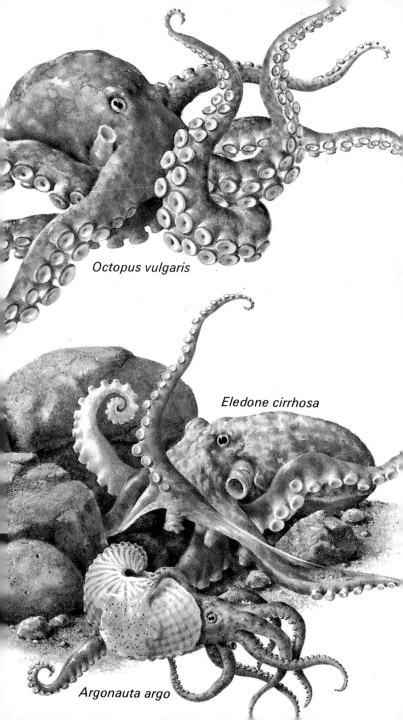

Octopus vulgaris

Eledone cirrhosa

Argonauta argo

Phylum Arthropoda

These are bilaterally symmetrical, segmented animals whose bodies are composed of three cell layers; the reduced body cavity forms a true coelom, and a large blood space may be present. Paired appendages are borne on at least some segments, and one pair functions as jaws. The exoskeleton is composed of chitin and other materials, being hard and jointed. A well-developed nervous system is present, but true nephridia are lacking. Sexes are usually separate.

This very important phylum is the largest in the animal kingdom. Its members owe their success to the combined effects of their exoskeleton, and to their particular style of metabolic processes. These factors permit ease of locomotion (including flight in insects) and maintain the correct balance of water and salts in the body even in quite hostile environments. The phylum is divided into a number of classes which together have invaded almost every type of environment on earth. Some of these classes (for instance the insects, the centipedes and the pseudoscorpions), are almost wholly terrestrial and so lie largely outside the scope of this book.

The major class of marine arthropods is the Crustacea, and it is very well represented in most marine habitats. A much smaller, but nevertheless interesting group, is the class Pycnogonida (sea-spiders). Pycnogonids are not closely related to the true land spiders, despite their name. Members of the class Crustacea have a body divided into three parts — head, thorax and abdomen. The exoskeleton is generally supported by calcium salts and is often heavy. The head bears two pairs of antennae (one pair on each of the second and third segments), and mandibles (jaws) on the fourth segment. Although the group is almost entirely aquatic, there are a few terrestrial exceptions, for instance, the familiar woodlouse. The Crustacea shows a diverse range of body forms and life styles, and is divided up into several subclasses and a number of orders. Some

Fig. 36 Planktonic crustacean larvae

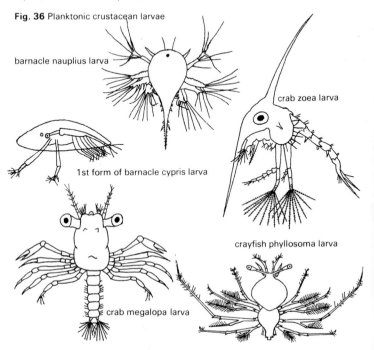

barnacle nauplius larva

crab zoea larva

1st form of barnacle cypris larva

crayfish phyllosoma larva

crab megalopa larva

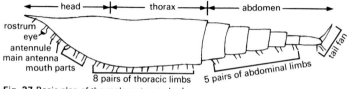

Fig. 37 Basic plan of the malacostracan body

of these comprise of microscopic, planktonic organisms, others are found solely in fresh water. Representatives of two subclasses (Cirripedia and Malacostraca) are commonly met with on the shore and in the shallow sea.

The basic crustacean body plan has been modified in a number of ways. In the Cirripedia (barnacles and their allies) the adults do not closely resemble other crustaceans, and for a long time they were classified elsewhere. Their larval development follows the typical crustacean form, however, and a small, free-swimming organism passes through two typically crustacean stages (nauplius and cypris) before leaving the plankton to settle and metamorphose on suitable rock or shell where it grows into an adult barnacle. Fig. 36 shows a number of different types of crustacean larvae which may be taken from the plankton at particular times of the year. Whilst they are clearly crustaceans, these larvae do not closely resemble the adult form into which they will grow. Crustaceans are found in almost all types of marine environment. The barnacles have evolved to lead a sessile life as adults, with their bodies protected by a number of massive plates of calcium carbonate which form the 'shell'. The type of shell base which attaches them to the rocks may help with identification; it may be calcareous or membranous, and can be seen if a specimen is removed from the rock. Effectively they are attached to the rocks by their head ends, and their thoracic appendages have become modified as filter-feeding organs. These can be projected outside the 'shell' and swept backwards and forwards through the water to collect any appropriate food particles.

The Malacostraca is a large and important subclass. It includes a great variety of organisms whose basic body plan is indicated in fig. 37. Many malacostracan appendages are biramous, i.e. they branch in two. Where this is the case one branch of the limb may have developed to carry out one function – for instance walking – and the other a different function – for instance respiration. This particular situation occurs in the thoracic legs of many malacostracans, where the shorter branch of the limb is modified to form a gill.

Members of the Malacostraca are generally free living and actively seek out their food using their well-developed eyes and chemoreceptors. This is especially true of many members of the order Decapoda such as crabs and lobsters, which often lead a scavenging or predatory life on the seabed. (They are arranged as a suborder Reptantia = creepers.) The prawns and shrimps also belong to this order, but their way of life is different in that they can swim as well as walk. Indeed, some members of this group (arranged as a suborder Natantia = swimmers) live entirely by swimming in the waters of the ocean, and never touch the seabed.

A swimming life is generally the rule for the malacostracan larvae of all groups. After fertilization, the female may carry the developing embryos attached to the outside of her body in a manner that allows her to keep them well aerated. When the larvae emerge from the egg cases they find their way to the surface waters and become members of the plankton where they feed and grow. During this period they may change their form once or more before they are finally ready for metamorphosis, and the juveniles develop to begin life as adults on the seabed or elsewhere.

195

Class Crustacea
Subclass Cirripedia Barnacles

Crustaceans which as adults have a calcified exoskeleton comprised of several chalky plates, forming a shell.

Lepas anatifera (Linnaeus) **Goose Barnacle** Shell about 5cm long with 5 translucent, nearly white plates which have a bluish-grey tinge. **Stalk** 10–20cm long, somewhat retractable, and with a brown-grey skin. **Habitat** pelagic; normally attached to boats and driftwood. **Distribution** Atlantic, English Channel and North Sea.

Lepas fascicularis Ellis & Solander **Buoy-making Barnacle** Shell about 3.5cm long with 5 translucent, brittle, white plates. **Stalk** secretes a spongy white float. **Habitat** pelagic; often washed ashore after south-westerly gales. **Distribution** Atlantic and English Channel.

Scalpellum scalpellum (Linnaeus) Shell about 2cm long with 14 small, hairy, grey-white plates. **Stalk** is covered with small scales. **Habitat** attached to hydroids, bryozoans and worm tubes. **Distribution** Mediterranean, Atlantic, English Channel and North Sea.

Verruca stroemia (O. F. Müller) Sessile. **Shell** asymmetrical, up to 0.5cm in diameter with 4 unequal, ribbed plates which may be grey, white or brown; base membranous if detached. **Habitat** under stones and attached to shells from lower shore down to about 70m. **Distribution** Mediterranean, Atlantic, English Channel and North Sea.

Chthamalus stellatus (Poli) **Star Barnacle** Sessile. **Shell** slightly asymmetrical, up to 1.2cm in diameter with 6 grooved plates arranged as a cone; lateral plates overlap terminal plates so that these appear narrow (in older specimens the fusion of plates may make their delineation difficult); kite-shaped opening; base membranous if detached. **Colour** usually whitish. **Habitat** on rocks on upper and middle shore; range dependent on exposure; always found above *Balanus balanoides* on the shore. **Distribution** Mediterranean, Atlantic and English Channel.

Balanus balanoides (Linnaeus) **Acorn Barnacle** Sessile. **Shell** symmetrical, up to 1.5cm in diameter with 6 plates; shape flat or steeply conical; lateral plates overlap one terminal plate, but are themselves overlapped by the other; 1 terminal plate appears narrow and the other wide; diamond-shaped opening; base membranous if detached. **Colour** usually dirty white. **Habitat** on rocks; in northern areas where *Chthamalus stellatus* is absent, from high water mark for neap tides downward; in southern areas where *C. stellatus* is present, below this species from about middle shore downward. **Distribution** Atlantic, English Channel, North Sea and west Baltic.

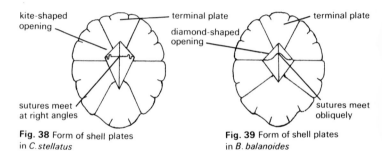

Fig. 38 Form of shell plates in *C. stellatus*

Fig. 39 Form of shell plates in *B. balanoides*

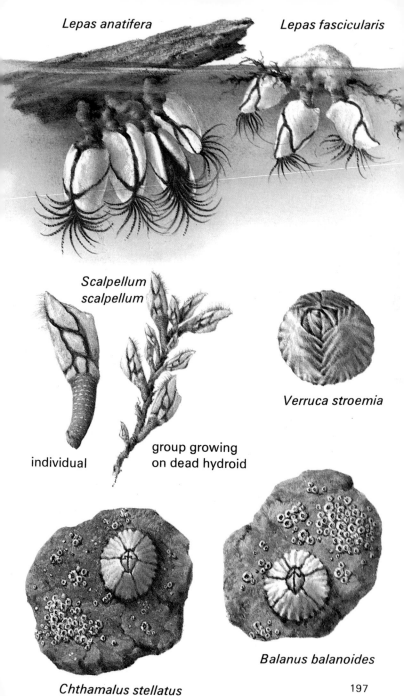

Lepas anatifera

Lepas fascicularis

Scalpellum scalpellum

Verruca stroemia

individual

group growing on dead hydroid

Chthamalus stellatus

Balanus balanoides

197

Balanus crenatus Bruguière Sessile. **Shell** conical, up to 2 cm in diameter and nearly as tall as it is round; body leans over when viewed sideways; 6 white-grey plates; base calcareous if detached; rim of inside movable plates yellow and purple. **Habitat** on the lower shore and in shallow water; not on exposed rock surfaces. **Distribution** Atlantic, English Channel, North Sea and west Baltic.

Balanus balanus (Linnaeus) (Not illustrated) Sessile. **Shell** large, conical, up to 3 cm in diameter with 6 stout, prominently ribbed plates; opening roughly triangular; base calcareous if detached. **Colour** whitish. **Habitat** on lower shore down to deep water on rocks and shells, e.g. *Pecten* (see page 173). **Distribution** Atlantic north from English Channel, North Sea and west Baltic.

Balanus perforatus Bruguière Sessile. **Shell** fairly symmetrical, up to 3 cm in diameter, tall and conical with 6 grey-purple-brown smooth or lined plates, often separated at the apex leaving a jagged lip; opening of shell off centre; base calcareous if detached. **Habitat** lower shore where it is not as numerous as *B. balanoides* and occupies the zone just below it. **Distribution** Mediterranean and Atlantic north to the English Channel.

Balanus improvisus Darwin Similar to *B. crenatus*. Sessile. **Shell** up to 1.5 cm in diameter, symmetrical; rim of inside movable plates white with purple bands; base calcareous if detached. **Habitat** in brackish water such as estuaries and lagoons. **Distribution** Atlantic, English Channel and North Sea regions; it is the only barnacle present in the Baltic Sea proper.

Acasta spongites Darwin Sessile. **Shell** up to 1.2 cm in diameter; easy to identify as it is always partially or totally embedded in a sponge and because its base is not flat, but convex. **Habitat** associated with a sponge (usually *Dysidea fragilis*) on extreme lower shore downward. **Distribution** Mediterranean, Atlantic and English Channel.

Pyrgoma anglicum Sowerby (Illustrated attached to *Caryophyllia smithii* on page 99) **Shell** up to 0.3 cm in diameter; easy to identify because it is always attached to a coral. **Colour** grey-green-brown. **Habitat** as for the coral; usually found on *Caryophyllia smithii*, but occasionally on other genera including *Cladocora*, *Dendrophyllia* and *Balanophyllia*. **Distribution** Mediterranean, Atlantic, and English Channel.

Elminius modestus Darwin Sessile. **Shell** flattened, up to 1 cm in diameter with 4 usually distinct plates in the shell; plates smooth with 2 slight depressions. **Colour** white-grey. **Habitat** attached to rocks on upper middle shore, sometimes near the influence of fresh water. **Distribution** this Australian barnacle first appeared near Southampton in the 1940s and is spreading rapidly in the Atlantic, English Channel and North Sea areas.

Chelonibia testudinaria (Linnaeus) Sessile. **Shell** flat, oval, up to 2.5 cm in diameter with 6 stout, smooth, whitish plates; only the tips of the plates reach the opening and there are pieces of exposed skin between. **Habitat** attached to turtle shells. **Distribution** Mediterranean. N.B. another closely related species *C. patula* occurs on crabs in the same area.

Sacculina carcini Thompson **Parasitic Barnacle** Parsitic and quite unlike the other barnacles; appears as a conspicuous lump covered with pale yellow-brown skin attached under the abdomen of the crab *Carcinus maenas* (see page 227), and sometimes to other species, in such a way as to prevent the abdomen from folding closely under the carapace; readily distinguished from the crab's own eggs which may be brooded in this position by the female, because the egg mass is *granular* in texture and *S. carcini* is smooth. **Habitat** and **Distribution** as for the host.

Balanus crenatus
detail of opening

Balanus perforatus

Balanus improvisus
detail of opening

Acasta spongites
in *Dysidea fragilis*

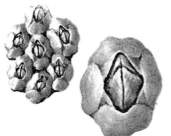

Elminius modestus

Chelonibia testudinaria

Sacculina carcini on the abdomen of
Carcinus maenas

Subclass Malacostraca

Crustaceans with compound eyes, 2 pairs of antennae, and with the head and thorax fused and usually covered by a carapace. The thorax has 8 segments each bearing appendages (first 3 pairs assist with feeding, and the remaining 5 pairs usually develop as legs). The abdomen usually comprises of 6 segments, with appendages variously modified for swimming, reproduction, etc.

Order Nebaliacea

Small malacostracans with stalked eyes separated by a rostral spine. The carapace enfolds all the thoracic and 4 pairs of abdominal appendages.

Nebalia bipes (Fabricius) **Length** up to 1 cm. Uppermost pair of antennae short, lowermost longer. **Habitat** middle and lower shore. **Distribution** Mediterranean, Atlantic, English Channel and North Sea.

Order Stomatopoda

Moderately sized malacostracans possessing a short, shield-shaped carapace. The last joint of the 2nd pair of thoracic legs forms a spiny crusher.

Squilla desmaresti Risso **Length** up to 12 cm. Last joint of 2nd pair of thoracic legs bears 4 conspicuous spines and terminates in a sharp point. **Habitat** in sand and mud from extreme lower shore down to deeper water. **Distribution** Mediterranean, Atlantic and English Channel.

Squilla mantis Fabricius **Mantis shrimp Length** up to 25 cm, often less. Similar to *S. desmaresti*, but with last joint of 2nd pair of thoracic legs bearing 5 spines; tail bears 2 dark spots. **Distribution** Mediterranean.

Order Cumacea

Small malacostracans with bodies compressed sideways. The distinctively shaped carapace covers only part of the thorax.

Pseudocuma longicornis (Bate) **Length** up to 0.5 cm. Anterior part of carapace appears ridged. **Habitat** burrowing in sand or mud on lower shore and in shallow water; sometimes swarming in surface waters. **Distribution** Mediterranean, Atlantic, English Channel and North Sea.

Order Tanaidacea

Small malacostracans with bodies compressed dorso-ventrally. The reduced carapace covers only the first 2 segments of the thorax; 2nd pair of thoracic appendages bears small pincers and these are followed by 6 pairs of similar legs. Abdominal appendages bear swimmerets, but a tail fan is lacking.

Apseudes latreillei (Milne-Edwards) **Length** up to 0.6 cm. Antennae branched; terminal appendages branched. **Habitat** often under stones or in mud among seaweeds on lower shore and in shallow water. **Distribution** Mediterranean, Atlantic, English Channel and North Sea.

Order Euphausiacea

Small, pelagic malacostracans with conspicuous eyes. The carapace bears a rostrum covering the thorax, but not shielding the thoracic appendages. The last 7 pairs of thoracic appendages are clearly branched near their points of origin; frequently they bear no pincers.

Meganyctiphanes norvegica (M. Sars) **Krill Length** up to 1.5 cm. Carapace bears rostrum, being about one-third of the body length; lower margins are smooth and not toothed nor horned as in some species; characteristic outgrowths on either side of the head behind the eyes. **Habitat** pelagic. **Distribution** Mediterranean, Atlantic, English Channel and North Sea.

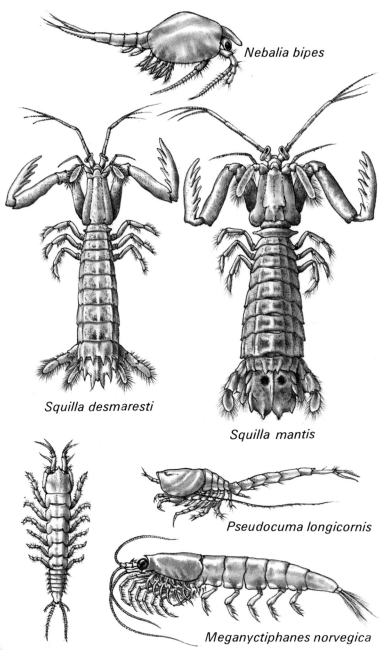

Nebalia bipes

Squilla desmaresti

Squilla mantis

Pseudocuma longicornis

Apseudes latreillei

Meganyctiphanes norvegica

Order Mysidacea Opossum shrimps

Small, swimming malacostracans which seldom reach more than 3cm in length. They possess a thin carapace and a long abdomen of 6 segments. The branched, thoracic appendages lack pincers, and the abdominal appendages are short. A tail fan is borne on the terminal segment, the precise form of which is useful in identification, and which is shown separately where the illustration is a side view. Conspicuous eyes are carried on movable eyestalks. These animals are often transparent and may remain suspended in the water by their swimming movements; females often carry a brood pouch on their under surfaces as the illustration of *Anchialina* shows.

Anchialina agilis (G. O. Sars) **Length** up to 0.9cm. Carapace relatively large, covering the whole thoracic region and reaching more than half the length of the abdomen; outer body surface covered with minute bristles or spines, especially noticeable on the terminal segment. **Habitat** on the seabed by day from shallow water down to 60m or deeper; migrating quickly to the surface for a relatively short period by night. **Distribution** Mediterranean, Atlantic, English Channel and southern North Sea.

Leptomysis gracilis (G. O. Sars) **Length** up to 1.3cm. Carapace short, does not cover the whole thoracic region, and is very little wider than the abdomen; entire body surface covered with minute scales (visible with a strong hand lens). **Colour** transparent and nearly colourless; abdominal region may have slight yellow-red tinge. **Habitat** lower shore in pools and on the seabed in shallow water; may be taken with plankton at certain times of the year. **Distribution** Mediterranean, Atlantic, English Channel and North Sea.

Leptomysis mediterranea G. O. Sars (Not illustrated) **Length** up to 1cm. Very similar to *L. gracilis*, but fine scales are totally absent on the opaque brown body surface. **Habitat** sometimes in great numbers from lower shore down to 100m. **Distribution** Mediterranean, Atlantic, English Channel and North Sea as far north as Scotland.

Mysis relicta Louvén **Length** up to 2cm. Carapace covers all but dorsal aspect of the last 2 thoracic segments and is about half the length of the slender abdomen; abdomen bent downwards in a characteristic posture giving a humped appearance. **Habitat** in fresh and brackish water, often in lakes and lagoons. **Distribution** Venice, Gulfs of Bothnia and Finland and in the Baltic generally north to 58° N.

Paramysis helleri (G. O. Sars) **Length** up to 1.1cm. Carapace not entirely covering the last thoracic segment and reaching slightly less than half the length of the abdomen. **Colour** transparent, with branching yellow, brown and pink markings. **Habitat** found in shallow water usually close to the coast and sometimes in estuaries. **Distribution** Mediterranean, Atlantic and English Channel.

Praunus flexuosus (O. F. Müller) **Length** up to 2cm. Eyes borne on relatively long eyestalks; carapace not entirely covering the last thoracic segment and reaching to slightly less than half the length of the abdomen. **Colour** very variable; from transparent colourless to nearly black according to the background. **Habitat** lower shore in pools and in shallow water, especially among *Zostera* beds over sandy substrates. **Distribution** Atlantic north of Biscay, English Channel, North Sea and Baltic.

Neomysis integer (Leach) **Length** up to 1.7cm. Carapace not quite covering the last thoracic segment and being about half the length of the body. **Habitat** often in shallow water where the salinity is reduced, e.g. estuaries and lagoons. **Distribution** Atlantic, English Channel and North Sea coasts and in the Baltic.

For fuller details of many European mysids see Tattersall, W. M. and Tattersall, O. F. 1951.

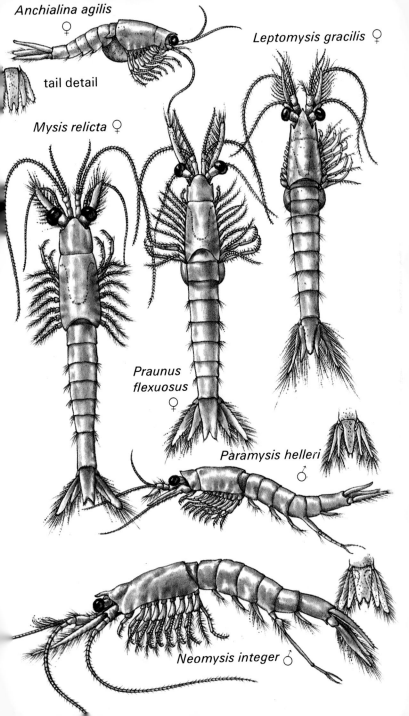

Anchialina agilis ♀

tail detail

Leptomysis gracilis ♀

Mysis relicta ♀

Praunus flexuosus ♀

Paramysis helleri ♂

Neomysis integer ♂

Order Isopoda

Resembling woodlice, isopods are small, dorso-ventrally flattened malacostracans lacking a carapace. The inner antennae are small, the outer antennae conspicuous, and the eyes are not stalked. The first pair of thoracic appendages are used as mouth parts, the remainder for locomotion. The first five pairs of abdominal appendages are leaf-like, functioning as gills, and the 6th segment bears branching swimming appendages which may combine with the telson. Naylor, E. 1972 provides a fuller account of many European isopods.

Anthura gracilis (Montagu) Length female up to 1.1 cm; male up to 0.4 cm. Head eyes relatively large; inner antennae short; outer antennae short in female and long and hairy in the male. Body long; thin thorax; terminal joint of the 1st leg folded back to form a pincer against the next joint; not so in the remaining legs; abdomen relatively short and fan-like. Habitat in crevices, worm tubes and among seaweeds; in shallow water. Distribution Mediterranean, Atlantic and west English Channel.

Eurydice pulchra Leach Length female up to 0.65 cm; male up to 0.8 cm. Head outer antennae nearly as long as head and thorax together. Body thorax oval, wider than abdomen, and about one and a half times as long; 6th pair of abdominal appendages short and not extending much beyond the edge of telson. Habitat in sand from middle shore downward. Distribution Atlantic, English Channel, North Sea and west Baltic.

Limnoria lignorum (Rathke) Length up to 0.35 cm. Head antennae short, together not wider than the abdomen. Body thorax slightly longer and wider than abdomen which has almost parallel edges; 6th pair of abdominal appendages small and just extending beyond edge of telson. Habitat boring in wood. Distribution Atlantic from English Channel north, North Sea and west Baltic.

Sphaeroma serratum (Fabricius) Length female up to 1 cm; male up to 1.2 cm. Head inner antennae about half the length of outer antennae; outer antennae about one-third of body length. Body oval; 6th pair of abdominal appendages terminate in conspicuous, oval, flat joints with serrated outer edges; telson has a smooth upper surface. Habitat in crevices and under stones, usually on middle shore. Distribution Mediterranean, Atlantic north to British Isles, and English Channel.

Sphaeroma rugicauda Leach (Tail only illustrated) Similar to *S. serratum*. Length female up to 0.75 cm; male up to 1 cm. Body outer edge of 6th abdominal appendages not serrated; upper surface of telson covered with tubercles. Habitat burrowing or under stones, etc., in estuaries and salt marsh pools. Distribution Atlantic, English Channel, North Sea and Baltic.

Idotea baltica (Pallas) Length female up to 1.7 cm; male up to 3 cm. Head inner antennae short; outer antennae about one-quarter body length. Body oblong with slightly convex sides; abdomen narrower than thorax, terminating in long telson with almost straight edges and keeled upper surface; rear of telson produced into 3 teeth. Habitat on seaweeds on lower shore and in shallow water. Distribution Mediterranean, Atlantic, English Channel, North Sea and Baltic.

Idotea granulosa Rathke Similar to *I. baltica*. Length female up to 1.3 cm; male up to 2 cm. Body telson narrows sharply at first and ends in a conspicuous central spine; no keel. Habitat on the shore among seaweeds. Distribution Atlantic from English Channel north, North Sea and Baltic.

Idotea chelipes (Pallas) (*=I. viridis*) Similar to *I. baltica*. Length female up to 1 cm; male up to 1.5 cm. Body telson slightly keeled and with one tooth at the tip, this is not as well developed as in *I. granulosa*. Habitat in brackish water. Distribution Mediterranean, Atlantic, English Channel, North Sea and Baltic.

head of ♂

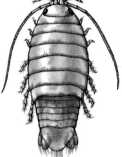

Anthura gracilis

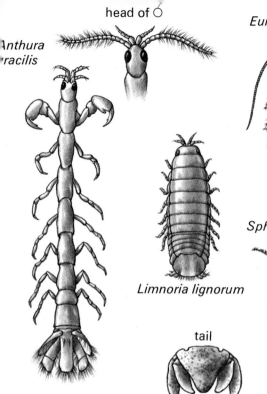

Eurydice pulchra

Limnoria lignorum

Sphaeroma serratum

tail

Sphaeroma rugicauda

Idotea baltica

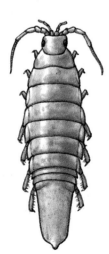

Idotea granulosa

Idotea chelipes

Astacilla intermedia (Goodsir) Length female about 3cm; male about 1cm. **Head** outer antennae long and conspicuous. **Body** slender and round; 4th thoracic segment much longer than the preceding ones and separating the 1st 4 pairs of thoracic limbs from the shorter, relatively hairless remaining 3 pairs which clasp the spines of the sea-urchin *Echinus esculentus* (see page 251) upon which this isopod lives as a commensal; abdomen terminates in a point. **Distribution** Atlantic, English Channel and North Sea.

Jaera albifrons Leach Length female up to 0.5cm; male up to 0.24cm. **Head** eyes quite large; inner antennae very short; outer antennae about half the length of the body. **Body** roughly oval in outline; sometimes deep notches between segments of thorax whose edges are fringed with spines; 6th abdominal appendages very short, set in a notch and just projecting from under the telson. **Habitat** on the upper shore under stones, and in estuaries. **Distribution** Atlantic, English Channel, North Sea and Baltic.

Ligia oceanica (Linnaeus) **Sea-slater** Strongly resembles a woodlouse. **Length** up to 2.5cm. **Head** outer antennae about two-thirds of body length. **Body** flat, oval; 6th abdominal appendages long and trailing behind the telson. **Habitat** on rocks above the intertidal zone. **Distribution** Mediterranean, Atlantic, English Channel and North Sea.

Order Amphipoda

Amphipods are small malacostracans lacking a carapace which are flattened laterally. The upper and lower antennae are variously developed, and the eyes are not stalked. The first pair of thoracic appendages are usually modified as mouth parts, the remaining six pairs being variously developed with pincers or claws for gripping. The abdomen bears three jumping legs, three swimming appendages and a telson, but sometimes it may be degenerate. Thorax and abdominal segments are less easy to distinguish than in isopods.

Bathyporeia pelagica (Bate) Length up to 0.6cm. **Head** upper antennae appear to be borne on an outgrowth of the head, being short with a small branch which can be distinguished under water; lower antennae as long as the body in the male and twice as long as the upper antennae in the female. **Habitat** lower middle shore, often burrowing in sand. **Distribution** Atlantic, English Channel, North Sea and west Baltic.

Haustorius arenarius (Slabber) Length up to 1cm. **Head** eyes difficult to distinguish; upper antennae with a small branch that can be distinguished under water, and which are slightly shorter than the lower antennae, the basal joints of which are flattened; both pairs of antennae appear suspended from the hood-like head segment. **Body** side-plates of body become larger towards the rear; last 3 pairs of thoracic legs with flattened plate-like joints. **Habitat** burrowing in sand on middle and lower shore. **Distribution** Atlantic, English Channel and North Sea.

Gammarus locusta (Linnaeus) Length female up to 1.4cm; male up to 2cm. **Head** upper antennae have a small branch which is visible under water, lower antennae are shorter. **Body** compressed laterally and somewhat curved; posterior margins of last 3 abdominal segments have small spinelets as does the telson; abdomen has 3 longer swimming appendages and 3 shorter jumping appendages; inner branch of the last pair of appendages more than half the length of the outer branch. **Habitat** abundant under stones, etc., on middle and lower shores. **Distribution** Mediterranean, Atlantic, English Channel, North Sea and Baltic.

Gammarus zaddachi Sexton; *G. chevreuxi* Sexton; *G. duebeni* Liljeborg (Not illustrated) 3 species which closely resemble *G. locusta*. Rasmussen 1973 provides notes for distinguishing them. Generally they occur in brackish conditions.

tacilla intermedia

Jaera albifrons

Ligia oceanica

Bathyporeia pelagica

austorius arenarius

Gammarus locusta

207

Talitrus saltator (Montagu) **Sand-hopper** Length up to 1.6 cm. **Head** upper antennae shorter than the large-jointed section of the lower antennae and lacking any branch; lower antennae terminate in a number of small joints which appear rough and toothed under a hand lens. **Body** 2nd thoracic leg terminates in a claw-like joint. **Habitat** upper shore associated with rotting seaweeds. **Distribution** Mediterranean, Atlantic, English Channel, North Sea and Baltic.

Orchestia gammarella (Pallas) **Sand-hopper** Length up to 2 cm. **Head** upper antennae shorter than the large-jointed section of the lower antennae and lacking any branch; lower antennae terminate in a number of small joints which appear smooth under a hand lens. **Body** 2nd thoracic leg terminates in a small claw which acts as a minute pincer against the next joint; 3rd thoracic leg terminates in a larger pincer, the penultimate joint being large, oval and relatively conspicuous. **Habitat** among stones and seaweeds, from upper to middle shore. **Distribution** Mediterranean, Atlantic, English Channel, North Sea and Baltic.

Jassa falcata (Montagu) Length up to 0.8 cm. **Head** upper antennae lacking a side-branch (which if present would be visible under water in a dish), being about three-quarters the length of the lower antennae which appear noticeably thicker. **Body** 1st thoracic leg terminates in a joint which is bent back as a pincer; 2nd thoracic leg does so too, but the pincer is larger and varies in shape from male to female (see inset illustration). **Habitat** middle and lower shores; often with seaweeds on floating objects. **Distribution** Mediterranean, Atlantic, English Channel and North Sea.

Corophium volutator (Pallas) Length up to 0.8 cm. **Head** upper antennae lacking a side-branch (which if present would be visible under water in a dish) and being about half the length of the lower antennae which are almost as long as the body, heavy and conspicuous. **Body** not compressed laterally like the preceding amphipods; the last pair of apparently functional walking legs is much longer than the preceding pairs. **Habitat** in U-shaped burrows in mud on the middle shore, estuaries and salt marshes. **Distribution** Atlantic, English Channel, North Sea and Baltic.

Chelura terebrans Philippi Length up to 0.6 cm. **Head** upper antennae with a minute branch halfway along (probably visible under water in a dish with a hand lens); lower antennae twice as long with somewhat flattened, hairy joints. **Body** not flattened; peculiar tail segment which is somewhat like the rudder of a jet-plane ending in a sharp point; of the last 3 pairs of abdominal appendages the 2nd is very conspicuous and long, exceeding the length of the tail segment and terminating in longish, oval plates, which are larger in the male than the female, and the 3rd is flattened into shorter plates. **Habitat** in bore holes in wood. **Distribution** Mediterranean, Atlantic, English Channel and North Sea.

Hyperia galba (Montagu) Length female up to 2 cm; male up to 1.2 cm. **Head** upper and lower antennae very small; eyes large and domed. **Body** somewhat curved. **Habitat** inside the umbrella of jellyfish (e.g. *Rhizostoma*, see page 85) in Summer, and living free on the seabed in Winter. **Distribution** Mediterranean, Atlantic, English Channel, North Sea and west Baltic.

Caprella linearis (Linnaeus) **Ghost Shrimp** Length female up to 1.4 cm; male up to 2 cm. **Head** upper antennae not branched and about twice as long as lower antennae, which have hairs all along them. **Body** thin and long; abdomen reduced; vestige of tail present. **Habitat** among hydroids, etc., on lower shore downward; sometimes swimming. **Distribution** Atlantic, English Channel, North Sea and west Baltic.

Chevreux, E. and Fage, L. 1925 provide a fuller account of the European amphipods.

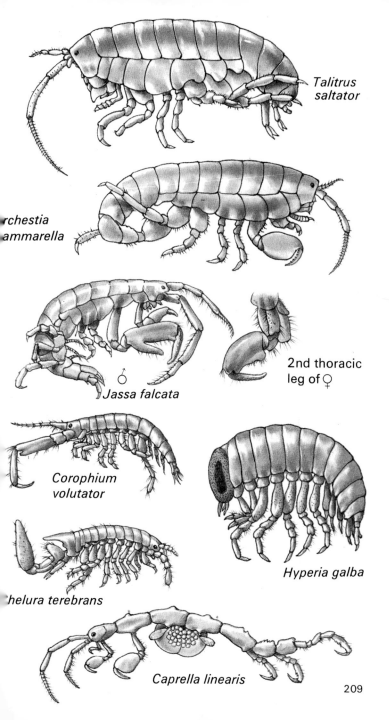

Talitrus saltator

rchestia ammarella

Jassa falcata ♂

2nd thoracic leg of ♀

Corophium volutator

helura terebrans

Hyperia galba

Caprella linearis

209

Order Decapoda

These malacostracans have the head and thorax fused and shielded by a carapace which bears a rostrum between the eyes, and the abdomen is clearly defined. There are eight pairs of thoracic appendages; the first and third pairs are developed as mouth parts, and the fourth to eighth pairs are used for walking and may terminate in a pincer or claw-like joint. Five pairs of abdominal appendages are used for swimming (and for brooding the eggs in the female), the last pair forming the tail fan on the terminal segment. The general malacostracan characteristics are shown in fig. 37.

Suborder Natantia Prawns and shrimps

These decapods, which can swim, have light exoskeletons, and their bodies are sometimes flattened laterally. One pair of antennae is distinctly larger than the other which is more obviously branched at its base. The rostrum may be prominent (as in most prawns where its form is of use in identification), or greatly reduced (as in the shrimps).

Lucifer acestra Dana Length up to 1 cm. Main antennae shorter than body; eye stalks conspicuously long; body flattened sideways; carapace small; thoracic legs delicate; swimmerets about half as long as thoracic appendages; tail with reduced fan. **Colour** transparent. **Habitat** pelagic. **Distribution** Mediterranean.

Pandalus montagui Leach **Aesop Prawn** Length up to 4 cm, sometimes more. Main antennae half as long again as body; rostrum as long as the carapace, curved and terminating in 2 teeth, has 10–12 teeth on the upper side, and 5–6 teeth on the lower side; 2nd pair of walking legs bears pincers, 2nd, 3rd and 4th pairs are the longest. **Colour** carapace red-grey with darker spots and stripes; main antennae ringed with dark and light colours. **Habitat** in rock pools on lower shore and in shallow water. **Distribution** Atlantic, English Channel and North Sea.

Pandalina brevirostris (Rathke) Length about 2 cm. Main antennae shorter than body; straight rostrum between a third and a half the length of the carapace, has about 5 teeth above and about 4 teeth below; carapace terminates in sharp point; 2nd pair of walking legs is the longest and bears pincers. **Colour** shiny with reddish colours showing through. **Habitat** in shallow water from 10–100m or more on clean, coarse gravel and sometimes among polyzoan colonies. **Distribution** Mediterranean, Atlantic and English Channel.

Hippolyte varians Leach **Chameleon Prawn** Length up to 2.5 cm. Main antennae half as long as body; rostrum straight, as long as carapace, and terminating in a single point, 2 widely spaced teeth above and 2 below which are closer together; 3rd pair of walking legs is the longest. **Colour** carapace variable depending on background – green, red or brown by day; transparent blue by night. **Habitat** on the lower shore among rocks and seaweeds and down to 100m. **Distribution** Mediterranean, Atlantic, English Channel and North Sea; not common from Scotland northwards.

Hippolyte prideauxiana Leach Similar to *H. varians*. **Length** up to 2 cm. No teeth on the top of the rostrum which terminates in a single point, and has 2 teeth close together below. **Habitat** among seaweeds and *Zostera* on lower shore and in shallow water; sometimes in river mouths. **Distribution** Mediterranean, Atlantic and west English Channel.

Alpheus ruber Milne-Edwards **Snapping Prawn** Length up to 3.5 cm. Main antennae about as long as body; rostrum small and untoothed; 1st pair of walking legs bears very large unequal pincers; 2nd pair bears minute pincers; the remaining pairs terminate in a claw-like joint. **Colour** pink-red. **Habitat** usually from 30–100m, often on soft substrates and among growths. **Distribution** Mediterranean, Atlantic and English Channel. N.B. by

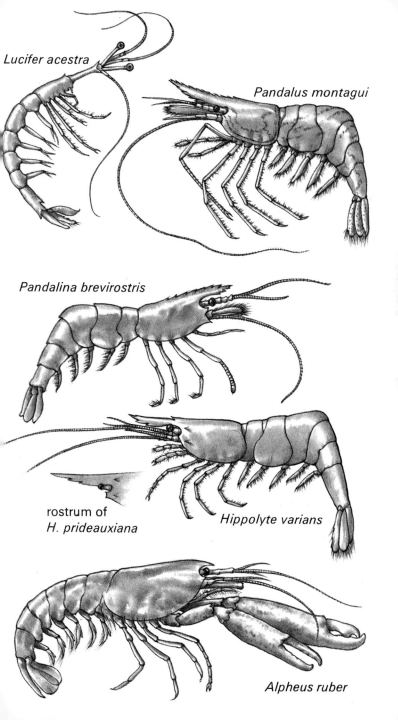

Lucifer acestra

Pandalus montagui

Pandalina brevirostris

rostrum of
H. prideauxiana

Hippolyte varians

Alpheus ruber

snapping its large pincers in the water this prawn produces audible vibrations which stun its prey.

Synalpheus laevimanus (Heller) **Snapping Prawn** Length up to 2 cm. Eyes borne on relatively short eye stalks; rostrum short with no teeth above or below, but with a large tooth on either side nearly as long as the rostrum itself; 1st pair of walking legs very unequal, with the left greatly enlarged and carrying an enormous pincer; 2nd pair bears minute pincers. **Habitat** from 15—30m, sometimes associated with plants or animals. **Distribution** Mediterranean.

Anthanas nitescens (Montagu) **Length** up to 2 cm. Main antennae half as long as body; short untoothed rostrum ends in a sharp point; 1st pair of walking legs as long as the 2nd; pincers of the 1st pair are much larger, and the right pincer is often greater than the left. **Habitat** in pools and among seaweeds on the lower shore and down to 70m. **Distribution** Mediterranean, Atlantic, English Channel, North Sea and west Baltic.

Leander squilla (Linnaeus) **Prawn** Length up to 5 cm. Main antennae one and a half times as long as the body; rostrum may be slightly upcurved and terminates in 1 sharp tooth, between 7 and 10 teeth on the upper side occupy the full length of the rostrum, 3 teeth below situated together near the tip; front edge of carapace has 2 teeth on each side; the largest pincers occur on the 2nd pair of walking legs, and the 2nd, 3rd and 4th pairs are the longest. **Habitat** in rock pools on the lower shore, often among seaweeds; also in shallow water. **Distribution** Mediterranean, Atlantic, English Channel, North Sea and west Baltic.

Leander serratus (Pennant) **Common Prawn** (Not fully illustrated) Similar to *L. squilla*. **Length** up to 6.5 cm, sometimes greater. Rostrum curves upwards and terminates in 2 small equal teeth; there are 6—8 teeth on the upper edge, set back from the tip, and 4—5 below. **Habitat** as for *L. squilla*. **Distribution** Mediterranean, Atlantic and English Channel.

Leander adspersus (Rathke) **Prawn** (Not fully illustrated) Similar to *L. squilla*. **Length** up to 5 cm. Rostrum slightly curved and terminating in 2 teeth, upper side has 5—7 teeth placed equally along its length, lower side has 3—4 grouped so that the 1st lies slightly in front of the 2nd tooth above. **Habitat** as for *L. squilla*. **Distribution** Mediterranean, Atlantic, North Sea and Baltic.

Crangon vulgaris Fabricius **Common Shrimp** Length up to 5 cm, sometimes greater. Main antennae almost as long as the body; rostrum reduced to a small tooth; carapace has 1 central spine and 1 on either side; 1st pair of thoracic legs bear the biggest pincers, 2nd pair carry minute pincers, while 3rd and 4th pairs are the longest. **Habitat** on the lower shore and in shallow water as well as in river estuaries. **Distribution** Mediterranean, Atlantic, English Channel, North Sea and Baltic.

Pontophilus fasciatus (Risso) **Length** up to 2 cm. Main antennae shorter than the body; rostrum greatly reduced, as in *Crangon vulgaris*; carapace carries a noticeable spine on the upper surface; 1st pair of walking legs bears quite large but strangely formed pincers, 2nd pair with pincers, but very short, others end in a claw, 4th and 5th being the longest; abdominal appendages are relatively short. **Habitat** on soft substrates sometimes with seaweeds from 4—40m. **Distribution** Mediterranean, Atlantic and English Channel.

Aegeon cataphractus (Olivi) **Length** up to 3.5 cm. Main antennae about half as long as body; carapace sculptured and bears several rows of conspicuous spines; some of the abdominal segments also carry spines; 1st pair of thoracic legs bear larger pincers similar to *Crangon vulgaris*, 2nd pair short and pincered, 4th and 5th pairs the longest. **Habitat** on sandy substrates from 10—50m. **Distribution** Mediterranean.

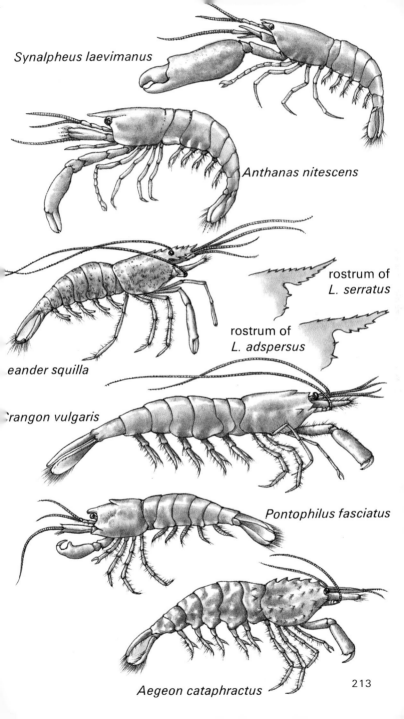

Synalpheus laevimanus

Anthanas nitescens

rostrum of
L. serratus

rostrum of
L. adspersus

Leander squilla

Crangon vulgaris

Pontophilus fasciatus

Aegeon cataphractus

213

Suborder Reptantia

Division Macrura True lobsters and crayfish

Walking decapods which live on the shore or seabed. They are strong and powerfully built often with heavy skeletons which are not flattened laterally. The rostrum is reduced. The first pair of walking legs sometimes carries large and conspicuous pincers, or terminates in a claw-like joint; the remaining four pairs of legs are strong with pincers or claws. The last pair of abdominal appendages is modified to form a tail fan, known as the telson.

Palinurus vulgaris Latreille **Crawfish** or **Spiny Lobster** Length 30—50cm overall. Easily recognized by the lack of pincers on any walking legs (except the 5th pair in the female which does have them); abdominal segments are sharply spined and can cause bad wounds if the animal is mishandled. **Colour** red, brown or shaded with plum colour. **Habitat** among rocks and in crevices, occasionally on stony substrates; from shallow water to 70m and deeper. **Distribution** Mediterranean, Atlantic and English Channel.

Scyllarides latus (Latreille) **Length** up to 35cm or more overall. Second antennae reduced to form 2 shield-shaped structures on either side of the head; relatively short walking legs and other appendanges give the animals a quaint appearance; walking legs lack pincers (except the 5th pair in the female which does have them); abdominal segments are sharply spined and can cause bad wounds. **Colour** brown to red. **Habitat** on rocks, stones and sand from about 3m downward. **Distribution** Mediterranean and Atlantic north to Portugal.

Scyllarus arctus (Linnaeus) Somewhat similar to *Scyllarides latus*. **Length** up to 15cm overall. Second antennae relatively more broad and produced into about 5 easily recognized processes along the front edge; walking legs lack pincers (except for the 5th pair in the female which does have them); abdominal segments are more rounded at their edges than in preceding species. **Habitat** among rocks with mud and on stony bottoms from 3m downward. **Distribution** Mediterranean and Atlantic north to English Channel approaches.

Nephrops norvegicus (Linnaeus) **Norway Lobster, Dublin Bay Prawn** or **Scampi Length** up to 15cm or more overall. Relatively long, slender and delicate by comparison with the other species illustrated here; 1st pair of walking legs long and slender and bearing slightly unequal pincers, 2nd and 3rd pairs of walking legs also with pincers. **Habitat** on soft substrates from about 50m downward. **Distribution** Mediterranean, Atlantic and North Sea.

Homarus gammarus (Linnaeus) **Common Lobster** Length up to 45cm, occasionally much longer; 1st pair of walking legs carry massive (but slightly unequal) pincers which can be formidable and dangerous. **Colour** blue-black on an orange background; turns red when boiled. **Habitat** among rocks, in cracks and holes and in caves. **Distribution** Mediterranean, Atlantic, English Channel, North Sea and west Baltic.

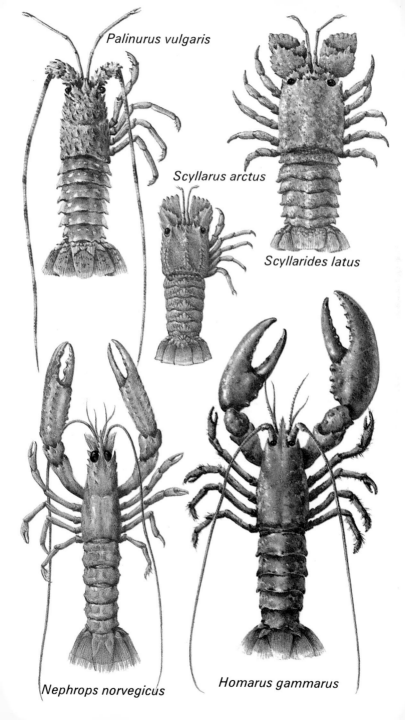

Palinurus vulgaris

Scyllarus arctus

Scyllarides latus

Nephrops norvegicus

Homarus gammarus

Division Anomura Squat lobsters, hermit crabs, etc.

Walking decapods which live on the shore or seabed. The abdomen is not greatly reduced, but is often twisted, as in the hermit crabs, or folded under the thorax, as in the squat lobsters. The last thoracic segment is free from the carapace.

Galathea intermedia Liljeborg Length up to 1cm. Rostrum tip (see fig. 40) slightly blunt, tip itself longer than the 4 small spikes on the side of the rostrum; 1st walking leg bears pincers and is about twice as long as the body. Colour bright red with blue spots. Habitat among stones and rocks on lower shore and down to 80m. Distribution Mediterranean, Atlantic, English Channel and North Sea.

Fig. 40 Rostrum of *G. intermedia*

Galathea dispersa Bate Length up to 4.5cm. Rostrum covered with hairs and with 4 points on the sides; 1st walking leg bears hairy pincers and is as long again as body. Colour dull orange or red; may be patterned. Habitat among stones and rocks on lower shore and down to about 60m. Distribution Atlantic, English Channel and North Sea.

Galathea squamifera Leach Length up to 4.5cm. Rostrum has 4 pairs of side-points and the hindmost pair is the smallest, the remaining side-points being all about the same size (see fig. 41); 1st walking leg one and a half times as long as body and bears pincers; pincer joints themselves have scales and spines on their outer edges, but the joints nearer the body have scales and spines on their inner or opposite edges. Colour generally green-brown, sometimes with a little red. Habitat under stones and rocks from lower shore down to 80m. Distribution Mediterranean, Atlantic, English Channel and North Sea.

Fig. 41 Rostrum of *G. squamifera*

Galathea strigosa (Linnaeus) Length up to 12cm, but often smaller. Rostrum pointed with 3 pairs of spines; 1st walking leg bears pincers about one and a half times as long as body; pincers and the 1st 3 pairs of legs are spiny. Colour red with blue lines across it. Habitat under stones and rocks from lower shore down to 35m. Distribution Mediterranean, Atlantic, English Channel and North Sea. N.B. aggressive when handled.

Munida rugosa (Fabricius) Length up to 6cm. Antennae not quite as long as pincers and the appendage which bears them (in most squat lobsters antennae are as long or longer than pincer-bearing legs); 1st pair of walking legs may be twice as long as body and bears delicate, long, thin pincers. Habitat normally in deep water on sandy or other soft substrates from 50–150m. Distribution Mediterranean, Atlantic and North Sea.

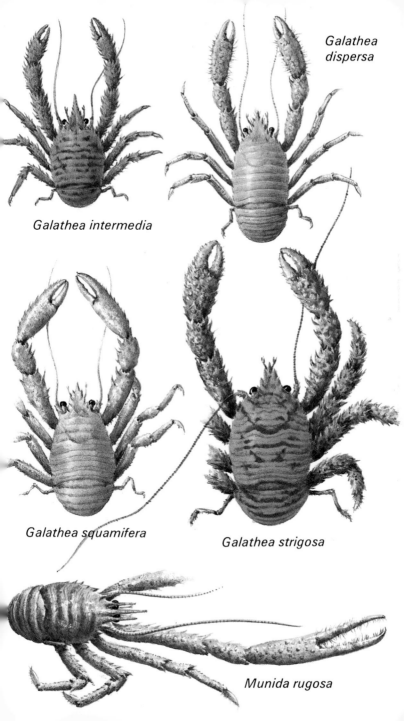

Galathea dispersa

Galathea intermedia

Galathea squamifera

Galathea strigosa

Munida rugosa

Note several groups of anomurans occur apart from the squat lobsters. Some of them resemble other divisions, such as the lobsters and true crabs, but their affinities with the squat lobsters and hermit crabs are indicated by their long and conspicuous antennae and by the miniature fifth pair of walking legs which is a key character of the porcelain 'crabs'.

Porcellana platycheles (Pennant) **Broad-clawed Porcelain 'Crab'** Length up to 1.2 cm. Carapace round and squat; 1st pair of walking legs about 2 cm long with thick and conspicuous pincers which are hairy on their outer edges; other legs hairy; abdomen folded tightly and out of sight under the carapace. **Colour** yellow-brown with dirty grey or reddish appearance. **Habitat** under stones among mud and gravel on middle shore down to shallow water. **Distribution** Mediterranean, Atlantic, English Channel and North Sea. N.B. not a true crab.

Porcellana longicornis (Linnaeus) **Long-clawed Porcelain 'Crab'** Similar to *P. platycheles* in overall appearance. **Length** up to 0.6 cm. Antennae longer than carapace; carapace round; pincers on the 1st walking legs long and relatively slender; animal is not hairy, but relatively 'clean' in appearance. **Colour** brown-red. **Habitat** under stones and in *Laminaria* holdfasts (see page 33) on lower shore and in shallow water. **Distribution** Mediterranean, Atlantic, English Channel and North Sea.

Jaxea nocturna (Chiereghin) Nardo Superficially prawn-like. **Length** about 5 cm. Eyes not apparent; pointed rostrum; 1st pair of walking legs bears strangely shaped, long, hairy pincers; remaining legs are slender and frail-looking, being slightly hairy; 2nd pair has small incomplete pincers; abdomen may be folded under thorax and terminates in a tail fan. **Colour** white, pink or brown. **Habitat** in mud from about 15 m downward. **Distribution** common in Adriatic, rare in Mediterranean, Atlantic and English Channel.

Callianassa subterranea (Montagu) Superficially prawn-like. **Length** about 4 cm. Eyes and rostrum are reduced; 1st pair of walking legs are unequal and hairy bearing pincers one of which is larger than the other; remaining walking legs are thin and hairy, and their terminal joints are sometimes spatulate; delicate and fragile-looking abdomen often folded under thorax. **Colour** white to pale red or bluish. **Habitat** burrows in sand or mud from about 2 m downward. **Distribution** Mediterranean, Atlantic and English Channel.

Upogebia deltaura (Leach) Superficially prawn-like. **Length** up to 10 cm. Head small; hairy rostrum; eyes reduced; 1st walking leg bears strange pincer with moving part longer than fixed part; other walking legs lack pincers, all are hairy; slender, delicate-looking abdomen may be folded under the thorax. **Colour** white-grey-yellow-green. **Habitat** burrowing in clay and muddy sand from lower shore to deep water. **Distribution** Mediterranean, Atlantic, English Channel and North Sea.

Porcellana platycheles

Porcellana longicornis

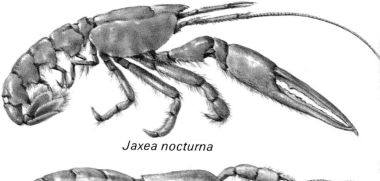

Jaxea nocturna

Callianassa subterranea

Upogebia deltaura

Hermit crabs

The Anomura includes a number of hermit crabs which are familiar seashore animals. They are easily recognized because of their association with empty gastropod shells which protect their delicate, soft-skinned abdomens. Sponges, hydroids and sea-anemones often grow on the outside of shells inhabited by hermit crabs.

Paguristes oculatus (Fabricius) Length up to 4cm; carapace up to 2cm. First pair of walking legs bears almost equal-sized pincers; 2nd and 3rd pairs of walking legs terminate in claws; 4th and 5th are greatly reduced. **Colour** yellow-orange eye stalks; antennae red; eyes clear blue; carapace red-brown; 2nd joint of 1st pair of walking legs with conspicuous dark violet spot. **Habitat** shells frequently occupied include those of *Murex, Cerithium* and *Turbo*; shell may be encrusted with the sponge *Suberites* (see page 73), or alternatively with hydroids such as *Hydractinia* (see page 79) or the sea-anemone *Calliactis* (see page 95) may be growing on the shell; from depths of 4m downward. **Distribution** Mediterranean.

Pagurus arrosor (Herbst) Length up to 10cm; carapace about 5cm. First pair of walking legs bears unequal pincers, the left being the larger; 2nd and 3rd pairs of legs terminate in claws, the 4th and 5th are greatly reduced. **Colour** carapace yellowish; eyes brown-black; pincers red with dark brown points on tips, 2nd and 3rd pairs red with black-brown claws. **Habitat** in gastropod shells from 20m downward. **Distribution** Mediterranean.

Diogenes pugilator (Roux) Length up to 2.5cm; carapace about 1cm (animal may be somewhat smaller). Hairy antennae; 1st pair of walking legs terminates in pincers, the left being the larger; 2nd and 3rd walking legs bear claws; 4th and 5th are greatly reduced. **Colour** eyes black; pincers with chalk-white tips. **Habitat** in gastropod shells usually in shallow water. **Distribution** Mediterranean, and Atlantic north to English Channel approaches.

Eupagurus bernhardus (Linnaeus) **Common Hermit Crab** Length up to 10cm; carapace up to 4cm. First pair of walking legs bears large, unequal, coarsely granulated pincers, the right being the larger; 2nd and 3rd walking legs terminate in claws which are spiny; 4th and 5th walking legs greatly reduced. **Colour** carapace grey-red; pincers red-brown. **Habitat** in gastropod shells, sometimes associated with sponges such as *Suberites* (see page 73), hydroids such as *Hydractinia* (see page 79), the anemone *Calliactis* (see page 95), and the polychaete *Nereis fucata* (see page 119); a yellowish lump may be visible on the underside of the tail – this is the parasitic barnacle *Peltogaster paguri*; from the lower shore down to deeper water. **Distribution** Mediterranean, Atlantic, English Channel, North Sea and west Baltic.

Eupagurus prideauxi (Leach) Length up to 6cm; carapace nearly 2cm. First pair of walking legs bears slightly bristled pincers with fine granules, the right being slightly larger; 2nd and 3rd pairs of walking legs bear claws which are grooved but not spiny; 4th and 5th pairs are greatly reduced. **Colour** carapace brown-red. **Habitat** in small shells often associated with the cloak anemone *Adamsia palliata* (see page 95); found on mud or sand from 10m downward. **Distribution** Mediterranean, Atlantic, English Channel and North Sea.

Anapagurus laevis (Thompson) Length up to 2cm; carapace almost 1cm. First pair of walking legs bears slightly hairy pincers, the right being the larger; 2nd and 3rd walking legs are slender and bear claws; 4th and 5th pairs are greatly reduced. **Colour** carapace yellow-white; pincers banded with orange. **Habitat** in small gastropod shells from 10m downward. **Distribution** Mediterranean, Atlantic, English Channel and North Sea.

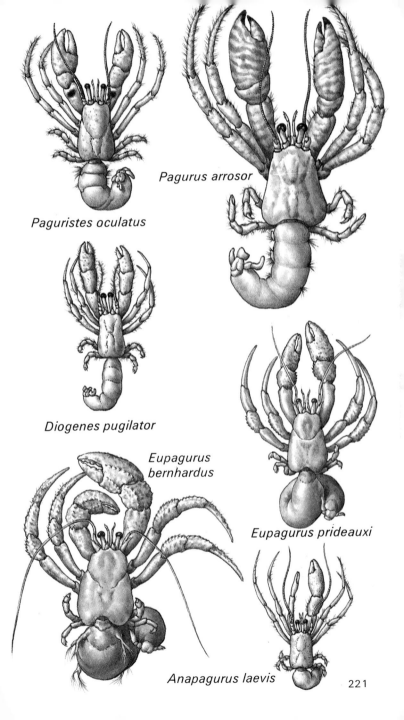

Paguristes oculatus

Pagurus arrosor

Diogenes pugilator

Eupagurus bernhardus

Eupagurus prideauxi

Anapagurus laevis

221

Division Brachyura True crabs

Walking decapods which live on the shore or seabed. True crabs are usually strong and powerfully built with a heavy skeleton. The carapace is flattened and rounded, forming the typical crab-shaped body, and the abdomen is much reduced and folded forwards under the carapace. The antennae are usually short. The first pair of walking legs bears conspicuous and often powerful pincers, while the other four pairs of walking legs are variously developed, ending normally in a claw-like joint.

Dromia vulgaris Milne-Edwards **Sponge Crab** Length up to 8 cm. Carapace slightly broader than it is long, and domed; whole body, including appendages, covered for the greater part by hairs which give the crab a furry appearance; 4th and 5th pairs of legs displaced, and the 5th pair appears to be carried on the crab's back; 5th pair terminates in small pincers. **Colour** hairs dark brown; tips of pincers bright pink. **Habitat** on sandy and rocky shores from low water down to 30 m. **Distribution** Mediterranean, Atlantic and English Channel. N.B. often found carrying a piece of sponge on its back.

Dorippe lanata (Linnaeus) **Length** up to 3 cm. Carapace pear-shaped, nearly as broad as long, with a flattened front edged with a number of teeth; carapace and legs hairy, but not as much as *Dromia vulgaris*; carapace with one conspicuous tooth halfway back on each side; 1st pair of walking legs small and pincered; 2nd and 3rd pairs are the largest; 5th pair almost on the crab's back. **Colour** carapace pink-brown. **Habitat** on soft substrates down to 50 m. **Distribution** Mediterranean.

Ethusa mascarone (Herbst) **Length** up to 1.6 cm. Carapace not as wide as long; anterior edge produced into two toothed points between the eyes, sides fairly straight, but bulging slightly towards the rear; delicate, slender, walking legs, the 1st pair thickest and bearing pincers, 2nd and 3rd pairs the longest, 4th and 5th pairs shorter and the 5th borne almost on the crab's back. **Colour** carapace brown-grey. **Habitat** on sandy and muddy substrates from 10–30 m, sometimes among *Zostera* beds (see page 65). **Distribution** Mediterranean.

Ebalia cranchi Leach **Length** up to 0.7 cm. Carapace granulated, with a rhomboidal outline when viewed from above; a notch is present in the posterior and anterior corners and bears 5 conspicuous knobs, 1 posteriorly, 2 laterally (1 left and 1 right) and 2 almost at the centre. **Colour** carapace yellow-red. **Habitat** on sand and gravel from 20–130 m; often uncommon. **Distribution** Mediterranean, Atlantic, English Channel and North Sea. N.B. at least 4 other species of *Ebalia* have been recognized from European waters all of which have somewhat rhomboidal carapaces, but differ in the presence or absence of granules and knobs, as well as in the shape and proportions of the 1st walking legs.

Ilia nucleus (Herbst) **Length** up to 3 cm. Carapace rounded and domed, almost as wide as it is long, slightly indented between the eyes and with several bumps on the posterior edge; 1st pair of walking legs bears long, slender pincers. **Colour** carapace yellow-brown-red. **Habitat** on muddy and stony substrates and among seaweeds from 5 m down to about 80 m. **Distribution** Mediterranean.

Calappa granulata (Linnaeus) **Length** up to 11 cm. Carapace almost oval in outline, being broader than it is long; front edge strongly convex and finely toothed, rear edge weakly convex with fewer, larger teeth; 1st pair of walking legs bear strongly built pincers which have a crest on their upper side reminiscent of a cock's comb. **Colour** carapace light grey to yellow, spotted with red. **Habitat** on muddy substrates from 30–100 m. **Distribution** Mediterranean and Atlantic north to Portugal.

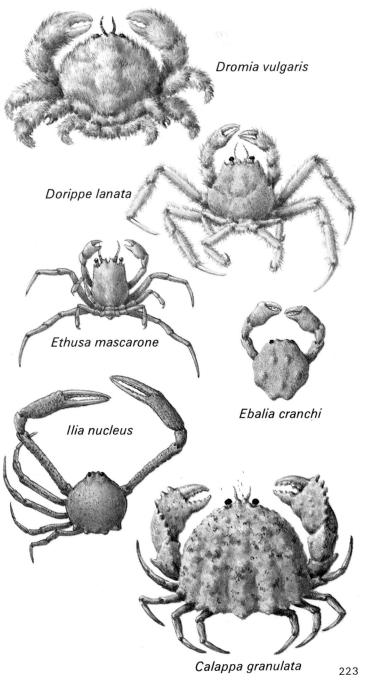

Dromia vulgaris

Dorippe lanata

Ethusa mascarone

Ebalia cranchi

Ilia nucleus

Calappa granulata

223

Macropodia longirostris (Fabricius) **Spider Crab** Length up to
1.5cm. Carapace triangular, not as wide as it is long; bears 7 thorny spikes and
is often encrusted with sponges and seaweeds; rostrum prominent and long,
being composed of 2 parallel spines joined all along; eyes borne on either side
of rostrum, but not retractable into their sockets; antennae have bristles at their
joints; 1st pair of walking legs bears pincers, other walking legs long and
slender; 2nd and 3rd pairs are the longest and terminate in a more-or-less
straight claw, 4th and 5th pairs shorter terminating in a more-or-less curved
claw; legs slightly hairy. **Colour** carapace yellow-red. **Habitat** in shallow water
camouflaged among seaweeds, etc., and in deeper water. **Distribution** Mediterranean, Atlantic, English Channel, North Sea and west Baltic.

Macropodia rostrata (Linnaeus) **Spider Crab** (Not illustrated)
Similar to *M. longirostris*. **Length** up to 1.7cm. Carapace triangular-shaped,
with about 8 conspicuous spines; rostrum much shorter; antennae lacking
bristles at their joints. **Colour** carapace yellow, grey, green or brownish. **Habitat**
and **Distribution** as for *M. longirostris*.

Inachus dorsettensis (Pennant) **Spider Crab** Length about 2.5cm.
Carapace triangular, about as wide as it is long, bears 4 small tubercles arranged
in a row across the front end with one large tubercle behind them; 2 large
tubercles at the back end with a smaller tubercle between them; 2 rostral spines
between the eyes not joined together; eyes can be retracted into their sockets;
1st pair of walking legs bears relatively stout pincers. 2nd pair is about three
times the shell length, and the remaining pairs become progressively smaller
towards the rear. **Colour** carapace yellow-brown. **Habitat** on stony substrates
and among seaweeds on lower shore, in shallow water and down to about
100m. **Distribution** Mediterranean, Atlantic, English Channel and North Sea.
N.B. often covered with sponges and pieces of seaweed.

Pisa gibbsi Leach Length up to 4cm. Carapace more or less triangular;
rough-topped, slightly domed, and with slightly concave sides; not quite as
wide at the rear as it is long; 2 rostral spines (parallel in the male, but diverging
in the female), with another smaller spine in front of each eye; usually 3
posterior tubercles, one pointing backward, and one to either side; 1st pair of
walking legs bears strong, but not large pincers; remaining pairs become
slightly shorter towards the posterior. **Colour** carapace brown. **Habitat** usually
below 20m. **Distribution** Mediterranean, Atlantic and English Channel. N.B.
may be encrusted with seaweeds, sponges or anemones.

Maia squinado (Herbst) **Spiny Spider Crab** Length up to 18cm.
Carapace not as wide posteriorly as it is long, somewhat triangular, but with
convex, rounded outline marked by large and small spines; covered with spines
and bristles; 2 spines between eyes; 1st pair of walking legs fairly long with
small, equal pincers, remaining legs hairy and long except the 5th pair. **Colour**
carapace red, pink or white, sometimes spotted. **Habitat** on sand and among
rocks from the lower shore down to about 50m. **Distribution** Mediterranean
and Atlantic north to the English Channel. N.B. may be encrusted with seaweeds
or sponges.

Hyas araneus (Linnaeus) **Spider Crab** Length up to 11cm. Carapace
somewhat pear-shaped, slightly domed and covered with small tubercles and
bristles; 2 rostral spines lie close together to make a triangular rostrum, on either
side of which is a smaller spine; 1st pair of walking legs bears pincers,
remaining legs of similar length. **Colour** carapace dull red to dull brown. **Habitat** among rocks and on sand, usually in shallow water and sometimes among
seaweeds. **Distribution** Atlantic from the English Channel northwards, North
Sea and Baltic. N.B. may be encrusted with seaweeds, sponges and hydroids.

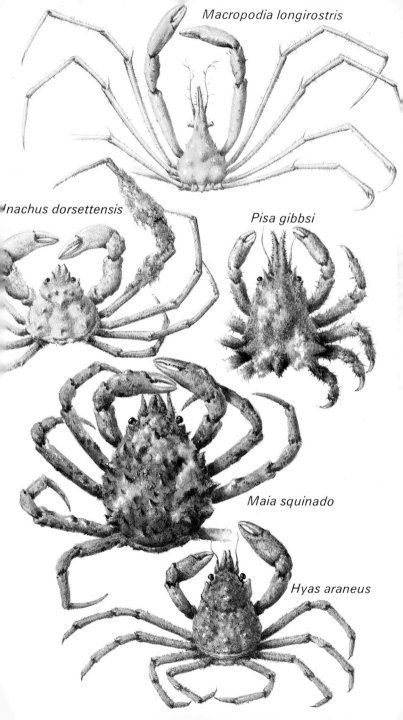

Macropodia longirostris

Inachus dorsettensis

Pisa gibbsi

Maia squinado

Hyas araneus

Lissa chiragra (Herbst) Length up to 4 cm. Carapace not as wide as it is long, basically pear-shaped, but produced into a number of nodular outgrowths around the perimeter and with 2 'humps' on top; outline sometimes disguised by encrusting organisms; 2 rostral spines appear to have grown together to produce a T-shaped rostrum, either side of which is a smaller spine; 1st pair of walking legs carry pincers and has knobbly joints like the other walking legs, 5th pair is the shortest. **Colour** carapace reddish. **Habitat** on soft substrates and among other organisms from 30–80m. **Distribution** Mediterranean.

Lambrus massena Roux Length up to 2 cm. Carapace shaped like a squat pear and as wide posteriorly as it is long, not strongly tuberculated; rostrum bears a rounded tip; 1st pair of walking legs very long and with conspicuous tubercles and pincers; remaining walking legs much smaller and roughly equal in size. **Colour** carapace light grey, yellow or greenish. **Habitat** on rocky and sandy substrates from 5–200m. **Distribution** Mediterranean.

Lambrus angulifrons (Latreille) (Not illustrated) Similar to *L. massena*. Carapace covered with rows of conspicuous tubercles; rostrum sharply pointed. **Colour** purple-red to blackish brown; 1st pair of walking legs violet on their inner faces. **Habitat** on muddy sand from 10m downward. **Distribution** Mediterranean.

Corystes cassivelaunus (Pennant) **Masked Crab** Length carapace up to 4 cm. Carapace not as broad as it is long, and relatively smooth; 1 small and 1 conspicuous border spine occur between the eyes and the origin of the 1st pair of walking legs, which themselves are twice as long as the carapace in the male, but shorter in the female; exceptionally long, hairy antennae which are held together throughout their length. **Colour** carapace drab brown-yellow. **Habitat** lower shore and in shallow water, usually buried in sand, using the joined antennae like a pipe to allow water to reach the gills. **Distribution** Atlantic, English Channel and North Sea.

Cancer pagurus Linnaeus **Edible Crab** Length up to 14 cm, frequently smaller and very occasionally larger. Carapace is lightly granulated and slightly domed, being half as wide again as it is long, oval in outline with about 9 rounded lobes on the edge of each side giving the animal an appearance reminiscent of a piecrust; 1st pair of walking legs bears massive pincers; 4 remaining pairs of walking legs are hairy, the 5th pair being the smallest. **Colour** carapace pink to brownish; pincers tipped with black. **Habitat** from lower shore down to about 100m, usually among rocks; really large specimens are normally found in deep water. **Distribution** Mediterranean, Atlantic, English Channel and North Sea.

Pirimela denticulata (Montagu) Length about 2.5 cm. Carapace bears 3 small projections between the eyes, the outer 2 being triangular and flattened, the middle longer and round; 7 more teeth developed on either side of the body; 1st pair of walking legs bears small pincers; all the other pairs have terminal joints which are pointed and not paddle-like. **Colour** carapace variable; green, brown, purple-red; may be mottled. **Habitat** rocky places or with gravel and seaweeds from lower shore down to about 60m. **Distribution** Mediterranean, Atlantic, English Channel and North Sea.

Carcinus maenas (Linnaeus) **Common Shore Crab** Length up to 4 cm, occasionally larger. Carapace up to half as wide again as it is long; 3 blunt teeth between the eyes; 5 sharp, well-developed teeth on either side of the body; 1st pair of walking legs bears moderately sized, powerful pincers, 2nd and 3rd pairs are the longest, 5th is the shortest and the terminal joints are flattened, but pointed. **Colour** carapace brown, olive or dark green above, green-yellow below. **Habitat** on sandy and rocky shores and in shallow water. **Distribution** Mediterranean, Atlantic, English Channel, North Sea and Baltic.

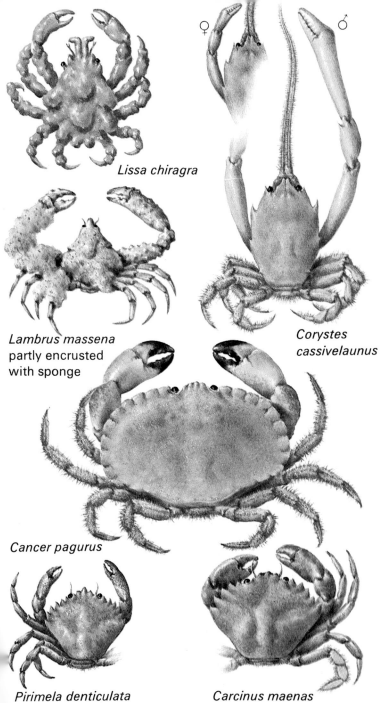

Lissa chiragra

♀ ♂

Lambrus massena
partly encrusted
with sponge

Corystes
cassivelaunus

Cancer pagurus

Pirimela denticulata

Carcinus maenas

Macropipus depurator (Linnaeus) **Swimming Crab** Length up to 4cm. Carapace slightly wider than it is long; carapace sometimes rough and scaly with some hairs; 3 sharp teeth between the eyes which are about the same size as the 5 on either side of the shell (sometimes there is an extra, smaller point at the inner corner of the eye socket); 1st pair of walking legs bears pincers, 5th pair has the last joint flattened and rounded into a paddle for swimming (not pointed as in *Carcinus*). **Colour** carapace reddish brown. **Habitat** often on sandy substrates from 5–20m. **Distribution** Mediterranean, Atlantic, English Channel and North Sea.

Macropipus puber (Linnaeus) **Velvet Swimming Crab** Length about 8cm or less. Carapace bears 8–10 small teeth between eyes of which the middle 2 are longest; 5 large, pointed teeth on either side of the edge of the shell towards the front; 1st pair of walking legs bears strong pincers; last joint of back legs is flat and rounded to act as a swimming paddle (not pointed as in *Carcinus*). **Colour** carapace red-brown; covered with fine hair giving a muddy-brown appearance; eyes red. **Habitat** among stones and rocks from the lower shore down to about 10m. **Distribution** Atlantic, English Channel and North Sea. N.B. may defend itself strongly when disturbed.

Pilumnus hirtellus (Linnaeus) **Hairy Crab** Length up to 2cm. Carapace anterior edge formed into 2 shallow lobes between the eyes; 5 points on the edge outside the eyes (including the eye-socket margin); carapace is wider than it is long, rounded in front, but tapering posteriorly; large, strong, unequal pincers on the 1st walking legs; whole animal is hairy. **Colour** carapace brownish red; pincers brown. **Habitat** on rocks and stones, in cracks and holes, sometimes among sponges; lower shore and in shallow water. **Distribution** Mediterranean, Atlantic and English Channel.

Xantho rivulosus Risso Length about 2cm. Carapace broad in front and tapering sharply to the posterior; shallow furrow runs in from between the eyes, 2 indentations on each side of the carapace; 1st pair of walking legs carries relatively large, unequal pincers; other legs become smaller towards the rear. **Colour** carapace variable; yellow, brown, green or red-brown. **Habitat** among sand, gravel and loose stones on lower shore and in shallow water. **Distribution** Mediterranean.

Xantho incisus Leach (Not illustrated) Similar to *X. rivulosus*. **Distribution** Atlantic and English Channel.

Pinnotheres pisum (Pennant) **Pea Crab** Length female up to 1.5cm; male smaller. Carapace spherical and smooth; no marks on the anterior lips of the carapace; last joint of the 5th pair of walking legs is hook-like. **Colour** female transparent yellow white; male less transparent and more brownish. **Habitat** inside bivalves such as oysters and mussels, usually in shallow water. **Distribution** Mediterranean, Atlantic, English Channel and North Sea.

Pachygrapsus marmoratus (Fabricius) Length up to 3cm. Antennae and eyes relatively far apart and almost at the corners of carapace which bears a straightish front edge which has about 3 slight hollows; carapace smooth; 2 or 3 pointed teeth occur on the sides; moderately large pincers occur on the 1st pair of walking legs, other legs are hairy. **Colour** carapace yellow-green; mottled. **Habitat** in rocky cracks and crevices from the lower shore downward. **Distribution** Mediterranean.

Eriocheir sinensis Milne-Edwards **Chinese Mitten Crab** Length up to 7cm. Carapace more or less square and wide-fronted, with 4 teeth and a shallow groove between the eyes; 1st pair of walking legs bears quite powerful pincers whose parts are invested with 'fur' giving the appearance of mittens; other legs long and hairy. **Colour** carapace olive-green; sometimes marked with blotches. **Habitat** in fresh water and estuaries. **Distribution** Atlantic north from the English Channel, North Sea and Baltic.

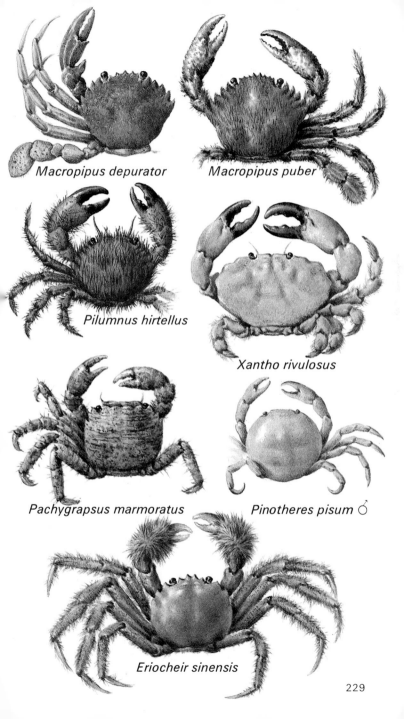

Macropipus depurator

Macropipus puber

Pilumnus hirtellus

Xantho rivulosus

Pachygrapsus marmoratus

Pinotheres pisum ♂

Eriocheir sinensis

229

Class **Chilopoda** Centipedes

Long, flattened arthropods with many similar body segments, and not more than one pair of appendages per segment. The head has antennae and simple eyes, and the first body segment bears poisonous claws.

Strigamia maritima (Leach) **Length** up to 4 cm. **Habitat** under stones and in rock crevices on the upper shore. **Distribution** Atlantic, English Channel, North Sea and west Baltic.

Class **Insecta** Insects

Arthropods in which the adult body is divided into three distinct regions : a head with a single pair of antennae ; a thorax with three pairs of legs and often one or two pairs of wings ; and an abdomen without walking appendages.

Petrobius maritimus (Leach) **Bristle-tail** **Length** up to 1.25 cm. **Head** conspicuous antennae which are about the length of the body ; it also has a pair of palps. **Body** thorax bears 3 pairs of legs but no wings ; abdomen terminates in a long bristle which itself is nearly as long as the body. **Habitat** upper shore and landward in rocky crevices and cracks. **Distribution** Mediterranean, Atlantic, English Channel and North Sea.

Lipura maritima (Laboulbène) **Length** about 0.3 cm. **Head** bears short antennae. **Body** thorax and abdomen quite plump ; thorax bears 3 pairs of short legs, but no wings ; abdomen broad towards the tail, but tapering to a blunt point at the tip. **Habitat** generally floating on the surface film of water in rock pools on the upper shore, or crawling on rocks and seaweeds. **Distribution** Mediterranean, Atlantic, English Channel and North Sea.

Class **Arachnida**
Order **Pseudoscorpiones** False scorpions

The adult body is made up of two primary divisions : a cephalothorax (head and thorax) of six segments bearing conspicuous pincers ; and a pair of appendages with fangs as well as 4 pairs of walking legs.

Neobisium maritimum (Leach) **Length** 0.2 cm. **Body** with the aid of a hand lens the characteristic pincers can easily be seen on the cephalothorax. **Habitat** generally found in rock crevices and under other cover on upper shore. **Distribution** Atlantic, English Channel and North Sea.

Class **Pycnogonida (sometimes regarded as a subphylum)** Sea-spiders

Exclusively marine arthropods with a cephalothorax (head and thorax) drawn out anteriorly into a proboscis which opens by a terminal mouth. The abdomen is reduced to a single segment. Four pairs of relatively long legs are borne by the thorax, into which the ovaries and digestive system extend.

Nymphon gracile Leach **Length** up to 1 cm, sometimes longer ; walking legs reach up to 2.5 cm. **Body** slender cephalothorax ; proboscis equipped on either side with a pair of pincer-like feeding appendages (chelicerae), behind which are a pair of 5 jointed palps ; in addition to the 4 pairs of walking legs there is one pair of 'ovigerous' legs (held below the body) on which the male carries the eggs after the female has laid them. **Habitat** middle and lower shores and in shallow water. **Distribution** Mediterranean, Atlantic, English Channel and North Sea.

Pycnogonum littorale (Ström) **Length** up to 2 cm. **Body** no palps or chelicerae, ovigerous legs only in males ; cephalothorax bears prominent proboscis ; relatively heavy body with thick legs. **Habitat** lower shore under stones, etc. **Distribution** Atlantic, English Channel and North Sea.

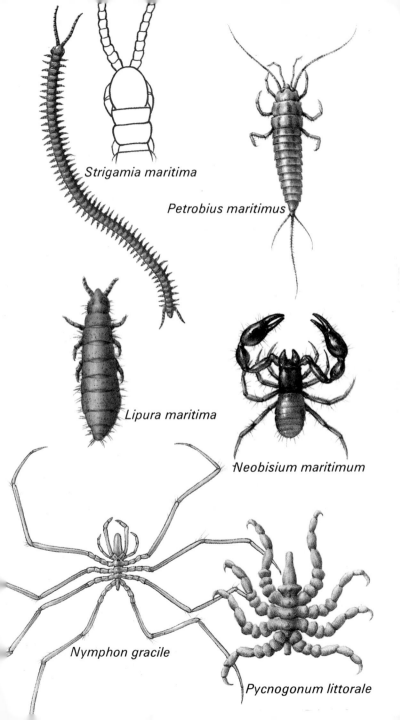

Strigamia maritima

Petrobius maritimus

Lipura maritima

Neobisium maritimum

Nymphon gracile

Pycnogonum littorale

Phylum Ectoprocta (= Bryozoa or Polyzoa)

Ectoprocts are minute, sessile, colonial animals. Individuals grow inside a secreted case called the *zooecium*. A true body cavity (coelom) is present, and the mouth is surrounded by a ring of hollow, ciliated tentacles (collectively called a lophophore), which can be retracted inside the zooecium. The anus lies outside the lophophore.

Ectoprocts are among the commonest animals inhabiting stony and rocky shores and seabeds, yet they are often neglected – probably on account of their small size and lack of commercial value. They are divided into three classes: Phylactolaemata, Stenolaemata and Gymnolaemata, of which the first class is exclusively freshwater and the second consists largely of fossil forms. The body plan is quite characteristic. Individuals dwell in a colony which has been developed by asexual budding from one ancestral animal. Colonies such as *Membranipora* often encrust rocks, shells or seaweeds, but other ectoprocts, like *Flustra*, grow largely unsupported, being attached only at their bases. The zooecium is sometimes hardened by chalky secretions from the body wall; and its shape may be flat and box-like, or tubular. The mouth leads to a U-shaped gut lying inside the zooecium, where the reproductive organs are also housed. Circulatory and excretory structures appear to be lacking. The general form of the ectoproct animal is shown below in fig. 42.

One striking feature of this phylum is the evolution of polymorphic individuals within a colony. Many members of the colony may be feeding individuals, but some are specialized to fulfil other roles. One type called *avicularia* resemble minute birds' beaks. They appear to defend the other members from small organisms which would otherwise creep over them and possibly clog them up. *Vibracula* are another variety of zooid; these bear miniature paddles which probably aid the circulation of water around the colony and discourage the accumulation of silt and other particles. The principal type of feeding individuals filter small food particles from the surrounding sea water by means of the ciliated tentacles of the lophophore. Fig. 43 shows the form of avicularia and part of a colony.

Although each colony develops by budding from an ancestral individual, sexual reproduction leads to the development and dispersal of free larvae. After a period in the plankton these larvae metamorphose into new ancestral individuals, assuming they can find a suitable place on which to settle, and then develop a new colony by asexual budding. In some species the developing embryos are brooded either inside the body or in special pouches called *ooecia*. Colonies usually contain both male and female zooids, but sometimes the zooids themselves are hermaphrodite. Ectoprocts do not generally flourish in

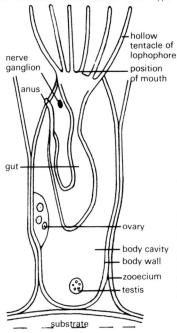

Fig. 42 Diagrammatic arrangement of an individual or zooid

hollow tentacle of lophophore
position of mouth
nerve ganglion
anus
gut
ovary
body cavity
body wall
zooecium
testis
substrate

brackish water, but a few species, for instance *Electra crustulenta*, can tolerate low salinities.

Some clue to the identification of an ectoproct colony will immediately be given by its overall appearance — e.g. erect or branching; flat or encrusting, etc. — but a good hand lens will be essential in order to show the fine details of the zooids themselves which are necessary to establish final identification. The general shape of the zooecium, the position of the opening through which the lophophore is protracted, the presence of an operculum (effectively a lid) for occluding the opening, the presence of ooecia, aviculariae, etc., are all very important in helping to make an identification. Some species also carry spines and bristles which also assist with their identification. Unfortunately, many more species of ectoproct occur in the European area than can be described here. Comprehensive references for the identification of ectoprocts are: Prenant, M. and Bobin, G. 1956 and 1966 *Faune de France* parts 60 and 68 *Bryozoaires* or Hincks, T. 1880 *A History of the British Marine Polyzoa*.

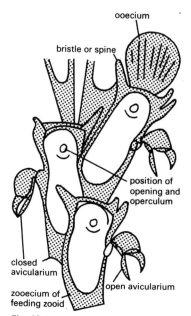

Fig. 43 Arrangement of a few individuals of *Bugula*

Class Stenolaemata

Ectoprocts with tubular zooecia, and with the zooecial walls calcified. The lophophore is often circular.

Order Cyclostomata

Zooecial opening rounded. No operculum, avicularia nor vibracula.

Crisia eburnea (Linnaeus) Branched, jointed colony up to 2 cm high; attached at base; a long spine grows behind each zooid. **Colour** grey-white. **Habitat** growing on red seaweeds, shells and rocks from middle shore down to 50m. **Distribution** Mediterranean, Atlantic, English Channel and North Sea.

Class Gymnolaemata

Zooecia tubular and box-like; the zooecial walls may be calcified. The lophophore is circular.

Order Ctenostomata

Zooecial walls not calcified; zooecial opening may be shut by a collar. No operculum, ooecia, avicularia nor vibracula are present.

Bowerbankia imbricata (Adams) Tufted, branching colony up to 7 cm high; attached at base; zooids at intervals along stems, often in groups. **Colour** grey-buff; golden embryos developing in zooecia may be seen with a hand lens. **Habitat** growing on seaweeds, e.g. *Ascophyllum* and *Fucus* (see page 39) on middle and lower shore and in shallow water. **Distribution** Mediterranean, Atlantic, English Channel and North Sea. N.B. related species grow on rocks, etc.

Zoobotryon verticillatum (Delle Chiaje) Branched, tufted colony up to 50 cm high; zooecia round or oval arranged spirally on branch tips. **Colour** opaque-white, occasionally greenish. **Habitat** growing in clusters on submerged objects, especially in harbours. **Distribution** Mediterranean and adjacent Atlantic. N.B. this is an important fouling organism.

Alcyonidium gelatinosum (Linnaeus) Gelatinous, smooth, sponge-like colony up to 30 cm long; individuals set into the mass. **Colour** yellow-green-grey-brown. **Habitat** growing on rocks and shells from lower shore down to about 100m. **Distribution** Mediterranean, Atlantic, English Channel, North Sea and west Baltic.

Alcyonidium polyoum (Hassall) Similar to *A. gelatinosum*, but more irregular. **Habitat** encrusting holdfasts of laminarians. N.B. not found in the Mediterranean.

Alcyonidium hirsutum Flemming Similar to *A. gelatinosum*, but surface of colony covered with small tubercles. **Habitat** on rocky overhangs and on seaweeds on middle and lower shore. **Distribution** Atlantic, English Channel, North Sea and west Baltic.

Order Cheilostomata

Zooecia generally flattened, and the zooecial walls are calcified. An anterior opening is present, with an operculum. Ooecia, avicularia and vibracula are present.

Membranipora membranacea (Linnaeus) **Sea-mat** Mat-like, encrusting colony of varying size, according to the substrate; round or irregular shape; zooids rectangular and beset with a blunt bristle on each side; elevated growths called 'towers' may occur (as illustrated). **Habitat** on laminarians and other seaweeds from middle shore down to shallow water. **Distribution** Mediterranean, Atlantic, English Channel and North Sea.

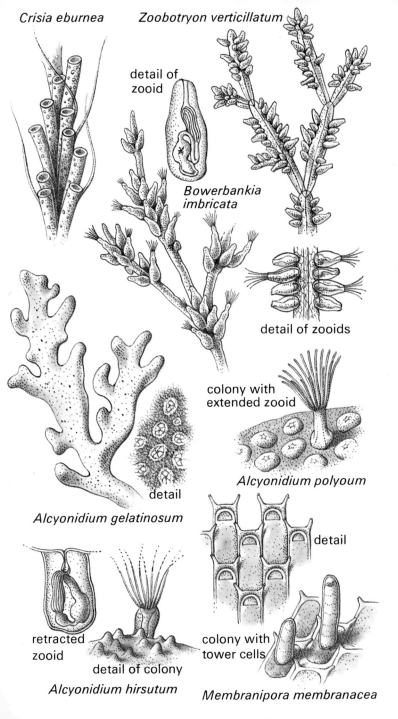

Crisia eburnea

Zoobotryon verticillatum

detail of zooid

Bowerbankia imbricata

detail of zooids

colony with extended zooid

Alcyonidium polyoum

detail

Alcyonidium gelatinosum

detail

retracted zooid

detail of colony

Alcyonidium hirsutum

detail

colony with tower cells

Membranipora membranacea

Electra pilosa (Linnaeus) **Hairy Sea-mat** Similar to *Membranipora membranacea*. Very irregular and angular in outline; zooids bear 2 blunt bristles at one end, 1 conspicuous spine at the other end, and various smaller bristles all round. **Colour** silver-grey. **Habitat** on laminarians, other seaweeds and stones from middle shore down to shallow water. **Distribution** Mediterranean, Atlantic, English Channel and North Sea.

Electra crustulenta (Pallas) Similar to *Membranipora membranacea*. Zooids of varying shape but often pear-shaped with 1 spine at one end. **Habitat** in shallow water often where salinity is low, encrusting stones, *Fucus*, *Zostera* and reeds. **Distribution** Atlantic, English Channel, North Sea and Baltic.

Cellaria fistulosa (Linnaeus) Forms large growths up to 10cm high; jointed and dichotomously branched; zooecium rounded to diamond-shaped. **Colour** ivory-white. **Habitat** on hard and soft substrates, sometimes associated with other bryozoans, from 20—200m. **Distribution** Mediterranean, Atlantic, English Channel and North Sea.

Flustra foliacea (Linnaeus) **Hornwrack** Leaf-like, branching colony up to 20cm high; almost rectangular zooids on both sides of colony; usually 2 short bristles on either side of zooecium at one end. **Colour** brown-green-yellow-grey; colour may fade if washed up. **Habitat** on rocks and stones where it may form extensive communities providing food and shelter for a variety of organisms; from shallow water down to 100m. **Distribution** Mediterranean, Atlantic, English Channel and North Sea.

Securiflustra securifrons (Pallas) Very similar to *Flustra foliacea*. Reaching up to 15cm high; colonies are divided into narrower 'leaves' and the zooecia are more oblong than those of *Flustra foliacea*. **Colour** pale yellowish. **Habitat** as for *Flustra foliacea* (above). **Distribution** some records from the Mediterranean, but generally Atlantic north of Wales, and North Sea.

Bugula turbinata Alder Tufted, branching colonies up to 5cm high; under a hand lens the spiral arrangement of the branches, small elongated zooids with 2 bristles at one end and the aviculariae may be seen. **Colour** usually orange. **Habitat** under overhanging rocks among red seaweeds and sponges on the lower shore and in shallow water. **Distribution** Mediterranean, Atlantic and English Channel.

Bugula neritina (Linnaeus) (Not illustrated) Similar to *B. turbinata*. Colonies up to 10cm high; stout and bushy; branching dichotomous; zooecia relatively large and rectangular; a short spine is present at the outer distal angle of each zooecium; large ooecia. **Colour** brownish. **Habitat** on lower shore and in deeper water. **Distribution** Mediterranean, Atlantic, English Channel and North Sea.

Myriozoum truncata (Pallas) **False Coral** Colony resembling a coral; branches have flat tips and lack the septa of true corals; reaching up to 10cm high; zooids embedded in the stems. **Colour** yellow-red. **Habitat** on rocks, in crevices and caves, usually in shallow, shaded places. **Distribution** Mediterranean.

Pentapora fascialis (Pallas) (**=*Hippodiplosia fascialis***) Large and conspicuous colonies reaching 20cm high; oval- to rhomboidal-shaped zooids tightly grouped. **Colour** orange-pink. **Habitat** on hard substrates, among corals, etc., down to about 25m. **Distribution** Mediterranean (especially Adriatic). N.B. in British waters the somewhat similar *P. foliacea* (Ellis & Solander) is usually found.

Margaretta cereoides (Ellis & Solander) (**=*Tubucellaria opuntioides***) Branching colony up to 5cm high; oval zooecia pressed together forming part of the stem. **Colour** yellow-brown. **Habitat** in shallow water among *Zostera* and *Posidonia* roots. **Distribution** Mediterranean.

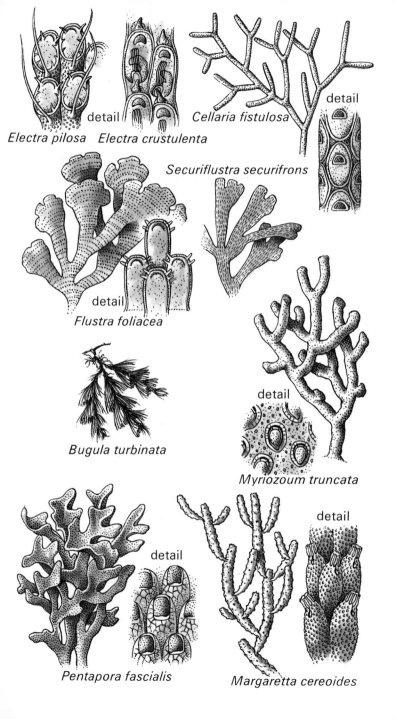

detail

Electra pilosa   *Electra crustulenta*

Cellaria fistulosa

detail

Securiflustra securifrons

detail

Flustra foliacea

Bugula turbinata

detail

Myriozoum truncata

detail

detail

Pentapora fascialis

Margaretta cereoides

Phylum Echinodermata

The Echinodermata constitute a most distinct phylum in the animal kingdom and have been regarded by some authorities as being related to the ancestors of the chordates. Echinoderms are exclusively marine, and they display in their adult form a unique type of symmetry. This is essentially radial, with a mouth in the centre on one side of the body, and the anus normally in the centre on the opposite side. The body may be disc-shaped or globular, as in the sea-urchins, or it may be drawn out into five or more radii, as in the starfishes and brittle-stars. This symmetry is known as *pentamerism*.

Present-day echinoderms are divided into five distinct classes, although fossil evidence shows that other groups existed. Each of these extant classes is represented in the European area: they are the Crinoidea (feather-stars); the Asteroidea (starfishes); the Ophiuroidea (brittle-stars); the Echinoidea (sea-urchins, sand-dollars and heart-urchins); and the Holothuroidea (sea-cucumbers). All of these animals have a number of features in common, which usually make it easy to recognize echinoderms as such, yet at the same time they have features sufficiently different to allow one to decide which group they represent.

Echinoderms are triploblasts (i.e. their bodies are composed of three cell layers: ectoderm, mesoderm and endoderm). The skeleton is basically internal, but it sometimes protrudes to the exterior as in the spines of a sea-urchin. The skeleton consists of many plates of calcium carbonate; some of these are linked together to form the *test* or so-called 'shell', while others are mounted on the test to form spines. In most species apart from the echinoids the test plates are loosely connected together so that the animals are relatively flexible. The outer surface of the test is covered by a thin layer of epidermal cells which are often highly pigmented. Most of the organ systems lie within the large body cavity carried inside the test. These include the digestive and reproductive systems as well as the greater part of the unique water-vascular system. There appears to be no distinct osmoregulatory system, and perhaps this is why echinoderms cannot tolerate reductions in salinity. The sexes are usually separate and synchronous spawning often takes place at certain times of the year. External fertilization occurs in the sea and leads to the formation of a pelagic larva which passes through several stages in the plankton before settling to metamorphose into a juvenile.

The water-vascular system is apparent on the outside of the test in the form of double rows of *tube-feet*. These rows of tube-feet are known as ambu-lacra, and there are usually five (one to each radius of the body). Each tube-foot is elastic and can extend by being filled with fluid under pressure from within the body. Muscles along the tube-foot shaft can contract, and empty the fluid, and these muscles can also cause the tube-feet to bend, thus allowing locomotory 'steps'. Most starfishes, as well as the sea-urchins and sea-cucumbers, have suckers on their tube-feet, and these can grip the substrate and serve as locomotory organs. This does not occur so much in the feather-stars and brittle-stars which move more by flexing their rays or arms. The internal anatomy of the water-vascular system is complex, and although it appears to open to the exterior by a special sieve-like test

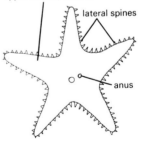

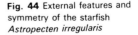

Fig. 44 External features and symmetry of the starfish *Astropecten irregularis*

plate (the madreporite) there is little evidence for water movements in and out of it. In addition to locomotion, the water-vascular system is involved with respiration and feeding.

In the crinoids the mouth and anus are borne on the same side of the disc and face away from the substrate. Crinoids anchor themselves to the substrate by means of special appendages (cirri) on their undersides, and use their tube-feet, which lack suckers and which occur in great numbers on the branching

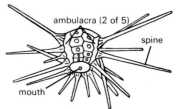

Fig. 45 External features of the sea-urchin *Cidaris cidaris* (some spines removed)

arms, to filter the sea water and collect from it small particles of suspended food matter. These particles are then passed down the arms to the mouth.

Asteroids hunt their prey by relying on a sense of smell to track it down. They frequently evert their stomachs over the prey or insert it inside gaping shells, etc. Digestion then occurs and the products can be absorbed. The mouth is on the underside and is thus well positioned for such behaviour. The small spines of asteroids are not as freely movable as those of the echinoids.

Ophiuroids are scavengers and use their suckerless tube-feet to pass food to their mouths. They move by means of their flexible arms. An anus is lacking and waste is passed out through the mouth.

Most round sea-urchins live by browsing on plant and animal growths which cover the rocks. A five-toothed chewing organ (the lantern of Aristotle) is carried inside the test, which also bears movable spines which serve a variety of functions including locomotion, defence and sensory detection. In some of these functions the spines are assisted by minute pincer-like organs (pedicellariae) which help to keep the test surface clean, and which also assist with defence. The tube-feet have suckers and can usually be extended considerable distances when they often resemble guy-ropes as they assist in posture and locomotion. The sand-dollars and heart-urchins are modified for burrowing and derive their food from organic substances in the sand and gravel where they live.

The skeletal elements of the holothuroids are often considerably reduced, giving the animals a softer texture. Modified tube-feet are arranged around the mouth to gather food either by filtering sea water or by sweeping organic matter from the surface of sand. The sea-cucumbers usually progress with one end leading, in the same manner as the sand-dollars and heart-urchins. In some cases (e.g. *Synapta*), the remaining tube-feet are not developed and the animal moves in a worm-like fashion.

Class Crinoidea Feather-stars

Echinoderms with 5 paired arms bearing branches and growing from a cup-shaped body. These arms, with their tube-feet, are used for filtering food from sea water and for creeping and swimming. The mouth and anus are situated on the upper side and below the body are a number of short appendages (cirri) which grip the substrate.

Antedon bifida (Pennant) **Feather-star** Diameter up to 15cm or more overall. **Body** bears inconspicuous disc with arms which often wave slowly in the water. **Colour** red-brown; arms sometimes banded with white. **Habitat** on rocks and in crevices, sometimes attached to other growths, on lower shore in pools and down to about 200m. **Distribution** Atlantic north from Portugal and as far as the Shetlands, English Channel and northern North Sea.

Antèdon mediterranea (Lamarck) (Not illustrated) Diameter up to 20cm overall. **Body** bears inconspicuous disc; arms with many branches. **Colour** yellow-red-brown. **Habitat** on rocks, stones and seaweeds when growing on soft substrates, as well as on gorgonians, down to 40m. **Distribution** Mediterranean.

Class Asteroidea Starfishes

Echinoderms in which the body is drawn out into distinct rays, generally 5 in number. The mouth is on the underside and an anus on the upper side. Locomotory organs (tube-feet) are carried on the underside of each ray, and are generally armed with suckers.

Luidia ciliaris (Philippi) Diameter up to 40cm or more overall. **Body** always has 7 flattened rays; tube-feet end in knobs rather than suckers. **Colour** orange-red on upper side; white below. **Habitat** on sand and mud, sometimes buried, from extreme lower shore (occasionally) down to 150m. **Distribution** Mediterranean, Atlantic, English Channel and North Sea.

Luidia sarsi Düben & Koren (Not illustrated) Diameter up to 20cm overall. **Body** similar in shape to *L. ciliaris*, but never having more than 5 rays. **Colour** yellow-red-brown above, with ray sides often darker. **Habitat** on soft substrates from 10m downward. **Distribution** Mediterranean, Atlantic, English Channel and northern North Sea.

Astropecten irregularis (Pennant) Diameter up to 12cm overall. **Body** flattened, with very distinct 5-rayed appearance; each ray is edged with 2 layers of distinct marginal plates; each upper plate bearing 1 or 2 small spines (visible when viewed from above), lower layer has distinctly longer spines; tube-feet lack true suckers. **Colour** orange-brown above; white below. **Habitat** on sandy substrates often burrowing from extreme lower shore downward. **Distribution** western Mediterranean, Atlantic, English Channel, North Sea and west Baltic. N.B. the polychaete *Acholoë astericola* may be living between the tube-feet.

Astropecten aurantiacus (Linnaeus) Diameter up to 60cm overall. **Body** similar in shape to *A. irregularis*; each upper edge plate bears 2 or 3 strong, conical spines (visible when viewed from above). **Colour** brown with reddish marks above; pale below. **Habitat** as for *A. irregularis*. **Distribution** Mediterranean and Atlantic north to Portugal. N.B. for a key to other species of *Astropecten* see Koehler, R. 1921.

Porania pulvillus (O. F. Müller) Diameter up to 10cm overall. **Body** fleshy and cushion-like with relatively short rays; smooth and rather sticky to the touch. **Colour** often brilliant scarlet or orange-white above; white below. **Habitat** on gravel from 10–250m, feeding on falling organic particles. **Distribution** Atlantic, English Channel and northern North Sea.

Ceramaster placenta (J. Müller & Troschel) Diameter up to 16cm overall. **Body** flat, pentagonal and very solid. **Colour** brown-yellow-red. **Habitat**

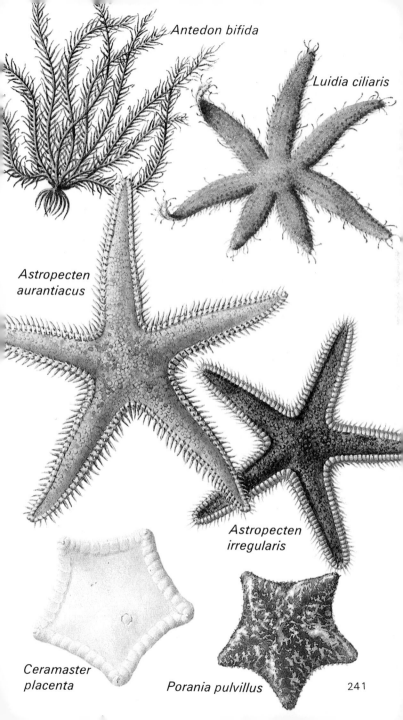

Antedon bifida

Luidia ciliaris

*Astropecten
aurantiacus*

*Astropecten
irregularis*

*Ceramaster
placenta*

Porania pulvillus

241

on soft substrates from about 30m downward. **Distribution** Mediterranean and Atlantic north to Biscay.

Ceramaster granularis (O. F. Müller) (Not illustrated) **Diameter** up to 8cm overall. **Body** pentagonal and similar to *C. placenta*, though more pointed. **Habitat** from 20–1400m. **Distribution** Atlantic from Morocco to Greenland, North Sea and Skagerrak.

Ophidiaster ophidianus Lamarck **Diameter** up to about 20cm overall. **Body** bears small disc with relatively long rays; cylindrical in section and not tapering until the tip; tube-feet with suckers and guarded by rows of short spines. **Colour** violet-red. **Habitat** on rocks and hard substrates from 1m downward. **Distribution** warmer parts of the Mediterranean, e.g. southern Italy.

Hacelia attenuata Gray **Diameter** up to 20cm overall, but often less. **Body** bears small disc with rounded arms which taper for most of their length to a fairly sharp point; tube-feet with suckers and guarded by rows of short spines. **Colour** brown-red-scarlet. **Habitat** on hard substrates. **Distribution** Mediterranean.

Anseropoda placenta (Pennant) **(=*Palmipes membranaceus*) Goose-foot Star** **Diameter** up to about 15cm overall. **Body** very flat and pentagonal; slightly concave edges which often look rather tattered. **Colour** brilliant, often with patterns of red and white above; yellow-white below (detailed distribution of pigment is variable). **Habitat** on sand and mud from 10–100m. **Distribution** Mediterranean, Atlantic, English Channel and northern North Sea.

Asterina gibbosa (Pennant) **Cushion-star** or **Starlet** **Diameter** up to 5cm overall, though occasionally more. **Body** star-shaped with rounded tips to the rays; not as flat as *Anseropoda placenta*. **Colour** green-pale brown on upper surface; more yellow below. **Habitat** on and under rocks and stones on the lower shore and down to 100m. **Distribution** Mediterranean, Atlantic and English Channel. N.B. possibly more tolerant to fresh water than most starfishes.

Echinaster sepositus Gray **Diameter** up to 20cm overall. **Body** small disc covered with soft skin; fairly conspicuous pockmarks on upper surface and larger disc distinguish it from *Ophidiaster ophidianus*; relatively long rays taper gradually; tube-feet with suckers. **Colour** scarlet. **Habitat** on rocks and softer substrates from 1–250m. **Distribution** Mediterranean and Atlantic north to Brittany.

Henricia oculata (Pennant) **(=*H. sanguinolenta* in part)** **Diameter** up to 10cm overall though occasionally nearly twice this size. **Body** relatively small disc with stiff rays which are nearly circular in section and continuously tapering. **Colour** blood-red-purple above; whiter below. **Habitat** on soft substrates and among pebbles and small stones. **Distribution** Atlantic from Biscay northward, English Channel, northern North Sea and west Baltic.

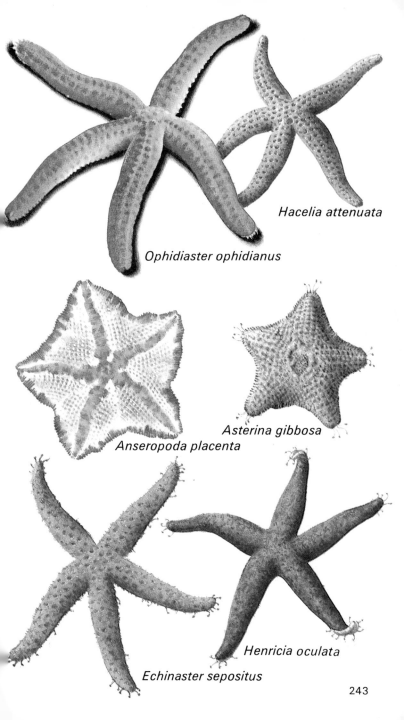

Hacelia attenuata

Ophidiaster ophidianus

Asterina gibbosa

Anseropoda placenta

Henricia oculata

Echinaster sepositus

243

Crossaster papposus (Linnaeus) (= *Solaster papposus*) **Common Sun-star** Diameter up to 25cm overall, but frequently smaller. **Body** bears large disc with between 8–13 blunt rays which are rarely longer than half the diameter of the disc; the whole surface of the animal is covered with small but distinct spines. **Colour** variable; brown-red with white markings above, yellow-white below; often beautifully patterned. **Habitat** on sand and stones and among mussel and oyster beds in the company of other starfishes from 10–40m; frequently preys upon other echinoderms. **Distribution** Atlantic from France northwards and to Greenland, English Channel, North Sea and west Baltic.

Solaster endeca (Linnaeus) **Purple Sun-star** Diameter up to 30cm overall, but frequently smaller. **Body** 7–13 rays; spines not as apparent as those of *Crossaster papposus*; upper surface has a fairly hard texture. **Colour** purple-orange above; white-orange below. **Habitat** on hard substrates from 20–90m. **Distribution** west and north Atlantic coasts of the British Isles and north to Greenland, North Sea and west Baltic.

Asterias rubens Linnaeus **Common Starfish** Diameter may reach up to 50cm, but frequently much smaller. **Body** has plump, rounded, tapering rays often slightly turned up at the tip when active; surface covered with irregularly arranged spines surrounded by pedicellariae (see *Marthasterias glacialis* below); tube-feet bear suckers. **Colour** brown-yellow above; paler below. **Habitat** on rocks and stony ground, in mussel and oyster beds from lower shore down to 200m; sometimes gregarious. **Distribution** Atlantic, English Channel, North Sea and west Baltic.

Marthasterias glacialis (Linnaeus) **Spiny Starfish** Diameter may reach up to 80cm overall, but frequently much smaller. **Body** rounded, gradually tapering rays often slightly turned up at tips when active; body surface is covered in conspicuous spines surrounded by rings of small, pincer-like organs (pedicellariae) which can easily be discerned with a hand lens; tube-feet bear suckers. **Colour** brown-yellow with green-grey markings above, white-yellow below. **Habitat** on rocks and stony substrates from the lower shore down to 180m. **Distribution** Mediterranean, Atlantic, western English Channel and North Sea.

Leptasterias mülleri (M. Sars) (Not illustrated) Diameter up to 10cm overall. **Body** somewhat similar in shape to *Asterias*, but with stouter dorsal skeleton due to crowding together of the plates; upper surface often with many knobby spines arranged in rows; pedicellariae present. **Colour** disc and inner part of rays red-violet above. **Habitat** among rocks from middle shore downward. **Distribution** Atlantic north of English Channel, and North Sea.

Coscinasterias tenuispina (Lamarck) Diameter up to 15cm overall. **Body** has relatively small disc, bearing 6–10 rays often of different lengths; surface covered with distinct spines each surrounded by pedicellariae (see *Marthasterias glacialis* above). **Colour** variable; basic shade may be white, red-brown or purple, with blue or brown spots. **Habitat** on rocks and stones from the lower shore down to 30m. **Distribution** Mediterranean and Atlantic, north to Portugal.

Stichastrella rosea (O. F. Müller) Diameter up to 15cm overall. **Body** small disc bearing long, tapering rays of equal length; surface covered with small spines in groups; pedicellariae present. **Colour** generally red-orange-yellow. **Habitat** on hard and soft substrates from 4–350m. **Distribution** Atlantic north from Biscay to Norway, Irish Sea and English Channel west to Devon.

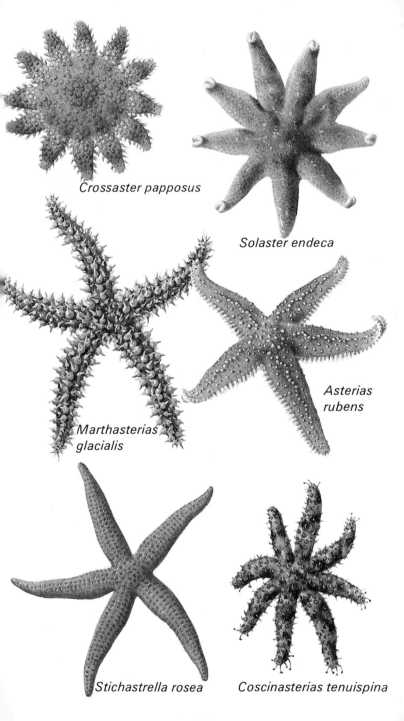

Crossaster papposus

Solaster endeca

Marthasterias glacialis

Asterias rubens

Stichastrella rosea

Coscinasterias tenuispina

Class Ophiuroidea Brittle-stars

Echinoderms normally with 5 unbranched, jointed arms bearing spines; the tube-feet on the underside of the arms lack suckers. The rounded disc is flattened, and the mouth is on the underside. There is no anus nor pedicellariae. The precise identification of brittle-stars is difficult unless account is taken of small structures best seen through a hand lens. A useful identification feature in the ophiuroids is the arm spine number (a.s.n.), which is the number of spines on one side only of one arm joint. Koehler, R. 1921 and Mortensen, T. 1927 provide good accounts of many European ophiuroids.

Ophiothrix fragilis (Abildgaard) **Common Brittle-star** Disc up to 2cm in diameter, often pentagonal with the points visible between the arms; upper surface has many minute spinelets, and some longer spinelets, arranged in 5 radiating, v-shaped groups over each arm and on either side of 2 naked, triangular plates. **Arms** not more than 5 times disc diameter; fragile and often broken or regenerating; arm spines conspicuous and finely thorned; lowermost arm spine hooked; a.s.n. = 7. **Colour** variable; bright red-brown-violet-purple or patterned above. **Habitat** under stones, seaweeds and shells from lower shore down to 350m. **Distribution** Mediterranean, Atlantic, English Channel and North Sea.

Ophiocomina nigra (Abildgaard) Disc up to 3cm in diameter, faintly pentagonal with arms borne at points, upper surface covered with fine granules. **Arms** tapering, and not more than 5 times disc diameter; arm spines fine and glassy and equal to 2 arm joints in length; lower arm spines shorter; a.s.n. = 5–7. **Colour** black-brownish grey. **Habitat** among rocks, seaweeds and sand, often shaded, from lower shore down to 400m. **Distribution** Mediterranean, Atlantic, English Channel and North Sea.

Acrocnida brachiata(Montagu) Disc up to 1cm in diameter. **Arms** exceptionally long, may reach 15 times disc diameter; a.s.n. = 8–10 on joints near the disc. **Colour** grey-brown. **Habitat** burrowing in sand with arms looped, coiled or twisted, from lower shore down to 40m. **Distribution** Atlantic north from Biscay, English Channel and North Sea. N.B. a related species, *A. neapolitana* (M. Sars) (not illustrated) occurs in the Mediterranean. A polychaete (*Harmothoë lunulata*) and a bivalve (*Montacuta bidentata*) may be associated with this species.

Amphipholis squamata (Delle Chiaje) Disc up to 0.5cm in diameter with 2 conspicuous pale plates above each arm. **Arms** up to 4 times disc diameter; arm spines short and conical; a.s.n. = 4, on joints near the disc. **Colour** bluish-grey-white. **Habitat** under rocks, pebbles and seaweeds (especially corallines) from lower shore down to 250m. **Distribution** Mediterranean, Atlantic, English Channel and North Sea. N.B. often present in great numbers.

Ophioderma longicauda (Retzius) Disc up to 3cm in diameter, granulated and leathery, apparently notched above the origin of each arm. **Arms** tapering, reaching about 4 times disc diameter; arm spines short and lying against the arm itself; a.s.n. = 15. **Colour** brownish with green marks. **Habitat** on sandy and rocky bottoms from extreme lower shore down to 70m. **Distribution** Mediterranean and Atlantic north to Biscay.

Ophiura texturata Lamarck Disc up to about 3cm, rounded from above and scaled; 2 conspicuous plates above the origin of each arm. **Arms** tapering, up to 4 times disc diameter; arm spines tapering, shorter than the arm width at that point and lying against the arm itself; a.s.n. = 3. **Colour** orange-brown above; pale below. **Habitat** burrowing in sand from lower shore down to 200m (may get washed to upper shore). **Distribution** Mediterranean, Atlantic, English Channel, North Sea and west Baltic. N.B. a closely related species *O. albida* may be found in similar habitats (see Koehler, R. 1921 and Mortensen, T. 1927 for differences).

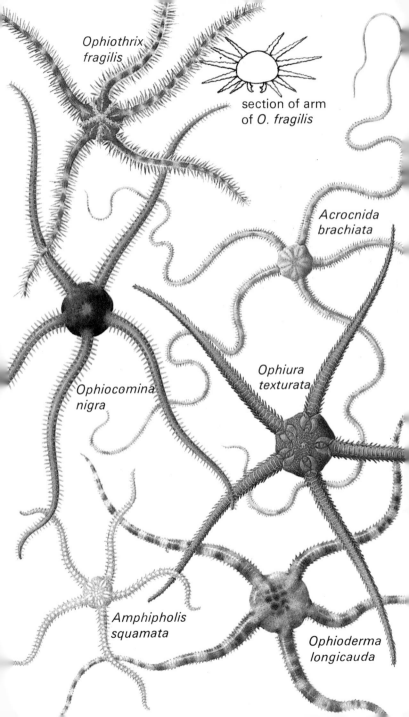

Ophiothrix fragilis

section of arm of *O. fragilis*

Acrocnida brachiata

Ophiura texturata

Ophiocomina nigra

Amphipholis squamata

Ophioderma longicauda

Class Echinoidea Sea-urchins, sand-dollars and heart-urchins

Subclass Perischoechinoidea Order Cidaroida and Subclass Euechinoidea

Superorders Diadematacea and Echinacea

Spherical echinoderms with a chalky, shell-like skeleton (the test) bearing mobile spines mounted externally on small knobs and being perforated by 5 double rows of pores which in life permit fluid to pass into the long tube-feet. The mouth is on the underside and has chewing teeth, and the anus is at the apex of the test.

Cidaris cidaris (Linnaeus) (***=Dorocidaris papillata***) Test up to 7cm in diameter. **Spines** both large and small; the large spines have longitudinal ridges (made up of rows of very fine thorns) reaching twice the test diameter and often encrusted with sponges, hydroids, etc.; the small spines are arranged around the bases of the large spines and on either side of the rows of tube-feet. **Colour** yellow-green-red-brown. **Habitat** various; from 30m downward. **Distribution** Mediterranean, Atlantic north to Biscay and in deep water off the west coast of Ireland.

Stylocidaris affinis (Philippi) (Not illustrated) Similar to *Cidaris cidaris* but smaller **Test** up to 4cm in diameter. **Spines** large and tapering; usually reach a little more than the test diameter and bear many visible small thorns. **Colour** orange-brown. **Habitat** on coralline seaweeds and rocks from the lower shore down to 30m. **Distribution** Mediterranean and Atlantic north to Portugal; not found in the Adriatic.

Centrostephanus longispinus (Philippi) Test up to 6cm in diameter. **Spines** long, hollow, slender and mobile. **Colour** spines patterned with brown and white bands; test red-brown. **Habitat** normally below 40m and often in very deep water. **Distribution** Mediterranean and adjacent Atlantic. N.B. the spines of this urchin may inflict painful wounds.

Arbacia lixula (Linnaeus) **Black Sea-urchin** Test up to 5cm in diameter. **Spines** up to 3cm long; solid and with sharp tips. **Colour** black spines; the cleaned test is pink with characteristic red lines marking the position of the tube-feet pores and the very large oral opening. **Habitat** on rocks and among coralline seaweeds from the extreme lower shore down to 40m. **Distribution** Mediterranean and Atlantic coasts to Portugal. N.B. this urchin is often confused with *Paracentrotus lividus* (see page 251) but in life the two may easily be distinguished by the extent of the soft membranes overlying the oral opening of the test. This opening is large in *A. lixula* and consequently the membrane is extensive; in *P. lividus* it is smaller and the membrane less apparent.

Sphaerechinus granularis (Lamarck) **Violet** or **Purple Sea-urchin** Test up to 12cm in diameter. **Spines** up to 2cm long; short and solid. **Colour** this urchin may easily be recognized by its colours, the spines often having white tips and purple shafts, or being entirely white and conspicuous against the purple of the test; the cleaned test can be recognized by the 10 narrow slits (each about 0.2cm long) which occur around the oral opening on the underside. **Habitat** on rocks and coralline seaweeds from the extreme lower shore down to 100m. **Distribution** Mediterranean and Atlantic north to Spain.

Strongylocentrotus droebachiensis (O. F. Müller) Test up to 5cm in diameter. **Spines** up to 2cm long; solid. **Colour** greenish. **Habitat** on rocks and seaweeds from sea level down to 1200m. **Distribution** north Atlantic coasts of Shetland and Norway, and North Sea. N.B. this urchin cannot be easily confused with *Paracentrotus lividus* (see page 251) because their distributions do not normally overlap.

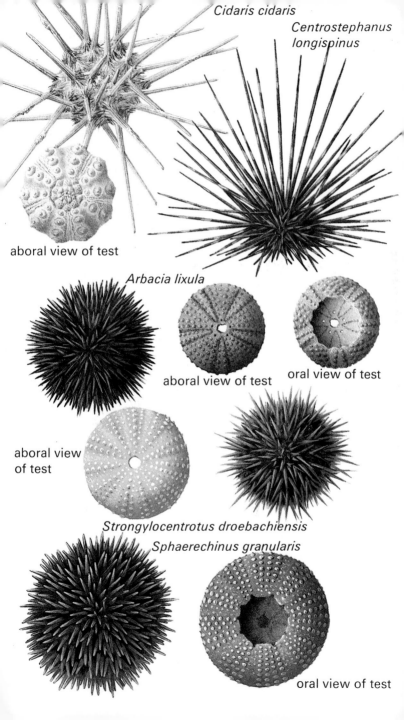

Cidaris cidaris

Centrostephanus longispinus

aboral view of test

Arbacia lixula

aboral view of test

oral view of test

aboral view of test

Strongylocentrotus droebachiensis

Sphaerechinus granularis

oral view of test

Paracentrotus lividus (Lamarck) **Test** up to 6 cm in diameter. **Spines** up to 3 cm long; smooth and solid. **Colour** variable; from green to dark brown; test when cleaned shows a relatively small oral opening (c.f. *Arbacia lixula*, page 249). **Habitat** on rocks and stones and among coralline seaweeds from lower middle shore in rock pools down to 30 m. **Distribution** Mediterranean and Atlantic north to Channel Islands and the west coast of Ireland; very rarely in the western English Channel. N.B. this species sometimes bores into the rocks of the shore, especially those on many western Irish beaches; it often covers itself with small fragments of seaweeds and shells, etc.; this species is somewhat gregarious and may occur in flocks, and in the Mediterranean it may be found associated with *Arbacia lixula*. In France the roes of this species are considered a delicacy.

Psammechinus miliaris (Gmelin) **Green Sea-urchin** Test up to 4 cm in diameter and very occasionally more. **Spines** up to 1.5 cm long; rather coarse. **Colour** spines have violet tips; test green when cleaned. **Habitat** on rocks and under stones often associated with coralline seaweeds and other encrusting organisms, from the lower middle shore down to 100 m. **Distribution** Atlantic, English Channel, North Sea and west Baltic.

Psammechinus microtuberculatus (Blainville) (Not illustrated) **Test** up to 3.5 cm in diameter. **Spines** up to 1.5 cm long; slender. **Colour** spines have reddish tips; test when cleaned is green-grey. **Habitat** on rocks and stones from 4–100 m. **Distribution** Mediterranean and Atlantic north to Portugal. N.B. this species could easily be confused with *P. miliaris* but for the fact that their distributions hardly ever overlap. It is also more delicate in form.

Echinus esculentus Linnaeus **Edible Sea-urchin** Test frequently up to 10 cm in diameter, but may reach 17 cm. **Spines** about 1.5 cm long; short and solid; not clearly divided into different size groupings (primaries and secondaries) and quite abundant on the test. **Colour** spines often have purple tips; test when cleaned is beautiful, with shades of red and purple, with white spine attachment points. **Habitat** on rocks and among seaweeds from extreme lower shore down to 50 m. **Distribution** Atlantic from Portugal to Norway, English Channel and North Sea. N.B. the polychaete *Flabelligera affinis* and the amphipod *Astacilla intermedia* (see pages 127 and 207) may be found living among the spines. This species has been used for food in various countries in Europe including Britain and Portugal, but the roes are rather coarse in comparison with those of *Paracentrotus lividus*.

Echinus acutus Lamarck Similar to *E. esculentus* **Test** up to 16 cm in diameter; noticeably more conical and not so well covered with spines which are rather scarce on the upper regions. **Spines** more readily divided into two size groupings (primaries and secondaries); longer than those of *E. esculentus*. **Colour** more reddish than in *E. esculentus* and often with white points. **Habitat** often on soft substrates from 20–1000 m. **Distribution** Mediterranean (not in the Adriatic), Atlantic and northern North Sea.

Echinus melo Lamarck (Not illustrated) **Test** up to 17 cm in diameter; there is some discussion as to the validity of this species which is very similar in many ways to *E. acutus*, but the test is globular rather than conical. **Colour** brownish red. **Habitat** on rocky substrates. **Distribution** Mediterranean (including the Adriatic) and Atlantic north to Portugal.

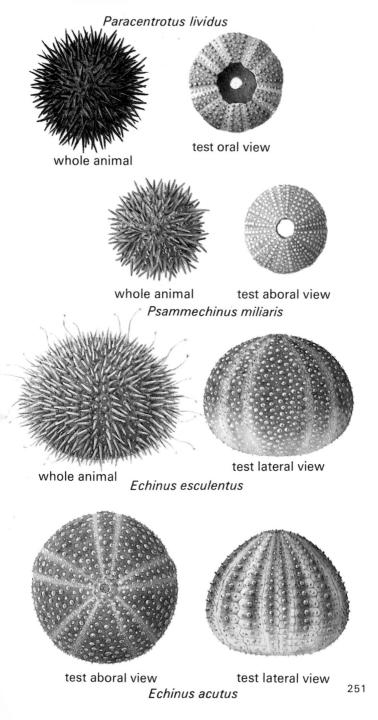

Paracentrotus lividus

whole animal

test oral view

whole animal

test aboral view

Psammechinus miliaris

whole animal

test lateral view

Echinus esculentus

test aboral view

test lateral view

Echinus acutus

251

Superorder Gnathostomata
Order Clypeasteroida Sand-dollars

Bilaterally symmetrical, disc-shaped echinoids with tube-feet which are mainly restricted to the upper side and are often arranged in petal-like patterns. The anus is on the underside, sometimes close to the mouth which bears chewing teeth.

Echinocyamus pusillus (O. F. Müller) **Pea-urchin** Test up to 1.5cm long. Spines short and thickly set. Colour green-grey. Habitat in sand and gravel from 1–800m. Distribution Mediterranean, Atlantic, English Channel, North Sea and west Baltic.

Superorder Atelostomata
Order Spatangoida Heart-urchins

Bilaterally symmetrical, heart-shaped echinoids with most tube-feet borne on the upper side but a few arranged below. The mouth and the anus are situated on the underside, towards the anterior and posterior ends respectively. The mouth lacks chewing teeth. The test is thickly covered with fine spines, often with a fur-like appearance. These urchins are highly adapted for burrowing.

Spatangus purpureus O. F. Müller **Purple Heart-urchin** Test up to 12cm long, bearing five rows of tube-feet of which the anterior row is the longest and lies in a pronounced but relatively shallow furrow leading towards the mouth. Spines mostly short, but some on the upper side are longer. Colour red-violet in life, but grey-white when cleaned. Habitat in coarse sand and shell gravel from 5–800m. Distribution Mediterranean, Atlantic, English Channel and North Sea.

Echinocardium cordatum (Pennant) **Sea-potato** Test up to 9cm long, but often smaller; bears 5 rows of tube-feet of which the anterior row is the longest, and appears modified considerably from the rest lying in a deep furrow reaching nearly to the mouth. Spines mostly short, but some are long and curved; densely distributed and directed backward. Colour yellow-brown in life, but yellow-white when cleaned. Habitat in sand from the lower shore to 200m. Distribution Mediterranean, Atlantic, English Channel and North Sea.

Echinocardium pennatifidum Norman (Not illustrated) Test up to 7cm long; bears 5 rows of tube-feet of which the anterior row is modified, being reduced and having relatively large pores; the frontal notch is inconspicuous and not severely furrowed as in *E. cordatum*. Colour white-yellow in life; white when cleaned sometimes showing grey blotches. Habitat in sand from 5–150m. Distribution Mediterranean, Atlantic, English Channel and North Sea; not present in the Adriatic.

Echinocardium flavescens (O. F. Müller) (Not illustrated) Very similar to *E. pennatifidum* but in life has yellow-pink spines. Habitat in sand from 20–325m. Distribution Atlantic, English Channel, North Sea and west Baltic.

Brissopsis lyrifera (Forbes) **Lyre-urchin** Test up to 7cm long; bears 5 rows of tube-feet, the posterior 2 rows being shorter and the anterior rows lying in a frontal notch which is not as deep as that of *Echinocardium cordatum*; the anus is fractionally above the edge of the test so as to appear slightly on the upper side. Spines short, dense and fur-like. Colour brown-red in life; yellow-grey when cleaned. Habitat buried in sand from 5–300m. Distribution Mediterranean, Atlantic and North Sea; not present in the Adriatic.

Brissus unicolor Klein Test up to 13cm long; bearing 5 rows of tube-feet all somewhat similar in length, but with the front row reaching up the mouth although not lying in a furrow; mouth well forward on the underside. Spines coat the test like fur. Colour yellow-brown in life; grey-light brown when cleaned. Habitat in muddy sand. Distribution Mediterranean.

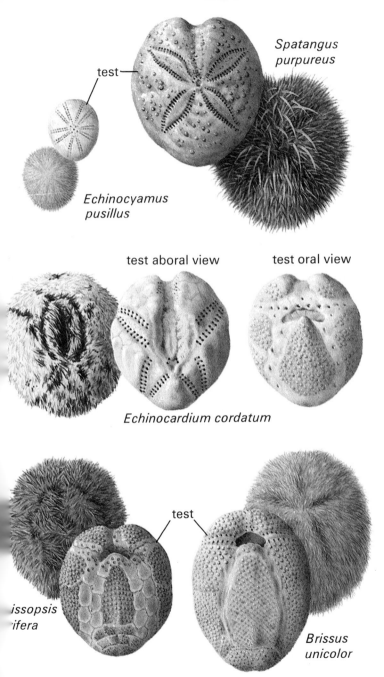

test

Spatangus purpureus

Echinocyamus pusillus

test aboral view

test oral view

Echinocardium cordatum

test

test

issopsis ifera

Brissus unicolor

253

Class Holothuroidea Sea-cucumbers

Bilateral echinoderms lacking conspicuous spines, arms or rays, and usually cucumber-shaped or worm-like. Tube-feet are present in many species, arranged in 5 rows along the sides of the animal; 3 rows are usually in contact with the substrate and these are equipped with suckers for locomotion, while the other 2 rows are borne away from the substrate. The anterior mouth is surrounded by modified tube-feet, and the anus is positioned posteriorly. A skeleton of loosely associated calcareous spicules is embedded in the 'skin'.

Stichopus regalis Cuvier **Length** up to 30cm. **Body** has well-developed, flattened, sole-like underside bearing locomotory tube-feet; rounded upper side is covered with warty protuberances and bumps; mouth opens on the underside and is not quite at the front of the body. **Colour** brownish with pale spots above; paler below. **Habitat** on sandy substrates and among corals and bryozoans, from 5–400m. **Distribution** Mediterranean and Atlantic.

Holothuria forskali Delle Chiaje **Sea-cucumber** or **Cotton-spinner** **Length** up to 20cm. **Body** cucumber-shaped; fairly well-defined lower surface bearing three rows of suckered, locomotory tube-feet; upper surface curved, warty and bearing irregularly arranged, suckerless tube-feet; around the mouth 20 feathery, modified tube-feet may be visible. **Colour** black above; pale brown-yellow below. **Habitat** on soft substrates and among *Zostera* (see page 65) from lower shore down to 70m. **Distribution** Atlantic and English Channel. N.B. if molested, this species may eject white sticky threads from the hind end as a defence mechanism.

Cucumaria normani Pace **Length** up to 15cm, but often less. **Body** generally more cylindrical than *Stichopus regalis* with lower surface not so clearly defined; well-developed locomotory tube-feet below arranged in double rows, upper tube-feet conspicuous but reduced; 10 special tube-feet around terminal mouth often extended and feather-like. **Colour** leathery skin is dirty white to brown. **Habitat** hidden under rocks and stones on the lower shore and down to 20m. **Distribution** Atlantic and English Channel.

Cucumaria elongata Duben & Koren **Length** up to 15cm. **Body** similar to *C. normani*; generally of curved shape and pointed towards the hind end; tube-feet apparently evenly distributed and arranged in 5 double rows. **Colour** usually dark brown. **Habitat** on muddy substrates from 5–150m. **Distribution** Mediterranean, Atlantic north to Norway, English Channel and North Sea. N.B. several other species of *Cucumaria* occur (see Mortensen, 1927 and Koehler, 1921).

Thyone fusus (O. F. Müller) **Length** up to 20cm, but often less. **Body** plump, tapering towards both ends; exterior covered by many irregularly arranged tube-feet; 10 modified oral tube-feet may be visible surrounding the mouth. **Colour** variable, but generally white-pink. **Habitat** on soft substrates from 10–150m. **Distribution** Mediterranean, Atlantic from Madeira to Norway and northern North Sea.

Leptosynapta inhaerens (O. F. Müller) **Worm-cucumber** **Length** up to 18cm. **Body** has no tube-feet apart from 12 around the mouth modified for feeding, each of these carries 5–7 pairs of minute, finger-like branches; minute, anchor-shaped skeletal spicules used in locomotion protrude through the soft skin making it adhesive. **Colour** usually pale pink. **Habitat** on or burrowing in mud and sand from 10–50m. **Distribution** Atlantic from French coast to Norway, English Channel and northern North Sea.

Labidoplax digita (Montagu) Similar in some respects to *Leptosynapta inhaerens* **Length** up to 18cm, though occasionally more. **Body** lacks locomotory tube-feet; oral tube-feet each have 2 pairs of minute, finger-like branches. **Habitat** on mud and sand from lower shore down to 70m. **Distribution** Mediterranean and Atlantic.

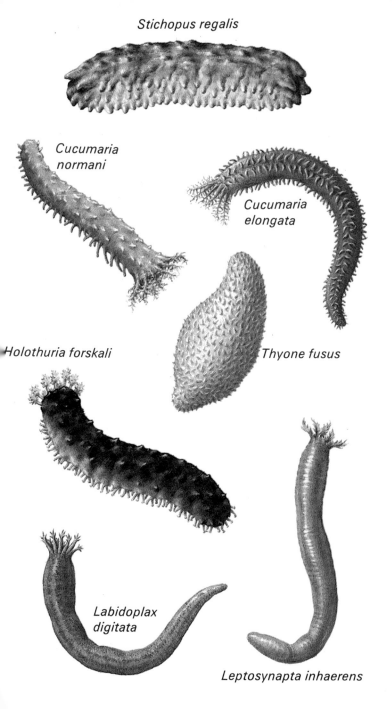

Stichopus regalis

Cucumaria normani

Cucumaria elongata

Holothuria forskali

Thyone fusus

Labidoplax digitata

Leptosynapta inhaerens

Phylum Chaetognatha

The chaetognaths are a small group of exclusively marine animals. Not more than fifty species have been identified, and these are all placed in one class. Their bodies are difficult to see unless they are held up to the light in a jar of sea water. Although they will be rarely met with on the seashore, they will be frequently encountered in plankton samples. About twelve or so species have been recorded from European waters, but because they are small and usually oceanic, only two are mentioned here.

Certain species of chaetognath are typically associated with particular currents of ocean water, and because of this they are important to oceanographers who need to trace the origins of planktonic communities. Such species are known as *indicator species*, one of which is *Sagitta setosa*, a common indicator for coastal waters in the North Sea and English Channel regions.

The body plan of the chaetognaths is quite characteristic. Essentially a small, bilaterally symmetrical, torpedo-shaped body bears paired side-fins and a tail fin. The anterior mouth is equipped with strong, grasping spines. Circulatory and excretory systems are lacking. The main variations in the body plan are the number of side-fins and the general shape of the body.

Chaetognaths are active predators. Typical items in their diet are small crustaceans called copepods. Chaetognaths appear able to detect the presence of prey by the vibrations that are sent out when swimming. The prey is then captured with the help of the grasping spines around the mouth.

Sagitta setosa J. Müller **Arrow Worm** (See page 259) **Length** up to 1.5 cm. **Body** narrow and transparent without colour; 2 pairs of lateral fins, the anterior being about halfway along the body, the posterior terminating a little in front of the tail. **Habitat** planktonic in coastal waters, sometimes stranded in rock pools. **Distribution** Mediterranean, Atlantic, English Channel, North Sea and west Baltic.

Spadella cephaloptera (Busch) (See page 259) **Length** up to 0.8 cm. **Body** less elongated than *Sagitta setosa*, but broader; 1 pair of lateral fins which are more or less continuous with the tail fin. **Habitat** unlike the majority of chaetognaths, this is a benthic species which attaches itself to rocks and seaweeds by means of suckers. It may be found on the seabed or in rock pools on the lower shore. **Distribution** Mediterranean, Atlantic and English Channel.

Phylum Hemichordata

The hemichordates are another small group of exclusively marine animals. Until recently they were classified as a subphylum within the Chordata. About eighty species are known, and these are divided into three classes: Enteropneusta, Pterobranchia and Planctosphaeroidea. Of these, only the first class falls within the scope of this book.

Hemichordates possess bilaterally symmetrical, worm-like bodies divided into three distinct zones, with or without gill slits. A circulatory system is present, but an excretory system is lacking. Tentacles may be present on the middle zone of the body. Both solitary and colonial forms occur.

Class Enteropneusta Acorn worms

These solitary marine worms should be quite easily distinguished from the other worms described in this book by the manner in which their bodies are divided into three regions or zones: an anterior proboscis, a short collar lying immediately behind the proboscis, and a long abdomen. The relative shapes of the various parts of the body are important in classification. The mouth opens at the junction of the proboscis and collar, and gives rise to the gut which passes back through the abdomen. The abdomen itself may be rounded or flattened. At the front of the abdomen are gills which communicate with the gut and facilitate respiration. Tentacles are lacking. In some species the gut forms a number of pockets towards the rear of the body and these can be discerned as small lumps arranged on either side of the posterior part of the abdomen. They are known as *hepatic pouches*. There is a simple circulatory system and a simple nervous system.

Enteropneusts live in U-shaped burrows in sand or mud, and may form characteristic casts reminiscent of polychaete worm casts. Like so many burrow-dwelling invertebrates, they are filter feeders extracting particulate food from sea water. The sexes are separate and the sperms and eggs escape into sea water by rupture of the body wall. A pelagic larva is formed after fertilization.

Saccoglossus cambrensis Stiasny (See page 259) **Length** up to 6cm. **Body** proboscis very long, and red-deep pink in colour; abdomen round, slightly paler and lacking hepatic pouches (see introduction to this group). **Habitat** burrowing in clean sand and gravel from lower shore downward. **Distribution** Atlantic.

Balanoglossus clavigerus Delle Chiaje (See page 259) **Length** up to 30cm. **Body** proboscis short, and yellow in colour; abdomen flattened and pale brown. **Habitat** burrowing in sand, mud and clay in shallow and deeper water. **Distribution** Mediterranean, Atlantic and English Channel.

Phylum Chordata

Chordates are animals possessing a single, hollow, dorsal nerve cord. A true body cavity (coelom) is present, as are gill slits and a notochord. The tail is post anal.

This phylum includes the fishes, which are the most familiar of all sea animals. A more detailed introduction is provided for them on pages 264–265. Far less familiar are the so-called invertebrate chordates (subphylum Urochordata), i.e. those animals whose evolutionary standing places them near the vertebrates, yet which as adults lack any trace of the diagnostic notochord or backbone, and which therefore resemble superficially the invertebrates. Two urochordate classes are treated here.

The class Thaliacea includes a number of organisms commonly known as salps. The adults lead a pelagic life, swimming amid their food supply (smaller planktonic organisms) which they filter by means of their gills. The body is surrounded by a number of muscle bands which can contract to force water out of the posterior exhalent opening, thus moving the animal forward. Water with food suspended in it is drawn in through the inhalent opening at the anterior end. The body structure is quite complicated, and a good deal of it is associated with the reproductive process. Thaliaceans have complex life cycles, and a very small tadpole-like larva with a notochord is formed. Some species are capable of forming associations or colonies. In some cases a species may be either colonial or solitary, and thus exists in two forms. Fig. 46 illustrates the basic characters of a solitary salp.

The class Ascidiacea comprises the sea-squirts. Unlike the salps, these are bottom dwellers as adults, and live attached to rocks or other organisms. They do retain a small, free-swimming tadpole-like larva, however. They also filter suspended food particles from the water which they take into their gills for respiration. The body is usually encased in a thick tunic made from cellulose-like material which often has a jelly-like consistency. As with the salps, there are inhalent and exhalent openings, but these are generally both situated towards the end opposite to the attachment point of the animal. The precise relationship of the two openings (the inhalent opening is normally terminal) is important in the identification of these animals. Another important feature is the proportion of body length which is occupied by the gill or branchial region, and the proportion which is occupied by the gastric region. In some species these areas

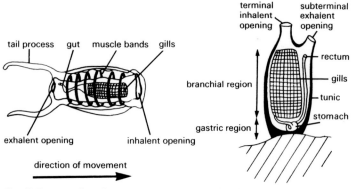

Fig. 46 Features of a solitary salp   Fig. 47 Features of a sea-squirt

are easier to discern than in others. Below the gills lie the stomach and reproductive systems as well as much of the circulatory system, but for simplicity the latter two systems have been omitted from the included diagram (fig. 47). Some sea-squirts, e.g. *Botryllus*, are colonial. Here, the individuals are arranged around common exhalent canals and are supported in a massive tunic.

Subphylum Urochordata

Class Thaliacea

Pelagic adults resemble floating, jelly-like barrels. A hollow, dorsal nerve cord and tail are present only in the larva. The nervous system is reduced.

Salpa maxima Forskål Solitary. **Length** up to 10cm long. **Body** barrel-shaped, with 9 conspicuous muscle bands arranged along the body. **Habitat** planktonic. **Distribution** Mediterranean and adjacent waters.

Salpa democratica Forskål **Length** solitary individuals up to 1.5cm; colonial individuals up to 0.6cm; colonial groups often have long streamers up to 30cm or more. **Habitat** planktonic. **Distribution** Mediterranean and adjacent waters.

See pages 256 and 257 for descriptions of the other species illustrated here.

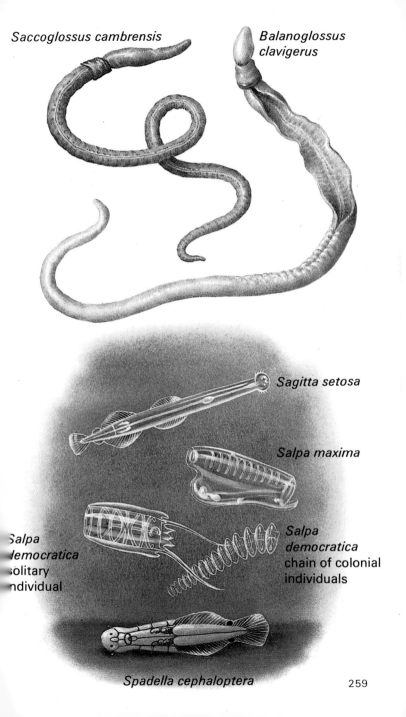

Saccoglossus cambrensis

Balanoglossus clavigerus

Sagitta setosa

Salpa maxima

Salpa democratica solitary individual

Salpa democratica chain of colonial individuals

Spadella cephaloptera

259

Class Ascidiacea

A hollow, dorsal nerve chord is present only in the larva, which resembles a small tadpole. Adults are sessile or pelagic, hermaphrodite, and covered with a tunic of cellulose. They may be solitary or colonial. Berrill, N. J. 1950, and Millar, R. H. 1970, provide a more detailed account of many European ascidians.

Clavelina lepadiformis (O. F. Müller) Sessile and colonial; individuals reach 2 cm in height and are easily distinguished from each other by being joined at the base only by thin stolons; inhalent and exhalent openings close together; branchial region markedly shorter than gastric region. **Colour** transparent and jelly-like, with pink-yellow-white marks. **Habitat** on stones, seaweeds and shells from extreme lower shore down to about 50m. **Distribution** Mediterranean, Atlantic, English Channel and North Sea.

Aplidium proliferum (Milne-Edwards) Sessile; individuals growing in fleshy colonies forming club-shaped growths; these may reach 5 cm in height and 5 cm across; individuals are not readily distinguished and are arranged rather irregularly around the common exhalent openings; colony is smooth and transparent with red individuals showing through. **Habitat** on stones, rocks, seaweeds, sponges and shells, etc., from the lower shore down to about 50m. **Distribution** Mediterranean, Atlantic, English Channel and North Sea. N.B. it is possible that this species may prove to be a variant of *Aplidium nordmanni*, which differs from it principally because it forms flat-topped, squat, encrusting colonies without club-shaped growths.

Didemnum candidum Savigny **(=*D. maculosum*)** Sessile; individuals growing in rough, leathery colonies which form irregular, encrusting growths about 0.2 cm thick and up to 4 cm across; individuals not easy to distinguish; 5–8 individuals share a common exhalent opening. **Colour** purple-yellow-white colonies contain calcareous spicules and are sometimes marked with purple lines. **Habitat** under stones and on seaweeds, especially laminarian holdfasts (see page 33), from lower shore down to deeper water. **Distribution** Mediterranean, Atlantic, English Channel and North Sea, but not further north than England.

Ciona intestinalis (Linnaeus) Sessile; solitary individuals with soft, cylindrical, retractile bodies reaching up to 12 cm in height; inhalent opening terminal, with exhalent opening close by; branchial region longer than gastric region. **Colour** transparent with yellow-green hues, edges of openings are yellow. **Habitat** often growing in great numbers on rocks, piers and piles as well as on seaweeds from lower shore down to 500m. **Distribution** Mediterranean, Atlantic, English Channel, North Sea and west Baltic.

Diazona violacea Savigny Sessile; individuals growing in globular or more flattened colonies reaching 20 cm in height and 40 cm across; individuals themselves may reach 5 cm high, and the branchial region of about 2 cm length usually protrudes from the colony; inhalent and exhalent openings are terminal and close together. **Colour** translucent yellow-green. **Habitat** attached to rocks and stones, often in strong currents, from 30–200m. **Distribution** Mediterranean, Atlantic and English Channel.

Ascidiella aspersa (O. F. Müller) Sessile; solitary, rough-looking individuals usually more than 6 cm high, but may occasionally reach 13 cm; inhalent opening terminal, exhalent opening about one-third of body height away. **Colour** brown-grey-black. **Habitat** in clay (where it may develop a stalk) or attached to stones and seaweeds or piles from lower shore down to 50m. **Distribution** Mediterranean, Atlantic north to Shetland, English Channel and west Baltic. N.B. sea-quirts of this and other species may grow on *A. aspersa*.

See page 262 for description of *Ascidia mentula*.

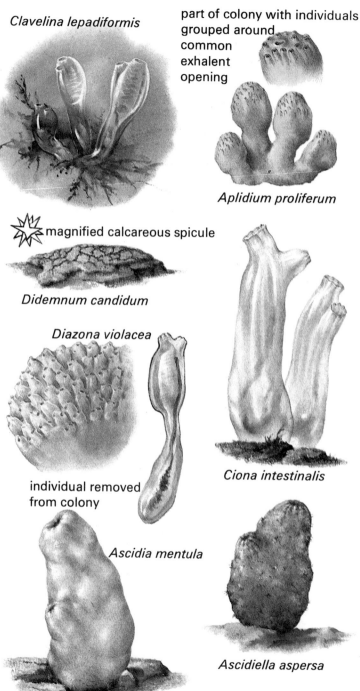

Clavelina lepadiformis

part of colony with individuals grouped around common exhalent opening

Aplidium proliferum

magnified calcareous spicule

Didemnum candidum

Diazona violacea

individual removed from colony

Ciona intestinalis

Ascidia mentula

Ascidiella aspersa

Ascidia mentula O. F. Müller (See page 261) Sessile; solitary individuals up to 10cm high, set in a thick, cartilage-like tunic; surface with swellings of low profile; exhalent opening more than half body length away from terminal, inhalent opening; branchial and gastric regions of similar size. **Colour** translucent with green hue. **Habitat** attached to rocks and sometimes shells from lower shore down to about 200m. **Distribution** Mediterranean, Atlantic, English Channel, North Sea and west Baltic.

Phallusia mammillata (Cuvier) Sessile; solitary individuals up to 14cm high, set in a thick, cartilage-like tunic with many conspicuous smooth swellings; inhalent opening terminal, exhalent opening less than half of the body length away from it. **Colour** varies with depth from white to brown. **Habitat** usually attached to stones buried in mud or clay from the lower shore down to about 180m. **Distribution** Mediterranean, and Atlantic to English Channel.

Styela plicata Leseur Sessile; solitary individuals up to 7cm high, set in a leathery, crinkled tunic; exhalent opening about one-quarter of body length from terminal inhalent opening. **Colour** white-brown. **Habitat** attached to stones, sometimes growing very close together; may be encrusted with seaweeds. **Distribution** Mediterranean and Atlantic.

Dendrodoa grossularia (van Beneden) Sessile, solitary or aggregated; individuals may be flattened to squat domes, or fairly upright and cylindrical, reaching 2.5cm high and 1.2cm across; exhalent opening about one-third of body length away from terminal inhalent opening. **Colour** red-brown. **Habitat** on rocks or shells from lower shore down to 100m or more; in sheltered places it often aggregates in large numbers and is more cylindrical in shape. **Distribution** Atlantic, English Channel, North Sea and west Baltic. N.B. avoid confusion with *Distomus variolosus* (below).

Distomus variolosus Gaertner Sessile and colonial; cylindrical-globular individuals reach up to 1cm high which are easily recognized within the colony, being clustered closely together; they aggregate by budding; inhalent opening of individual is terminal, exhalent opening is close by; tunic has rough surface. **Colour** red-brown. **Habitat** encrusting rocks and holdfasts of *Laminaria*, and hydroids on the extreme lower shore and in shallow water. **Distribution** Atlantic, English Channel and northern North Sea. N.B. avoid confusion with *Dendrodoa grossularia* (see above).

Botryllus schlosseri (Pallas) **Star Ascidian** Sessile; individuals arranged in characteristic, star-like groups of 3–12 or more within the colony; colonies of various shapes and sizes, often flat, but sometimes thicker and fleshy; individuals about 0.2cm long and arranged around a common exhalent opening. **Colour** very variable; often brown-yellow-green or reddish with 'stars' standing out in contrasting colours. **Habitat** encrusting stones, rocks and seaweeds, and sometimes hydroids and other ascidians, on lower shore and in shallow water. **Distribution** Mediterranean, Atlantic, English Channel and North Sea.

Botrylloides leachi (Savigny) General appearance similar to *Botrylus schlosseri* but individuals, which are about 0.15cm long, are arranged in irregular rows on either side of an elongated common exhalent cavity; they do not resemble stars. **Colour** orange-yellow-grey. **Habitat** encrusting stones and other ascidians on the lower shore and in shallow water. **Distribution** Mediterranean, Atlantic, English Channel and North Sea.

Molgula manhattensis (de Kay) Sessile and solitary; rounded, soft body up to 3cm high, inhalent and exhalent openings both terminal; tunic covered with small fibrils and sometimes with sand grains. **Colour** blue-green. **Habitat** on a variety of substrates and in areas of normal and reduced salinity from the lower shore down to about 100m. **Distribution** Atlantic, English Channel, North Sea and west Baltic.

Phallusia mammillata

Styela plicata

Dendrodoa grossularia

Distomus variolosus

Botrylloides leachi

Botryllus schlosseri

Molgula manhattensis

Subphylum **Vertebrata** Vertebrates

In addition to possessing chordate features, vertebrates have a backbone composed of many articulated body units, or vertebrae, arranged segmentally along with the main body musculature. The distinct head has associated sense organs, and the brain is protected by a brain case of skeletal material. Vertebrates often have paired front (pectoral) and rear (pelvic) appendages.

In terms of known species (about 46 700 species), the vertebrates are but a fraction of the whole animal kingdom. However, they include many of the most familiar organisms, and they range from the lowly lampreys to Man himself. In this book there is room to treat only one section of the vertebrates, the fishes, although seabirds, and mammals such as the porpoise and seal, are also familiar marine organisms. Several classes of vertebrates may be described as fishes. These are the Agnatha (fishes lacking true jaws), which include the lampreys and hagfishes; the Placodermi (an extinct class of primitive jawed fishes); the Chondrichthyes (cartilaginous fishes lacking hard bones), which include the sharks and rays; and the Osteichthyes which includes all the higher bony fishes of which the salmon and the goldfish are examples. The following account will include all these groups apart from the Placodermi.

The class Agnatha are primitive fishes represented today by one living order – the Cyclostomata. This name refers to the circular, sucker-like area armed with rasping teeth which surrounds the mouth. It includes two groups, the lampreys and the hagfishes. Lampreys which exist in fresh water and in the sea live as parasites by attaching themselves to other fishes, rasping a hole in them and sucking out the blood. Hagfishes are entirely marine and feed on dead and dying fishes and a variety of bottom-living organisms. The whole of the hagfish life cycle is passed in the sea, but the sea lamprey enters fresh water to spawn, and may be taken in estuaries. The river lamprey also spawns in fresh water, but spends at least one year in the sea during its growth to maturity before it returns to fresh water.

Although in general terms the cyclostomes show a low level of vertebrate development (simple, unpaired fins; poorly developed sense organs, etc.), they show special modifications to their way of life. These include the mouth and surrounding teeth, and the arrangement of the gills which may permit respiration even when part of the head is buried in the host's tissues.

The class Chondrichthyes contains some of the largest and most voracious marine animals, and in European waters it is represented by a range of forms including the smaller dogfishes, various skates and rays, and the very large basking sharks. The sharks, unlike the cyclostomes mentioned above, are all rapid and powerful swimmers, often leading lives as voracious carnivores. They frequently prey on shoaling fishes like herring and mackerel. Some of the smaller species are scavengers, while the basking sharks are filter feeders, straining the surface waters for small, planktonic organisms in the manner of many whales. The skates and rays are bottom dwellers, feeding on invertebrates living on or in the sand and mud, as well as preying on flatfishes. Fig. 48 shows the main external features of a male shark. It will be noted that the pelvic fins are

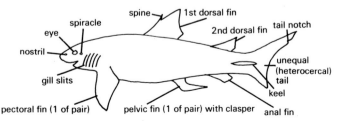

Fig. 48 External features of a generalized male shark

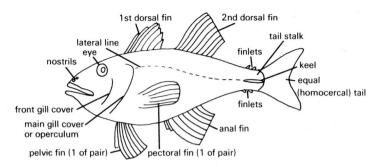

Fig. 49 External features of a generalized teleost

modified for use as claspers — structures which allow the transfer of sperms to the female. Females lack claspers. The eggs are normally retained within the female body and, after fertilization, the embryos may develop there until they are sufficiently mature to lead an independent life after birth. In the case of certain species, such as the dogfishes, the embryos are extruded from the female body in special egg cases known as mermaids' purses (see page 305). These egg cases are attached to seaweeds, and eventually the juveniles hatch from them. Many rays and skates reproduce in a similar fashion. In these species the males can also usually be distinguished by the possession of claspers.

As would be expected from a group of predatory organisms, the senses are well developed, particularly those of vibration and smell which enable the sharks and their allies to track down their prey.

Most of the important food fishes in the world belong to the class Osteichthyes, although in many countries sharks and skates are fished commercially. The Osteichthyes are divided into a number of subgroups of which two concern us here. The first of these is the Chondrostei, which are rather primitive, with unequally developed tail fins. An example is the sturgeon, but there are many fossil forms. The second subgroup is the Teleostei, which includes the dominant fishes of the present day, and of most recent geological eras. They are immediately distinguished externally by the equal tail, and internally by the possession of a swim bladder or buoyancy mechanism which enables them to maintain a particular position in the water without swimming. Fig. 49 indicates the principal external features of a teleost. In many cases it is not easy to distinguish between the sexes except by colour at certain times of the year. Most marine teleosts lay thousands of eggs which are fertilized externally by the male. In a number of cases the eggs float, and after fertilization they develop in the plankton as embryos, the juveniles feeding on the yolk supply of the egg. When this is exhausted they can often take small items of planktonic food. The teleosts have evolved to occupy almost all possible niches in the marine habitat, from the open ocean to the rock pool, from the surface waters to the abyssal depths. A great variety will be encountered on the seashores and in the shallow seas of Europe. Readers requiring more information should turn to Hardy, A. C. 1970; Muus, B. J. and Dalstrom, P. 1974; Lythgoe, J. and Lythgoe, G. 1971; Marshall, N. B. 1965 or Wheeler, A. 1969.

Because of variability both in life and after death, references to colour for identification purposes have been kept to a minimum.

Class Agnatha Lampreys and hagfishes

Vertebrates lacking true jaws

Petromyzon marinus Linnaeus **Sea Lamprey** Length up to 90cm when adult. **Head** bears small eyes; 7 pairs of gills; mouth opens to form an oval, sucker-like structure armed with many teeth arranged in several circlets; large centre tooth with 2 points. **Body** long, slender and eel-like; 2 dorsal fins and 1 tail fin; skin smooth and lacking scales. **Habitat** often near river mouths and fresh water, from shallow water down to 400m or more. **Distribution** Mediterranean, Atlantic, English Channel, North Sea and Baltic.

Myxine glutinosa Linnaeus **Hagfish** (Not illustrated) **Length** up to 40cm when adult. **Head** bears no eyes; 2 barbels each side of terminal nostril and 2 more each side of mouth; 1 gill opening on each side. **Body** eel-like; 1 fin continuous around posterior. **Habitat** on muddy substrates in burrows from 25m downward; often attached to other fishes on which it preys. **Distribution** Atlantic, English Channel and North Sea.

Class Chondrichthyes Sharks, skates and rays

Vertebrates with true jaws and cartilaginous skeletons, and lacking bony fin rays. The mouth is on the under surface. The skin generally feels hard and rough when stroked from the tail towards the head. The tail usually has two unequal lobes.

Isurus oxyrinchus Rafinesque **Mako** Length up to 4m when adult. **Head** mouth has powerful jaws armed with large, sharply pointed teeth lacking cusps or notches; 5 large gill slits in front of pectoral fins. **Body** typically shark-like; fairly slender; 2 dorsal fins, the first being immediately behind the posterior edge of the pectoral fin; tail has side-keels and a notch. **Habitat** open water near the surface. **Distribution** Atlantic north to the approaches to the English Channel.

Lamna nasus (Bonnaterre) **Porbeagle** or **Mackerel Shark** Length up to 3.5m when adult. **Head** teeth have notches or cusps on either side of the main triangular point. **Body** somewhat similar to *Isurus oxyrinchus* but with a fuller shape and upper part of tail fin longer; dorsal fin begins where pectoral fin bones terminate. **Habitat** from shallow water down to about 150m. **Distribution** Mediterranean, Atlantic, English Channel and North Sea. N.B. illustration shows a female, identifiable by the lack of claspers on the pelvic fins (see page 264).

Cetorhinus maximus (Gunnerus) **Basking Shark** Length up to 15m when adult; great size gives easy identification. **Head** pointed snout; tiny teeth; small eyes; 5 long gill slits in front of the pectoral fin; gill slits run from near the top of the body almost to the mid-line below; gills have rakers which strain plankton from the sea water passing through them, so providing food. **Body** 1st dorsal fin lies between pectoral and pelvic fins. **Habitat** usually in open surface water, migrating to deeper water in Winter. **Distribution** Mediterranean, Atlantic, English Channel, northern North Sea and western Baltic.

Alopias vulpinus (Bonnaterre) **Thresher** Length up to 4m when adult. **Head** not as pointed as in some species. **Body** the exceptionally long upper lobe of the tail fin gives easy identification. **Habitat** open surface water. **Distribution** Mediterranean, Atlantic and northern North Sea.

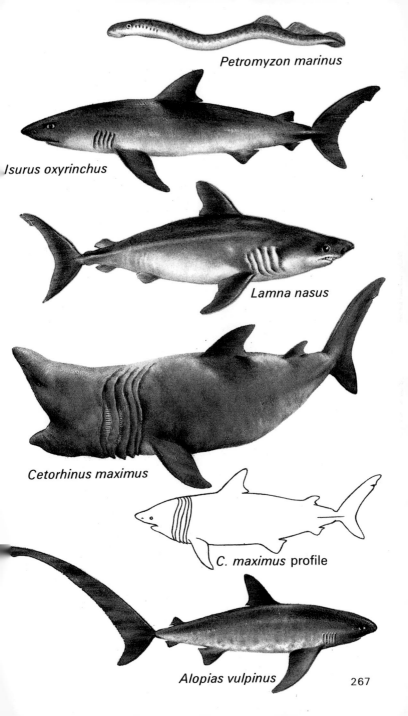

Petromyzon marinus

Isurus oxyrinchus

Lamna nasus

Cetorhinus maximus

C. maximus profile

Alopias vulpinus

267

Scyliorhinus canicula (Linnaeus) **Lesser-spotted Dogfish, Rough Hound** or **Rock Salmon** Length up to 70cm when adult. **Head** blunt, rounded snout; nostrils connected to the mouth by a conspicuous, fairly straight external groove visible on the underside of the snout; 5 pairs of small gill slits, the posterior 2 pairs overlap the pectoral fins; 1 pair of spiracles. **Body** 2 dorsal fins, the second lying just behind the anal fin. **Habitat** near or on sandy and muddy substrates, from shallow water down to 100m or more. **Distribution** Mediterranean, Atlantic, English Channel and North Sea.

Scyliorhinus stellaris (Linnaeus) **Large-spotted Dogfish** or **Nurse Hound** Length up to 1m when adult. **Head** very similar to *S. canicula*; may be distinguished by the nostril grooves on the underside of the snout which do not connect the nostrils to the mouth, but terminate short of it and then run towards the mid-line almost meeting to form a w-shape. **Body** 2nd dorsal fin begins over the centre of the anal fin. **Habitat** often on rocky ground in sheltered places, from shallow water down to about 50m. **Distribution** Mediterranean, Atlantic, English Channel and North Sea.

Mustelus mustelus (Linnaeus) **Smooth Hound** Length up to 1.5m when adult. **Head** sharp, tapering snout; jaws with flat, unpointed teeth somewhat resembling diamond-shaped tiles and adapted for crushing the prey rather than tearing it to pieces; 5 gill slits, the last overlapping the pectoral fin. **Body** 1st dorsal fin starts posterior to pectoral fins; 2nd dorsal fin starts just anterior to anal fin; conspicuous tail notch. **Habitat** on soft substrates from 5–100m. **Distribution** Mediterranean, Atlantic, English Channel and North Sea.

Mustelus asterias Cloquet **Stellate Smooth Hound** (Not illustrated) **Length** up to 2m when adult. **Head** pointed. **Body** not quite as slender as *M. mustelus*, but resembling it in most respects apart from the presence of white markings on the sides and back. **Habitat** on sandy and muddy substrates, from shallow water down to about 150m. **Distribution** Mediterranean, Atlantic, English Channel and North Sea.

Prionace glauca (Linnaeus) **Blue Shark** Length up to 4m when adult. **Head** pointed snout; triangular teeth with serrated edges; 5 pairs of small gill slits, the last pair overlapping the long blade-like pectoral fins. **Body** 1st dorsal fin larger than 2nd; no keels; tail fin with notch on dorsal lobe; relatively smooth skin because scales are reduced in size. **Habitat** open surface water. **Distribution** Mediterranean, Atlantic north to Norway and the extreme west of the English Channel.

Galeorhinus galeus (Linnaeus) **Tope** Length up to 2m when adult. **Head** conspicuously pointed snout; sharp, pointed teeth with small accessory points on the posterior sides; 5 gill slits, the last pair overlapping the large pectoral fins. **Body** 1st dorsal fin lies between pectoral and pelvic fins and is considerably larger than the 2nd dorsal fin; 2nd dorsal fin lies slightly in front of the anal fin. **Habitat** on gravel or sandy substrates, from shallow water down to about 250m. **Distribution** Mediterranean, Atlantic, English Channel and North Sea.

Squalus acanthias (Linnaeus) **Spiny Dogfish** Length up to 1.2m when adult. **Head** rounded snout; spiracle behind eyes; 5 gill slits, all in front of pectoral fins. **Body** 1st and 2nd dorsal fins with an anterior spine; pelvic fins lie in front of 2nd dorsal fin; anal fins lacking; no keels or notch in tail. **Habitat** on a variety of substrates, from shallow water downward. **Distribution** Mediterranean, Atlantic, English Channel and North Sea.

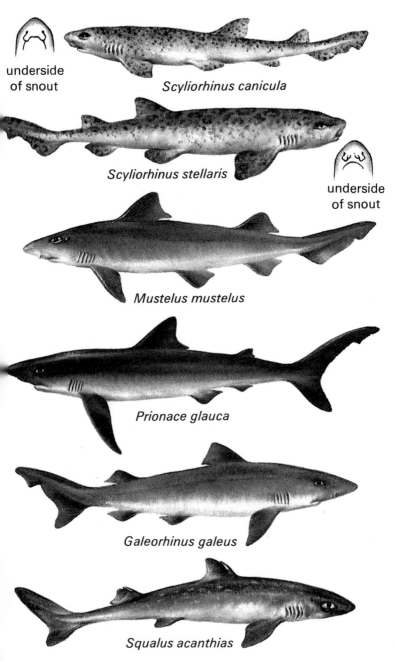

underside
of snout

Scyliorhinus canicula

Scyliorhinus stellaris

underside
of snout

Mustelus mustelus

Prionace glauca

Galeorhinus galeus

Squalus acanthias

Squatina squatina (Linnaeus) **Monkfish** or **Angel Shark** Length up to 2m when adult. **Head** blunt in outline with 2 nostrils and small barbels; conspicuous spiracles lie behind eyes. **Body** flattened and resembling that of a ray; very large pectoral fins, pelvic fins smaller; 2 dorsal fins; no anal fin; upper lobe of tail is smaller than lower. **Habitat** on sand and gravel, sometimes partly buried, usually in shallow water and down to 100m. **Distribution** Mediterranean, Atlantic and English Channel. N.B. two other species of *Squatina* occur in the Mediterranean and nearby Atlantic but are not illustrated. *S. aculeata* (Linnaeus) is distinguished from *S. squatina* by a row of conspicuous spines running down its back; *S. oculata* Bonaparte has large black spots on the pectoral fins and on the body towards the tail.

Torpedo marmorata Risso **Electric Ray** Length up to 60cm when adult. **Head** bears conspicuous spiracles behind the eyes, fringed on their inner margins by small protrusions of skin. **Body** banjo-shaped; pectoral fins form edges of body; smaller pelvic fins; anal fins lacking; smooth skin lacks scales. **Habitat** on sandy substrates, sometimes partly buried, from shallow water down to 200m. **Distribution** Mediterranean, Atlantic north to south-west Britain and Ireland and English Channel. N.B. this fish can give quite powerful shocks when touched, by discharging its electric organs which are modified muscles. Two similar species occur in the same regions as well as further afield. *T. torpedo* (Linnaeus) may be distinguished by its possession of about 5 large, blue spots set in dark rings on the predominantly brown back. The spiracles are generally large and unfringed. *T. nobiliana* Bonaparte is dark grey to black all over and has unfringed spiracles.

Raja clavata Linnaeus **Thornback Ray** Length up to 80cm when adult. **Head** bears conspicuous spiracles. **Body** pectoral fins form edges of the body which are wing-like; pelvic fins set close-by; dorsal fins lacking; very rough skin with conspicuous spines on the upper surface of the body and tail. **Habitat** on soft substrates from shallow water down to 100m or more. **Distribution** Mediterranean, Atlantic, English Channel, North Sea and west Baltic.

Raja batis (Linnaeus) **Common Skate** Length up to 2m when adult. **Head** snout tends to be more pointed than that of *R. clavata*. **Body** row of conspicuous spines along tail. **Habitat** sandy and muddy substrates, from shallow water down to about 500m. **Distribution** rarely in Mediterranean, Atlantic, English Channel and North Sea. N.B. about ten other species of *Raja* occur in the European area and may be difficult to identify. Wheeler, A. 1969 gives identification details.

Dasyatis pastinaca (Linnaeus) **Common Stingray** Length up to 2.3m overall. **Head** fairly pointed snout; eyes smaller than spiracle situated just behind them. **Body** pectoral fins form edge of body; pelvic fins adjacent; no dorsal fins; long tapering tail about 1.5 times length of body and bearing conspicuous toothed spine; female illustrated here. **Habitat** on soft substrates sometimes partly buried and often in sheltered places in shallow water down to 50m. **Distribution** Atlantic, English Channel, southern North Sea and rarely west Baltic. N.B. the tail spine is associated with a venom sac and extremely painful (but not fatal) wounds may be inflicted.

Myliobatis aquila (Linnaeus) **Eagle Ray** Length up to 2m overall. **Head** more distinct from body than in *Dasyatis pastinaca*; eyes and spiracles set sideways. **Body** diamond-shaped, with pectoral, pelvic and small dorsal fins, the last situated just in front of tail spine; tail about twice as long as body. **Habitat** in surface water and on soft substrates down to about 250m. **Distribution** Mediterranean, Atlantic north to Scotland and English Channel.

Squatina squatina

Raja batis ♀

Raja clavata ♂

Torpedo marmorata

Dasyatis pastinaca

Myliobatis aquila

Class Osteichthyes Bony fishes

Fishes with true jaws and bony skeletons

Subclass Actinopterygii
Infraclass Chondrostei

Primitive fishes with bony rays in the fins, the gill openings covered by a gill cover or operculum, and with unequally developed tail lobes.

Acipenser sturio Linnaeus **Sturgeon** Length up to 1.5m when adult, though occasionally up to 4m. **Head** pointed snout with 4 barbels; oval sucker-mouth. **Body** has 5 rows of large bony plates running along it; upper lobe of tail larger than lower. **Habitat** on sandy and muddy substrates, often in brackish water, and penetrating far up rivers to spawn. **Distribution** Mediterranean (especially Adriatic), Atlantic, English Channel, North Sea and Baltic. N.B. a closely related species *A. huso* Linnaeus (not illustrated) may be found in the eastern Mediterranean and Adriatic. Adults reach up to 6m in length and have crescent-shaped mouths and much smaller bony plates.

Infraclass Teleostei

More advanced fishes having bony rays in the fins, gill openings covered by an operculum, equally developed tails and an internal swim bladder.

Sprattus sprattus (Linnaeus) **Sprat** Length up to 15cm when adult. **Head** operculum with radial ridges. **Body** 1 dorsal fin set slightly back from mid-line; pelvic fins begin just in front of dorsal fin; forked tail fin; sharp scales give belly a serrated keel; large scales easily lost from body. **Habitat** open water in shoals coming in shore towards Winter; from 10–150m. **Distribution** Mediterranean, Atlantic, English Channel, North Sea and Baltic. N.B. the Mediterranean and Baltic races do not generally interbreed with those found in the Atlantic, English Channel and North Sea.

Clupea harengus Linnaeus **Herring** Length up to 40cm when adult. **Head** operculum smooth. **Body** very similar to *Sprattus sprattus* but with dorsal fin in middle of back; pelvic fins begin just behind start of dorsal fin; sharp scales on belly form a weak ridge only. **Habitat** open water in vast shoals migrating into shallow inshore waters towards Winter. **Distribution** Atlantic north from Biscay, English Channel, North Sea and Baltic. N.B. several races of herring are recognized from the north Atlantic and Baltic. Mixed shoals of young Herrings and young Sprats are known as whitebait. Much scientific work has been carried out on the habits of this important food fish, see Muus, B. J. and Dahlstrom, P. 1974 or Hardy, A. C. 1970 for brief reviews.

Sardina pilchardus (Walbaum) **Sardine** (when small) or **Pilchard** (when large) **Length** up to 26cm when adult. **Head** operculum with radial ridges. **Body** 1 dorsal fin set a little forward of the mid-line; pelvic fins start below the middle of the dorsal fin; last rays of the anal fin are long; forked tail; no sharp keel; large scales; may show a few darker spots on flanks. **Habitat** in coastal waters in Spring and Summer, moving to deeper water in Winter. **Distribution** Atlantic north to Ireland and northern England, English Channel and North Sea.

Salmo salar Linnaeus **Salmon** Length male up to 150cm, female up to 1.2m when adult. **Head** large jaws, the upper extending back to the posterior margin of the eye; in breeding condition the jaws of old males may become hooked. **Body** 2 dorsal fins, 2nd lacks bony rays and is called the *adipose* fin. **Habitat** open sea, migrating via coastal waters to spawn in rivers. **Distribution** Atlantic north from Biscay, English Channel, North Sea and Baltic. N.B. migration and breeding habits are frequently described in books.

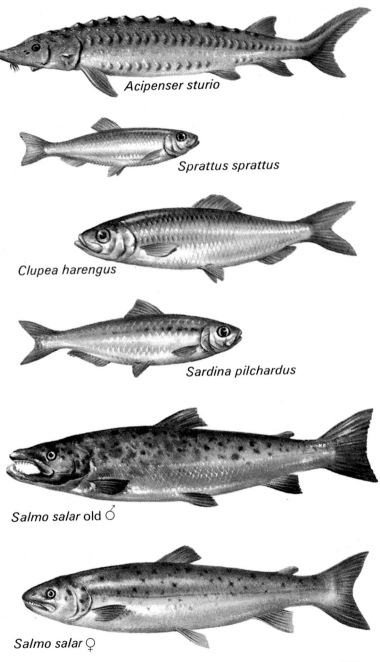

Acipenser sturio

Sprattus sprattus

Clupea harengus

Sardina pilchardus

Salmo salar old ♂

Salmo salar ♀

273

Salmo trutta Linnaeus **Sea Trout** (Not illustrated) **Length** up to 1 m when adult. **Head** upper jaw usually reaches back beyond posterior limit of eye. **Body** similar to *S. salar* (illustrated on page 273), but deeper, and tail stalk deeper. **Habitat** coastal waters, but entering rivers to spawn. **Distribution** Atlantic north of Spain, English Channel, North Sea and Baltic.

Note on the freshwater fishes Apart from several species which occur in both fresh and sea water throughout the European area and which will be treated below, a number of typical freshwater fishes occur in the Baltic where the salinity is low enough for them to exist. They include *Abramis brama* (Linnaeus), Bream; *Alburnus alburnus* (Linnaeus), Bleak; *Leuciscus idbarus* (Linnaeus), Ide; *Rutilus rutilus* (Linnaeus), Roach; *Tinca tinca* (Linnaeus), Tench; *Perca fluviatilis* (Linnaeus), Perch; and *Stizostedion lucioperca* (Linnaeus), Pike-perch. A description of these fishes is beyond the scope of this book and reference should be made to an appropriate text such as *The Collins Guide to Freshwater Fishes* by Muus, B. and Dahlstrom, P. 1971.

Esox lucius Linnaeus **Pike** **Length** up to 1 m when adult. **Head** the extended snout and long jaws give easy identification. **Body** single dorsal fin set far back on the powerful body; slightly forked tail. **Habitat** freshwater lakes and rivers and sea areas of low salinity. **Distribution** throughout the European area and Baltic.

Anguilla anguilla (Linnaeus) **Common Eel** **Length** up to 1.4m when adult. **Head** upper jaw shorter than lower one; gill slit. **Body** dorsal fin starts about a quarter of the way back from snout and well behind pectoral fins; no pelvic fins; minute scales embedded in skin. **Habitat** in lakes, rivers and coastal waters as well as in the ocean depths. **Distribution** Atlantic, English Channel, North Sea and Baltic. N.B. the lengthy migration made by this species to the Sargasso Sea to spawn is described in many books dealing with fishes. The illustrations show two forms, the younger or yellow form which has a swollen head when viewed from above and the older or silver form which has lost its swollen headed appearance and is ready for its journey to the Sargasso Sea. There are many intermediate forms.

Conger conger (Linnaeus) **Conger Eel** **Length** up to 2m when adult. **Head** large mouth; upper jaw fractionally longer than lower jaw; 1 gill slit. **Body** more massive and powerful than *Anguilla anguilla*; dorsal fin starts just behind pectoral fins; no pelvic fins; no scales. **Habitat** among rocks and wrecks in shallow and very deep water. **Distribution** Mediterranean, Atlantic, English Channel, North Sea and west Baltic. N.B. this is a truly marine species.

Muraena helena Linnaeus **Moray Eel** **Length** up to 1.3m when adult. **Head** long, powerful jaws; gill opening surrounded by a black ring. **Body** no pectoral or pelvic fins; dorsal fin starts just in front of gill opening. **Habitat** in cracks of rocks and reefs and in old amphorae (as illustrated) in both shallow and deeper water. **Distribution** Mediterranean and Atlantic north to Biscay.

Belone belone (Linnaeus) **Garfish** or **Garpike** **Length** up to 80cm when adult. **Head** fine, tapering jaws, the upper being the shorter. **Body** long, slender; 1 dorsal fin set far back near forked tail; pectoral and pelvic fins; anal fin situated under dorsal fin; no finlets between these fins and tail. **Habitat** open surface water in shoals, occasionally inshore. **Distribution** Mediterranean, Atlantic, English Channel, North Sea and Baltic.

Scomberesox saurus (Walbaum) **Skipper** (Not illustrated) **Length** up to 50cm when adult. Similar to *Belone belone* in appearance and details; about 5 finlets between dorsal fin and tail and about 6 finlets between anal fin and tail (see fig. 49).

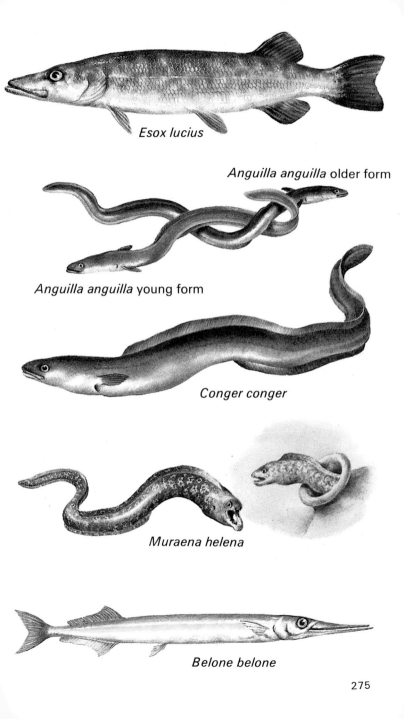

Esox lucius

Anguilla anguilla older form

Anguilla anguilla young form

Conger conger

Muraena helena

Belone belone

275

Trisopterus luscus (Linnaeus) **Pout, Whiting** or **Bib** Length up to 30cm when adult. **Head** upper jaws slightly longer than lower; conspicuous barbel on lower jaw. **Body** deep; 3 dorsal fins; pelvic fins lie in front of pectoral fins which have blackish spot at base; anus set vertically beneath centre of 1st dorsal fin; 2 anal fins; very short spaces between dorsal fins and anal fins. **Habitat** on rocky and sandy substrates from shallow water down to about 100m. **Distribution** Atlantic north from Biscay, English Channel, North Sea and west Baltic.

Trisopterus minutus (Linnaeus) **Poor Cod** Length up to 20cm when adult. **Head** upper jaw longer than lower jaw. **Body** similar to *T. luscus* but not quite as deep and lacking vertical colour bands; anus lies slightly further back, behind the hind part of the 1st dorsal fin. **Habitat** around piles, piers and rocks from shallow water down to 100m. **Distribution** Atlantic north from Brittany, English Channel, North Sea and west Baltic.

Pollachius pollachius (Linnaeus) **Pollack** Length up to 1.2m when adult. **Head** upper jaw shorter than lower jaw, which lacks barbel. **Body** 3 dorsal fins and 2 anal fins with distinct spaces between each; lateral line (see fig. 49) curves over pectoral fins and meets horizontal plane of fish just below start of 2nd dorsal fin; 1st anal fin starts below 1st dorsal fin and ends short of terminal part of 2nd dorsal fin. **Habitat** among piers and rocks inshore in shallow water and down to 100m. **Distribution** west Mediterranean, Atlantic, English Channel, northern North Sea and west Baltic.

Pollachius virens (Linnaeus) **Saithe** or **Coley** Length usually up to 60cm, but may be twice this size. **Head** minute barbel on lower jaw (may not be visible). **Body** similar to *P. pollachius* but distinguished by pale, nearly straight lateral line; 1st anal fin starts vertically beneath the start of 2nd dorsal fin. **Habitat** among piers and rocks inshore and down to 200m. **Distribution** Atlantic north from Biscay, English Channel, North Sea and west Baltic.

Gadus morhua Linnaeus **Cod** Length up to 1m when adult. **Head** lower jaw shorter than upper; conspicuous barbel. **Body** lateral line curves over pectoral fin and does not straighten out until it passes under the trailing edge of 2nd dorsal fin; 1st anal fin starts more or less directly under start of 2nd dorsal (this is similar to the Saithe, but curved lateral line and barbel identify Cod). **Habitat** on soft substrates from shallow water down to 600m. **Distribution** Atlantic north from Biscay, English Channel, North Sea and Baltic.

Molva molva (Linnaeus) **Ling** Length up to 1m when adult. **Head** lower jaw shorter than upper and bearing simple barbel. **Body** long, gradually tapering to tail. **Habitat** among rocks from 10—400m. **Distribution** Atlantic from Biscay northwards.

Gaidropsarus mediterraneus (Linnaeus) **Shore Rockling** Length up to 25cm when adult. **Head** 3 barbels; upper jaw does not reach back beyond eye. **Body** 1st dorsal fin has pronounced leading ray, others reduced; 2nd dorsal fin long; long anal fin. **Habitat** among rocks, in pools and shallow water down to 30m. **Distribution** Mediterranean, Atlantic and English Channel.

Ciliata mustela (Linnaeus) **Five-bearded Rockling** Length up to 20cm when adult. **Head** 5 barbels. **Body** similar to *Gaidropsarus mediterraneus*. **Habitat** on the shore and in shallow water in sandy places. **Distribution** Atlantic north to Portugal, English Channel, North Sea and west Baltic. N.B. several other species of cod-like fishes and Rocklings occur in the European area. These include the Whiting (see page 279); for descriptions of Haddock, Hake and Three- and Four-bearded Rocklings, etc., see Wheeler, A. 1969.

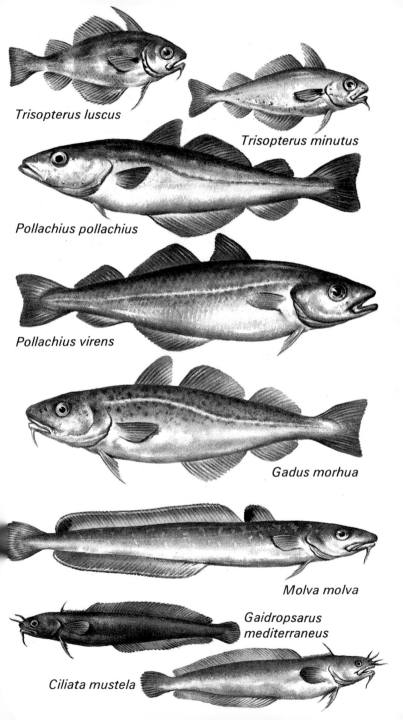

Trisopterus luscus

Trisopterus minutus

Pollachius pollachius

Pollachius virens

Gadus morhua

Molva molva

Gaidropsarus mediterraneus

Ciliata mustela

Merlangius merlangus (Linnaeus) **Whiting** (Not illustrated) Length up to 50cm when adult. **Head** upper jaw longer than lower jaw, which normally lacks barbel. **Body** similar in shape to *Trisopterus minutus* and *T. luscus* on previous page, but less deep; 1st anal fin starts vertically beneath centre of 1st dorsal fin and terminates level with end of 2nd dorsal fin. **Colour** blue-green-brown above, sides silvery with grey-black spot at the base of pectoral fin. **Habitat** near soft substrates from 20–150m. **Distribution** western Mediterranean, Atlantic north from Spain, English Channel, North Sea and west Baltic.

Hippocampus ramulosus Leach **Seahorse** Height up to 15cm when adult. **Head** snout is more than one-third of the total head length. **Body** 'mane' or crest of appendages runs from behind the eyes to the dorsal fin on the 'back'; the horse-like appearance gives easy identification. **Habitat** among seaweeds and sea-grasses especially *Posidonia* (see page 65). **Distribution** Mediterranean and Atlantic north to English Channel approaches.

Hippocampus hippocampus Linnaeus **Seahorse** Height up to 15cm. **Head** snout is one-third or less of the total head length. **Body** similar to *H. ramulosus*. **Habitat** as for *H. ramulosus*. **Distribution** Mediterranean and Atlantic north to English Channel approaches.

Syngnathus acus Linnaeus **Greater Pipefish** Length up to 50cm when adult. **Head** tapering snout occupies more than half total head length; small hump over gill opening. **Body** very long and slender; pectoral fins present; about 18 body rings between pectoral fin base and start of dorsal fin; small tail fin. **Habitat** among sand, pebbles and rocks in shallow water. **Distribution** Mediterranean, Atlantic, English Channel, North Sea and west Baltic.

Syngnathus rostellatus Nilsson **Lesser Pipefish** (Not illustrated) **Length** up to 17cm when adult. **Head** snout occupies less than half head length. **Body** similar to *S. acus*; about 15 body rings between pectoral fin base and start of dorsal fin; tail fin. **Habitat** among seaweeds in shallow water. **Distribution** Atlantic north of Spain, English Channel, North Sea and west Baltic.

Syngnathus typhle Linnaeus **Broad-nosed Pipefish** Length up to 35cm when adult. **Head** snout not tapering and nearly as tall along its length as rest of head, also very flattened sideways. **Body** about 19 body rings between pectoral fin base and start of dorsal fin; tail fin. **Habitat** often in brackish water among seaweeds and in shallow places. **Distribution** Mediterranean, Atlantic, English Channel, North Sea and Baltic.

Syngnathus phlegon Risso Length up to 20cm when adult. **Head** snout more than half total head length. **Body** pectoral fin; dorsal surface very rough when stroked from back to front; tail fin. **Colour** varies from bluish to yellow with darker spots or stripes. **Habitat** open surface water and down to 600m. **Distribution** Mediterranean and Atlantic.

Entelurus aequoreus (Linnaeus) **Snake Pipefish** Length up to 60cm when adult. **Head** snout more than half total head length. **Body** very long and slender; no pectoral fin; very small tail fin; anus situated below and towards hind end of dorsal fin. **Habitat** among seaweeds in shallow water down to about 25m. **Distribution** Atlantic, English Channel, North Sea and west Baltic.

Nerophis ophidion (Linnaeus) **Straight-nosed Pipefish** Length up to 30cm when adult. **Head** snout about half total head length with a straight ridge up to the eyes. **Body** no pectoral or tail fins; anus situated below and towards the front end of the dorsal fin. **Colour** variable; dark to pale green sometimes with vertical lines or spots. **Habitat** among seaweeds in very shallow water. **Distribution** Mediterranean, Atlantic, English Channel, North Sea and west Baltic.

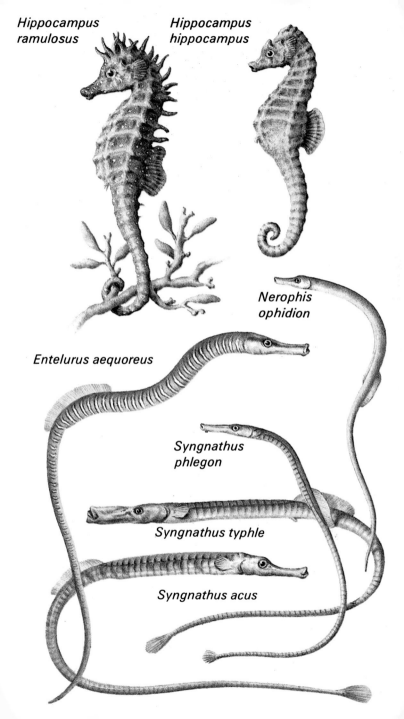

Hippocampus ramulosus

Hippocampus hippocampus

Nerophis ophidion

Entelurus aequoreus

Syngnathus phlegon

Syngnathus typhle

Syngnathus acus

Zeus faber Linnaeus **John Dory** Length up to 40cm when adult. **Head** has extendable mouth. **Body** dorsal fin with long anterior rays and edged on each side by spiny scales; anterior part of anal fin has conspicuous rays; this fin is also edged by spiny scales; conspicuous blackish spot on side of body. **Habitat** among rocks and seaweeds from shallow water down to 200m. **Distribution** Mediterranean, Atlantic, English Channel and rarely in the North Sea and west Baltic.

Chelon labrosus (Risso) **Thick-lipped Grey Mullet** Length up to 60cm when adult. **Head** relatively small mouth at the front; very thick lip on upper jaw; small teeth. **Body** 1st dorsal fin with 4 conspicuous rays; large scales. **Habitat** among rocks and seaweeds in shallow water and estuaries, often near sewage outfalls. **Distribution** Mediterranean, Atlantic, English Channel and southern North Sea. N.B. several other species of Grey Mullet occur in European waters, see Wheeler, A. 1969 or Riedl, R. 1963. The Grey Mullet is not a close relative of the Red Mullet *Mullus surmuletus* (see page 285).

Atherina presbyter Valenciennes **Sand Smelt** Length up to 15cm when adult. **Head** has large mouth. **Body** narrow, 2 clearly separated dorsal fins; forked tail; anal fin starts a little in front of 2nd dorsal fin; characteristic silvery line along sides. **Habitat** in coastal waters, estuaries and in brackish water. **Distribution** western Mediterranean, Atlantic, English Channel and North Sea.

Sphyraena sphyraena (Linnaeus) **Barracuda** Length up to 50cm when adult. **Head** has strong jaws, upper shorter than lower; many sharp teeth. **Body** narrow, powerful, 2 dorsal fins clearly separated; anal fin below 2nd dorsal fin; adults usually have dark, vertical markings. **Habitat** in open water often over sandy substrates; normally in shoals. **Distribution** Mediterranean and Atlantic north to Biscay.

Maena chryselis Valenciennes **Picarel** Length up to 20cm when adult. **Head** extendable mouth. **Body** ovoid; resembles the sea-breams (see page 285), but is distinguished from them by the extendable mouth and the black ovo-rectangular-shaped spot on the side of the body; long dorsal fin somewhat bilobed and spiny in the front; spiny anal fin. **Habitat** often over muddy substrates from 50–150m. **Distribution** Mediterranean. N.B. several closely related species occur in the Mediterranean and nearby Atlantic.

Apogon imberbis (Linnaeus) **Cardinalfish** Length up to 15cm when adult. **Head** has large mouth; very large eye with 2 cross bands. **Body** fins small and short, with pelvic fins well in front of pectoral fins. **Colour** bright red with darker areas including the fin tips. **Habitat** in darkish places such as cave entrances, and among rocks from 10–200m; nocturnal. **Distribution** Mediterranean and neighbouring Atlantic. The slightly forked tail distinguishes this fish from *Anthias anthias* (see page 283).

Chromis chromis (Linnaeus) **Damselfish** Length up to 15cm when adult. **Head** small mouth at front of head. **Body** dorsal fin has 2 sections, the rays in the hinder part being longer and finer; forked tail. **Colour** adults darkish brown, younger specimens vivid blue. **Habitat** among rocks in shallow water. **Distribution** Mediterranean and adjacent Atlantic.

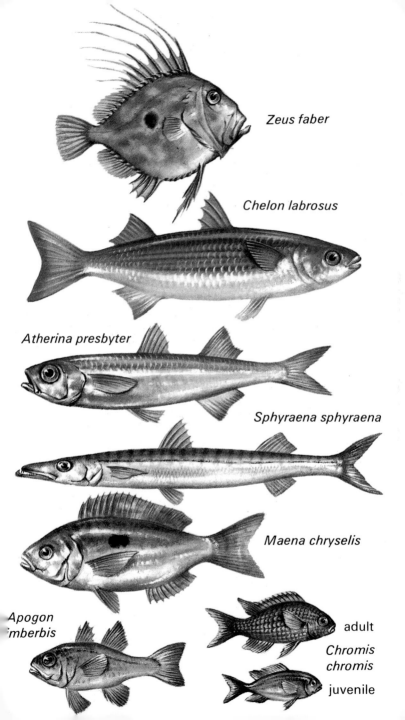

Zeus faber

Chelon labrosus

Atherina presbyter

Sphyraena sphyraena

Maena chryselis

Apogon imberbis

Chromis chromis

adult

juvenile

Dicentrarchus labrax (Linnaeus) **Bass** Length up to 80cm when adult. **Head** front gill cover has toothed hind edge; dark mark on main gill cover which has 2 spines. **Body** long, ovoid; 2 separated dorsal fins each about the same length, the first with prominent rays. **Habitat** over sand, shingle and rocks from shallow water down to about 100m, sometimes in estuaries. **Distribution** Mediterranean, Atlantic, English Channel, North Sea and Baltic.

Polyprion americanum Bloch & Schneider **Wreckfish** Length up to 2m when adult. **Head** large; upper jaw shorter than lower; shape of forehead over eyes is important in identification: there is a slight dip in the outline just above the eyes; there are swellings between the eyes and on the brow; front gill cover is toothed on hind edge; main gill cover has a conspicuous horizontal ridge running across it approximately level with the eye. **Body** dorsal fin bilobed with large spines at front. **Habitat** among floating objects, wreckage, seaweeds, etc., from shallow water down to 200m and sometimes much deeper. **Distribution** Mediterranean, Atlantic north to Ireland and English Channel.

Epinephelus guaza (Linnaeus) (*=Serranus gigas*) **Grouper** or **Dusky Perch** Length up to 1.4m when adult. **Head** upper jaw just shorter than lower jaw; front gill cover has toothed hind edge; main gill cover has about 3 trailing points lying a little above origin of pectoral fin. **Body** deep, ovoid; fins darker than the patterned body and with pale edges, but dorsal fin has orange edge. **Habitat** among rocks and caves from shallow water down to about 400m. **Distribution** Mediterranean and Atlantic north to Biscay.

Serranus cabrilla (Linnaeus) **Comber** Length up to 25cm when adult. **Head** front gill cover has toothed hind edge; main gill cover has 2 points on it near the horizontal mid-line of the fish. **Body** elongated; one dorsal fin with prominent rays in the anterior part; about 8 conspicuous, upright brown bands and 2 blue-green horizontal lines as well as yellow-orange markings. **Habitat** among rocks, sand and sea-grasses, from shallow water down to 50m; sometimes much deeper. **Distribution** Mediterranean, Atlantic north to western English Channel.

Serranus scriba (Linnaeus) **Painted Comber** Similar to *S. cabrilla* but not as long. **Length** up to about 20cm when adult. **Body** 4—7 conspicuous upright brown bands; pale blue marking above anal fin; red marks on head. **Habitat** among rocks, sand and sea-grasses down to about 30m. **Distribution** Mediterranean and Atlantic north to Biscay.

Serranus hepatus (Linnaeus) **Brown Comber** Length up to 13cm when adult. **Body** shorter and relatively deeper than either of the two preceding species; about 4 conspicuous, upright brown bands; dark pigment in the dorsal fin where the anterior spines end and the smaller rayed section begins. **Habitat** among rocks, sand and sea-grasses from shallow water down to about 100m. **Distribution** Mediterranean and Atlantic north to Portugal.

Anthias anthias (Linnaeus) **Length** up to 20cm when adult. **Head** mouth low down; front gill cover has toothed hind edge; main gill cover has about 3 points. **Body** oval; dorsal fin divided into two parts, front with conspicuous spines, especially the 3rd which is very tall; deeply cleft tail fin distinguishes this species from *Apogon imberbis* (see page 281); long pelvic fins; first 3 rays of anal fin spiny. **Habitat** among rocks and around cave mouths, in shoals as illustrated, from 25m downward. **Distribution** Mediterranean north to Biscay.

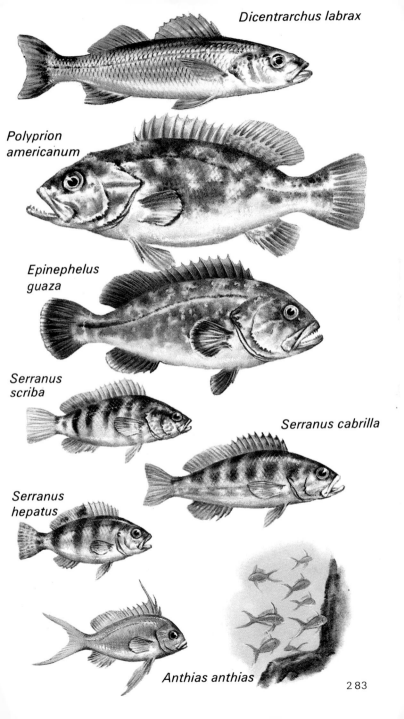

Dicentrarchus labrax

Polyprion americanum

Epinephelus guaza

Serranus scriba

Serranus cabrilla

Serranus hepatus

Anthias anthias

283

Boops boops (Linnaeus) **Bogue** Length up to 20cm when adult. **Head** small mouth; teeth notched, upper teeth with 4 points and lower with 5 points each; front gill cover not toothed; no spines on the main gill cover. **Body** shallow; upper and lower edges have similar curvature; dorsal fin long, anterior rays more spiny than posterior; anal fin has spiny anterior rays and terminates approximately level with hind edge of dorsal fin; lateral line is a dark curved mark following the profile of the fish's back; about 3 darkish lines lie below it; blackish spot at pectoral fin base. **Habitat** among rocks, sand and sea-grasses from shallow water down to 150m. **Distribution** Mediterranean and Atlantic north to Biscay, and occasionally further north.

Sarpa salpa (Linnaeus) (= ***Boops salpa***) **Saupe** Length up to 30cm when adult. **Head** teeth in upper jaw notched, those in lower jaw are triangular and saw-edged; gill covers untoothed and lacking spines. **Body** more ovoid than *Boops boops* (above); upper and lower edges have similar curvature. **Colour** about 11 yellow-gold stripes run horizontally from head to tail; blackish spot near pectoral fin base. **Habitat** among rocks and seaweeds, in shoals in shallow water. **Distribution** Mediterranean and Atlantic north to Biscay.

Pagellus bogaraveo (Brünnich) **Red Sea-bream** Length up to 35cm when adult. **Head** mouth on lower side; front teeth small and sharp; rear ones small but blunter; eye large and conspicuous; gill covers untoothed and lacking spines. **Body** ovoid; upper edge of body more strongly convex than lower edge; in most adults there is a conspicuous blackish spot at the anterior end of the lateral line just behind the gill. **Habitat** among rocks and seaweeds, in shoals, in shallow water and down to 250m or more. **Distribution** Atlantic north to Ireland and occasionally as far as Scandinavia and northern North Sea.

Dentex dentex (Linnaeus) **Dentex** Length up to 1m when adult. **Head** large; mouth on extreme lower side; front teeth long and conspicuous, rear teeth smaller; eye small; gill covers untoothed and lacking spines. **Body** ovoid; upper edge more strongly convex than lower edge. **Colour** somewhat variable, but generally as illustrated with about 5 vertical darker bands which are usually indistinct; very large specimens greater than 1m may be reddish all over. **Habitat** among rocks from shallow water down to 200m. **Distribution** Mediterranean and Atlantic north to Biscay.

Sparus aurata Linnaeus **Gilthead** Length up to 70cm when adult. **Head** steep snout and 'forehead'; upper jaw protrudes slightly; large lips; strong sharp pointed teeth in front of jaw, with crushing teeth behind; gill covers untoothed and lacking spines. **Body** ovoid; darkish patch where lateral line meets gill cover. **Habitat** in shallow water among rocks; will tolerate brackish conditions. **Distribution** Mediterranean and Atlantic north to Biscay.

Mullus surmuletus Linnaeus **Red Mullet** Length up to 30cm when adult. **Head** mouth low; 2 long sensory barbels on the lower jaw; 2 conspicuous scales run from end of jaw to below the eye. **Body** long and somewhat compressed. **Habitat** among rocks and sand from shallow water down to 100m. **Distribution** Mediterranean and Atlantic, north to Scotland. N.B. this fish is not a close relation of the Grey Mullet. It can change its colour considerably according to situation, stress, time of day, etc. *Mullus barbatus* Linnaeus is distinguished by its more vertically inclined 'forehead' and 3 conspicuous scales which run from the end of the jaw to below the eye. Authorities are not all in agreement as to the status of this species, which some feel is a variety of *M. surmuletus*.

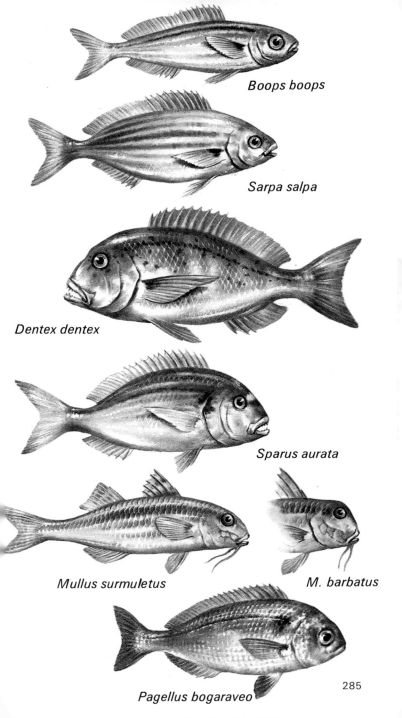

Boops boops

Sarpa salpa

Dentex dentex

Sparus aurata

Mullus surmuletus

M. barbatus

Pagellus bogaraveo

285

Sciaena umbra Linnaeus **Corb** or **Brown Meagre** Length up to 50cm when adult. **Head** large, rounded. **Body** deep, ovoid; 2 dorsal fins, 1st with conspicuous spines, 2nd just connected to it by a fine piece of skin; 2nd spine of anal·fin is conspicuous; tail fin straight-ended in adults. **Habitat** among rocks and caves, seaweeds and sea-grasses often in shoals; generally in shallow water. **Distribution** Mediterranean and Atlantic north to Biscay.

Trachurus trachurus (Linnaeus) **Scad** or **Horse Mackerel** Length up to 35cm when adult. **Head** large, pointed, with a conspicuous mouth. **Body** slim; 2 dorsal fins, 1st taller than 2nd; deeply cleft tail fin; anal fin preceded by 2 spines; pectoral fin wing-like and when folded, stretches back to the 2 spines; lateral line curves back from the gill and straightens out under the 2nd dorsal fin; large, pointed scales form a 'keel' along the lateral line on each side of the fish. **Habitat** in shoals in open water from the surface down to 200m or more; sometimes close inshore over sand. **Distribution** Mediterranean, Atlantic, English Channel, North Sea and west Baltic. N.B. this fish is easily distinguished from the true Mackerel by its lack of finlets (see fig. 49).

Naucrates ductor (Linnaeus) **Pilotfish** Length up to 40cm when adult. **Head** rounded. **Body** shallow, ovoid; 1st dorsal fin reduced to a few isolated spines in front of 2nd dorsal fin; forked tail; anal fin preceded by 2 spines; keels on tail stalk over lateral line; dark, vertical bands on the body extend on to the anal, dorsal and tail fins; tail edged with white. **Habitat** open water, often accompanying large fish such as sharks, as well as turtles, floating objects, etc.; young specimens may keep company with jellyfishes. **Distribution** Mediterranean, Atlantic and English Channel.

Scomber scombrus Linnaeus **Mackerel** Length up to 40cm when adult. **Head** pointed. **Body** long, shallow, but plump; 2 dorsal fins, 1st has 11–13 spines; anal fin lies under 2nd dorsal fin; about 5 finlets (see fig. 49) between 2nd dorsal fin and tail fin, and between anal fin and tail fin; deeply cleft tail; characteristic stripes along back. **Habitat** pelagic in shoals, coming inshore in Summer and Autumn. **Distribution** Mediterranean, Atlantic, English Channel, North Sea and west Baltic.

Scomber japonicus Houttuym **Spanish Mackerel** Length up to 30cm when adult. **Head** pointed. **Body** very similar to *S. scombrus*; 9–10 spines in first dorsal fin; beneath lateral line there is a clear row of darker spots; golden-yellow stripe runs along side of fish. **Habitat** pelagic in shoals. **Distribution** Mediterranean and Atlantic north to English Channel.

Sparisoma cretense (Linnaeus) **Parrotfish** Length up to 30cm when adult. **Head** blunt; small mouth reveals apparently massive teeth (composed of a number of fused teeth) which resemble a parrot's beak. **Body** ovoid; two colour varieties are known, the one illustrated probably being the female; there is a grey form (probably the male) which has a blackish patch behind the gill cover. **Habitat** among rocks and seaweeds, often in shallow water. **Distribution** Mediterranean and Atlantic north to Portugal.

Balistes carolinensis Gmelin **Triggerfish** Length up to 25cm when adult. **Head** large; small mouth. **Body** deep, ovoid-diamond shape; 1st dorsal fin has massive front spine followed closely by another, and then by a 3rd a little way back; 2nd dorsal fin over anal fin; top and bottom rays of tail fin may be extended back as trailers. **Colour** variable; from green-brown-blue. **Habitat** among rocks and seaweeds in coastal waters. **Distribution** Mediterranean, Atlantic north to Ireland, and English Channel. N.B. the 1st ray of the 1st dorsal fin may be raised and locked into position. It is often used to wedge the fish in crevices.

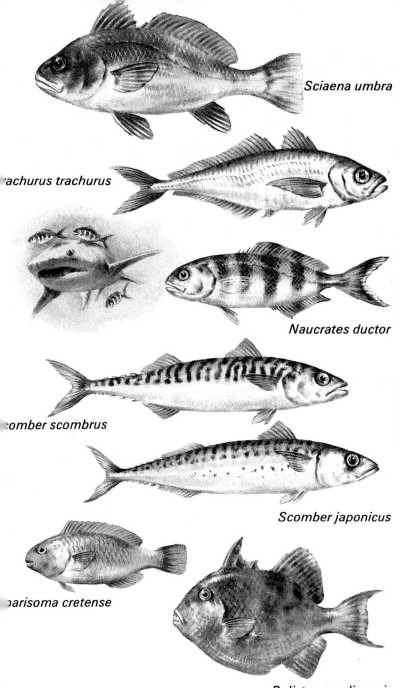

Sciaena umbra

Trachurus trachurus

Naucrates ductor

Scomber scombrus

Scomber japonicus

Sparisoma cretense

Balistes carolinensis

Note on the wrasses This large group of fishes includes many common and familiar inhabitants of coastal waters. Some of them are most brilliantly coloured and patterned. Often the appearance varies with the time of year, courtship, etc., and frequently the males and females are differently marked. The basic body shape is ovoid and somewhat elongate. The mouth is at the extreme tip of the head. The front gill cover is often toothed, but the main cover never bears spines. The dorsal fin is often divided into two sections with the front few rays of the first part spiny. In this group of fishes there are a number of hermaphrodite species that start life as females and then, as they age, change their sex to become males. This is a familiar condition in many invertebrates but is less common in vertebrates.

Labrus mixtus Linnaeus **Cuckoo Wrasse** Length up to 35cm when adult. **Head** front gill cover untoothed. **Body** fairly long and shallow; front of dorsal fin sometimes slightly lower than rear. **Colour** immature males orange-red colour; mature males have bright blue heads and sides, blue extending to front of dorsal fin and blue stripe on tip of tail fin; white heads indicate courtship coloration; females orange-red with 3 dark patches on rear of back. **Habitat** among rocks from about 10m downward. **Distribution** Mediterranean, Atlantic and English Channel.

Labrus merula Linnaeus **Brown Wrasse** Length up to 40cm when adult. **Head** small mouth with thick lips; gill covers untoothed and lacking spines. **Body** tail fin may have a small 'snip' out of the centre. **Colour** less variable than in some species; olive-grey dorsal, tail and anal fins with bluish edges. **Habitat** among rocks and sea-grasses in coastal waters. **Distribution** Mediterranean and Atlantic north to Portugal.

Labrus bergylta Ascanius **(** = *L. maculatus***) Ballan Wrasse** Length up to 40cm when adult. **Head** large; large lips; slightly humped 'forehead'; gill covers untoothed and lacking spines. **Body** front of dorsal fin may be slightly lower than rear when fully erect; large scales usually having a paler centre and darker posterior edge. **Colour** varies according to age and stress; two colour forms are illustrated here. **Habitat** among rocks and seaweeds in coastal waters down to about 20m. **Distribution** western Mediterranean, Atlantic, English Channel, North Sea and west Baltic.

Coris julis (Linnaeus) **Rainbow Wrasse** Length up to 20cm when adult. **Head** pointed snout with mouth at tip; eye relatively inconspicuous. **Body** longer and less deep than many wrasses; 1st 2 rays of long dorsal fin spiny in male; front of dorsal fin about same height as the rear; like a number of wrasses this species is hermaphrodite; the first (female) phase is distinguished by a blue spot on the bottom edge of the gill cover and a yellowish line running from the snout towards the tail; the second (male) is distinguished by the spiny rays and a blackish spot on the dorsal fin; the male also has a characteristic double saw-toothed orange pattern along the side and a dark mark about half way along the body. **Habitat** among rocks and seaweeds from shallow water down to 120m. **Distribution** Mediterranean and Atlantic north to Biscay.

Thalassoma pavo (Linnaeus) **Rainbow Wrasse** Length up to 20cm when adult. **Body** longish; lateral line follows the profile of the upper surface of the fish for part of the length of the dorsal fin, and then becomes straight towards the tail; hermaphrodite. **Colour** of first (female) phase is brown-green with a number of brighter vertical bands; there is also a broad blackish spot in the middle of the dorsal fin; second (male) phase distinguished by pale green body colour with a contrasting vertical stripe behind the pectoral fin; intermediate forms occur. **Habitat** among rocks and seaweeds down to 20m. **Distribution** Mediterranean and Atlantic north to Biscay.

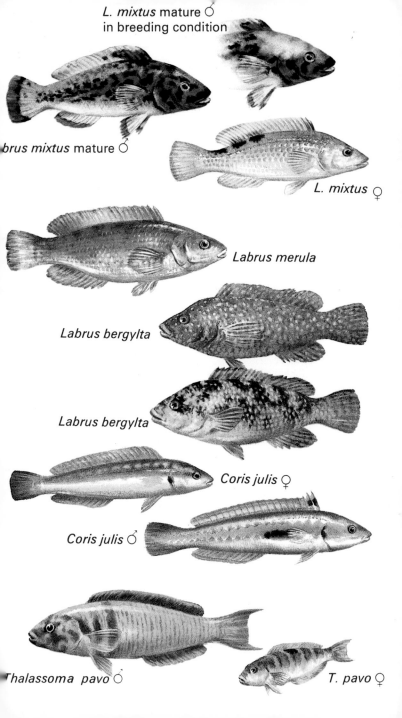

L. mixtus mature ♂
in breeding condition

brus mixtus mature ♂

L. mixtus ♀

Labrus merula

Labrus bergylta

Labrus bergylta

Coris julis ♀

Coris julis ♂

Thalassoma pavo ♂

T. pavo ♀

Crenilabrus mediterraneus (Linnaeus) **Axillary Wrasse** Length up to 15cm when adult. **Head** conspicuous lips; lower jaw shorter than upper; front gill cover toothed. **Body** dorsal fin drawn out towards rear as a lobe; lateral line has similar curvature to upper edge of body. **Colour** conspicuous dark marks on pectoral fin base and above lateral line in front of tail fin; in the male the pectoral mark is dark blue, set in a thin gold ring; in the female it is brown. **Habitat** over sand and among sea-grasses. **Distribution** Mediterranean.

Crenilabrus melops (Linnaeus) **Corkwing Wrasse** Length up to 20cm when adult. **Head** front gill cover toothed. **Body** fuller shape than most wrasses; lateral line less curved and straightening out towards rear of dorsal fin; about 3 spiny rays at front of anal fin. **Colour** very variable according to age and conditions (male illustrated with breeding coloration); a dark spot in front of the tail fin, over or just below the lateral line, is a characteristic feature of this species. **Habitat** among rocks and seaweeds in rock pools and in shallow water. **Distribution** Mediterranean, Atlantic, English Channel, North Sea and west Baltic.

Centrolabrus exoletus (Linnaeus) **Rock Cook** Length up to 15cm when adult. **Head** front gill cover toothed. **Body** about 5 spiny rays at front of anal fin. **Colour** varies with age and conditions; most characteristic distinguishing feature is the dark bar on the tail and the paler trailing edge; male illustrated with breeding coloration. **Habitat** among rocks and seaweeds in shallow water. **Distribution** Atlantic from Biscay northwards, English Channel and North Sea.

Centrolabrus rupestris (Linnaeus) **Goldsinny** Length up to 15cm when adult. **Head** fine serrations on the front gill cover. **Body** back somewhat flattened; lateral line follows a more or less straight course under the front part of the dorsal fin but curves downwards towards the tail under the hind lobe of the dorsal fin; reddish-brown colour distinguishes this species; blackish spot in front of the tail fin, well above the lateral line; sometimes a similar spot on the front of the dorsal fin. **Habitat** among rocks from shallow water down to about 30m. **Distribution** Mediterranean, Atlantic and English Channel.

Trachinus draco Linnaeus **Greater Weever** Length up to 35cm when adult. **Head** flattened sideways; large oblique mouth; eyes almost on top of head; about 2 small spines on upper edge of eye socket; large, conspicuous poison spine on main gill cover. **Body** notch in pectoral fin; front dorsal fin has about 3 spines and a blackish spot towards the front; 2nd dorsal fin long; diagonal stripes on side of body. **Habitat** often buried in sand, from shallow water down to 100m. **Distribution** Mediterranean, Atlantic, English Channel and North Sea.

Trachinus vipera Cuvier **Lesser Weever** Length up to 12cm when adult. **Head** similar to *T. draco*, but lacking spines above eye socket; poison spine on gill cover. **Body** also similar, though deeper; pectoral fin lacks notch; 1st dorsal fin is black with about 6 spines. **Habitat** and **Distribution** similar to *T. draco*. N.B. the spines on the dorsal fins and on the gill covers of these two species are venomous and cause exceedingly painful wounds. Allow wounds to bleed freely before cleaning them carefully.

Uranoscopus scaber Linnaeus **Star Gazer** Length up to 25cm when adult. **Head** large, with eyes on upper surface; small process on lower jaw. **Body** similar in shape to the weevers; pectoral fin bases in front of the beginning of the dorsal fin; large sculptured gill covers with 1 sharp venomous spine behind; 1st dorsal fin has about 4 rays. **Habitat** often buried in sand, in shallow water. **Distribution** Mediterranean and Atlantic north to Spain.

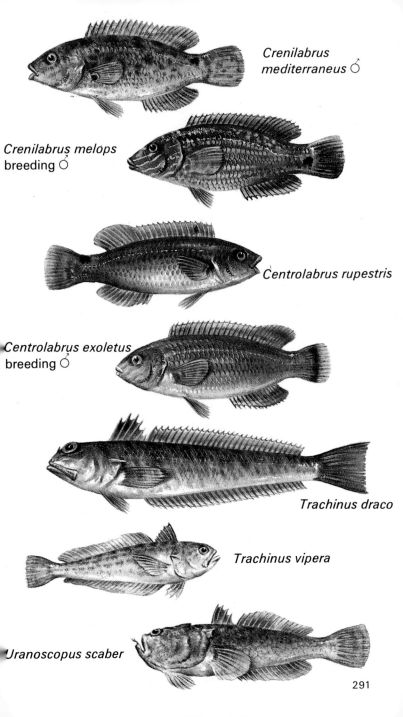

*Crenilabrus
mediterraneus* ♂

Crenilabrus melops
breeding ♂

Centrolabrus rupestris

Centrolabrus exoletus
breeding ♂

Trachinus draco

Trachinus vipera

Uranoscopus scaber

291

Callionymus lyra Linnaeus **Dragonet** Length up to 25cm when adult. **Head** longish pointed snout; mouth set low; quite large lips; frog-like eyes; front gill cover with 4 spines. **Body** long, thin and somewhat compressed vertically; 1st dorsal fin very long and sail-like in the mature male, but no longer than the 2nd in the juvenile male and female. **Habitat** on soft substrates from shallow water down to about 100m. **Distribution** Mediterranean, Atlantic, English Channel, North Sea and west Baltic. N.B. spawning takes place in mid water with the female swimming vertically beside the male as he displays to her (see inset illustration). Several closely related species occur in the European area (see Wheeler, A.1969).

Hyperoplus lanceolatus (Lesauvage) **(=*Ammodytes lanceolatus*)** Length up to 32cm when adult. **Head** the dark mark on the snout just in front of the eye gives easy identification; upper jaw is not extendable. **Body** long and slender; the oblique folds in the skin lack scales (hand lens useful here). **Habitat** on sandy substrates, from shallow water down to 150m. **Distribution** Atlantic, English Channel, North Sea and west Baltic.

Ammodytes tobianus Linnaeus **(=*A. lancea*)** **Lesser Sand-eel** Length up to 20cm when adult. **Head** similar to *Hyperoplus lanceolatus* but lacking black spot on snout, in front of eye; upper jaw is extendable. **Body** also similar to *H. lanceolatus* but there are scales present on the oblique folds in the skin (hand lens useful). **Habitat** on sandy bottoms in shallow water down to about 30m. **Distribution** Atlantic north from Portugal, English Channel, North Sea and west Baltic. N.B. several other species of sand-eel occur in the area. See Lythgoe, J. and Lythgoe, G. 1971, or Wheeler, A. 1969.

Pholis gunnellus (Linnaeus) **Butterfish** Length up to 20cm when adult. **Head** small, rounded; thick lips. **Body** compressed sideways; very long dorsal fin with about 11 dark spots ringed by pale pigment; dorsal fin about twice length of anal fin; pelvic fins level with pectoral fins and greatly reduced; distinct tail fin. **Colour** predominantly brown, as illustrated, and grey. **Habitat** in mud, sand and among rocks, from the lower shore down to about 50m. **Distribution** Atlantic north from English Channel, English Channel, North Sea and west Baltic.

Zoarces viviparus (Linnaeus) **Eelpout** or **Viviparous Blenny** Length up to 40cm when adult. **Body** longish, tapered, and more massive than *Pholis gunnellus*; reduced pelvic fins in front of pectorals; long dorsal fin is continuous with anal fin, but there is a notch in the dorsal fin just before the tail; regular darker patches along the back. **Colour** illustration shows a male with breeding coloration; otherwise pectoral fins are brownish and fringed with orange-yellow. **Habitat** on sand, mud and under stones in shallow water and sometimes down to about 50m. **Distribution** Atlantic north from mid-Wales and Northern Ireland, eastern English Channel, North Sea and Baltic.

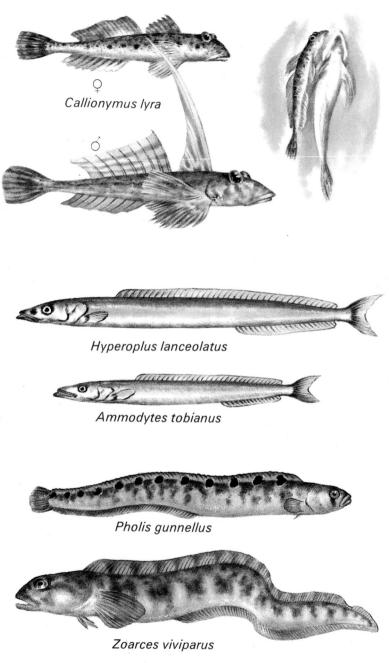

♀
Callionymus lyra

♂

Hyperoplus lanceolatus

Ammodytes tobianus

Pholis gunnellus

Zoarces viviparus

Note on the blennies This large group of fishes has a number of European representatives. They lack scales, and their bodies are typically long and rounded in section. They bear superficial similarity to the gobies (see following page), but can be distinguished from them because: **1.** their pelvic fins, which are set well in front of the pectorals, consist of a few rays only and are not united to form a ventral sucker as in the gobies; **2.** gobies have scales; **3.** the dorsal fin is single but may be divided into 2 lobes by a notch or 'dip' whereas in the gobies the 1st dorsal fin is usually clearly separated from the 2nd dorsal fin.

Blennius pholis Linnaeus **Shanny** Length up to 15cm when adult. **Head** sharply rising snout with 'brow' over eye; no head tentacles. **Body** typical dorsal fin with a poorly defined blotch of darker pigment towards the front. **Colour** ground colours vary from brown to green, but the male becomes much darker in the breeding season. **Habitat** among rocks and stones on the lower shore and in shallow water. **Distribution** Atlantic north from Portugal, English Channel and North Sea.

Blennius ocellaris Linnaeus **Butterfly Blenny** Length up to 17cm when adult. **Head** bears 2 short divided appendages above the eye and 1 more very small one on either side of the front of the dorsal fin. **Body** fairly deep; compressed sideways; 1st ray of dorsal fin very long and there is a conspicuous dark mark surrounded by a white ring towards the rear of the front lobe. **Habitat** usually in shallow water, often associated with coralline algae, e.g. *Lithothamnion* (see page 51). **Distribution** Mediterranean, Atlantic and English Channel.

Blennius gattorugine Brunnich **Tompot Blenny** Length up to 25cm when adult. **Head** eyes well up towards 'brow'; 1 much-divided tentacle above each eye socket. **Body** fairly deep; typical dorsal fin with spiny rays at front, rays in posterior part are the tallest. **Habitat** among stones and kelps from lower shore downward. **Distribution** Mediterranean, Atlantic and English Channel.

Blennius pavo Risso Length up to 10cm when adult. **Head** shape and position of eyes somewhat similar to *B. pholis*; 1 minute eye tentacle; mature males usually have a conspicuous bump over the eye; in both sexes a clear dark spot behind the eye is bordered by a blue ring. **Body** typical of group. **Habitat** among rocks and mud in shallow water and brackish places. **Distribution** Mediterranean.

Blennius rouxi Cocco **Striped Blenny** Length up to 7cm when adult. **Head** tentacles above the eye socket and on the nostrils. **Body** grey-white; the horizontal dark stripe running from gill cover to tail distinguishes the species from others in the area. **Habitat** among rocks in holes and crevices, usually in shallow water. **Distribution** Mediterranean.

Coryphoblennius galerita (Linnaeus) (= *B. montagui*) **Montagu's Blenny** Length up to 8cm when adult. **Head** a fringe of tentacles runs crossways over the head just behind the eyes and a crest of small projections (larger in the male) runs back towards the start of the dorsal fin. **Body** slender, tapering; front and rear lobes of dorsal fin separated by a dip. **Habitat** among rocks and seaweeds, usually in pools on the lower shore and in shallow water. **Distribution** Mediterranean (rarely), Atlantic north to south-west Britain and western English Channel.

Tripterygion tripteronotus (Risso) **Black-faced Blenny** Length up to 8cm when adult. **Head** pointed snout; unbranched tentacle above each eye and on each nostril. **Body** 3 dorsal fins, anterior well separated; in the male, 1st ray of 2nd dorsal fin long, giving a sail-like appearance; unlike the true blennies, this species has scales. **Colour** black head coloration of the male becomes most distinct in the breeding season; female lacks this black coloration. **Habitat** among rocks from the extreme lower shore down to about 10m. **Distribution** Mediterranean.

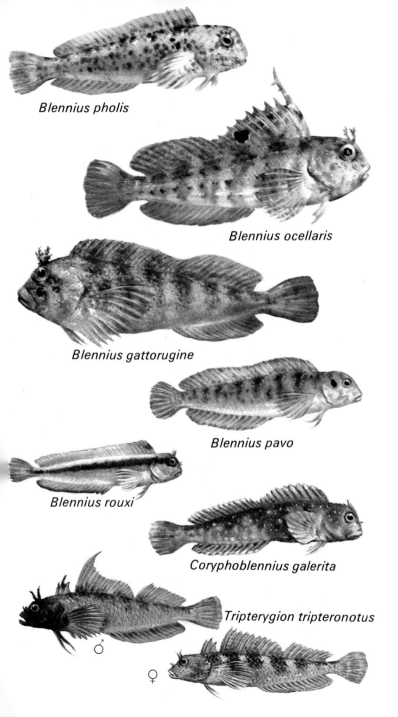

Blennius pholis

Blennius ocellaris

Blennius gattorugine

Blennius pavo

Blennius rouxi

Coryphoblennius galerita

Tripterygion tripteronotus

♂

♀

Note on the gobies These small, generally inshore fishes form a large group which includes about 50 European species. To distinguish them from the blennies, see the preceding page. For species not treated below, see Wheeler, A. 1969 and Riedl, R. 1963.

Gobius niger Linnaeus (= *G. jozo*) **Black Goby** Length up to 15cm when adult. **Body** slightly fuller than many gobies; 1st dorsal fin taller and more crest-like in male (illustrated) than in female; pectoral fins have a few short, spiny, upper rays which do not reach up to the base of the 1st dorsal fin; tail stalk relatively short. **Colour** dark, with various markings. **Habitat** over soft substrates and among sea-grasses in shallow water and down to 60m; can tolerate brackish water. **Distribution** Mediterranean, Atlantic, English Channel, North Sea and west Baltic.

Gobius paganellus Linnaeus **Rock Goby** Length up to 12cm when adult. **Body** thickset; 1st dorsal fin characterized by a band of orange, or a paler brown stripe, and having leading 4 rays about the same height; pectoral fins have several conspicuous, free, spiny upper rays which may reach to the base of the 1st dorsal fin; tail stalk relatively short. **Habitat** among seaweeds in rock pools on lower shore and in shallow water. **Distribution** Mediterranean, Atlantic north to Ireland and Scotland and western English Channel.

Thorogobius ephippiatus (Lowe) **Leopard-spot Goby** Length up to 13cm when adult. **Body** fairly slender; 1st dorsal fin rounded, front ray tallest; pectoral fins lack spiny upper rays; tail stalk quite long; characteristic blotches of red-brown pigment, becoming larger towards the rear; blackish spot at hind base of 1st dorsal fin. **Habitat** among rocks, extreme lower shore and shallow water down to about 35m. **Distribution** Mediterranean and Atlantic north to south-west Britain.

Pomatoschistus minutus (Pallas) (= *Gobius minutus*) **Sand Goby** Length up to 9cm when adult. **Body** slender; 1st dorsal fin has its anterior rays tallest; small, dark blue spot at hind end of dorsal fin in male; upper edge of pectoral fins not spiny; tail stalk quite long; characteristic markings include about 4 indistinct vertical bands of darker pigment along the sides. **Habitat** in shallow, sandy places. **Distribution** Mediterranean, Atlantic, English Channel, North Sea and west Baltic.

Lesueurigobius friesii (Collett) (= *Gobius friesii*) **Fries' Goby** Length up to 12cm when adult. **Body** slender; this genus is immediately distinguished by the short tail stalk and diamond-shaped tail fin; anterior rays of 1st dorsal fin spiny and tall; no spiny rays on pectoral fin. **Habitat** in deep water from 50m downward, where it may share the burrows of *Nephrops norvegicus* (Norway Lobster, see page 215); quite rare but may be taken in dredges, etc. **Distribution** Mediterranean, Atlantic, English Channel and North Sea.

Zosterisessor ophiocephalus (Pallas) **Grass Goby** Length up to 25m when adult. **Body** fairly full; 1st dorsal fin has prominent rays and is well separated from 2nd dorsal fin; there may be a dark mark on the upper side of the pectoral fin base and a fairly prominent mark at the base of the tail; tail stalk short. **Habitat** among sea-grasses in shallow water, sometimes in brackish areas like the Venice Lagoon. **Distribution** Mediterranean.

Gobiusculus flavescens (Fabricius) **Two-spotted Goby** Length about 6cm. **Head** eyes quite widely separated. **Body** 2nd dorsal fin slightly longer than 1st, which has about 7 rays; these fins are well separated; upper edges of pectoral fins not spiny; conspicuous spots below 1st dorsal fin and at base of tail; long tail stalk. **Habitat** above the seabed, among seaweeds, etc., in shallow places. **Distribution** Atlantic north from Spain, English Channel, North Sea and Baltic.

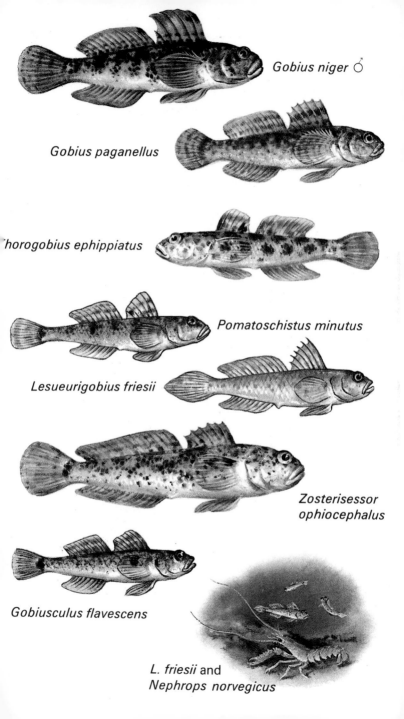

Gobius niger ♂

Gobius paganellus

horogobius ephippiatus

Pomatoschistus minutus

Lesueurigobius friesii

Zosterisessor ophiocephalus

Gobiusculus flavescens

L. friesii and
Nephrops norvegicus

Eutrigla gurnardus (Linnaeus) **Grey Gurnard** Length up to 40cm when adult (rather smaller in Mediterranean). **Head** sharply pointed snout; 3 or 4 spines above mouth. **Body** tapers towards tail; 1st dorsal fin spiny and well separated from 2nd; anal fin starts a little behind 2nd dorsal fin and is shorter; pectoral fin rays divided; lowermost 3 rays hang down and are used as sense organs to test substrate; remainder form a more normally rounded fin which does not reach start of anal fin; short spine above pectoral fin; pelvic fins start about level with pectoral fins; sides of dorsal fins edged by row of spines, and spine scales overlie lateral line; Mediterranean specimens are more brown-red and have a dark mark on 1st dorsal fin. **Habitat** on soft substrates and among rocky outcrops, from shallow water down to 200m. **Distribution** Mediterranean, Atlantic, English Channel, North Sea and west Baltic.

Aspitrigla cuculus (Linnaeus) **Red Gurnard** Length up to 30cm when adult. **Head** pointed snout somewhat 'dished' in front of eye and with about 3 spines on either side. **Body** tapers towards tail; 1st dorsal fin tall in front and sail-like, with spiny rays; anal fin in about same relative position and of same length as 2nd dorsal fin; pectoral fins divided, with 3 sensory rays hanging down; rounded swimming section (see above) reaches back as far as start of anal fin; several small spines above start of pectoral fin; pelvic fins below pectoral fins; sides of dorsal fins edged by row of spines; lateral line covered by vertically arranged, smooth, scaly ridges. **Habitat** generally over soft substrates, from shallow water down to about 250m. **Distribution** Mediterranean, Atlantic, English Channel, North Sea and west Baltic.

Myoxocephalus scorpius (Linnaeus) (= *Cottus scorpius*) **Father Lasher** or **Short-spined Sea-scorpion** Length up to 20cm when adult. **Head** large, spiny and somewhat flattened; large mouth and jaws; front gill cover has 2 spines and its lower edge is extended as a flap which reaches under chin. **Body** rounded, tapering towards tail; 2 spiny dorsal fins; anal fin starts just behind start of 2nd dorsal fin and ends just before it; pectoral fin extends back to start of anal fin; pelvic fins small with about 3 rays. **Colour** varies according to conditions and season; here a male is illustrated in breeding coloration; the upper surface of the female is usually grey-brown with darker markings, and the under surface is orange. **Habitat** usually over soft substrates and among seaweeds, in shallow water and down to 60m. **Distribution** Atlantic north from Biscay, English Channel, North Sea and west Baltic.

Scorpaena porcus Linnaeus **Scorpionfish** Length up to 25cm when adult. **Head** large and spiny; large mouth; feather-like tentacles over eye; no tentacles under chin; gill covers spiny. **Body** fairly full; long dorsal fin, front lobe having spiny rays, rear part with smooth outline, and slightly more lobed; short anal fin terminates about level with end of dorsal fin; camouflage of this fish makes it difficult to see against substrates. **Habitat** among rocks in shallow water. **Distribution** Mediterranean and Atlantic north to Biscay. N.B. the spines on the dorsal fin and gill covers are very poisonous and can inject a powerful venom if touched. The affected part of the body should be treated with very hot water to relieve pain and then well cleaned.

Agonus cataphractus (Linnaeus) **Pogge** or **Armed Bullhead** Length up to 15cm when adult. **Head** large with barbels beneath. **Body** tapers to a very slender tail stalk; large pectoral fin; 2 dorsal fins; body entirely cased in bony plates. **Habitat** on soft substrates in shallow water and down to about 500m; often burrows under mud or sand; may occur in estuaries. **Distribution** Atlantic north from south-west Britain, English Channel, North Sea and west Baltic.

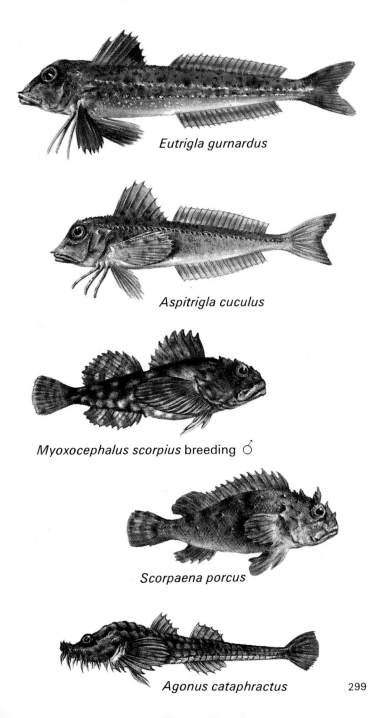

Eutrigla gurnardus

Aspitrigla cuculus

Myoxocephalus scorpius breeding ♂

Scorpaena porcus

Agonus cataphractus

299

Cyclopterus lumpus Linnaeus **Lump Sucker** or **Sea Hen** Length up to 55 cm when adult. **Head** mouth and eyes relatively small. **Body** large, thickset and traversed by 4 rows of bony plates; no scales; 2 dorsal fins, but in older specimens the 1st appears reduced and incorporated in the body; anal fin about equal in length to 2nd dorsal fin; pelvic fins form a sucker under the body. **Colour** adult male in breeding coloration illustrated, otherwise males and females are grey-blue below; small immature specimens may be greenish. **Habitat** usually on rocky substrates from extreme lower shore down to about 300 m; may be attached to rocks by the ventral sucker formed from the pelvic fins. **Distribution** Atlantic north from Portugal, English Channel and North Sea.

Liparis montagui (Donovan) **Montagu's Sea-snail** Length up to 7 cm when adult. **Head** rounded, blunt. **Body** relatively long and tapering towards tail; hind parts somewhat compressed sideways; body covered with slippery, loose skin; long dorsal fin; shorter anal fin, not connected to tail fin; pectoral fins somewhat extended under chin; pelvic fins form a ventral sucker. **Habitat** among rocks and stones, from the middle shore down to about 30 m. **Distribution** Atlantic north from south-west Britain, English Channel, North Sea and west Baltic. N.B. a very similar fish *Liparis liparis* (Linnaeus), Common Sea-snail, differs from *L. montagui* principally in that its anal fin joins the tail fin.

Gasterosteus aculeatus Linnaeus **Three-spined Stickle-back** Length up to 6 cm when adult. **Head** pointed with small mouth and large eyes. **Body** long and laterally compressed; 3 dorsal spines precede dorsal fin which is slightly larger than the anal fin; pelvic fins reduced to 1 spine and 1 ray. **Colour** male in breeding coloration illustrated, otherwise the sides are silver and the underparts whitish. **Habitat** in shallow water, often among seaweeds where the nest is built. **Distribution** throughout Europe in conditions of varying salinity, Atlantic north from Biscay, English Channel, North Sea and Baltic. N.B. this familiar freshwater fish also inhabits brackish and fully marine areas.

Spinachia spinachia (Linnaeus) **Fifteen-spined Stickle-back** Length up to 16 cm when adult. **Head** tapering snout with tiny mouth. **Body** long and tapering; pelvic fins reduced to 1 spine and 1 small ray; anal fin about level with, and equal in length to, the dorsal fin, which is preceded by about 15 spines; extremely fine tail stalk. **Habitat** this sea fish is often found among rocks in inshore waters and estuaries, in pools on the lower shore, and down to about 10 m. **Distribution** Atlantic north from Biscay, English Channel, North Sea and Baltic.

Lepadogaster lepadogaster (Bonnaterre) **Clingfish** or **Cornish Sucker** Length up to 7 cm when adult. **Head** long pointed snout; quite long jaws; upper jaw bigger than lower which is covered when the mouth is shut; tentacle over nostril. **Body** flat below and curved above; anal fin shorter than dorsal fin and, like it, linked to the tail fin; rounded pectoral fins; pelvic fin modified to form a sucker. **Habitat** often in pools among rocks and seaweeds from the middle shore down to a few metres. **Distribution** Mediterranean, Atlantic north to Scotland and western English Channel.

Lophius piscatorius (Linnaeus) **Anglerfish** Length up to 2 m when adult. **Head** huge, grotesque, with an enormous crescent-shaped mouth just on the upper surface; very much broader than rest of body; about 3 long spines borne in a row from above the upper lip to between the eyes, the foremost spine having a fleshy tip which acts as a lure to bring small fishes within reach of the mouth; gill slits directly behind pectoral fins. **Body** somewhat flattened top to bottom and tapering towards the tail; dorsal fin well back. **Habitat** from shallow water down to about 500 m. **Distribution** Mediterranean, Atlantic, English Channel and North Sea.

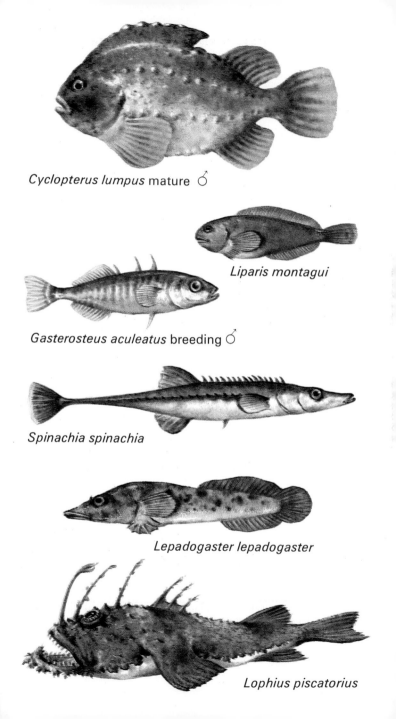

Cyclopterus lumpus mature ♂

Liparis montagui

Gasterosteus aculeatus breeding ♂

Spinachia spinachia

Lepadogaster lepadogaster

Lophius piscatorius

Scophthalmus maximus (Linnaeus) **Turbot** Length up to 60cm when adult. **Head** long dorsal fin commences between mouth and eyes. **Body** rounded; left-hand side uppermost; pectoral and pelvic fins; separate anal fin; scales lacking; upper side bears a number of hard raised platelets which give a rough surface; lateral line curves steeply over the pectoral fin. **Colour** upper side varies according to substrate and the need for camouflage; tail fin spotted; underside pale. **Habitat** on mud, sand and gravel substrates, from shallow water down to about 100m. **Distribution** Mediterranean, Atlantic, English Channel, North Sea and Baltic.

Scophthalmus rhombus (Linnaeus) **Brill** (Head end only illustrated) Very similar to *S. maximus*. **Length** up to 50cm when adult. **Body** lacks bony platelets on upper surface, but has scales; anterior rays of dorsal fin tufted. **Colour** may be darker with fins lighter and the tail fin less spotted. **Habitat** and **Distribution** similar to *S. maximus* but not penetrating as far into the Baltic.

Zeugopterus punctatus (Bloch) **Topknot** Length up to 20cm when adult. **Head** dorsal fin starts between mouth and eyes. **Body** oval; left-hand side uppermost; pelvic fin attached to anal fin; belts of darker pigment extend either side of eye sockets and there is a dark patch posterior to the curve in the lateral line; the hind edges of the scales are toothed (hand lens useful here). **Habitat** among rocks from shallow water down to about 40m. **Distribution** Atlantic north from Biscay, English Channel, North Sea and west Baltic.

Platichthys flesus (Linnaeus) **Flounder** Length up to 20cm when adult. **Head** long dorsal fin commences near the eye. **Body** less rounded than the Turbot, and with the right-hand side uppermost; pelvic and anal fins separate; row of hard knobs follows the outline of the body where it joins the dorsal and anal fins; shallow curve to the lateral line over pectoral fin; scales lack toothed edges. **Colour** upper side green-brown, and may be speckled with darker spots or even orange; underside pale. **Habitat** on soft substrates, from shallow water down to 50m; this species can tolerate brackish or fresh water, so it may be found far up-river also. **Distribution** Mediterranean, Atlantic, English Channel, North Sea and Baltic.

Pleuronectes platessa Linnaeus **Plaice** Length up to 55cm when adult. **Body** very similar in general outline to *Platichthys flesus* but tail is rounded rather than almost square cut; no hard bony knobs at edge of body under dorsal and anal fin bases; upper left side patterned with conspicuous orange blotches. **Habitat** on soft substrates, from shallow water down to about 350m. **Distribution** western Mediterranean, Atlantic, English Channel, North Sea and west Baltic.

Solea solea (Linnaeus) **Sole** Length up to 30cm when adult. **Head** blunt, with mouth not at the front extremity. **Body** elongated and with the right-hand side uppermost; long dorsal fin; pelvic fin just separate from anal fin; dorsal and anal fins reaching tail fin. **Habitat** on soft substrates from shallow water, but also down to about 200m; sometimes in river mouths. **Distribution** Mediterranean, Atlantic, English Channel, North Sea and west Baltic.

A number of other species of flatfish may be encountered in the European area, for which reference should be made to Lythgoe, J. and Lythgoe, G. 1971, Wheeler, A. 1969, or Riedl, R. 1963.

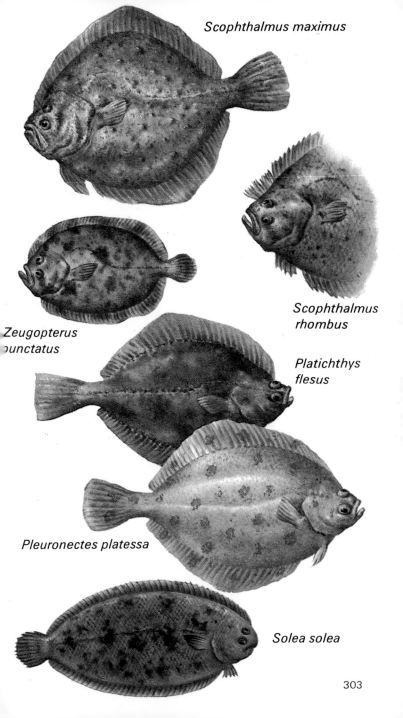

Scophthalmus maximus

Scophthalmus rhombus

Zeugopterus punctatus

Platichthys flesus

Pleuronectes platessa

Solea solea

303

Flotsam and Jetsam

A variety of objects may be found cast up by the sea and they usually accumulate at the high tide mark to form the strandline. In many cases they include the remains of dead or dying animals; sometimes wreckage with attached animals will be found. It must be remembered that on shingle beaches the objects that occur may have been pounded by the action of pebbles so altering their form. The following list is by no means exclusive.

Egg mass of *Buccinum undatum* Linnaeus Spongy looking masses usually reaching about the size of an apple. These consist of a great number of egg capsules laid in coils which form a spherical mass. In most cases the individual egg capsules will be empty when found, for the embryos of this species develop inside the egg case after fertilization and hatch out when they are ready to lead an independent existence. Because of this, some people might reasonably argue that the capsules should be termed embryo capsules.

Egg capsules of *Nucella lapillus* (Linnaeus) Small, flask-like capsules about 7mm tall attached to rocks or shells. These are normally laid in groups and bear a very superficial resemblance to some small sponges. A number of other gastropods lay their eggs intertidally in this way.

Egg mass of *Archidoris pseudoargus* (Rapp) Coiled, gelatinous streamer-like egg mass. Close examination reveals that the individual egg capsules are embedded in a transparent jelly. The mass may reach several centimetres in length. A number of other nudibranchs lay egg masses similar to this.

Egg capsule of *Eulalia viridis* (O. F. Müller) (see page 121) Shaped like a miniature, greenish pear, this jelly-like object has an attachment strand at one end. It is usually about 2.5cm long. It is often found lying on sand on the middle and lower shore.

Mermaids' Purses   Egg capsules of *Scyliorhinus canicula* (Linnaeus) Capsule length about 6cm. These horny egg capsules are usually attached to seaweeds by means of the twisted tendrils which arise from each corner. Those that are washed up on the shore are generally empty because the embryo has hatched.

Mermaids' Purses   Egg capsules of *Scyliorhinus stellaris* (Linnaeus) (Not illustrated) Similar to the above, only about twice as long.

Mermaids' Purses   Egg capsules of *Raja clavata* (Linnaeus) (Not illustrated) Capsule length about 6cm. Similar to that of *Scyliorhinus canicula* above, but with four tapering points rather than tendrils and with a slightly hairy covering.

Mermaids' Purses   Egg capsules of *Raja batis* Linnaeus (Not illustrated) Capsule length about 13cm, with four points rather than tendrils. They are often covered with quite long, sticky hairs.

Hornwrack   Fronds of the ectoproct *Flustra foliacea* (Linnaeus) Leafy fronds reaching up to 6cm long, often washed up after storms.

Cuttlebone of *Sepia officinalis* (Linnaeus) (see also page 191) Length up to about 18cm. This structure forms the internal skeleton for the cuttlefish. It is a porous structure which in life can be partly filled with gas to form a buoyancy organ which regulates the vertical position of the cuttlefish in the water. After death and decay of the cuttlefish the bone is often washed up.

Sea-balls Matted, fibrous balls 4—6cm in diameter (see page 65).

egg mass of *Buccinum undatum*

egg capsules of *Nucella lapillus*

egg mass of
Archidoris pseudoargus

egg capsule of
*Scyliorhinus
canicula* –
mermaid's
purse

Flustra foliacea

cuttle bone of *Sepia officinalis*   305

Bibliography

The following list of reference works, which is by no means exclusive, includes a variety of monographs, fauna lists and guides to specific areas as well as a few scientific papers published in journals. The author has referred to these books in the course of preparing the present volume. In order to guide the reader further, * denotes references which are recommended for assisting with identification of particular groups of organisms; † denotes those which are fauna lists for particular areas; ‡ denotes those which are other important books of the field guide nature; and § denotes references of historical interest.

Admiralty Tide Tables *Vol* 1 *European Waters*. Hydrographic Department, Admiralty, Ministry of Defence, Taunton, Somerset. Contains tidal predictions for many major ports in Europe, and is of great use for planning field excursions. Published annually.

*Alder, J. and Hancock, A. 1845–1855 *A Monograph of the British Nudibranchiate Mollusca* (with a supplement by Sir Charles Eliot, 1910). Ray Society, London.

* Alder, J. and Hancock, A. 1905–1912 *The British Tunicata*. 3 vols. Ray Society, London. This work is now superseded by that of Berrill, N. J. 1950, but it still contains useful coloured illustrations.

‡ Barrett, J. and Yonge, C. M. 1958 *Collins Pocket Guide to the Sea Shore* (1972 revised edition). Collins, London.

* Bate, C. Spence and Westwood, J. O. 1868 *A History of the British Sessile-eyed Crustacea*. 2 vols. J. Van Voorst, London.

* Bell, T. 1853 *A History of the British Stalk-eyed Crustacea*. J. Van Voorst, London. Both this volume, and the preceding one, are somewhat outdated, but they contain information on some groups which are not treated in modern texts.

* Berrill, N. J. 1950 *The Tunicata, with an account of the British Species*. Ray Society, London. A detailed guide to the ascidians.

† Bruce, J. R., Colman, J. S. and Jones, N. S. 1963 *Marine Fauna of the Isle of Man*. L.M.B.C. Memoir No. 36. Liverpool University Press.

* Brunberg, L. 1964 On the nemertean fauna of Danish Waters *Ophelia* 1, 77–112. A useful, illustrated guide to this group.

* Burton, M. 1963 *Revision of Classification of Calcareous Sponges*. British Museum (Natural History), London.

* Chevreux, E. and Fage, L. 1925 *Faune de France 9: Amphipodes*. Paul Lechevalier, Paris. One of the few specialist accounts of this group of crustacea with identification details. Text in French.

† Crothers, J. H. 1966 *Dale Fort Marine Fauna* (second edition). Field Studies Council, London. A fauna list for the Dale Peninsula and adjacent areas of Pembrokeshire, Wales.

* Cuenot, L. 1922 *Faune de France, 4; Sipunculiens, Echiuriens, Priapuliens*. Paul Lechevalier, Paris. Provides a comprehensive reference text for the minor marine worms. Text in French.

* Darwin, C. 1851–1854 *A Monograph of the sub-class Cirripedia*. 2 vols. Ray Society, London. A classical reference work on barnacles.

‡ Dickinson, C. I. 1963 *British Seaweeds*. The Kew Series, Eyre & Spottiswoode, London. A useful illustrated guide to marine algae.

* Duncan, U. K. 1959 *A Guide to the Study of Lichens*. T. Buncle & Co. Ltd., Arbroath.

† Eales, N. B. 1967 *The Littoral Fauna of the British Isles; A Handbook for Collectors* (fourth edition). A source of many detailed references to the various monographs; also contains a great deal of information on identification.

Eltringham, S. K. 1971 *Life in Mud and Sand*. English Universities Press Ltd, London. A very useful account of the ecology of sandy and muddy habitats which have hitherto been somewhat neglected.

* Fauvel, P. 1923 *Faune de France 5: Polychètes errantes*. Paul Lechevalier, Paris. An essential text for the serious student of polychaetes. Together with the companion volume *Polychetes sedentaires* it has superseded the Ray Society monograph by McIntosh. Text in French.

* Fauvel, P. 1927 *Faune de France 16: Polychètes sedentaires*. Paul Lechevalier, Paris.

* Ferry, B. W. and Sheard, J. W. 1969 Zonation of Supralittoral Lichens on Rocky Shores around the Dale Peninsula, Pembrokeshire (with key for their identification). *Field Studies, 3*, 1, 41–67.

* *Fiches d'Identification du Zooplankton*. Conseil Permanent International pour l'exploration de la mer 1949–1965. A useful series of sheets providing keys and figures for identification of many planktonic animals.

§ Forbes, E. 1841 *A history of British Starfishes*. J. Van Voorst, London. Includes an early discussion of zonation which is now only of historical interest.

§ Forbes, E. 1859 *Natural History of the European Seas*. J. Van Voorst, London. See introduction for details.

* Forbes, E. and Hanley, S. 1848–53 *A History of the British Mollusca and their Shells*. 4 vols. J. Van Voorst, London. Despite its age, this large and rare book contains a great deal of specialist information on British molluscs which can be found nowhere else.

Forsman, B. 1972 Evertebrater vid svenska osterjokusten *Zoologisk Revy*, 34, 32–56. An account of the bottom-dwelling invertebrates of the Baltic. Text in Swedish.

Fretter, V. and Graham, A. 1962 *British Prosobranch Molluscs*. Ray Society, London. An important work dealing with the biology of prosobranchs.

Gibson, R. 1972 *Nemerteans*. Hutchinson University Library, London. An excellent general account of the biology of nemertines.

§ Gosse, P. H. 1853 *A Naturalist's Rambles on the Devonshire Coast*. J. Van Voorst, London. See Introduction for details.

§ Gosse, P. H. 1854 *The Aquarium*. J. Van Voorst, London. See Introduction for details.

§ Gosse, P. H. 1856 *Tenby, A Sea-side Holiday*. J. Van Voorst, London. See Introduction for details.

§ Gosse, P. H. 1860 *Actinologia Britannica. A History of the British Sea-anemones and Corals*. J. Van Voorst, London. The classical work on British sea-anemones and corals. To a great extent it has been superseded by the two Ray Society volumes by T. A. Stephenson.

§ Gosse, P. H. 1865 *A Year at the Shore*. Alexander Strahan, London. See Introduction for details.

* Graham, A. 1971 *Synopses of the British Fauna (New Series) No. 2: British Prosobranch and other operculate gastropod molluscs*. The Linnean Society of London, Academic Press, London and New York. A most useful guide to many of the marine and freshwater gastropods of the north Atlantic region.

* Grimpe, G. and Wagler, E. (editors) 1927–1940 *Die Tierwelt der Nord-und Ostsee*. Akadmische Verlagsgesellschaft, Leipzig. An important series giving accounts of the fauna of the North Sea and the Baltic, containing many detailed identification keys and general ecological descriptions. Issued in many parts with many authors. Text in German.

Hardy, A. C. 1970 *The Open Sea: Part 2. Fish and Fisheries* (new edition). New Naturalist series, Collins, London. An important book on fish and bottom-dwelling animals.

Hardy, A. C. 1971 *The Open Sea: Part 1. The World of Plankton* (revised edition). New Naturalist series, Collins, London. An excellent account of planktonic life.

‡ Haas, W. de and Knorr, F. 1966 *The Young Specialist Looks at Marine Life*. Burke, London. An introductory guide to sea life with many excellent line drawings.

Heller, J. 1975 The taxonomy of some British *Littorina* species, with notes on their reproduction (Mollusca: Prosobrancia). *Zoological Journal of the Linnean Society*, 56, 2, 131–151.

* Hincks, T. 1868 *A History of British Hydroid Zoophytes*. 2 vols. J. Van Voorst, London. While much of the nomenclature has been changed since it was published, this book still remains an important work on hydroids for the serious student.

* Hincks, T. 1880 *A History of the British Marine Polyzoa*. 2 vols. J. Van Voorst, London. Still a most important work on the subject of marine ectoprocts. To some extent it has been superseded by the *Faune de France* volumes by Prenant and Bobin.

* Jeffreys, J. G. 1862–1869 *British Conchology*. 5 vols. J. Van Voorst, London. An old but remarkably useful book on molluscs which inhabit the British Isles and the surrounding seas.

* Kerrich, G. J., Meikle, R. D. and Tebble, N. (editors) 1967 *Bibliography of Key Works for the Identification of the British Fauna and Flora*. Systematics Association, British Museum (Natural History), London. This book is a directory to the principal existing publications for identifying all organisms found in Britain. It also has considerable application to Europe.

* King, P. E. 1974 *Synopses of the British Fauna (New Series) No. 5: British Sea Spiders: Arthropoda: Pycnogonida*. The Linnean Society of London, Academic Press, London and New York. An excellent guide to this little-known group.

* Koehler, R. 1921 *Faune de France 1: Echinodermes*. Paul Lechevalier, Paris. A comprehensive account of many Mediterranean, Atlantic and Channel echinoderms with keys for identification. Text in French.

† Laverack, M. S. and Blackler, M. 1974 *Fauna and Flora of St Andrews Bay*. Scottish Academic Press, Edinburgh and London.

Lewis, J. R. 1964 *The Ecology of Rocky Shores*. English Universities Press, London. See Introduction for details.

‡ Luther, W. and Fiedler, K. 1967 *Die Unterwasserfauna der Mittelmeer-kusten* (second edition). Paul Parey, Hamburg and Berlin. A compact guide book to the Mediterranean. Text in German.

* Lythgoe, J. and Lythgoe, G. 1971 *Fishes of the Sea*. Blandford, London. A comprehensive identification manual for fishes in the coastal waters of northern Europe and the Mediterranean.

† Marine Biological Association, 1957 *Plymouth Marine Fauna* (third edition). A fauna list for Plymouth and adjacent areas of south-west England, containing many important references.

Marshall, N. B. 1965 *The Life of Fishes*. Weidenfeld and Nicolson, London. This book provides much information on the biology of fishes and is written by a great authority on the subject.

* Matthews, G. 1953 A Key for use in the Identification of British Chitons. *Proceedings of the Malacological Society, London, 29*, 241–248.

* McIntosh, W. C. 1873–1923 *A Monograph of the British Marine Annelids*. 4 vols. Ray Society, London. This extensive work, which is illustrated with many beautiful colour plates, is largely out of date as far as the nomenclature is concerned. It does, however, include at the start a comprehensive section on the nemerteans, which may be of use simply because there are few alternatives. For normal use the reader is directed to Fauvel, P. in the *Faune de France* series.

† Micallef, H. and Evans, F. 1968 *The Marine Fauna of Malta*. Malta University Press.

* Millar, R. H. 1970 *Synopses of the British Fauna (New Series) No. 1 : British Ascidians; Tunicata: Ascidiacea*. The Linnean Society of London, Academic Press, London and New York. An alternative guide to the sea-squirts; more compact and readily available than that by Berrill.

* Mortensen, T. 1927 *Handbook of the Echinoderms of the British Isles*. Oxford University Press. A very complete account of most of the north Atlantic species together with good identification keys.

* Muus, B. J. and Dahlstrom, P. 1974 *Collins Guide to the Sea Fishes of Britain and north-western Europe*. Collins, London. This useful book provides identification details of many fishes and describes methods for their capture in addition to aspects of their biology.

* Naylor, E. 1972 *Synopses of the British Fauna (New Series) No. 3 : British Marine Isopods*. The Linnaean Society of London, Academic Press, London and New York. An excellent account of these crustaceans which supersedes the relevant section in Bate and Westwood.

† Newell, G. E. 1954 The Marine Fauna of Whitstable. *Annals and Magazine of Natural History Series 12*, 7, 321–350.

* Newell, G. E. and Newell, R. C. 1973 *Marine Plankton* (revised edition). Hutchinson, London. Provides a very useful and practical account of planktonic organisms together with many illustrations of species not treated in this book.

Newell, R. C. 1970 *Biology of Intertidal Animals*. Elek, London. Discusses in great detail many important aspects of life on the shore.

* Newton, L. 1931 *A Handbook of the British Seaweeds*. British Museum (Natural History) Publications, London. This book, although somewhat out of date, provides an important account of the marine algae, their distribution and structure, and can be used in conjunction with Parke and Dixon.

Nicol, J. A. 1967 *The Biology of Marine Animals* (second edition). Pitman & Sons Ltd., London. Contains a great deal of information on the organization and physiology of marine animals.

Nichols, D. 1969 *Echinoderms* (fourth edition). Hutchinson University Library, London. A very good account of the structure and evolution of these animals.

* Nordsiech, F. 1969 *Die Europaischn Meeresmuscheln*. 2 vols. Fischer, Stuttgart. A comprehensive and up-to-date account of the marine molluscs of Europe. Text in German.

* Organization for Economic Co-operation and Development (O.E.C.D.) Catalogues of marine fouling organisms dealing with ascidians, barnacles, and Serpulids. H.M.S.O., London. These handy pamphlets contain useful identification keys and coloured illustrations.

† Parke, M. and Dixon, P. S. 1968 Check-list of British Marine Algae, second revision. *Journal of the Marine Biological Association of the United Kingdom*, 48, 783–832. Rationalizes and updates much of the terminology.

* Prenant, M. and Bobin, G. 1956 *Faune de France 60; Bryozaires pt. 1*. Federation Francaise des Societies de Science Naturelles, Paris. An excellent work for the serious student which together with the companion volume covers many of the species known from the European area. Text in French.

* Prenant, M. and Bobin, G. 1966 *Faune de France 68; Bryozaires pt. 2*. Federation Francaise des Societies de Science Naturelles, Paris.

* Rasmussen, E. 1973 Systematics and ecology of the Isefjord marine fauna (Denmark). *Ophelia*, 11, 1–495. Includes descriptions and ecological data for many species occurring in the Kattegat region of Denmark.

‡ Riedl, R. 1963 *Fauna und Flora der Adria*. Paul Parey, Hamburg and Berlin. An excellent account of many species which occur in the Mediterranean area, particularly those in the Adriatic Sea.

* Russell, F. S. 1953 and 1970 *The Medusae of the British Isles*. 2 vols. Cambridge University Press. An up-to-date monograph on hydromedusae and scyphozoans with many illustrations, some in colour.

Russell, F. S. and Yonge, C. M. 1975 *The Seas* (revised edition). Warne & Co., London. A good book for further reading which describes most aspects of marine biology.

* Ryland, J. S. 1962 The biology and identification of intertidal Polyzoa. *Field Studies, 1, 4*, 33–51. A handy paper for identification of ectoprocts which is available as an offprint from the Field Studies Council, London.

Ryland, J. S. 1970 *Bryozoans*. Hutchinson University Library, London. An excellent account of the general biology of the ectoprocts.

* Smith, S. M. 1974 Key to the British Marine Gastropoda. *Royal Scottish Museum*; *Information Series*; *Natural History No. 2*. A useful key in pamphlet form.

Steers, J. A. 1969 *The Sea Coast* (fourth edition). New Naturalist series, Collins, London. Provides an excellent account of the geography and geology of coastlines, and discusses the ways in which they are built up and broken down.

* Stephenson, T. A. 1928 and 1935 *The British Sea Anemones*. 2 vols. Ray Society, London. Much more up-to-date than Gosse 1860, and beautifully illustrated. It does not include corals.

Stephenson, T. A. and Stephenson, A. 1949 The universal features of zonation between tide marks on rocky coasts. *Journal of Ecology, 38,* 289–305. See introduction for details.

* Tattersall, W. M. and Tattersall, O. S. 1951 *The British Mysidacea*. Ray Society, London. An excellent account of the mysids with many line drawings.

* Tebble, N. 1966 *British Bivalve Seashells*. British Museum (Natural History) Publications, London. An excellent handbook for identification.

* Vosmeyer, G. C. J. 1935 *The Sponges of the Bay of Naples, Porifera Incalcarea*. 3 vols. Martinus Nijhoff, The Hague. A large and distinguished account of non-calcareous sponges. Many of these occur outside the Mediterranean. The work is beautifully illustrated with coloured plates.

Wallentinus, I. 1972 Makroskopiska alger och vattenlevande fanerogamer vid svenska osterskokusten *Zoologisk Revy*; 34, 69–84. An account of the larger marine plants of the Baltic. Text in Swedish.

* Watson, W. 1953 *Census Catalogue of British Lichens*. Cambridge University Press. Contains important references to the distribution of maritime lichens.

* Wheeler, A. 1969 *The Fishes of the British Isles and North West Europe*. MacMillan, London. An excellent reference book on fishes.

Yonge, C. M. 1949 *The Sea Shore* New Naturalist series, Collins, London. Provides an excellent account of life on the shore. Well illustrated. Published by Fontana as a paperback in 1971.

* In addition to the references specifically cited here, many useful works directly relating to the fauna of the European seas have been published in the series *Fauna und Flora des Golfes von Neapel*; *Faune de France*; and *Synopses of the British Fauna* (Old and New Series), Linean Society of London.

Glossary

Aboral describes the surface of the body opposite that which bears the mouth.

Ambulacrum (of echinoderms) usually a groove, with a row of tube-feet on either side; generally five per animal.

Antenna usually a long, slender, sensory appendage on the heads of some arthropods and some annelids.

Asymmetrical without symmetry, being irregular or unequal; used to describe the growth form of some animals, e.g. certain sponges.

Benthic dwelling in or on the seabed.

Bilateral symmetry symmetry of an organism (e.g. a fish) which can be divided into two equal and complementary left and right halves, but which has dissimilar front and hind ends.

Brackish describes water usually containing less, but occasionally more, salt than is usually found in the sea.

Byssus hair-like filaments which attach some bivalves to rocks or plants.

Calcareous being made of calcium carbonate or chalk.

Cell smallest functional unit of a plant or animal, consisting of a nucleus surrounded by cytoplasm and bounded by a membrane, and sometimes a cell wall.

Cephalothorax region combining the head and thoracic segments of advanced crustaceans.

Chaeta bristle of polychaetes.

Chela leg of crustaceans which bears pincers or nippers.

Chemoreceptor sense organ for detecting chemical stimuli as in smell or taste.

Chitin organic constituent of cuticle, as found in arthropods.

Chitinous made of chitin.

Chordate animal with at least a simple form of backbone (the notochord) at some stage in the life cycle; includes the vertebrates.

Cilia minute, filamentous structures which, by beating, may create a current and provide locomotion; visible only under the high power of a microscope.

Cirrus small, tentacular or finger-like appendage found in certain arthropods and polychaetes.

Class major subdivision of a phylum.

Coelom fluid-filled cavity, formed within the middle cell layer of animals.

Commensal organism of one species which lives in close association with one or more different species.

Crenulate having the edge cut into very small scallops.

Cuticle exterior skeleton of chitin and protein; may be tanned as in insects.

Detritus particles of decaying organisms accumulating, for example, on the seabed; forms the food of many invertebrate animals.

Disc (or an anemone) either the mouth disc which bears the tentacles, or the basal, sucker-like attachment disc; (of an ophiuroid) body excluding the arms.

Dorsal upper side of a bilaterally symmetrical animal (c.f. Ventral).

Ectoparasite parasite living on the outer surface of another organism.

Epiphyte plant which grows on the outer surface of another organism.

Epizoic describes an animal which grows on the outer surface of another organism.

Eulittoral zone biologically defined zone on the seashore whose uppermost limit is marked by the highest point at which barnacles occur, and whose lowermost limit is marked by the highest point at which laminarians occur (see Lewis, J. R. 1964); equivalent to the term *middle shore* as used in this book.

Evert turn inside out; often applied to the process of extending the proboscis of worms.

Exhalent breathing out; applied to respiratory streams of water in organisms or the anatomical structures by which they are conveyed.

Foot (of molluscs) organ on the underside of the body used in gastropods for creeping, and in bivalves for various functions including secretion of byssus, digging and burrowing.

Free tooth tooth not attached to jaws; as teeth on the proboscis of polychaetes such as *Nereis*.

Free living living unattached to any other structure.

Frond (of alga) all of the plant except the holdfast.

Gamete sperm or egg.

Gametophyte (of plants) generation which produces sperms and eggs.

Genus group of related species; many genera may form one order.

Growth line recognizable line or mark on a shell which indicates the start or end of a period of shell growth.

Hermaphrodite organism which has reproductive organs of both sexes and thus produces sperms and eggs.

Heteromorphic (of plants) condition where the gametophyte and sporophyte generations are dissimilar in form (c.f. Isomorphic).

Holdfast attachment organ of seaweeds.

Inhalent breathing in; applied to respiratory streams of water in organisms or the anatomical structures by which they are conveyed.

Invertebrate without a backbone.

Isomorphic (of plants) condition where the gametophyte and sporophyte generations are similar in form (c.f. Heteromorphic).

Lamella thin, plate-like structure or layer.

Larva developmental phase of an organism which usually does not resemble the adult or lead a way of life similar to it; a phase often associated with an entirely different manner of feeding from the adult and which provides a dispersive mechanism in many sedentary marine species; always terminates with the process of metamorphosis.

Littoral pertaining to the shore; a biologically defined zone on the seashore comprising of the eulittoral zone and the littoral fringe.

Littoral fringe a biologically defined zone on the seashore whose uppermost limit is marked by the highest point at which periwinkles of the genus *Littorina* occur, and whose lowermost limit is marked by the highest point at which barnacles occur (see Lewis, J. R. 1964); equivalent to the term *upper shore* as used in this book.

Lusitanian applied to water masses and plankton originating from the Mediterranean and Atlantic region of Portugal.

Mandible jaw, especially as applied to arthropods.

Mantle special region of the body wall, particularly of molluscs, which secretes the shell and encloses the mantle cavity.

Medusa the jellyfish phase in the life cycle of hydrozoan and scyphozoan cnidarians.

Metamorphosis the act of transformation of a larva into an adult.

Neap tide tide with the smallest range between high and low water.

Nekton (c.f. Plankton) swimming animals which are able to determine their position in the sea.

Nematocyst special cell of cnidarians which discharges threads to sting or ensnare the prey.

Nephridium excretory organ of many invertebrates.

Niche limiting resources and habitat of a species; determined by its interaction with a wide variety of biological, physical and chemical environmental factors.

Notochord skeletal tube running from front to back in some simple chordates; forerunner of the backbone of vertebrates.

Ocellus simple light receptor.

Oral relating to the mouth; in echinoderms that side of the body on which the mouth is situated (c.f. Aboral).

Order major subdivision of a class.

Papilla small outgrowing structure on the surface of an organism.

Paragaster main cavity inside a sponge.

Parapodium segmental, flap-like appendage of a polychaete annelid; usually bears chaetae or bristles.

Parasitism condition whereby one organism, the parasite, lives on or in another, its host, at the expense of the latter.

Pelagic inhabiting the surface waters of the sea.

Pentamerism five-fold symmetry found in echinoderms.

Perisarc thin, tubular, skeletal structure investing the outer surface of many hydroid polyps.

Peristalsis form of motion resulting from the interaction of circularly and longitudinally arranged muscles in organs like intestines and in whole animals like worms.

Pharyngeal relating to the pharynx.

Pharynx anterior region of the alimentary canal; it adjoins the gills in chordates.

Phylum major division of the animal kingdom which includes those animals thought to have a common evolutionary origin.

Phytoplankton planktonic plants (generally microscopic).

Plankton drifting organisms or swimming organisms which are not able to determine their position in the sea.

Planula simple larva (for instance) of cnidarians resembling a ball of cells; usually ciliated and hence able to move.

Pneumatophore organ of flotation containing gas, or a modified individual in a siphonophoran colony which subserves this function.

Polymorphism the occurrence of different forms of the same species, for instance in a life cycle (polymorphism in time), or in a colony (polymorphism in space).

Polyp sedentary, individual cnidarian such as *Hydra*, basically with a sac-like body opening only by the mouth which is generally surrounded by tentacles.

Proboscis special structure at the anterior end of some animals; in nemertines it is generally everted through the mouth but is itself not part of the alimentary canal; in polychaetes it is everted through the mouth and is part of the alimentary canal.

Radial symmetry symmetry of an organism (e.g. a cnidarian) in which the body parts are equally arranged around a median vertical axis which passes through the mouth; lacking definite front and rear ends and hence left and right sides.

Rhizoid root-like structure.

Rostrum pointed projection at the extreme anterior end of the crustacean head.

Salinity measure of the salt concentration of water.

Segment one of a (generally fixed) number of functional units of the body and normally bearing a pair of appendages; applied particularly to annelids and arthropods.

Sessile commonly meaning living attached to a structure such as a rock or a shell of another organism.

Siphon tube leading into or out of the bodies of invertebrates and used for conducting water currents; found especially in molluscs and sea-squirts.

Species reproductively isolated group of interbreeding organisms; usually defined by morphological characteristics.

Spicule minute fragment or crystal of skeletal material.

Spiracle vestigial gill slit found in fishes such as sharks.

Splash zone zone on the shore above the highest point to which the tides flow but which is under the influence of spray and salt.

Spore minute reproductive germ or particle produced by the asexual generation of plants, i.e. the sporophyte.

Sporophyte (of plants) that generation which produces asexually reproductive spores; alternates with the gametophyte.

Spring tide tide with the greatest range between high and low water.

Stolon root-like structure found in some animals and linking up individuals in a colony; in plants a horizontal branch which produces its own roots and subsequently a new individual.

Sublittoral biologically defined zone on the seashore which lies below the highest point to which laminarians grow, and only uncovered at the lowest tides and extending down from the shore to the shallow seabed; equivalent to the term *lower shore* as used in this book.

Symbiotic describes an organism of one species which lives in close association with one of another species and to the advantage of both.

Telson terminal, flap-like appendage of many crustaceans.

Test 'shell' of a sea-urchin or starfish which, strictly speaking, is an internal skeleton.

Thallus entire body of a lower plant, such as an alga or lichen.

Theca cup-shaped skeleton of a hydroid or coral polyp; the cup-shaped test of a feather-star (crinoid).

Thecate possessing a theca.

Thixatropic condition in which sand contains much water and becomes slushy when compressed, and so is able to flow.

Torsion twisting of the body; particularly applied to an event in the development of certain larvae, e.g. gastropods and holothuroids.

Tube-foot hydraulic appendage of echinoderms and part of the water vascular system.

Tunic the proteinaceous coat surrounding the bodies of sea-squirts and salps.

Umbilicus aperture in the central pillar of a snail shell.

Umbo part of the shell of a bivalve mollusc.

Ventral underside of a bilaterally symmetrical animal (c.f. dorsal).

Vertebrate animal with a backbone made up of vertebrae.

Viscera organs inside the body cavity, especially intestines, heart, liver, etc.

Visceral hump part of the gastropod body where most of the internal organs are housed.

Water vascular system hydraulic system unique to the echinoderms comprising a system of vessels and organs like the tube-feet, and fulfilling various functions, especially locomotion.

Zoecium casing surrounding an individual ectoproct zooid.

Zonation separation of plants and animals into discrete zones or communities on the shore related to the tidal levels.

Zooid individual animal in a colony; usually applied to the Cnidaria and Ectoprocta.

Zooplankton animals of the plankton.

Index

Page numbers in bold type refer to illustrations

318